CAMBRIDGE

OPEN WORLD

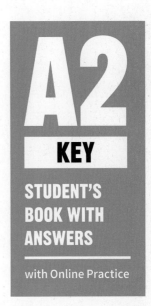

A2

KEY

STUDENT'S
BOOK WITH
ANSWERS

with Online Practice

Anna Cowper

with Sheila Dignen and Susan White

Cambridge University Press
www.cambridge.org/elt

Cambridge Assessment English
www.cambridgeenglish.org

Information on this title: www.cambridge.org/9781108753012

First published 2019

20 19 18 17 16 15 14 13 12 11 10 9 8 7 6 5 4 3

Printed in Italy by Rotolito S.p.A.

A catalogue record for this publication is available from the British Library

ISBN 978-1-108-75301-2 Student's Book with answers with Online Practice

CONTENTS

SPEAKING	GRAMMAR	VOCABULARY	REAL WORLD
Personal information	*Be* *Have got* *Can* Present simple – *he/she/it*	Countries and nationalities Families	
What you do and what you like	Present simple Question forms Adverbs of frequency	Things I do Jobs B1 Applying for a job	Talking about yourself in Mexico City
Describing a photo	Present continuous Present simple or present continuous?	Seasons and months Weather Geography and the natural world Pronouncing months B1 Weather collocations	Asking about the weather in Vancouver
Talking about the weekend	Past simple of *to be* Past simple Pronouncing *-ed* endings	TV and the Internet Time expressions B1 Adjectives to describe films	Buying tickets for a show in New York
Telling a story	*Can* and *can't*; *could* and *couldn't* *Should/shouldn't* for giving advice Stressed and unstressed *can* and *could*	The body Illness and injury Linking words B1 Parts of the body	If you're ill in Dublin
Part 2 Different types of holiday	Past continuous Past simple and past continuous B1 *When, while* and *as* Pronouncing *was* and *were*	Travel Easily confused words	Going on a sightseeing tour in Berlin
Making suggestions	Countable and uncountable nouns *A/an, some* and *any* Expressions of quantity Pronouncing *-s* endings	Food and meals B1 Preparing food	Buying a coffee and a snack in Vienna
Part 1 Talking about your hobbies	Present perfect: *Have you ever…?* Present perfect with *just* Pronouncing *Have you ever…?*	Free time The theatre Music performers B1 Linking words	Spending your free time in London
Describing where you live B1 Describing a picture	Present perfect with *for* and *since* Present perfect with *yet* and *already* Present perfect vs past simple	Houses Kitchen items Prepositions Pronouncing prepositions	Living and learning in Malta
Giving advice	Verbs/adjectives + *to* + infinitive Verbs + *-ing* B1 More expressions with *-ing* and *to* Unstressed *to*	Feelings and emotions	Meeting people in Melbourne
Part 1 Talking about where you live	*Will/may/might* *Will/shall* for offers and promises	Places in a town Directions B1 City words Intonation	Visiting tourist sites in Rome
Shopping habits	The present continuous for fixed plans The present simple for schedules and timetables *Going to* Unstressed *to* in *going to*	Spending and saving Shopping B1 Money and shopping	Dealing with money in Stockholm
A job interview Intonation in questions	Zero conditional First conditional The passive B1 *Unless* and *when*	School subjects Jobs and work	Planning to study in Geneva
Appearance and personality	Comparative adjectives Superlative adjectives B1 Equal comparisons with *(not) as … as* Pronouncing *-est* endings	Personality adjectives *Look like* and *be like*	Shopping for clothes in Dubai
Part 2 Talking about sports	*Can, must, have to, need to* Tenses review The /ɔː/ sound	Sports *Do, play* and *go* with sports B1 Adverbs	Going to a sports event in Madrid

HOW TO USE THIS BOOK

WELCOME TO OPEN WORLD
THE COURSE THAT TAKES YOU FURTHER

Learn about the features in your new Student's Book

Large images at the start
of each unit introduce the
topic and get you talking

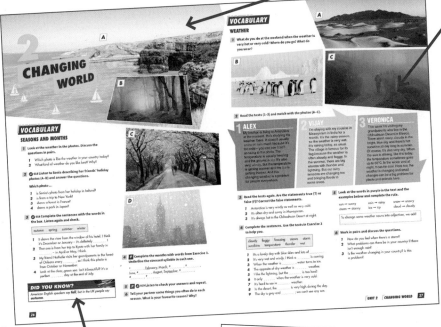

EXAM TRAINING

'Training' exam tasks provide
guidance and tips on each part
of the exam

DID YOU KNOW?

Learn the differences between British
English and American English

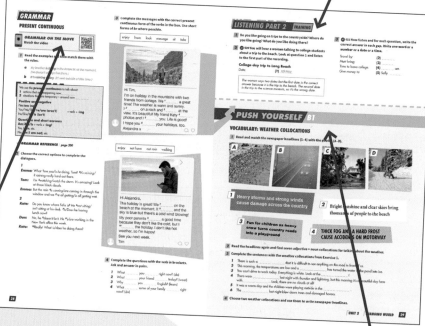

GRAMMAR ON THE MOVE

Scan the QR codes to watch grammar animations in
your free time to learn about each grammar point

PUSH YOURSELF

Learn and practise more challenging
language and skills that take you to
the next level

EXAM FOCUS

Read exam tips and facts and do two complete practice exam tasks after every unit

EXAM CHECKS

test what you remember about the exam

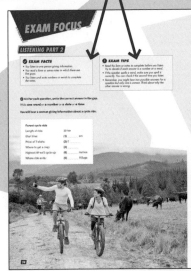

REAL WORLD

pages take you outside the classroom and into the real world

PHRASES YOU MIGHT USE AND HEAR

Learn and practise phrases you might use and hear when you are using English in the real world

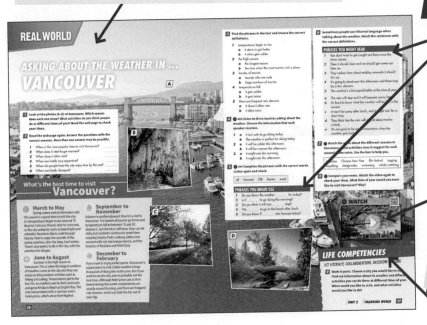

Scan the QR codes to watch videos of different locations around the world on your mobile phone

LIFE COMPETENCIES

Develop important skills, knowledge and attitudes that you can use in your daily life

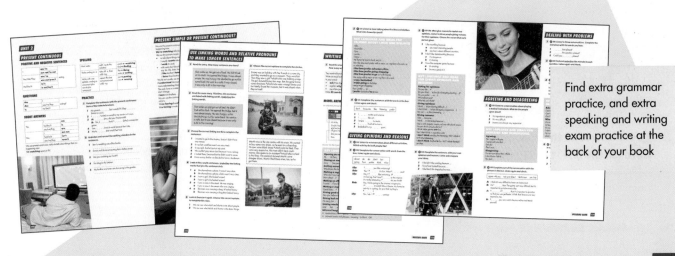

Find extra grammar practice, and extra speaking and writing exam practice at the back of your book

S WHO I AM

GRAMMAR

BE

1 Work in pairs and discuss the questions.

1 Where can you meet new people? What do you say when you meet new people?
2 Does English help you to meet new people? Why?

2 002 Listen to the people. Where are they? Match the places in the box with the photos and the dialogues.

> on holiday   in an English class   at a sports centre

A
1 Hi, I _____ Ben. What's your name?
2 Hello, Ben. My name _____ Jim. Nice to meet you.
3 Nice to meet you, too, Jim. _____ this the basketball club?
4 No, it _____ . It _____ five-a-side football.

B
5 _____ you British?
6 No, we _____ . We _____ Canadian.
7 Oh, that _____ interesting. Where _____ you from in Canada?

C
8 _____ he our English teacher?
9 Yes, he _____ . His name is Mr Robinson.
   He _____ very nice. _____ you a new student?
10 Yes, I _____ . This is my first lesson.
11 Where _____ you from?

3 002 Now read the dialogues and complete them with the words in the box. Then listen again and check your answers.

> am   are   aren't   is   isn't   'm   's   're

➡ **GRAMMAR REFERENCE** / page 196

VOCABULARY

COUNTRIES AND NATIONALITIES

Complete the dialogues with the words in the box.

> American   French   Italian
> Mexican   Spanish   Chinese

1 **A:** Who's that girl over there?
  B: That's Mia. She's in my class. She's very nice.
  A: Is she _____ ?
  B: No, she isn't from Italy. She's from New York. She's _____ .

2 **A:** Are Juana and Carlos _____ ?
  B: Carlos is, but Juana isn't from Spain. She's from Mexico so she's _____ .

3 **A:** Where are you from in France? Are you from Paris?
  B: No, I'm not _____ , I'm Canadian. What nationality are you?
  A: I'm _____ . I'm from Shanghai in China.

READING

1 Read the information about Karl's family. Look at the photos and write the names.

Karl is 33 and he's a sports teacher. He's married and his wife's name is Zadie. She's 31 and she's a computer programmer. Their son, Adam, is seven years old.

Karl's father is a sports teacher, too. His name is Robert and he's 62. Karl's mother's name is Adi. She's 64 and she doesn't work.

Karl's brother's name is Leroy. He's 28 and he's a nurse in a hospital. He's single.

Karl has also got a sister. Her name is Lily. She's an actor. She's married and her husband is an actor, too. His name is Marco. Lily and Marco are 30. Marco is Italian and he comes from Naples.

1	3	5	7 ....
2	4	6	8 ....

2 Read the text again and match the questions and answers.

1 **How old** is Karl's son?
2 **Who** is Leroy?
3 **What** is Zadie's job?
4 **Where** is Marco from?
5 **Whose** husband is an actor?
6 **How many** children have Karl's parents got?

a She's a computer programmer.
b He's seven.
c He's Karl's brother.
d Lily's
e They've got three.
f He's from Italy.

3 Look at the questions in Exercise 2. Which question word(s) in pink do we use to:

1 ask a question about a person?
2 ask about a place?
3 ask a question about a thing?
4 ask a question about a person's age?
5 ask about something that belongs to someone else?
6 ask about the number of things or people?

> Karl's family = **the family of Karl**
> He's a sports teacher. = **He is a sports teacher.**
> His parents' names are … = **The names of his parents are …**
> The children's book is new. = **the book of the children is new.**

➡ **GRAMMAR REFERENCE** / page 197

VOCABULARY

FAMILIES

1 Look at Luca's family tree and read the texts. Then complete the sentences with the pink words.

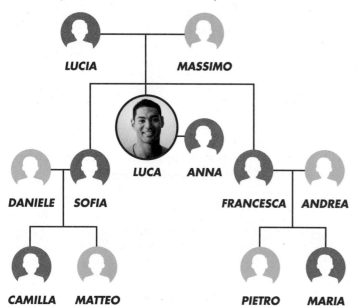

LUCIA MASSIMO

LUCA ANNA

DANIELE SOFIA FRANCESCA ANDREA

CAMILLA MATTEO PIETRO MARIA

- Luca's parents' names are Lucia and Massimo. They**'ve got** three children and four grandchildren: two **grandsons** and two **granddaughters**.
- Luca **hasn't got** a brother, but he**'s got** two sisters. They are both married and they**'ve** both **got** a son and a daughter. This means that Luca and Anna are the **uncle** and **aunt** of two **nephews** and two **nieces**. Their nephews are Pietro and Matteo (the boys) and their nieces are Camilla and Maria (the girls).
- Massimo and Lucia are the **grandfather** and **grandmother** of Sofia's and Francesca's children.
- Camilla and Matteo **have got** two **cousins**: Pietro, and Maria.

1 Your parents' parents are your _____ .
2 If your brother has a son, he's your _____ .
3 My _____ is my mum or dad's brother.
4 If your sister has two daughters, they are your _____ .
5 Your mum's sister is your _____ .
6 If your mum or dad's brothers or sisters have children, they are your _____ .
7 I'm a girl. I'm my grandmother's _____ and my brother's her _____ .

2 Complete the sentences with the words in the box.

Grandad	Dad	Mum	Grandma
Grandpa	Granny		

1 In families, people often call their mother _____ .
2 People also often call their father _____ .
3 Many people call their grandmother _____ or _____ .
4 Many people call their grandfather _____ or _____ .

GRAMMAR

HAVE GOT

 GRAMMAR ON THE MOVE
Watch the video

1 Read the examples and the rules and then choose the correct answers.

*They**'ve got** three children and four grandchildren. Luca **hasn't got** a brother, but he**'s got** two sisters.*

	I/You/We/They	He/She/It
Positive	have got/'ve got	has got/'s got
Negative	have not got/haven't got	has not got/ hasn't got
Questions	Have … got?	Has … got?
Short answers	Yes, I/you/we/they have. No, I/you/we/they haven't.	Yes, he/she has. No, he/she hasn't.

➡ **GRAMMAR REFERENCE** / *page 196*

1 He's/'ve got four brothers and two sisters.
2 We *hasn't/haven't* got a big house.
3 *Have/'ve* you got a dog? Yes, I *have/I've got*.
4 *Has/have* your mum got a computer? Yes, she's/has.

2 Complete the questions with the correct form of *have got*. Ask and answer in pairs.

1 _____ you _____ any brothers and sisters?
2 _____ your best friend _____ a car?
3 How many children _____ your grandfather _____ ?
4 _____ your friend _____ a cat or a dog?

READING

1 Look at the photo. What do you think his job is? What languages do you think he can speak?

2 Now read the text and check your answers.

Miguel is 30 years old. He **comes** from Porto in Portugal, but he **doesn't live** there. He **lives** in New York. He **works** at a dance school as a dance teacher. He **can speak** English and Portuguese and of course he **can dance** very well! Miguel isn't married and he hasn't got any children. He's got a family in Portugal. His parents live in Porto and he's got two sisters. He **can** phone his family but he **can't** visit them. New York is very interesting and Miguel **loves** the city. He's got lots of friends and he **likes** his job.

3 Read the text again and choose the correct answers.

1 Miguel comes from *New York/Porto*.
2 He can speak *two languages/three languages*.
3 He's *a Portuguese teacher/a dance teacher*.
4 Miguel has got *two sisters/two daughters*.
5 Miguel can *dance/visit his family*.

GRAMMAR

CAN

GRAMMAR ON THE MOVE
Watch the video

1 Read the examples and complete the rules.

*He **can speak** English and Portuguese.*
*He **can dance** very well.   He **can't visit** his family.*
***Can** he visit his family? No, he **can't**.*

Positive	I/You/He/She/It/We/They ¹_____
Negative	I/You/He/She/It/We/They ²_____/cannot
Questions	³_____ I/you/he/she/it/we/they?
Short answers	Yes, I/you/he/she/it/we/they can.
	No, I/you/he/she/it/we/they ⁴_____.

➡ **GRAMMAR REFERENCE** / page 197

2 Use the words and phrases to make questions with *can*. Ask and answer with a partner. Think of three more questions to ask.

speak English   dance   swim   play tennis   cook

Can you speak Chinese?

Yes, I can, a little.   No, I can't.

PRESENT SIMPLE – *HE/SHE/IT*

3 Read the sentences and complete the rules with *like*.

He **comes** from Porto.   He **loves** the city.
He **doesn't live** there.   He **likes** his job.
Does he **work** at a dance school?   Yes, he **does**.

Positive	He/She/It ¹_____
Negative	He/She/It ²_____
Questions	³_____ he/she/it ⁴_____?
Short answers	Yes, he/she/it ⁵_____.
	No, he/she/it ⁶_____.

➡ **GRAMMAR REFERENCE** / page 197

4 Read the information about Polly and complete the sentences with the verbs in the box.

come   like   live   work

POLLY OLIVER

Home: London
Job: chef – pizza restaurant
From: Ireland
Languages: English, Italian
Likes: cooking, music, films, snakes, cats
Doesn't like: cars (has got a bike!), computers

1 Polly _____ in South London.
2 Polly _____ from Ireland.
3 Polly _____ cooking and music.
4 Polly _____ at a pizza restaurant.

5 Match the questions and answers a–c.

1 Where **does** Polly **come** from?
2 **Does she like** computers?
3 **Does she like** cats?

a No, she **doesn't**.
b Yes, she **does**.
c She **comes** from Ireland.

6 Complete the sentences and questions about Polly with the verbs in brackets. Write answers for the questions.

1 Polly _____ _____ in Ireland. (not live)
2 _____ Polly _____ Italian? (can/speak)
3 _____ she _____ a job? (have got)
4 Where _____ Polly _____? (work)
5 _____ Polly _____ snakes? (like)
6 Polly _____ _____ cars. (not like)

LISTENING

PERSONAL INFORMATION

1 **P** Work in pairs. Can you say the alphabet in English? Are there any letters that you don't know how to say? Which ones?

A B C D E F G H I J K
L M N O P Q R S T
U V W X Y Z

2 **P** ● 003 Listen and repeat.

3 **P** ● 004 Work in pairs. Practise saying these groups of letters. What do you think they mean? Listen and check your answers.

1 UK *2* USA *3* EU *4* DOB *5* LOL

DID YOU KNOW?

British English speakers pronounce the letter **z** *as /zed/, but American English speakers say /ziː/.*

4 Have you got: a passport/a driving licence/a national ID card? What information is on it?

5 ● 005 Listen to George giving information about himself. Where is he?

6 ● 005 Listen again and complete part 1.

> **1** First name ....
> Surname ....

7 ● 006 Now listen to the rest of the conversation and complete part 2.

> **2** DOB ....
> Address ....
> ....
> Phone number ....

8 Read the answers and complete the questions.

1 What's your .... ?
My name's Jane Fairley.
2 How do you .... that?
J–A–N–E   F–A–I–R–L–E–Y
3 How .... are you?
I'm 18.
4 What's your .... ?
It's the 18th of March, 1999.
5 What's your .... ?
It's 24 Lea Road, Littletown, NR4 8GJ.
6 What's your .... ?
It's 0721 883 6458.

9 Work in pairs. Take turns to ask for and give your personal information. Ask your partner the questions in Exercise 8 and write down what they tell you.

SPEAKING

PERSONAL INFORMATION

1 Look at the photos of the famous people. Discuss in pairs.

   1 What are their jobs? Why are they famous?

   2 Where are they from?

2 ● 007 Work in pairs. Match the people in Exercise 1 with their dates of birth. Listen and check your answers.

> 19 February 2004   4 September 1981
> 29 November 1990

3 Write down three dates that are important to you. Your partner has to guess why they are important.

> Is it someone's birthday?

> Yes, it is.

> Is it your birthday?

> No, it isn't.

WRITING

A PROFILE

1 What can you remember about the dance teacher Miguel who lives in New York? Complete the information. Then turn to page 11 to check your answers.

Name:	Likes:
Lives:	Age:
Family:	Is from:
Languages:	Things he can do:

2 Choose a famous person or someone who you know and find out about them. Copy the list in Exercise 1 and complete it with information about this person.

3 Use the information to write a profile for your person. Use as much language from this unit as you can.

> He/She lives … His/Her family is/isn't big.
> He/She likes/doesn't like …
> He/She comes from … He/She has/hasn't got …
> He/She can/can't …

1 Beyoncé

2 Diego Boneta

3 Millie Bobby Brown

A BUSY LIFE

VOCABULARY

THINGS I DO

1 **What is a perfect day for you? Discuss in pairs.**

- Is it on holiday, at the weekend, at the beach or in the city?
- Are you alone or with friends or with family?
- Do you go shopping, relax at home or do sport?

2 **Look at the people in the photos. Match the photos A–F with the activities in the box.**

| go shopping   play or watch sport   play video games |
| relax at home   spend time alone |
| spend time with friends |

3 🔊 008 **Listen to four people talking about their perfect day. Match the speakers with the photos.**

Speaker 1 ....
Speaker 2 ....
Speaker 3 ....
Speaker 4 ....

4 🔊 008 **Answer the questions. Then listen again and check your answers.**

1 Where does Speaker 1 like to be on her perfect day?
2 What does Speaker 2 do when he and his friends get tired?
3 What does Speaker 3 enjoy doing on his perfect day?
4 What does Speaker 4 do with her friends in the evening at the end of her perfect day?

5 **Do you do any of the things in the photos? When do you do them?**

LISTENING

ROUTINES

1 Write the correct time under each clock.

> quarter past eight   half past nine
> one o'clock   quarter to six

1

....

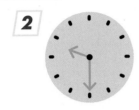
2

....

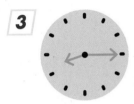
3

....

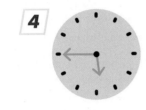
4

....

2 **P** 🔊 009 **Listen and repeat these times.**

at half past six   at quarter to seven
at half past two   at quarter past nine
at quarter to four   at quarter past eleven

3 **P** 🔊 009 **Listen again and answer the questions.**

1 Which words are stressed?
2 Which letter is silent in the pronunciation of *half* (/hɑːf/)?
3 How do we pronounce the unstressed *o* in *to* (/tə/) and the unstressed *a* in *at* (/ət/)?

4 **Where are you at these times on weekdays (Monday to Friday)? Tell your partner.**

1 8.00 in the morning
2 1.30 in the afternoon
3 7.45 in the evening

5 🔊 010 **Listen to Amy talking about her day and answer the questions.**

1 What's her job?
2 What's her sister's job?
3 Where do they live?

6 🔊 011 **Now listen to the whole interview. Are these statements true (T) or false (F)? Correct the false statements.**

1 Amy wakes up at 7.30.
2 She gets dressed after she has breakfast.
3 Amy usually goes to work by bus.
4 She starts teaching at 8.45.
5 Amy often has lunch with her friends from work.
6 She gets home at 5.15.
7 After dinner, she always watches TV.

7 **Complete the sentences with the verbs in the box from Amy's interview.**

> get dressed   get on   get up
> put on   take off   wake up

1 My brothers have a lot of clothes and they take a long time to .... in the morning.
2 Please .... your shoes when you come inside.
3 Before you .... the bus, ask the driver if it stops at the correct bus stop.
4 Sometimes I .... during the night and can't go back to sleep again.
5 The teacher told us to .... our sports clothes and go to the gym.
6 It's Sunday, so we don't need to .... early. We can stay in bed.

BEFORE AND AFTER

I do my homework **after** school. (First I go to school, then I do my homework.)
I put on my shoes **before** I go to work. (First I put on my shoes, then I go to work.)

GRAMMAR

PRESENT SIMPLE

GRAMMAR ON THE MOVE
Watch the video

1 Read the sentences and then choose the correct options to complete the rules.

*I usually **wake up** at quarter past seven, but I **don't get up**!*
*No, she **doesn't catch** the bus. She **goes** by car.*
*We both **drink** coffee for breakfast. We **don't like** tea.*

> **1** We use the **present simple** to talk about things that happen *regularly/at the moment of speaking*.
> **2** We also use the **present simple** to talk about things that are *always true/happening now*.
>
> | | |
> |---|---|
> | **Positive** | I/you/we/they + verb |
> | **Negative** | I/you/we/they + don't + verb |
> | **Question** | **Do** I/you/we/they + verb? |
> | **Short answers** | Yes, I/you/we/they **do**. |
> | | No, I/you/we/they **don't**. |
>
> Go back to page 11 for *he/she/it*.

⇒ **GRAMMAR REFERENCE** / page 198

2 Choose the correct options to complete the information about Olivia's day.

I ¹*don't/doesn't* have the same working hours every day. Sometimes I start work at 6.00 am and so I ²*get up/gets up* at 4.00 am! After breakfast, I drive to the police station and ³*meet/meets* my partner, Joe. Joe ⁴*don't/doesn't* like getting up early. He ⁵*feel/feels* very tired!

All the police officers ⁶*has/have* a meeting at the beginning of the day. After that, Joe and I ⁷*go/goes* to the police garage and collect our car. We ⁸*don't/doesn't* come back to the police station until the afternoon.

3 Complete the sentences, questions and short answers with the verbs in the box in the correct form.

> | catch | go | have | not eat |
> |---|---|---|---|
> | not get dressed | | not write | walk |

1 My sister _____ when she gets up. She puts on her clothes after breakfast.

2 He usually _____ a cup of coffee for breakfast, but no toast or cereal. He _____ in the morning.

3 My dad doesn't have a car, so he _____ to the station every day at 7.30 and catches the train to London.

4 '_____ you _____ to work by train, too?'
'No, I _____ the bus.'

5 I _____ emails to my friends. I text them or talk to them on the phone.

4 How is your weekend different from your week? Tell your partner:

• what you do during the week that you don't do at the weekend.

• what you do at the weekend that you don't do during the week.

QUESTION FORMS

5 Read these questions and complete the rules.

*What time **do** you **get up**?*   *I get up at half past seven.*
*How **does** Olivia **go** to work?*   *She goes by car.*
*Where **do** you **have** lunch?*   *I have lunch in a café.*

> **1** To make questions with the present simple we use **do** and _____ in front of the main verb.
> **2** We use question words such as **Who, Where, When, Why,** _____ and _____ at the beginning of the question.

⇒ **GRAMMAR REFERENCE** / page 198

6 Match the questions (1–6) with the correct answers (a–f).

1 What job do you do?
2 Where do your friends work?
3 How does your sister get to school?
4 Who do you have lunch with?
5 When does your brother finish work?
6 Why do you go for a walk after dinner?

a I eat with my colleagues in the café.
b She walks or catches the bus.
c Late – just before midnight.
d Because it helps me to sleep.
e I'm a teacher.
f In the city centre.

7 Write questions with *do* and *does* for these answers about a young man called Sergio.

NAME: SERGIO AGUZZI   AGE: 21

1 What _____ ?
He's an apprentice.

2 Where _____ ?
He works for a telephone company in Rome.

3 Where _____ live?
He lives in a small flat near the university.

4 Who _____ with?
He lives with two friends. They're students.

5 How _____ work?
He cycles. He doesn't like walking.

6 What time _____ work?
He starts work at 9.00 am and finishes at 5.00 pm.

7 What _____ evening?
He watches TV or listens to music. He doesn't like studying for his job after 9 pm.

8 Why _____ his job?
He likes it because it's interesting.

SPEAKING

WHAT YOU DO AND WHAT YOU LIKE

1 🔊 012 **Listen to Sergio and complete the sentences.**

1 I like _____ TV and I love _____ to music.

2 I don't like _____ in the evenings. And I hate _____ .

2 Look at the verbs which follow *like*, *love* and *hate* in Exercise 1. Complete the rule.

> After the verbs *love/like/hate*, the second verb in the sentence ends in _____ .

3 Complete the text with a verb in the box.

> dancing   having   listening to   meeting
> playing   shopping   staying   watching

At the weekend, I love ¹_____ in bed in the morning. I like ²_____ music and then going downstairs and ³_____ a big breakfast. On Saturdays, I like going into town and ⁴_____ my friends. In the evening, we like going to clubs and ⁵_____ . On Sundays, I like ⁶_____ sports or ⁷_____ a film. I also buy food for the week. I hate ⁸_____ for food, so I usually only go to the supermarket once a week.

4 Tell your partner. What do you like/love/not like doing at the weekends/at school/at work?

5 Interview your partner and use the question words from Exercise 7. Ask them about their job, school or university.

> Where do you work/study/go to school?

> How do you go to school?

> Why do you like/don't you like your school?

6 Look at the photos (A & B). Where are the people? What jobs do they do?

A

Karen

B

Roman

7 Work in pairs. Student A, turn to page 192, Student B, turn to page 194. Read the information. Take turns to ask and answer questions to complete the missing information.

1 Do you know anybody who works at night? What job do they do? What are the good things and the bad things about working at night?

2 Look at the photos below and match the jobs with the people. Then read and check your answers.

the DJ   the security guard   the nurse

A I don't like working at night, but it's part of my job. I'm a nurse at a large hospital in Valencia. **I work five nights a month**, from 11 pm to 7 am. The hospital isn't busy at night and I like the quiet. I have more time for the patients and like talking to the ones who can't sleep. I don't usually feel hungry during the night so I just have a sandwich or some fruit at 2 or 3 am.

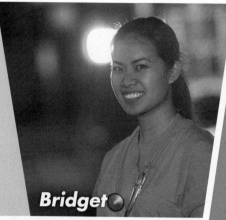

Bridget

B I work at the Divo Club, Berlin. **I work four nights a week** from 10 pm to 6 am. I'm a DJ and I love playing music. I also enjoy working at night. I like being awake when most other people are asleep! I see a different side of Berlin. I never have time to eat at work, but I have a big breakfast in the morning when the club closes. I often go to a café with the others from the club and watch the sunrise.

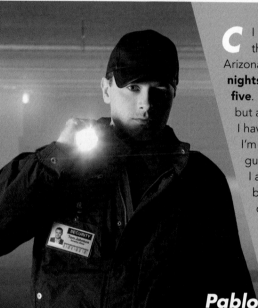

C I work from 10 pm until 8 am at the Plaza shopping Mall in Reno, Arizona. **I <u>sometimes</u> work six nights a week, but <u>usually</u> I work five**. I'm often busy until midnight but after that, it's very quiet. I have time to write my book – I'm a writer as well as a security guard. I stop to eat at 2 am and I always go to the all-night burger restaurant. It's the only time I speak to other people! But that's OK. I'm happy working alone.

Pablo

Tobi

3 Look at question 1 below and read the tip. Then read questions 2–6 and choose the correct answers.

		Bridget	Tobi	Pablo
1	Which person doesn't always work the same number of nights?	A	B	C

Look at the three texts and find the sentence where the people talk about how many nights they work. This is what they say: Bridget works 'five nights a month'. Tobi works 'four nights a week'. Pablo says he 'sometimes' works 'six nights a week' but he 'usually' works 'five'. So C is the correct answer.

		Bridget	Tobi	Pablo
2	Which person likes working at night?	A	B	C
3	Which person has breakfast after finishing work?	A	B	C
4	Which person enjoys talking to people at work?	A	B	C
5	Which person has more than one job?	A	B	C
6	Which person doesn't eat a lot at work during the night?	A	B	C

4 Discuss in pairs.

1 Can you think of any other jobs where people work at night?
2 Would you like to work at night? Why?/Why not?

GRAMMAR

ADVERBS OF FREQUENCY

GRAMMAR ON THE MOVE
Watch the video

1 Read the sentences and choose the correct options to complete the rules.

*I **sometimes work** six nights a week.*
*I **don't usually feel** hungry.*
*I'm **often busy** until midnight.*

We use **adverbs of frequency** to say how often something happens. In a sentence, the adverb of frequency comes:
1 before/after all verbs except the verb **be**.
2 before/after the verb **be**.
3 before/between/after **don't** or **doesn't** and the main verb.

always	usually	often	sometimes		never
100%	←	←	50%	→	0%

→ **GRAMMAR REFERENCE** / *page 199*

2 Complete the sentences about Bridget, Tobi and Pablo with these words.

always	never	often	sometimes	usually

1 Most of the time, Pablo works five nights a week, but he _____ works six nights.
2 Tobi _____ eats at work – he's too busy.
3 Pablo _____ eats at a fast food restaurant – he goes there every night.
4 Most of the time, Bridget doesn't want to eat much during the night. She isn't _____ very hungry.
5 After he finishes work, Tobi _____ has breakfast with his friends. He does this a lot.

3 Now complete these sentences about you. Then tell your partner.

1 I don't usually _____ at the weekends.
2 I never _____ in the evenings.
3 I sometimes _____ in the summer.
4 I don't always _____ in the morning.
5 I often _____ on holiday.

ONCE/TWICE A ...

4 Read the interview with Tobi and complete the rules.

Interviewer:	How often do you exercise, Tobi?
Tobi:	Well, I sometimes dance all night! But I also go to the gym **once** or **twice** a week.
Interviewer:	Do you ever leave the city and visit the beach or mountains?
Tobi:	Not very often. I like the city! I go to the countryside **three** or **four times** a year.

We can answer the question **How often?** with an adverb of frequency, or we can say how many times we do something **a day/a week/a month/a year**.
one time = ¹ _____   two times = ² _____
three/four/five times, etc.

5 Tell your partner about how often you do these things.

- go running
- go to the cinema
- cook a meal
- go to the beach
- buy new clothes
- dance

I don't often go to the cinema – maybe twice a year.

I go out dancing about once a month.

VOCABULARY

JOBS

1 🔊 013 Listen to these people talking about their jobs. Number the photos in the order you hear them and write the jobs.

mechanic	photographer	pilot	police officer

_____

2 Complete the descriptions with the correct jobs.

1 A _____ repairs machines.
2 A _____ takes interesting photos.
3 A _____ flies planes.
4 A _____ helps to keep people safe.

VOCABULARY: APPLYING FOR A JOB

So you want to be a journalist? For many young people it seems a glamorous job but remember the salary is low and the hours are long, especially at the beginning! You can study to get a qualification in journalism at some universities, but the most important thing really is to get experience writing articles for a small local or student newspaper, or for an online magazine or blog.

Newspapers usually select new employees using recruitment web sites first, so it's important to write a good CV too. An interesting CV that gets the employer's attention is the thing that gets you a personal interview, then at the interview you can show them some of your writing and hope they like it!

Read the text about how to become a journalist. Match the beginnings of the definitions (1–6) with the endings (a–f).

1 A job interview is a meeting where you have to answer questions
2 Your salary is the money
3 You have experience of something
4 An employee is a person
5 Your CV is a written description
6 A qualification is something you get

a when you have done it before.
b who is paid to work for a company.
c of your education and other jobs.
d you get for doing your job.
e after you pass an exam.
f to show that you are the right person for a job.

LISTENING PART 1 TRAINING

1 Discuss the questions in pairs.

1 What's your idea of a perfect job? Why?
2 What is important for you in a job?

2 🎧 014 You are going to hear a journalist on the radio asking some people about work. Listen and choose the correct answer for question 1.

1 What job does the woman want to do when she finishes her studies?

Read the question carefully. The woman will talk about all three jobs, but the question is asking about when she finishes her studies. Listen to the recording.

A is wrong because she is studying to be a nurse now but she doesn't want to work as a nurse. B is wrong because she will only become a teacher if she can't make any money as a DJ. C is correct because she wants to become a DJ after her course ends.

DID YOU KNOW?

*American English speakers say **sales clerk** instead of **shop assistant**.*

3 🎧 015 Look at questions 2 and 3. In each question underline the important information you need to listen for. Then listen and choose the correct answer.

2 What does the police officer do first when he gets home from work?

3 What time does the man get up in the morning?

WRITING

AN EMAIL ABOUT A JOB

1 How do you communicate with friends and family who you don't see every day? Who do you send emails to? Is there anyone you send emails to in English?

2 Read the email from Tori, a student, to a friend. What's her new job? Why does she like it?

To: Emily
From: Tori Kotzamani
Subject: My job

Reply Forward

Hi Emily,

How are you? I'm really happy because I've got a new job! Of course I still go to college, but from Thursday to Saturday I work in a pizza restaurant from 5.00 to 10.00 pm. I'm a waitress so I wear a uniform – a pink and white shirt and jeans. It's hard work but it's fun. I like talking to the customers.

Next year, I want to go to the police college and study to become a police officer. My parents want me to be a teacher but I don't want to work with children and I hate working inside. I like helping people, so I think it's the perfect job for me.

What about you? Tell me about your job. What do you want to do in the future? Write soon!

Love, Tori.

3 Read the email again and underline the expressions Tori uses to begin and end her email. Add them to the table.

BEGINNING AN EMAIL	ENDING AN EMAIL
Dear Hello	Best wishes All the best

4 You are a student and work as a shop assistant in a games store at the weekends. You want to be a photographer in the future. Write to Tori and tell her about the job you do now and the job you want to do in the future. Complete these notes.

	YOUR JOB NOW	THE JOB YOU WANT TO DO
What's the job?	Shop assistant	
Where do you work?	In a games store	
What time do you start/finish?	9 am/5 pm	
Do you wear a uniform?	Yes	
Do you work inside/outside/with people/alone?	Inside, with people	
What do you like/ not like about this job?	I like playing new games I don't get a lot of money	
Why do you want to do this job?	....	

5 Write an email in reply to Tori. Use this plan to help you.

Begin:
Dear Tori,
Let me tell you about my job …

Paragraph 1:
Your job now:
I work in/at, I work from … to …

Paragraph 2:
The job you want to do:
In the future I want to … because …

Paragraph 3:
Ask Tori to tell you about her free time and what she does at weekends when she's not working:
What about you …? What do you …?

End:
Ask Tori to write soon and end your email.

✓ EXAM FACTS

- You read three short texts.
- You answer seven questions about the texts.
- The answer to each question will be A, B or C.

! EXAM TIPS

- Read the questions carefully.
- Underline or highlight words in the texts that mean the same as words in the questions.
- For each question (1–7), find the answer (A, B or C) which answers the question.
- Remember that the question may not use the same words as the text, but it will have the same meaning.

For each question, choose the correct answer.

	Marta	Gia	Rosa
1 Which person plans her day during her journey?	A	B	C
2 Which person starts her journey earlier than she needs to?	A	B	C
3 Which person enjoys having time alone while she's travelling?	A	B	C
4 Which person hates being late for work?	A	B	C
5 Which person never uses her phone during her journey?	A	B	C
6 Which person works while she's travelling?	A	B	C
7 Which person reads the news while she's travelling?	A	B	C

My journey to work

Marta

I travel to work by train. When I first started, I left home at eight and hurried to get to work by nine. I was never late, but I didn't enjoy hurrying. So now I make sure I'm out of the house by seven thirty. I go slowly, buy a coffee and chat to people in the coffee shop. On the train I use my phone to send emails, which saves time when I get to the office.

Gia

I usually have to run to the station to catch my train – I should probably plan my mornings better and get up earlier! My train isn't busy, and it's nice to be on my own for a while, just to think or read a book. I know lots of people play games or read the news on their phones, but I just check mine quickly when I get to work. And I don't work on the train – I'm a nurse, so I can't do that!

Rosa

I like to read about what's happening around the world, so I use the internet to do that when I'm on the train – usually on my phone. I can't really work on the train, but I make a list of the things I have to do when I get to work, and I think about what I'm going to do first. The worst kind of day for me is when there are delays on the trains, and I arrive after the time I should. That makes me really angry.

🔊 016 **For each question, choose the correct answer.**

1 What time does the man start work?

2 Where did the woman go with her friend?

3 How should the man contact Eva?

4 What does the man need to buy?

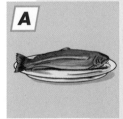 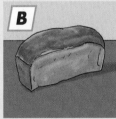 

5 Why was the woman late for work?

HOW WAS IT?

Gave it a go ☐

Getting there ☐

Aced it! ☐

REAL WORLD

A

TALKING ABOUT YOURSELF IN ...
MEXICO CITY

1 Look at the photos (A–C) of Mexico city. What can you see? What do you know about Mexico City?

2 Work in pairs. What can you learn when you stay with a family in another country? Discuss and then read the information about homestays. Which of your ideas does it talk about?

3 Read about four families you can stay with in Mexico City. Which family ...

 1 doesn't have any children?
 2 has a pet?
 3 wants to show you the city?
 4 lives near some places that are popular with tourists?

FAMILY HOMESTAY

Everyone likes visiting other countries. But staying in hotels isn't always fun because you don't learn about the country you are in. At Family Homestay, we can find the perfect family for you. We check all our families carefully, so we know they will look after you well.

With our families, you can:
- learn the language of the country
- make new friends
- enjoy the food that people in the country eat
- get help with any problems you have
- understand the way local people live

Book <u>here</u> to find your perfect Family Homestay.

B

A Hi! We live in a big apartment right in the middle of the city, and it's within walking distance of many of the tourist sites like the National Palace and all the museums. We have three children, all teenagers. All meals are included in the price.

B Hello. There are four people in our family. We live in a small house in a quiet part of the city. We do a lot of things together, and we always eat together in the evenings. We know a lot about the city. We can take you to visit some interesting places and tell you about them. We also offer airport pickup.

C We are the Ruiz family from Mexico City. There are five people in our family, me, my husband, our two children and our little cat. We love having students from other countries living in our home! We live in the south of the city. There's good public transport, like buses and trains, so you can get to the city centre easily.

D We are a young couple in Mexico City. There are just the two of us, so our home is very quiet. We would love to welcome you. Your room has a bed and a desk, and you have your own bathroom. We have wi-fi at home, and there's a very nice park nearby. You can enjoy our home cooking, or you have free use of the kitchen to make your own food.

4 Find the phrases in the text and choose the correct definitions.

1 within walking distance
   a it's too far to walk there
   b you can walk there
2 all meals are included
   a you don't pay extra for meals
   b you pay extra for meals
3 airport pickup
   a we live near the airport
   b we can come and meet you at the airport
4 good public transport
   a lots of buses and trains
   b we have a good car
5 the city centre
   a the middle part of the city
   b the area outside the city
6 enjoy our home cooking
   a cook your own food in our home
   b eat food that we cook at home

5 🔊 017 Listen to three conversations. Where is the student in each conversation? There is one extra answer which you do not need to use.

a at a party   *c* on public transport
b at the airport   *d* with the host family

6 🔊 017 Complete the phrases with the correct words in the box. Listen again and check.

allergic   from   I'll   I'm staying   I've got
really like   student   very excited

PHRASES YOU MIGHT USE

1 .... be here for five weeks.
2 .... with a family.
3 .... one brother.
4 I'm .... to be here.
5 I'm not .... to anything.
6 I'm .... Harrow, in the UK.
7 I'm a ....
8 I .... the city.

7 Sometimes people use words and phrases that you don't know when they ask about you. Choose the correct definitions.

PHRASES YOU MIGHT HEAR

1 What's the purpose of your visit?
   a Why are you here?
   b How long will you be here?
2 Is that convenient for you?
   a When would you like to do that?
   b Is that OK for you?
3 What do you think of Mexico?
   a Do you like Mexico?
   b Why did you choose to come to Mexico?
4 Maybe we should go and get some food.
   a Do you have any food?
   b Would you like some food?

8 ▶ Watch the video. What do you learn about these things? Make notes.

- Mexico City
- family life
- homestays

9 ▶ Compare your notes. Watch the video again to check your ideas.

▶ WATCH

C

LIFE COMPETENCIES

COMMUNICATION, UNDERSTANDING AND CULTURE

10 Work in groups and make a list of the most important things for people to know if they come to live in your city. Compare your ideas with other groups.

2 CHANGING WORLD

A

B

VOCABULARY

SEASONS AND MONTHS

1 **Look at the weather in the photos. Discuss the questions in pairs.**

    1 Which photo is like the weather in your country today?

    2 What kind of weather do you like best? Why?

2 🎧 018 **Listen to Sonia describing her friends' holiday photos (A–D) and answer the questions.**

Which photo ...

    1 is Sonia's photo from her holiday in Ireland?

    2 is from a trip to New York?

    3 shows a forest in France?

    4 shows a park in Japan?

C

3 🎧 018 **Complete the sentences with the words in the box. Listen again and check.**

autumn   spring   summer   winter

    1 It shows the view from the window of his hotel. I think it's December or January – it's definitely _____ !

    2 That one is from her trip to Kyoto with her family in _____ – in April or May, I think.

    3 My friend Nathalie visits her grandparents in the forest of Orléans every _____ , so I think this photo is from October or November.

    4 Look at the clear, green sea. Isn't it beautiful? It's a perfect _____ day at the end of July.

DID YOU KNOW?

*American English speakers say **fall**, but in the UK people say **autumn**.*

D

4 **P** **Complete the months with words from Exercise 3. Underline the stressed syllable in each one.**

    ¹ _____ , February, March, ² _____ , ³ _____ , June, ⁴ _____ , August, September, ⁵ _____ , ⁶ _____ , ⁷ _____

5 **P** 🎧 019 **Listen to check your answers and repeat.**

6 **Tell your partner some things you often do in each season. What is your favourite season? Why?**

VOCABULARY

WEATHER

1 What do you do at the weekend when the weather is very hot or very cold? Where do you go? What do you wear?

A

B

C

2 Read the texts (1–3) and match with the photos (A–C).

1 ALEX

My brother is living in Antarctica at the moment. He's studying the weather there. It doesn't usually **snow** or **rain** much because it's too cold – you can see it isn't snowing in the photo. The temperature is usually freezing and the ground is **icy**. It's also very **windy**. But the temperature is getting warmer and the **ice** is getting thinner. And this changing weather is a problem for people everywhere.

2 VIJAY

I'm staying with my cousins in Mawsynram in India for a month. It's the **rainy** season, so the weather is very wet. It's raining today, as usual. The village is famous for its **fog** because the weather is often **cloudy** and **foggy**. In the summer, there are big **storms** with thunder and lightning. But our rainy seasons are changing too and bringing floods to some areas.

3 VERONICA

This week I'm visiting my grandparents who live in the Chihuahuan Desert in Mexico. There aren't many **clouds** in the bright, blue sky and there's hot sunshine all day long in summer. Of course, it's also very dry. When the **sun** is shining, like it is today, the temperature sometimes goes up to 50°C. In the winter and at night, it can be cool. Here too, the weather is changing and small changes can be a big problem for plants and animals here.

3 Read the texts again. Are the statements true (T) or false (F)? Correct the false statements.

1 Antarctica is very windy as well as very cold.
2 It's often dry and sunny in Mawsynram.
3 It's always hot in the Chihuahuan Desert at night.

4 Complete the sentences. Use the texts in Exercise 2 to help you.

cloudy	foggy	freezing	snows	storm
sunshine	temperature	thunder	wet	

1 It's a lovely day with blue skies and lots of _____ .
2 It's very wet and windy. I think a _____ is coming.
3 When the weather is _____ , water turns to ice.
4 The opposite of dry weather is _____ weather.
5 I like the lightning, but the _____ is too loud!
6 It only _____ when the weather is very cold.
7 It's hard to see in _____ weather.
8 In the desert, the _____ is very high during the day.
9 The sky is grey and _____ ; we can't see any sun.

5 Look at the words in **purple** in the text and the examples below and complete the rule.

sun → sunny	rain → rainy	snow → snowy
storm → stormy	ice → icy	cloud → cloudy

To change some weather nouns into adjectives, we add _____ .

6 Work in pairs and discuss the questions.

1 How do you feel when there's a storm?
2 What problems can there be in your country if there isn't enough rain?
3 Is the weather changing in your country? Is this a problem?

PRESENT CONTINUOUS

GRAMMAR ON THE MOVE
Watch the video

1 Read the examples and then match them with the rules.

a *My brother **is living** in the Antarctic at the moment. (He doesn't always live there.)*

b *It's raining today. (It's wet outside at this time.)*

We use the **present continuous** to talk about:
1 actions that are happening now. _____
2 situations that are temporary – around now. _____

Positive and negative
I'm/am (not)
You/We/They're/are (aren't)   + verb + **-ing**
He/She/It's/is (isn't)

Questions and short answers
Am/Are/Is + verb + **-ing**?
Yes, I **am**, etc.
No, **I'm (I am not)**, etc.

➡ **GRAMMAR REFERENCE** / page 200

2 Choose the correct options to complete the dialogues.

1
Emma: What ¹*are you/is he* doing, Tom? ²*It's raining/ It raining* really hard out there.
Tom: I'm ³*watching/watch* the storm. It's amazing! Look at those black clouds.
Emma: But the rain ⁴*is coming/are coming* in through the window and we ⁵*'re all getting/is all getting* wet.

2
Kate: Do you know where Felix is? He ⁶*not sitting/ isn't sitting* at his desk. ⁷*Is/Does* he having lunch now?
Dan: No, he ⁸*doesn't/isn't*. He ⁹*'s/are* working in the New York office this week.
Kate: ¹⁰*Really!* What *is/does* he doing there?

3 Complete the messages with the correct present continuous form of the verbs in the box. Use short forms of *be* where possible.

enjoy	have	look	message	sit	take

Hi Tim,

I'm on holiday in the mountains with two friends from college. We ¹_____ a great time! The weather is warm and sunny. I ²_____ on a rock and ³_____ at the view. It's beautiful! My friend Katy ⁴_____ photos and I ⁵_____ you. Life is good! I hope you ⁶_____ your holidays, too.

Alejandra x

enjoy	not have	not rain	walking

Hi Alejandra,

The holiday is great! We ⁷_____ on the beach at the moment. It ⁸_____ and the sky is blue but there's a cold wind blowing!

My poor parents ⁹_____ a good time because they don't like the cold, but I ¹⁰_____ the holiday. I don't like hot weather, so I'm happy!

See you next week.

Tim

4 Complete the questions with the verb in brackets. Ask and answer in pairs.

1 What _____ you _____ right now? (do)
2 What _____ your friend _____ today? (wear)
3 Why _____ you _____ English? (learn)
4 What _____ some of your family _____ right now? (do)

1 Do you like going on trips to the countryside? Where do you like going? What do you like doing there?

2 🎧 020 You will hear a woman talking to college students about a trip to the beach. Look at question 1 and listen to the first part of the recording.

College day trip to Long Beach

Date: **(1)** *6th May*

> The woman says two dates but the first date is the correct answer because it is the trip to the beach. The second date is the trip to the science museum, so it's the wrong date.

3 🎧 021 Now listen and for each question, write the correct answer in each gap. Write one word or a number or a date or a time.

Travel by:	**(2)** _____
Must bring:	**(3)** _____
Time to leave college:	**(4)** _____ am
Give money to:	**(5)** Sally _____

PUSH YOURSELF `B1`

VOCABULARY: WEATHER COLLOCATIONS

1 Read and match the newspaper headlines (1–4) with the photos (A–D).

1 Heavy storms and strong winds cause damage across the country

2 Bright sunshine and clear skies bring thousands of people to the beach

3 Fun for children as heavy snow turns country roads into a playground

4 THICK FOG AND A HARD FROST CAUSE ACCIDENTS ON MOTORWAY

2 Read the headlines again and find seven adjective + noun collocations for talking about the weather.

3 Complete the sentences with the weather collocations from Exercise 1.

1 There is such a _____ _____ that it is difficult to see anything on the road in front of us.

2 This morning, the temperatures are low and a _____ _____ has turned the water in the pond into ice.

3 You can't drive to work today. Everything is white. Look at the _____ !

4 There were _____ last night with thunder and lightning, but this morning it's a beautiful day here with _____ . Look, there are no clouds at all!

5 It was a warm day and the children were playing outside in the _____ _____ .

6 The _____ last night blew down trees and damaged houses.

4 Choose two weather collocations and use them to write newspaper headlines.

READING

1 Would you like to spend time living in a different country or city? Where would you like to go? Why?

2 Read about Koon-Sung and Carla and answer the questions.

   1 Where do they usually live? Where are they living now?

   2 Why are they spending time in a different place?

KOON-SUNG

My name is Koon-Sung. I'm an engineer and I'm from Singapore. At the moment, I'm living in Turin in the north of Italy. I'm working on a project to make a road in the mountains. My life here is very different from my life at home. I'm staying in a big house on a hill so I have a great view of the city. The house is near a forest with lots of beautiful trees. From my bedroom window, I can also see the mountains. At the weekend, I enjoy walking in the Aosta Valley and taking photos of waterfalls, rivers and lakes. At home in Singapore, all the buildings are very tall and I can only see the street from my window!

I'm Carla and I'm studying to be a doctor. I'm from Mexico City, but this year I'm on a student exchange programme in the United Arab Emirates. At home in Mexico, I usually go to classes and study a lot, but here I'm working as a doctor in a hospital.

This week I'm on holiday, which is fun. I'm staying on the east coast. My hotel is by the sea and I can spend all day at the beach if I want. There are also lots of boat trips, so I'm visiting the little islands along the coast this week. Today I'm sandboarding in the desert. I'm having a great time!

3 Read the texts again and choose the correct answers.

   1 At the moment Koon-Sung is living in
      a a big city in the mountains.
      b an apartment in a valley.
      c a house on a hill.

   2 From the window of his apartment at home, he can see
      a the valley.
      b the city.
      c the mountains.

   3 This year, Carla is
      a studying hard.
      b working in a hospital.
      c spending a lot of time in class.

   4 Today, she's
      a sandboarding in the desert.
      b in Dubai.
      c on a boat trip.

VOCABULARY

GEOGRAPHY AND THE NATURAL WORLD

1 Complete the sentences with the words in red in the text. There is one word you don't need.

   1 People enjoy hiking up big _____ in the summer and doing sports on them in the snow in winter.

   2 _____ often have lots of beaches and are great places to go on holiday.

   3 From the top of the mountain, you can look down into the _____ .

   4 I love the sea and I would like to live on the _____ one day.

   5 Many people say that a _____ becomes a mountain if it is more than 300 metres high.

   6 In the summer, I love lying under the green trees in the _____ .

   7 There are lots of fish in the _____ because the water is so clean.

   8 You can't take the boat there because there are two big _____ where the river goes down into the valley.

CARLA

2 Work in pairs and discuss.

What would you tell a tourist in your country who wants to:

a visit a waterfall?

b walk in the hills or mountains?

c visit some beautiful places on the coast?

Are they in the north, south, east or west?

3 Do you prefer the mountains, the coast or the desert? Why?

PRESENT SIMPLE OR PRESENT CONTINUOUS?

 GRAMMAR ON THE MOVE
Watch the video

1 Read the examples and match them with the rules.

1 I**'m** from Singapore.

2 I **work** in an office every day.

3 I**'m sandboarding** in the desert!

4 At the moment, I**'m living** in Turin.

a We use the present simple for a habit or regular action.	....
b We use the present continuous for something temporary – happening around now.	....
c We use the present simple for a fact – something that is always true.	....
d We use the present continuous for an action happening at the moment of speaking.	....

➡ *GRAMMAR REFERENCE* / *page 201*

2 Choose the correct answer.

1 It often *rains/is raining* in the spring.

2 I *'m staying/stay* at my friend's house at the moment.

3 Look it *snows/'s snowing*!

4 London is my home. I *live/'m living* there all the time.

3 Complete the text with the verbs in the box in the present simple or present continuous tense.

go	learn	not like	play
practise	stay	travel	wear

Leila Bruni ¹_____ the guitar and sings in a rock band. She lives in Rome but she ²_____ to different countries a lot with the band.

This week she's in America. She ³_____ in a hotel in Los Angeles. At the moment, she ⁴_____ with the band before their concert. They ⁵_____ some new songs.

The band gives concerts once or twice a week. After a concert, Leila always ⁶_____ to bed very late. She ⁷_____ getting up early the next day and sometimes she gets dressed too quickly. Today she ⁸_____ one red sock and one black one!

4 Work in pairs and discuss.

1 What are you doing at the moment? What do you usually do at this time on other days?

2 What clothes do you usually wear at school/work? What are you wearing today?

3 What things make you feel good? What are you feeling good about at the moment?

WRITING PART 6 `TRAINING`

INVITATIONS AND REPLIES

1 How do you invite your friends to do things? Do you usually call them/send texts/write emails? What are you doing with friends or family in your free time this week?

2 Look at the emails (1–3). What are the writers inviting their friends to do? Where and what time do they want to meet?

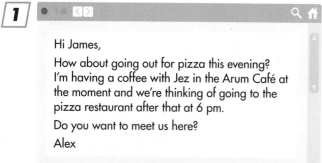

> **1**
>
> Hi James,
>
> How about going out for pizza this evening? I'm having a coffee with Jez in the Arum Café at the moment and we're thinking of going to the pizza restaurant after that at 6 pm.
>
> Do you want to meet us here?
>
> Alex

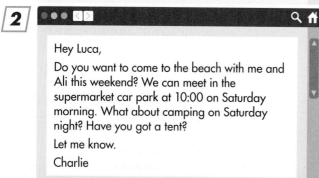

> **2**
>
> Hey Luca,
>
> Do you want to come to the beach with me and Ali this weekend? We can meet in the supermarket car park at 10:00 on Saturday morning. What about camping on Saturday night? Have you got a tent?
>
> Let me know.
>
> Charlie

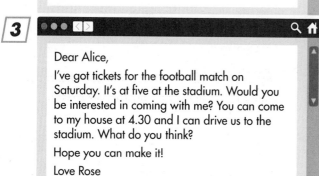

> **3**
>
> Dear Alice,
>
> I've got tickets for the football match on Saturday. It's at five at the stadium. Would you be interested in coming with me? You can come to my house at 4.30 and I can drive us to the stadium. What do you think?
>
> Hope you can make it!
>
> Love Rose

3 Look at how the writers begin and finish their emails.

1 Write the different ways they begin the emails. Can you think of any others?

2 Write the different ways they finish the emails. Do you know any others?

4 Match the answers (a–c) with the invitations in Exercise 2.

a I'd love to come, but I'm afraid I've got a music exam on Saturday afternoon. Can we meet for a coffee after the match instead? ....

b Thanks, that sounds great. I'd love to come, but I haven't got a tent. I need to get one. Can I let you know tomorrow? ....

c Thanks for asking but I'm babysitting at the moment so I can't come out for a pizza tonight. Maybe next week? ....

5 Which expressions do the writers use to say 'yes' and 'no' to the invitations.

PHRASES FOR SAYING 'YES'	PHRASES FOR SAYING 'NO'

6 Complete the invitations and the answers with the phrases in the box.

> about   afraid   come   interested   like   sounds

1 I know you like music so would you be .... in going to a concert tonight?

2 How .... going for a boat trip along the river on Sunday?

3 Would you .... to come for a picnic in the park at lunchtime?

4 I'm .... I'm away in London all weekend. Another time perhaps?

5 That .... great! What time does the film start?

6 I'd love to .... but I'm afraid I don't finish work until 9.30 this evening.

7 Look at the exam question and answer. Does the answer include all the 3 points?

> You would like to go camping next weekend. Write an email to your English friend, Morgan.
>
> In the email:
> * invite Morgan to come with you
> * say where you are going to camp
> * tell Morgan what to bring
>
> Write **25 words** or more.
>
> | Hi Morgan | |
> | Would you like to go camping with me next weekend? I'm planning to go to a campsite near the river. I have a tent and all the cooking equipment, so you only need to bring clothes and a sleeping bag. Let me know if you want to come. | invite Morgan

say where

what to bring |

8 You would like to play tennis next Saturday with your English friend Jo. Write an email to Jo.

In your email:
* ask Jo to play tennis
* say where you want to play tennis
* say what she needs to bring

Write **25 words** or more.

SPEAKING

DESCRIBING A PHOTO

1 Do you like taking photos? What do you take photos of? Do you take a lot of selfies? Where/when do you take them? Discuss in pairs.

2 Look at the photos (A and B). What can you see? Take turns with a partner to describe them. Try to say at least four sentences about each one. Think about:

- what you can see in the photo.
- where different things are in the photo.
- what is happening in the photo.
- what you think/feel/like etc. about the photo.

3 🎧 022 Listen to Irina describing one of the photos. Which photo is it?

4 🎧 022 Listen again and complete the sentences from the description.

1 The man's got .... and a ....
2 The man is wearing a .... and .... He looks ....
3 He's holding his phone on a selfie stick and he's ....
4 Maybe he's visiting the .... with ....
5 I think the fence is to stop people from falling .... the ....

5 Find three expressions in Exercise 4 which Irina uses to say what she thinks and give her own ideas about the photo.

1 He (She/It) looks …
2 ....
3 ....

6 Complete the expressions Irina uses for describing where things are in the photo. Use the words in the box.

> behind   bottom   middle   next   top

1 I can see a man who is standing .... to a big, beautiful waterfall.
2 The man is in the .... of the photo.
3 At the .... of the photo we can see a fence.
4 .... the fence is the river.
5 At the .... of the photo we can see the trees of a big forest.

7 Prepare to describe a photo. Student A and B look at page 192. Make notes using the box below.

USEFUL LANGUAGE

Think about what's in the photo.
In the photo, I can see … There is/there are …
Think about where things are in the photo.
At the top/bottom/in the middle/on the right/left …
Talk about the weather in the photo.
The sun is shining … There are clouds in the sky …
Think about how to say what is happening using the present continuous.
A man is standing … The people are looking at …
A woman is sitting …
Think of adjectives to describe the objects and people and more details to give.
He/She/It is … They're wearing …
Give your opinions/say what you think.
He/She/It could … Perhaps they are …

Describe your photo to your partner.

EXAM FOCUS

✓ EXAM FACTS

- You listen to one person giving information.
- You read a form or some notes in which there are five gaps.
- You listen and write numbers or words to complete the notes.

! EXAM TIPS

- Read the form or notes to complete before you listen. Try to decide if each answer is a number or a word.
- If the speaker spells a word, make sure you spell it correctly. You can check it the second time you listen.
- Remember, you might hear two possible answers for a question but only one is correct. Think about why the other answer is wrong.

🔊 023 **For each question, write the correct answer in the gap.**

Write **one word** or **a number** or **a date** or **a time**.

You will hear a woman giving information about a cycle ride.

Forest cycle ride

Length of ride:	30 km
Start time:	**(1)** .... am
Price of T-shirts:	**(2)** £ ....
Where to get a map:	**(3)** ....
Highest hill we'll cycle up:	**(4)** .... metres
Where ride ends:	**(5)** .... Village

WRITING PART 6

Read the email from your English friend, Harley.

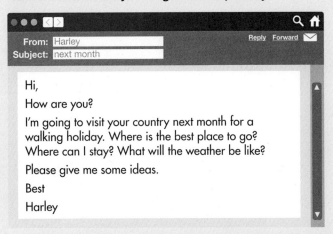

From: Harley
Subject: next month

Reply Forward

Hi,

How are you?

I'm going to visit your country next month for a walking holiday. Where is the best place to go? Where can I stay? What will the weather be like?

Please give me some ideas.

Best

Harley

Write an email to Harley and answer the questions. Write 25 words or more.

➡ **WRITING BANK** / pages 233–234.

HOW WAS IT?

Gave it a go ☐

Getting there ☐

Aced it! ☐

ASKING ABOUT THE WEATHER IN ...
VANCOUVER

A

1 Look at the photos (A–D) of Vancouver. Which season does each one show? What activities do you think people do at different times of year? Read the web page to check your ideas.

2 Read the web page again. Answer the questions with the correct seasons. More than one answer may be possible.

1 When is the most popular time to visit Vancouver? ....

2 When does it start to get warmer? ....

3 When does it often rain? ....

4 When are hotels very expensive? ....

5 When do people from the city enjoy time by the sea? ....

6 When are hotels cheapest? ....

B

What's the best time to visit
Vancouver?

March to May

Spring comes early in Vancouver and this season is a good time to visit the city. As temperatures begin to rise (around 15 degrees Celscius), flowers start to come out, so the city suddenly starts to look bright and colourful. Residents like to walk through Stanley Park to enjoy the warmth of the spring sunshine, after the long, hard winter. There's also plenty to do in the city, with fun activities for all ages.

June to August

Summer is the high season in Vancouver. This is when the largest numbers of travellers come to the city and they can enjoy exciting outdoor activities such as hiking and sailing. Temperatures get to the low 20s, so residents put on their swimsuits and go to Kitsilano Beach at English Bay. The only real problem with a summer visit is hotel prices, which are at their highest.

September to November

Autumn is another pleasant time for a visit to Vancouver. The hordes of tourists go home and temperatures fall to between 15 and 20 degrees C, but the city is still busy. Days can be chilly, but residents continue to spend time enjoying Stanley Park's walking paths (now covered with red and orange leaves), and the beaches of Kitsilano and Point Grey.

December to February

If you want to enjoy winter sports, Vancouver is a great place to visit. Colder weather brings thousands of skiing fans to the area. But if you want to see the city, now is probably not the best time. Although hotel prices are at their lowest during the winter, temperatures are usually around freezing, and there are frequent rain showers, which can take the fun out of your trip.

C

3 Find the phrases in the text and choose the correct definitions.

1 temperatures begin to rise
  a it starts to get hotter
  b it often gets colder
2 the high season
  a the longest season
  b the time when the most tourists visit a place
3 hordes of tourists
  a tourists who are rude
  b large numbers of tourists
4 temperatures fall
  a it gets colder
  b it gets hotter
5 there are frequent rain showers
  a it doesn't often rain
  b it often rains

4 024 Listen to three tourists asking about the weather. Choose the information that each speaker receives.

1 a It isn't safe to go skiing today.
  b The weather is perfect for skiing today.
2 a It will be colder this afternoon.
  b It will be warmer this afternoon.
3 a It might rain this morning.
  b It might rain this afternoon.

5 024 Complete the phrases with the correct words. Listen again and check.

| all | forecast | OK | there's | want |

PHRASES YOU MIGHT USE

1 Do you know the weather _____ for today?
2 Is it _____ to go skiing this morning?
3 Do you think it will rain _____ day?
4 We _____ to go to the beach after lunch.
5 Do you know if _____ rain forecast today?

6 Sometimes people use informal language when talking about the weather. Match the sentences with the correct definitions.

PHRASES YOU MIGHT HEAR

1 You don't want to get caught out there once the storm comes.
2 Then it should clear and we should get some sun later on.
3 They reckon from about midday onwards it should dry up.
4 It's going to cloud over this afternoon and there may be a few showers.
5 The weather's a bit unpredictable at this time of year.

a The rain will stop and it will become sunny later.
b It's hard to know what the weather will be like in this season.
c It won't be sunny after lunch, and it might rain for a short time.
d They think that the rain will stop at about twelve o'clock.
e It's not good to be on the mountains when the weather gets bad.

7 Watch the video about the different seasons in Vancouver. What activities does it suggest for each season? Make notes. Use the box to help you.

| beaches | Chinese New Year | film festival | jogging |
| kayaking | sledge rides | swimming | whale watching |

8 Compare your notes. Watch the video again to check your ideas. What time of year would you most like to visit Vancouver? Why?

▶ WATCH

D

LIFE COMPETENCIES
ICT LITERACY, COLLABORATION, DECISION-MAKING

9 Work in pairs. Choose a city you would like to visit. Find out information about its weather and different activities you can do there at different times of year. When would you like to visit, and what activities would you like to do?

PROGRESS CHECK 1

UNITS S–2

1 Look at the photos and complete the sentences about what these people do each day. Use the verbs in the box.

get dressed   get on   get up
put on   take off   wake up

1 The man _____ at _____ .
2 The boy _____ at _____ .
3 The man _____ at _____ .
4 The woman _____ her jacket and leaves the house at _____ .
5 The girl _____ the bus at _____ .
6 The boy _____ his shoes when he arrives home at _____ .

2 Look at this family tree and complete the sentences.

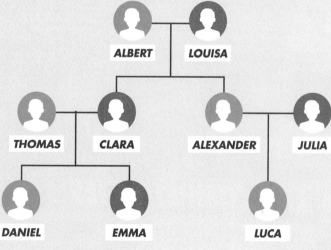

1 Louisa is Luca's _____ .
2 Emma is Julia's _____ .
3 Alexander is Emma's _____ .
4 Luca is Thomas' _____ .
5 Daniel is Luca's _____ .
6 Albert is Emma's _____ .

3 Complete the sentences about Emma's family, using the correct form of the verbs *be* and *have got*.

1 Emma _____ (have) one brother.
2 Albert and Louisa _____ (have) two children.
3 Luca _____ (be) Daniel's cousin.
4 Thomas and Clara _____ (be) Daniel and Emma's parents.
5 Luca _____ (not have) any brothers or sisters.
6 _____ Emma _____ (have) any sisters?

4 Choose a place from box A and a season from box B to match each sentence (1–4).

A | lake   coast   mountain   forest |

B | spring   summer   autumn   winter |

1 This is high, and you can ski on it when it's cold and there is snow. **A:** _____ **B:** _____
2 People go here to enjoy the sun and swim in the sea when it's hot and sunny. **A:** _____ **B:** _____
3 This is full of trees and is a nice place to go for a walk when the leaves change colour. **A:** _____ **B:** _____
4 If you go to a park when the weather starts to get warmer, you will often see ducks on this area of water. **A:** _____ **B:** _____

5 Complete the sentences with words in the box.

desert   hills   island   north
valley   waterfall   west

1 Great Britain is an _____ – an area of land with water all around it.
2 The sun comes up in the east and goes down in the _____ .
3 A _____ is a low area of land between _____ , and often has a river going through it.
4 Niagara is a famous _____ between Canada and the USA.
5 Germany is a country in the _____ of Europe, but Greece is in the south.
6 A _____ is a very dry place where it doesn't rain very often.

6 Put the letters in the correct order to make a country or nationality.

1 eFarnc   _____
2 niatlal   _____
3 oxMeci   _____
4 pinSahs   _____

7 Put the adverbs in the box in the correct place in each sentence.

| always | every day | never |
| often | sometimes | usually |

I work at night a lot.

1 Nurses have to work at night.

I practise from Monday to Sunday.

2 Musicians need to practise.

I work from Monday to Friday.

3 Teachers go to school at the weekend.

I have to wear these clothes for school.

4 Some school children wear a uniform.

My shop is often busy on Saturdays and Sundays.

5 Is your shop busy at weekends?

I travel to other countries about once a month.

6 Business people travel to other countries.

8 Choose the correct option to complete the sentences.

1 I *drink/I'm drinking* coffee when I get up in the morning.
2 I don't want to go out today – *it rains/it's raining*.
3 I *wake up/I'm waking up* at seven thirty every day.
4 In my country *it never snows/it's never snowing*.
5 Where's Jack? *Does he play/Is he playing* football?
6 *We go/We are going* to the beach every summer.

9 Read the sentences and correct any mistakes in the verb tense or adverb of frequency.

1 I am sorry that I can't coming to the class tomorrow.
2 She have green eyes and blonde hair.
3 The people there is very friendly.
4 I usually can write twice a month.
5 The club is open always.
6 I sell a bike that I bought two years ago.

10 Read the text about Olivia, and choose the correct answer (A, B or C) for each gap.

Olivia works in a hospital. She is a *1*_____ . She gets *2*_____ at six o'clock every morning. For breakfast she *3*_____ some toast and a cup of coffee. After breakfast she *4*_____ her shoes and coat and *5*_____ the house. Olivia can't drive to work because she doesn't have a *6*_____ . If the weather is nice, she walks, but she doesn't like getting wet, so if it's *7*_____ , she walks to the bus stop and *8*_____ for the bus.

1	**A**	shop assistant	**B**	photographer	**C**	nurse
2	**A**	on	**B**	up	**C**	off
3	**A**	has	**B**	does	**C**	takes
4	**A**	brings back	**B**	goes in	**C**	puts on
5	**A**	misses	**B**	leaves	**C**	goes
6	**A**	driving licence	**B**	passport	**C**	ID card
7	**A**	foggy	**B**	rainy	**C**	sunny
8	**A**	hopes	**B**	stays	**C**	waits

3
FREE TIME, SCREEN TIME?

TV AND THE INTERNET

1 How many hours a week do you use screens, watch TV or play video games? Discuss in pairs.

HOW WE SPEND OUR FREE TIME

- 📺 54%
- 👍 20%
- ▶ 12%
- 🎮 8%
- 🎾 6%

2 Look at the diagram about how people usually spend their leisure time. In pairs, match the activities below with the percentages.

> playing sports and doing exercise   watching TV
> watching videos online   using social media
> playing video games

3 🎧 025 Listen and check. Were you correct? Are you surprised by any of the answers?

4 🎧 026 Read the quiz below. Then listen to Roz and answer the questions.

1 What is Roz's score for each activity?
2 What is Roz's final score? What does it mean?

MY SCREEN LIFE

How much time do you spend in front of screens and on the internet?

How often do you ...

- chat online?
- message friends?
- upload photos?
- download films?

- watch an episode/series?
- write or follow a blog?
- watch vlogs?
- stream music?

Choose from 0–5:
0 = less than once a month
1 = several times a month
2 = once a week
3 = several times a week
4 = once a day
5 = several times a day

5 🎧 026 **Complete the sentences. Then listen again and check.**

1 I _____ _____ with you every evening!

2 I _____ my _____ all day. That's how we talk to each other if we aren't together.

3 I like _____ _____ to social media sites to share them with my friends.

4 I usually _____ an _____ from my favourite series every day.

5 I _____ music all the time.

6 **Work in pairs and do the quiz. Turn to page 192 and calculate your scores. Ask questions to find out more about what your partner watches and listens to.**

What kind of music do you stream?

Which series do you watch?

Who do you message the most?

Who's your favourite blogger?

7 **Work in pairs and discuss the questions. Use the words in the box.**

action film	comedy	crime drama
documentary	horror	news
quiz show	cartoon	

1 What kind of programmes do you often/ sometimes/never watch?

2 Talk about a programme you like. What's it called? When do you watch it? What genre is it? Who's in it? Why do you like it?

VOCABULARY: ADJECTIVES TO DESCRIBE FILMS

1 **Read the reviews and answer the questions.**

1 Which one is about a science-fiction film? a horror film? a comedy?

2 Which films did the writer enjoy/not enjoy?

1 If you like amusing stories, you will love this funny film about a woman who is looking for her lost love. The story is silly and hard to believe, but the actors are great and play their roles well. I know it isn't like real life, but the brilliant ending will make you laugh out loud and feel good.

2 I was excited about watching this film. I expected it to be really scary, but it was actually very disappointing. The actors were awful and the story was just boring.

3 I'm someone who usually doesn't enjoy films like this. I find them uninteresting and a bit too serious, but this one was fantastic. Most of the story is set on a spaceship far away from Earth, with only four characters. However, it's never dull and the excellent actors and the exciting story make this a very enjoyable film.

2 **Match the beginnings of the definitions with the correct endings.**

1 If something is disappointing

2 A scary film

3 If I say something is awful

4 If we say something is silly

5 Uninteresting means that

6 If something is enjoyable

7 If something is never dull

8 If I say something is brilliant

9 A serious film or book

10 The opposite of an amusing film

a doesn't try to be funny but it makes you think.

b makes you feel frightened.

c it makes you feel good.

d it is not as good as we hoped it to be.

e it isn't ever boring.

f I think it's very good.

g is a film that isn't funny.

h something is not interesting.

i we mean that it isn't clever, but it might be funny.

j I think it's very bad.

GRAMMAR

PAST SIMPLE OF *TO BE*

GRAMMAR ON THE MOVE
Watch the video

1 **Look at the examples and complete the rules.**

> It **wasn't** very funny – it **was** a bit boring actually.
> We **were** at home on Friday night.
> The action films **weren't** very exciting.
> **Was** it good? No, it **wasn't**.

1 The past form of **is/am** = _____ .	
2 The past form of **are** = _____ .	

Positive and Negative	
I/He/She/It **was/wasn't**	
You/We/They **were/weren't**	
Questions and short answers	
Was I/he/she/it there yesterday?	Yes, I/he/she/it **was**.
	No, I/he/she/it **wasn't**.
Were you/we/they there yesterday?	Yes, you/we/they **were**.
	No, you/we/they **weren't**.

➡ **GRAMMAR REFERENCE** / page 202

2 **Read the conversation and complete with *was*, *wasn't*, *were* and *weren't*.**

Charlie:	Were you at home last night?
Steve:	No, I ¹_____ . I was at Joel's party.
Charlie:	²_____ you? Was it good?
Steve:	It was OK.
Charlie:	Were there many people there?
Steve:	Yes, there ³_____ .
Charlie:	And what about Gabi? ⁴_____ Gabi there?
Steve:	No she ⁵_____ . Where were you anyway? Why ⁶_____ you there?
Charlie:	Because I was at Leila's party. It was fantastic!

3 **Work in pairs and ask and answer.**

Where was/were you/your best friend/your parents …
- at six/eight o'clock this morning?
- at lunchtime?
- on Saturday?
- at ten o'clock yesterday evening?
- at 3 o'clock yesterday morning?
- this time yesterday?

LISTENING PART 5 | TRAINING

1 **What do you enjoy doing at the weekend? Where were you last weekend?**

2 🔊 027 **For these questions, choose the correct answer.**

You will hear Abby talking to Sophie about what they and their friends did on Saturday. Where were they? Listen to the first part of the recording.

> *You might hear words from several of the options (A–G) below. This does not always mean they will be the correct answer.*
>
> *Sophie talks about the football stadium, but A is wrong because she didn't go to see a football match. She says she went to see (= visited) her cousin (= a family member), who lives near the football stadium.*

Example:
0 Sophie   Answer: F

3 🔊 028 **For questions 1–4, choose the correct answer.**

People	**Activities**
1 **Alice**	**A** at a football match
2 **Meg**	**B** at work
3 **Ben**	**C** in bed
4 **James**	**D** shopping
	E studying at home
	F ~~visiting a family member~~
	G watching videos

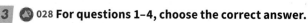

GRAMMAR

PAST SIMPLE

▶ **GRAMMAR ON THE MOVE**
Watch the video

1 **Look at the examples and complete the rules.**

*She **phoned** me to say she was feeling sick.*
*She **went** to bed.*
*You **didn't play** tennis yesterday. What **did you do** instead?*

---

1 We use the past simple to talk about past time, e.g. *last weekend, yesterday, last year,* etc.
2 To make the past simple form of regular verbs, we add _____ to the end of the verb.
3 Many verbs are irregular, eg:
take – took   think – thought   become – became   speak – spoke
eat – ate   get – got   feel – felt   make – made
4 We use _____ before the main verb to make negative forms and _____ to make questions in the past for both regular and irregular verbs.

Positive
subject + play**ed** / decid**ed** / **felt** / **made**

Negative
subject + **didn't** + verb

Questions and short answers
Did + subject + verb?
Yes, subject + **did**.
No, subject + **didn't**.

➡ **GRAMMAR REFERENCE** / **page 202**

2 **Write the past forms of the verbs.**

1 see _____
2 get up _____
3 come _____
4 go _____
5 say _____
6 have _____

3 **Use the words to make sentences in the past simple.**

1 She / say / 'good morning' / when / she / see / us.
2 I / not see / her / there.
3 They / have / a / really good time.
4 She / stay / with / you / last week?
5 No / she / not.
6 He / play / video games / until midnight.

4 **Complete the text about what Hugo did last weekend. Use the correct past simple form of the verbs in brackets.**

I ¹_____ (visit) my grandmother last weekend. She lives on a farm and she works very hard. So I ²_____ (not stay) in bed late like I usually do in the morning! We ³_____ (get) up early and ⁴_____ (work) in the fields. I ⁵_____ (help) her look after the sheep and vegetables. We ⁶_____ (not stop) until midday. Then my grandmother and I ⁷_____ (come) back to the house. She ⁸_____ (make) lunch and I ⁹_____ (clean) the kitchen.
My cousins, uncles and aunts arrived at one o'clock to eat with us. We ¹⁰_____ (not finish) lunch until late in the afternoon!

5 **P** 🔺 029 **The -*ed* ending of verbs is pronounced in different ways. Listen and repeat the examples.**

1 -*ed* is pronounced /d/ when a verb ends in a voiced sound: *b, g, l, m, n, r, v, w, z.*
*I pho**ned** my friend.   We lo**ved** the film.*
2 -*ed* is pronounced /t/ when a verb ends in an unvoiced sound: *c, ch, k, f, p, s, sh, x.*
*She coo**ked** lunch.   I hel**ped** my grandmother.*
3 -*ed* is pronounced /ɪd/ when a verb ends in *t* or *d.*
*She invi**ted** my cousins.   We downloa**ded** a film.*

6 🔺 030 **Practise saying these sentences with a partner. Then listen, check your answers and repeat.**

1 I uploaded lots of photos.
2 We cooked lunch.
3 They started early.
4 He streamed some music.
5 I liked the film.
6 We enjoyed the party.

7 **Use the words to make questions in the past simple. Ask and answer with your partner.**

1 What / do / last weekend?
2 Where / go / on your last holiday?
3 How / you / come / to class / today?
4 What / be / the last / really good film / you see?

VOCABULARY

TIME EXPRESSIONS

1 Look at the questionnaire and then read some of Maria's answers to it. Write which questions she answered.

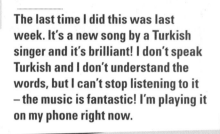

When was the last time you ...?

... read a really good book?
   ... downloaded a great song?
... watched a film that made you cry?
      ... posted a comment on social media?
... phoned a friend?
      ... played a game/sport?
... walked more than 5 km?

1 The last time I did this was last week. It's a new song by a Turkish singer and it's brilliant! I don't speak Turkish and I don't understand the words, but I can't stop listening to it – the music is fantastic! I'm playing it on my phone right now.

2 I phoned my friend Joe about five minutes ago to say 'happy birthday' to him. Most of the time, I text my friends, but this was different. A birthday is special! I wanted to speak to him in person.

3 The last time I cried in the cinema was about two years ago. If I know a film has a sad ending, I usually don't go to see it! I prefer happy films and books.

4 I usually go everywhere by bike, I hardly ever walk. I think the last time I walked a long distance was last year when I went on holiday in the mountains.

2 Read Maria's answers again and answer the questions.

1 What is Maria listening to at the moment?
2 Why did she phone Joe instead of texting him?
3 What kind of films doesn't Maria like?
4 What did Maria do when she was on holiday in the mountains?

3 Find the expression in each of Maria's answers that tells us **when** she did the actions.

1 last week   *3* ....
2 ....   *4* ....

4 Put the time expressions in the boxes in the correct places on the time lines.

| an hour ago   yesterday afternoon |

¹ .... last night   ² .... five minutes ago

← ——————————————————— →
past   **now**

| last month   last year   the day before yesterday |

³ .... 3 months ago ⁴ .... a week ago ⁵ ....

← ——————————————————— →
past   **now**

5 Look at the questionnaire below. Find someone in your class who did these things.

Find someone who ...

• went to bed after 11.00 pm last night.
• didn't use social media yesterday.
• listened to music last night.
• watched a film last weekend.
• didn't have breakfast this morning.
• did some exercise last week.

1 Write a question to ask about each activity.
2 Ask questions with *What/Where/When/Why did you ...* to get more information.

Did you go to bed after 11.00 pm last night?

Yes, I did.

What time did you go to sleep?

At 12.00 pm.

6 Now work with a partner and tell him or her what you found out about your classmates.

READING PART 3 `TRAINING`

1 Do you enjoy playing video games? Why?/Why not? Are you a good player? What's your favourite game?

2 Read the information about e-sports. Does anything surprise you? Would you like to watch or take part in e-sports?

> E-sports or electronic sports are competitions using video games. The first big e-sports competitions were in South Korea but now they are in lots of countries. Most players are professional gamers, which means that they play video games as their job. If you win a big competition, you can get a lot of prize money.

3 In pairs, discuss what the words in the box mean.

competition	prize	professional	win

4 Read the text about Haiyun Tang, a professional female gamer. Which games does she play?

Haiyun Tang is a gamer from Shanghai. When she was a teenager, she loved playing video games, and her favourite game was *World of Warcraft*. She became really good at playing this game and, after a few years, she joined *STARS*, a special club for excellent players. This meant she could begin playing in national competitions in China, and she soon won a number of these.

Later Haiyun decided that she would like to enter international competitions, so she learned a new game called *Hearthstone* and practised 12–16 hours a day. In 2015, an American professional team called *Tempo Storm* saw Haiyun playing in a Chinese competition. They invited her to join them. She chose the professional name 'Eloise' for herself and became a professional Hearthstone player.

Eloise won $16,000 in prize money in her first two years with the team *Tempo Storm*. She also started playing on *Twitch TV*, an online service where people can stream video game competitions. At first, playing on *Twitch TV* was hard for Hiayun because she didn't speak much English, but now thousands of people pay to watch her playing. They also chat with her online, and she can make $4,000 per month on Twitch TV.

5 Read the text again. For each question, choose the correct answer.

> *Look at Question 1. Think about the order of what happened: First, she was playing games when she was a teenager. A few years later she joined STARS. Then she played in competitions. So B is the answer.*

1 Hiayun started playing in important competitions in China
   A before she was a teenager.
   (B) after she joined the games club STARS.
   C as soon as she started playing *World of Warcraft*.

2 Why did Hiayun learn to play *Hearthstone*?
   A She thought the game could help her improve.
   B She saw a team called *Tempo Storm* playing this game.
   C She wanted to play against people from other countries.

3 In her first two years with *Tempo Storm*, Hiayun
   A was the only woman on the team.
   B earned $16,000 from winning competitions.
   C played in more games than her team mates.

6 Work in pairs and discuss the questions.

1 What do you think are the good and the bad things about being a professional gamer?

2 Would you like to be a professional gamer? Why?/Why not?

WRITING

A REVIEW

1 Are you watching a series on TV or the internet at the moment? Which one(s)? What kind of programmes do you like/not like?

2 Read a review of a TV series. What did the writer enjoy most about it?

Home   About   **Reviews**   Search

The Originals

I downloaded a really enjoyable series at the weekend and watched it with some friends. It's called *The Originals* and it's a science-fiction comedy-drama. The **setting** is the city of Madrid in the future and the story is about a group of young people. They are students and are all studying science at university. One night, they do a science experiment in their flat. They all get special powers and lots of strange but very funny things start to happen.

My favourite **character** is Valeria. She's clever and makes jokes all the time but she also does some very silly things! For a long time, she doesn't know what her special power is. My favourite **scene** is when she falls out of a window and finds out that she can fly.

I like *The Originals* because it's so unusual. The **plot** is sometimes difficult to understand but it's always funny and very exciting. But for me, the best thing about the series is the characters: they are just like real people. Some of them are like my friends. I also really enjoy the **dialogue**. The characters always say interesting things that make me think and laugh at the same time!

3 Match the words in blue in the review with the definitions (a–e) below.

a the story – what happens in the series
b what the people in the story say to each other
c a person in the story
d a moment in the story when something happens
e the place where the story happens

4 Read the review again and find this information.

1 What is the title of the series?
2 What is the setting of the series.
3 What sort of people are the characters?
4 What is the genre of the series?
5 Who is the writer's favourite character and why?
6 What is the writer's favourite scene?
7 Why does the writer like the plot?
8 Why does the writer enjoy the dialogue?

5 Read the review again and answer the questions.

1 Which paragraphs talk about the things in the box?
2 Write the key words from the review that describe each thing.

| setting | genre | why the writer likes it |
| favourite scene | plot | characters |

		KEY WORDS
paragraph 1	setting	*The city of Madrid in the future*
paragraph 2		
paragraph 3		

6 Now plan your own review. Choose a series you want to write about. Copy the table in Exercise 5 and use it to plan what you want to say.

7 Write your review. When you have finished, exchange reviews with a partner and check each other's work.

- Did your partner include enough information?
- Can you find any grammar or spelling mistakes?
- Is the review interesting? Would you like to watch this programme? Why?/Why not?

SPEAKING

TALKING ABOUT THE WEEKEND

1 Have you got any friends or family who live in other countries? Where do they live? How often do you speak to them? What kind of things do you talk about?

2 🎧 031 Listen to Sara, who lives in England, talking online to her sister Iman, who works in New York. Who had a fun weekend?

DID YOU KNOW?

*Some British English speakers say that they are watching **telly**, but American English speakers always say that they are watching **TV**.*

3 Put the words in order to make questions for asking about the weekend.

1   a / you / have / weekend? / Did / nice
2   was / weekend? / your / How
3   up / did / get / Sunday? / to / on / What / you
4   the / do / at / did / weekend? / you / What

4 🎧 031 Listen again. Who gave these answers to questions about the weekend? Write I (Iman) or S (Sara).

It was …
☐ really good   ☐ not great   ☐ really quiet   ☐ quite busy

What did you do?
☐ not much   ☐ this and that

5 Match the questions (1–6) with the correct answers (a–f). Which are in the present and which are in the past tense?

1   So how was your Saturday?
2   What did you get up to at the weekend?
3   What did you do on Friday night?
4   Did you have a good weekend?
5   What do you usually do at the weekend?
6   Do you see your friends at the weekends?

a   I met some friends after work and we went to the cinema.
b   I go shopping and clean the house but I try to do something interesting too.
c   Not great. I was sick and stayed in bed all day.
d   What weekend? I worked all day Saturday and Sunday!
e   No, they work at the weekends, but I usually see them during the week.
f   Yes, I did, thanks. It was really quiet, but it was nice to stay at home.

6 Write at least five questions to ask your partner about the weekend, then ask and answer.

• Include some present tense questions about what he/she normally/usually does.
• Include some past tense questions about last weekend.
• Include a mixture of *yes/no* questions (with *do/did*) and *Wh-* questions with *What/Where/When/Who/Why*.

✓ **EXAM FACTS**

- You read a long text.
- You answer five questions about the text.
- One question might be about the whole text, not just a section of the text.

! **EXAM TIPS**

- Look at the question numbers to find out which part of the text the answer is in.
- Read the question carefully and underline the part of the text where you can find the answer.
- Look at all three options A, B and C and decide which one is the correct answer to the questions.
- Remember that words from A, B and C may all be in the text, but only one is the correct answer.

For each question, choose the correct answer.

Working in the theatre

By Grace Mellor

I love my job! I studied dance at university, but I was never sure I wanted to be a dancer. One day, when I was reading an entertainment magazine, I saw advertisements for stage managers. 'That's what I want to do,' I thought. I've got a friend who does make-up in a small theatre, so I contacted her. I was lucky because the stage manager there needed an assistant.

My boss, the stage manager, tells me what everyone needs to do, and it's my job as assistant stage manager to see that they do it when they should. She seems to spend her day answering questions from people – actors, writers, and everyone else who works here. And they all want her to decide immediately!

Most people don't really understand my job. They think it's all about moving heavy things on and off stage. It isn't, which is good because I'm not that strong! People say, 'Are you doing this until you get better-paid work as a dancer?' They can't believe I want to work behind the scenes, not as the star of the show.

Some of my colleagues think we work too much. They want to go out with friends more. I have so many friends in the theatre, I don't feel like that. But one thing that is difficult is how hot it gets behind the stage. I didn't know that until I started here. I also didn't know just how many different jobs a stage manager – or the assistant – has to do. But that's one of the things I enjoy.

1 How did Grace get her job?
   A She saw an advertisement in a theatre.
   B She knew someone who worked in the theatre.
   C She had help from a friend at university.

2 As assistant stage manager, Grace has to
   A work with different types of people.
   B decide quickly what needs to be done.
   C make sure things happen at the right time.

3 Grace says other people are often surprised that
   A she doesn't want to be a dancer.
   B she isn't looking for a job with more money.
   C she is not very strong.

4 What doesn't Grace like about being an assistant stage manager?
   A the long hours that she works
   B the temperature behind the stage
   C having to do so many different things

5 What is Grace doing in this text?
   A explaining a job that not everyone knows about
   B giving information about different jobs in the theatre
   C helping people choose which job they want to do

✓ EXAM FACTS

- You listen to a conversation between two people.
- You see two lists (1–5 and A–H), and you match the people, places or things in the list 1–5 with the options A–H.
- You hear the conversation twice.

! EXAM TIPS

- Remember that you hear about the people from list 1–5 in the order that you read them and you will hear their names BEFORE you hear the answer for that person.
- You might hear about the things on list A–H more than once, but each is the correct answer for only one person.
- There is always an example for this task, with the answer given. Cross this answer off in the A–H list, as you won't need to use it again.
- There are two options in the list A–H that you will not need to use.

For each question, choose the correct answer.

🔊 032 **You will hear Luis talking to his friend about a weekend trip to the city. What activity is each person going to do?**

Example:

0   Luis   D

People		Activities	
1	Stella ☐	**A**	go shopping
2	Marco ☐	**B**	go to a concert
3	Lili ☐	**C**	go to the theatre
4	Richard ☐	**D**	meet a friend
5	Clara ☐	**E**	take a bus tour
		F	take a river trip
		G	visit a museum
		H	walk with a guide

HOW WAS IT?

Gave it a go ☐

Getting there ☐

Aced it! ☐

REAL WORLD

BUYING TICKETS FOR A SHOW IN ... NEW YORK

A

1 Look at the people in the photos (A–C). Where are they? What do you think they are doing?

2 Read the text about going to see a show on Broadway. Match the headings with the paragraphs.

| What to buy | What to see | Where to eat before the show | Where to get tickets | Where to sit |

BROADWAY SHOWS

Want to watch a Broadway show? Here's everything you need to know!

1

To help you decide, think about who is going to the show with you. If you're going with younger brothers and sisters, don't choose something too scary. And think about when you want to go, too. Some popular shows are booked up for months ahead. Check that there are tickets available before you start planning your trip.

2

Once you've chosen your show, book as early as possible. Prices are high, but discounts are available, so you don't have to pay full price. You can often get cheaper tickets online. If you're happy to go in the afternoon rather than the evening, matinee tickets are often half price. The TKTS Discount Booths sell same-day theatre tickets for 50% off. And many shows have standing tickets for sale a few hours before each performance.

3

Many theatre fans think that it's best to choose orchestra seats as close to the stage as possible. But this isn't always true. Sometimes you want to be further away, to get a bigger picture of what's happening. The mezzanine is higher up, and you usually get a good view. If you're tall, choose an aisle seat because you get extra space for your legs.

4

There are lots of restaurants around Times Square, but they are usually expensive, and the food isn't great. Look at restaurant reviews to find cheaper places to eat that are a bit further away from the theatres. These are often the places where New Yorkers eat and you'll get a much better meal.

5

Nothing! All theatres sell merchandise for their shows, but it costs a lot! If you really want a T-shirt or something else to help you remember your trip, look at the merchandise in the theatres, then look online to see if you can find the same thing at a lower price.

B

C

3 Read the text again. Decide if the statements are true (T) or false (F). Correct the false statements.

1 You have to wait a long time to see some shows.
2 It's usually more expensive to watch a show in the afternoon.
3 It's always a good idea to choose tickets that are near the stage.
4 You can get cheap meals in restaurants around Times Square.
5 The things that theatres sell to help you remember the show are usually expensive.

4 Find the phrases in the text and choose the correct definitions.

1 some shows **are booked up**
  a all the tickets are sold
  b there are lots of tickets that you can book
2 **discounts** are available
  a the prices are all the same
  b you can get cheaper tickets
3 **matinee tickets**
  a tickets for an evening show
  b tickets for an afternoon show
4 **orchestra seats**
  a seats that are high up in the theatre
  b tickets in the lowest part of the theatre
5 **an aisle seat**
  a a seat that is on the end of a line of seats
  b a seat that is in the middle of a line of seats

5 🔊 033 Listen to three tourists booking tickets for a Broadway show. Complete the details for the tickets that each tourist buys.

Speaker	Show	Day	Evening or matinee	Seats
1			evening	
2		Tuesday		
3	Charlie and the Chocolate Factory			Mezzanine

6 🔊 033 Complete the phrases with the correct words. Listen again and check.

Can I	Do you sell	I'd like	Is there	these vouchers

PHRASES YOU MIGHT USE

1 .... to book four tickets for *Wicked* on Thursday.
2 .... tickets for *School of Rock* here?
3 .... a discount for students?
4 .... book tickets for *Charlie and the Chocolate Factory* here?
5 Can I use .... to pay for the tickets?

7 Sometimes people use certain phrases when talking about theatre bookings. Match the sentences with the correct definitions.

PHRASES YOU MIGHT HEAR

1 The matinee's sold out.
2 I don't have four in a block.
3 I have two twos.
4 We don't offer any concessions.
5 Do you mind the back row?

a There aren't four seats together.
b Are you happy to sit far away from the stage?
c There are no tickets left for the afternoon show.
d There are two groups of two seats.
e There are no discounts.

8 ▶ Watch the video about Broadway. Match the numbers with the correct facts.

1 40
2 1,933
3 11,400
4 79
5 70%
6 20–50%

a the number of times a popular show was performed
b the amount of money (in millions) that one show cost
c the number of theaters in the Theater District
d the discount you can get if you buy tickets at a TKTS booth
e the number of seats in the Gershwin Theater
f the number of seats that tourists buy

9 ▶ Discuss the questions. Watch the video again to check your ideas.

LIFE COMPETENCIES

MAKING NOTES AND GIVING INFORMATION

10 Work in groups. Find out what shows you can see in your city, or a city near you. Find information about the prices, the different seats available, and discounts. Discuss the shows and agree on which one you would all like to see. Tell your classmates about your show and why you chose it.

4

KEEP FIT, FEEL GOOD

READING

1 Can you swim? How often do you swim? Do you like running? Have you got a bike? How often do you use it?

2 Our bodies can do lots of amazing things. Read the quiz and match the photos (A–F) with the questions. Then complete the quiz.

BRILLIANT BODIES

We hang out with our bodies all the time, so it's easy to forget how amazing they are. Did you know:

1 There are athletes who can run up to:

a 44 km per hour   b 37 km per hour   c 24 km per hour

2 Basketball players and dancers can jump nearly:

a 0.3 m   b 1 m   c 1.3 m

3 In one hour, it's possible for a cyclist to cycle:

a 25 km   b 54 km   c 75 km

4 There is a freediver who can stay under water for:

a 13 minutes   b 22 minutes   c 33 minutes

5 Speed skiers can ski up to:

a 150 km per hour   b 200 km per hour   c 250 km per hour

6 It's possible for a person to lift up to:

a 284 kg   b 2,840 kg   c 28,400 kg

3 🔊 034 Listen and check your answers. Does anything surprise you?

4 You are going to read interviews with some people who can do amazing things with their bodies. Read the texts. Which of the things can you do? Which would you like to be able to do?

AMAZING ATHLETES

Which athletes have the fittest bodies and can do the most amazing things?
We spoke to two top athletes to find out.

MIKHAIL – BALLET DANCER

'Ballet is great exercise: it's good for the **heart** because you are moving all the time and also jumping a lot.
I can jump one metre in the air when I'm dancing. My dance partner, Inna, can't jump as high as I can, but she can dance en pointe – on her **toes** – which I don't do. You need to have very strong feet for this: it takes years to learn and your feet hurt!
I need to have strong arms and a strong **back** because I sometimes lift Inna over my head as part of a dance. We usually practise for six to nine hours every day. We get very tired but we love dancing!'

OSCAR – QUARTERBACK

The great thing about American football is that there is a position for everyone. Players are often big and strong, but if you are small and fast, you can play American football too. I'm a quarterback and this position is very important. I need to play with my **brain** and my body. I have big hands and strong **fingers**, so I can throw the ball a long way. It's a very physical sport and there are often injuries. **Neck**, shoulder and **knee** injuries are a big problem and last year I couldn't play for three months after another player hit me in the **stomach** with his helmet.

---

5 Read the texts again. Are the sentences true (T) or false (F)? Correct the false sentences.

1 Ballet dancers jump a lot when they dance.
2 Only men dance on their toes.
3 It's important for Mikhail to have strong arms.
4 Small athletes can't play American football.
5 Oscar thinks a lot when he's playing.
6 Oscar could play in every game last year.

6 Which parts of the body can:

1 dancers sometimes hurt? ....
2 American footballers often hurt? ....

VOCABULARY

THE BODY

1 Label the diagram of the body with words in **red** from the text.

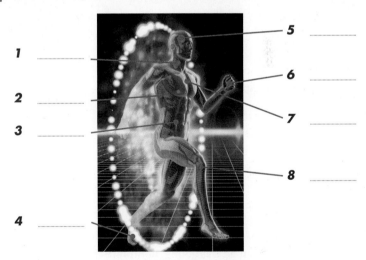

1 ....
2 ....
3 ....
4 ....
5 ....
6 ....
7 ....
8 ....

2 Complete the sentences with the correct words from Exercise 1.

1 People who can't use their hands and fingers can learn to write with their ....
2 It's very easy to hurt your .... when you lift something heavy.
3 Your .... joins your head to the rest of your body.
4 My .... hurts. I think I ate my sandwich too quickly.
5 A person's .... moves blood around their body.
6 People who have long .... can play the piano more easily.
7 We use our .... to think and control our bodies.
8 Your .... is in the middle part of your leg.

GRAMMAR

CAN AND CAN'T; COULD AND COULDN'T

GRAMMAR ON THE MOVE
Watch the video

1 Look at the examples and complete the rules for *can* and *could*.

*I **can** jump one metre in the air when I'm dancing.*
*Inna **can't** jump as high as I can.*
*Last year I **couldn't** play for three months.*
*I **could** throw the ball a long way when I was a young player.*
***Could** you skateboard when you were a child? No, I **couldn't**.*

---

1 We use _____ for things we are able to do in the present.
2 We use _____ for things we were able to do in the past.

Positive/Negative
Subject + **can/can't** + verb
Subject + **could/couldn't** + verb

Questions and short answers
Can + subject + verb?
Yes/No + subject + **can/can't**.

➡ **GRAMMAR REFERENCE** / *page 204*

2 Match the beginnings of the sentences (1–6) with the endings (a–f).

1 Can you finish the work by tomorrow
2 When I was a child I could stand on my head
3 He spoke very quietly
4 Be careful when you take Ben to the beach
5 There was so much food
6 Could you speak English

a that they couldn't eat it all.
b or do you need more time?
c when you were a child?
d because he can't swim.
e and I couldn't hear what he said.
f but I can't do it now.

3 Musician Ivan Morrison is talking about his life now and his life when he was young. Complete the sentences with *can, can't, could* or *couldn't*.

Now *and* then

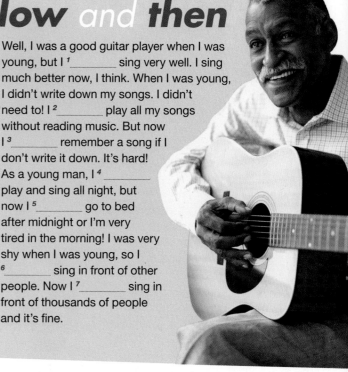

Well, I was a good guitar player when I was young, but I ¹_____ sing very well. I sing much better now, I think. When I was young, I didn't write down my songs. I didn't need to! I ²_____ play all my songs without reading music. But now I ³_____ remember a song if I don't write it down. It's hard! As a young man, I ⁴_____ play and sing all night, but now I ⁵_____ go to bed after midnight or I'm very tired in the morning! I was very shy when I was young, so I ⁶_____ sing in front of other people. Now I ⁷_____ sing in front of thousands of people and it's fine.

4 **P** 🔊 035 Read and listen to the dialogues. Notice which words are stressed. Circle the two unstressed examples of *can* in dialogue 1 and *could* in dialogue 2. How are *can* and *could* pronounced differently when they are unstressed?

1 **A:** Can you stand on your head?
 B: No, I can't. Can you?
 A: Yes, I can and I can walk on my hands, too!

2 **A:** Could you read when you were six years old?
 B: Yes, I could, a little. Could you?
 A: Yes, I could and I could write quite well, too.

5 Use the words in the box to make questions with *can* and *could*. Ask and answer in pairs. Be careful of the pronunciation!

| speak more than one language | play the guitar |
| swim 500 metres | ride a bike | cook | drive a car |

Can you cook?

Yes, I can. I'm a good cook!

Could you ride a bike when you were six years old?

No, I couldn't.

VOCABULARY

ILLNESS AND INJURY

1 🔊 036 **Listen and match the people (1–8) with the photos (A–H). What health problems have they got? Who hasn't got a health problem?**

 A

 B

 C

 D

 E

 F

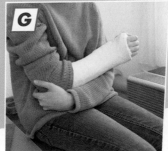 G

 H

1	Jack ☐		5	Harry ☐
2	Alissa ☐		6	Jenna ☐
3	Mina ☐		7	Daniel ☐
4	Luca ☐		8	Sally ☐

2 🔊 036 **Listen again and complete the information. Use the words in the box.**

> ache   arm   backache   cold   feels
> fine   head   hurt   stomach ache

1 Jack's got a _____ache.
2 Alissa broke her _____ yesterday.
3 Mina's got _____ .
4 Luca _____ his leg at football training.
5 Harry's got a _____ .
6 Jenna has got a _____ and she _____ sick.
7 Daniel's got tooth_____ .
8 Sally feels _____ !

3 🔊 036 **Match the beginnings of the sentences (1–7) with the endings (a–g). Listen again to check your answers.**

1 Jack's headache is
2 Alissa's friend called an **ambulance**
3 Mina needs to sit down
4 Luca hurt his leg
5 Harry went to the **pharmacy**
6 Jenna is ill because
7 Daniel's friend thinks

a to get some **medicine** for his cold.
b he should go to the **dentist**.
c she ate some bad fish.
d and she went to hospital.
e because of the sun.
f but he didn't break it.
g and have a rest.

4 **Complete these expressions with one word.**

> better   hurt   matter   sorry   well   your

1 Are you OK, Roy? What's the _____?
2 How are you, Sally? Are you _____?
3 Does your arm _____?
4 I'm _____ to hear that.
5 I hope she gets _____ soon.
6 How's _____ knee?

5 **Which of the expressions in Exercise 4 do we use:**

1 to ask about a person's health?
2 to respond to information about a person's health?

6 **Work in pairs and discuss the questions.**

1 When was the last time you felt ill?
2 What do you do when you:
   a have a headache?
   b have a cold?
3 What number do you ring for an ambulance in your country?
4 How often do you go to the dentist?

GRAMMAR

SHOULD/SHOULDN'T FOR GIVING ADVICE

 GRAMMAR ON THE MOVE
Watch the video

1 Do you think you have a healthy lifestyle? Discuss the questions in pairs.

1 Do you eat fruit and vegetables every day?
2 How many hours do you sleep at night?
3 Are you fit? How often do you exercise?
4 How much water do you drink every day?

2 Read the information about how to be fit and healthy and complete with the numbers in the box.

| 1.6 | 10 | 25 | 9 | 5 | 30 |

FACT FILE: HOW TO BE FIT AND HEALTHY

» FOOD:

You should eat at least ¹_____ pieces of fresh fruit and vegetables per day.

You shouldn't eat more than 60g of fat, ²_____ g of sugar and 2g of salt per day.

» WATER:

It's important to drink enough water, but you shouldn't drink too much.

Men should drink 2 litres of water a day and women should drink ³_____ litres.

» SLEEP:

Teenagers should sleep 8–⁴_____ hours a night and adults should sleep 7–⁵_____ hours.

» EXERCISE:

Everybody should do some form of exercise for 20–⁶_____ minutes per day.

3 Look at the examples of *should* and *shouldn't* and complete the rules.

Men **should** *drink two litres of water a day.*
You **shouldn't** *eat more than 60g of fat.*

---

1 We use **should** and **shouldn't** to give advice.
You ¹_____ do this. = 'It's a good idea to do this'.
You ²_____ do this. = 'It's not a good idea to do this'.
2 In questions, **should** goes in front of the subject,
e.g. ³_____ he do this?
Yes, he should. / No, he ⁴_____ .

➡ *GRAMMAR REFERENCE / page 205*

4 Complete the sentences with the correct form of *should* and one of the verbs in the box.

| drink | drive | eat | exercise | walk |

1 He's always hungry: he _____ more for breakfast.
2 'I don't have any energy and I feel unfit.
I _____ more?' 'Yes, you _____!'
3 I _____ more water during the day!
4 He needs to exercise more: he _____ to the shop, he _____ there. It's not far!

5 What changes should you make to have a more healthy lifestyle? Tell your partner.

> I should drink more water.

> I shouldn't stay up late at night.

SPEAKING

GIVING ADVICE

1 🔊 037 Look at the photos and read the questions. Listen to a health and fitness expert giving advice to two people. Do you think she gives good advice?

A
> I love fast food – I eat it all the time. Is it really bad for me?

B
> I want to get fit so I started running but I hate it! It makes me feel terrible. What should I do?

2 🔊 037 Listen again and complete the expressions she uses to give advice.

| you should | how about … | why don't you … |
| you shouldn't | what about | |

1 Perhaps _____ start exercising more slowly.
2 To begin with, _____ walking for half an hour every day?
3 _____ try some different types of exercise?
4 It's OK to eat fast food sometimes, but _____ eat it all the time.
5 _____ try some other types of food?
6 If you really want a burger, _____ having a salad with it?

3 Work in pairs. Take turns to give each other advice about a healthy lifestyle.

1 🔊 038 **Listen to three conversations about people with different types of health problems. For each question, choose the correct answer.**

First look at question 1 and the options. Listen to the first part of the recording.

> *The women talk about the ideas in the three options (A, B and C), but they don't always use the same words that you read in the question. Think about how to say each idea using different words. For example, I'm tired = I need to sleep, or I'm worried = I'm thinking about problems and feel stressed.*
>
> ***A** is correct because she <u>didn't sleep last night</u> and she <u>can't keep her eyes open</u>. **B** is wrong because she was sick yesterday but her stomach's better today. **C** is wrong because she has finished all her work today.*

1   Annie is talking to her friend at work. What's the matter with Annie?
   (A) She's feeling very tired.
   B She's got a stomach ache.
   C She's worried about her work.

2 🔊 039 <u>Underline</u> **the important information you need to listen for in questions 2 and 3 and the A, B, C options. Then listen and choose the correct answer.**

2   You will hear Victor phoning his friend Karen. Why is Victor phoning?
   A He can't leave his house today.
   B He can't take her to the doctor's.
   C He can't go for a walk.

3   You will hear Jake talking to his friend Naomi. What's the matter with Jake?
   A His tooth hurts.
   B He has a headache.
   C There's a problem with his neck.

VOCABULARY: PARTS OF THE BODY

1 **Read the interview with Dr Jones, a specialist sports doctor. Do sports people usually injure the same parts of their bodies as ordinary people?**

Interviewer:	So, Dr Jones, your job is looking after sports people. Are their bodies very different from ordinary people?
Dr Jones:	Well, sports people are always fit and strong but in different ways. For example, if you run or swim a lot, your lungs get stronger because they need to hold more air. Swimmers also get very strong muscles in their arms and shoulders, and runners, of course, have strong legs, feet and ankles.
Interviewer:	And do sports people hurt themselves in different ways from us?
Dr Jones:	Yes, sports people hurt the parts of their bodies that they use a lot for their particular sport. So for example, tennis players have more problems with their elbows and their wrists than the rest of us because they use their arms so much. Skiers are another example. They often have problems with their hips – where the legs join the body – because of how they move when they ski. Sports players also break their bones more often than ordinary people.

2 **Match the words in orange in the interview with these definitions.**

1   Your _____ are where your feet join the body.
2   We use our _____ to breathe and bring air into our bodies.
3   Your _____ are where your arms join your body, near your neck.
4   We need strong _____ to move all different parts of our bodies and to carry things.
5   The _____ are the parts of the body between the hands and the arms.
6   _____ are hard things inside the body that support it.
7   The _____ are in the middle of the arms.
8   Your _____ are at the top of your legs where they join the body.

VOCABULARY

LINKING WORDS

1 When was the last time you had an accident? Where? When? What happened?

2 Read two stories about an accident and answer the questions.

A

Last year I was on holiday in the mountains with my family. One day, we went skiing. It was a lovely sunny day and we went to the top of the hill. I put on my skis and looked around. I felt very happy. 'I love skiing!' I thought and I started to ski slowly down the hill.

Suddenly a man skied in front of me! I tried to stop but I couldn't. I bumped into him and then I fell over. The man was OK, but he didn't stop.

I hurt my leg and my family took me to hospital. After that, I couldn't go skiing for the rest of the holiday. It was really boring!

B

One sunny afternoon, I was reading in our garden and I saw Sam, my nephew, climb a big tree. Sam didn't come back down so I went to have a look. He was stuck! I wanted to help Sam so I climbed the tree to get him.

When I got to the top, I took the boy in my arms and I started to climb down the tree but then I got stuck too. I couldn't move up or down.

Suddenly, Sam got frightened; he started to move in my arms and I fell out of the tree. I broke my arm when I hit the ground but Sam was fine! After that, he didn't climb any more trees!

1 Where were the people?
2 When did the accident happen?
3 How did it happen?
4 What part of their body did they hurt?

3 Look at the words and expressions in blue in the stories. They help us to link the different parts of the story. Which one(s) tell us:

1 when the story happened?
2 in what order events in the story happened?
3 that something happened quickly and was a surprise?

4 Find these verbs in the stories and then complete the sentences with the correct form.

bump into	fall over	get stuck	hit

1 The little boy ran so fast that he .... and hurt his leg.
2 When I threw the ball it .... the sports teacher on his head. He was very angry!
3 My dog went into a hole after a rabbit. He was too big to get out and he ....!
4 It was dark and I couldn't see anything, so I .... my friend.

WRITING PART 7   TRAINING

> In this exam task, you see three pictures, which together tell a story. You can write the story in the present or the past. Try to use linking words and time expressions and don't forget to write full sentences and check your spelling.

1 Read the sentences from a story about an accident and put them in order. Use the words in bold to help you.

    a   'Don't worry!' said Emily.

    b   'Sorry. We didn't know he was such a crazy horse!' said Joanna.

    c   **One afternoon**, Martha went horse riding with her friends Emily and Joanna.

    d   But when they got to the field, the horse **suddenly** went really fast, and Martha fell off.

    e   **When** Martha got on the horse, she asked, 'Are you sure this horse is safe to ride?'

    f   **After that** Martha had to go to hospital because her leg was broken.

2 Look at the three pictures. Write the story shown in the pictures. Write 35 words or more. Use the words below to help you.

> Useful words:
> Time expressions: suddenly, one day, after that, one afternoon
> Picture 1: swimming pool, water polo, sign, no running, fell, wet floor
> Picture 2: hurt, arm, ambulance, hospital
> Picture 3: the next week, couldn't swim, arm, broken, watch his friends, bored

 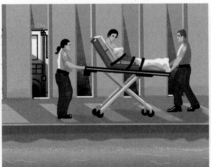 

SPEAKING

TELLING A STORY

1 🔊 040 You are going to hear Alex telling a story. Listen and fill in the table about what happened.

When and where?	
Who with?	
What did they do?	
How did he feel?	
What happened?	
What happened after that?	

2 Prepare to tell your partner a story about an accident. Make some notes using the questions in the table in Exercise 1.

3 Work in pairs and take turns to tell your stories. Ask your partner at least one question about their story.

EXAM FOCUS

✔ EXAM FACTS

- You listen to five short recordings in which one person or two people are speaking.
- For each recording, you read a question and choose the correct answer, A, B or C.
- You hear each recording twice.

❗ EXAM TIPS

- Before you listen, read each situation and question carefully.
- Don't worry if you hear words that you don't understand. You can choose the correct answer without understanding every word you hear.
- Remember, the speakers may use words from all three options, but only one is the correct answer to the question.
- When you listen the second time, check your answers.

🔊 041 **For each question, choose the correct answer.**

1 You will hear two friends talking about doing exercise. What does the man say about it?

A He thinks exercise is better with other people.

B He thinks he should exercise more.

C He thinks doing exercise is boring.

2 You will hear a woman leaving a message for a doctor's receptionist. Why did the woman call?

A She's forgotten the time of her appointment.

B She wants to change her appointment.

C She needs to make an appointment.

3 You will hear a woman called Lara talking to a friend about going shopping. What does Lara want her friend to do?

A help her choose something

B lend her some money

C give her a lift

4 You will hear a man talking about his new job. How does the man feel about his new job?

A He's glad he's earning more money.

B He likes his working hours.

C He thinks the boss is good.

5 You will hear two friends talking about an exhibition of photographs. Where will the exhibition be?

A in a train station

B in a hospital

C in a hotel

✓ EXAM FACTS

- You see three pictures which, together, tell a story.
- You write the story which is shown in the pictures.
- You write at least 35 words.

! EXAM TIPS

- You can write the story in the present or in the past, but use the same tense for the whole story.
- Write in full sentences, and join your ideas with words like and, so, because, and when.
- When you finish, check your spelling.

Look at the three pictures.

Write the story shown in the pictures.

Write 35 words or more.

➡ *WRITING BANK* / pages 235–236.

HOW WAS IT?

Gave it a go ☐

Getting there ☐

Aced it! ☐

REAL WORLD

IF YOU'RE ILL IN ...
DUBLIN

A S ...ARE ST. MEDICAL CENTRE DOCTOR PRESENT

1 Look at the photos (A–C) of places in Dublin. Why do people go to the places in these photos?

2 Read the webpage about what to do if you get ill or have an accident in Dublin. Match the photos with the paragraphs.

HOME | ABOUT | Q SEARCH

Being sick in Dublin is no fun, just like anywhere else in the world. So where should you go if you need prescription medicines or a consultation with a doctor?

1 Where can I buy medicine?

You can buy medicines in lots of different places. Supermarkets, small shops and petrol stations will probably sell a few standard medicines for headaches, sore throats and coughs. Many also sell medicines for allergies. Pharmacies are the only places that sell prescription medicines. Note that you will need an Irish prescription to get these.

2 What should I do if I need a doctor?

If you need to see a doctor during the day, ask your hotel who your nearest GP (general practitioner) is, and phone the medical centre to book an appointment. You will probably have to pay cash for the consultation, but this should not be more than €60. Remember, if you are an EU member, take your EHIC card (European Health Insurance Card) with you. Most doctors are open from nine to five, Mondays to Fridays. Outside these times, you will need to find a DOC (Doctor on Call), who will probably be at one of the larger medical centres. If you have an injury such as a broken bone, you can also go to the A&E (Accident and Emergency) department of a hospital.

3 What should I do in an emergency?

In any life-threatening emergency, you should call 112 or 999 and ask for an ambulance. An ambulance will be sent immediately and you will be taken to the nearest hospital. A nurse will decide how bad your illness or injury is and you will then wait to see a doctor. You may have to pay €100. Remember, when you are travelling, it's always a good idea to have travel insurance to pay for medicines or to see a doctor abroad.

3 Find the words and phrases in the text and match them with the correct definitions.

1 consultation
2 prescription medicines
3 GP
4 medical centre
5 EHIC card
6 DOC
7 life-threatening emergency
8 travel insurance

a a doctor who sees people with lots of different medical problems
b an agreement in which you pay money to a company and they agree to pay if something bad happens to you
c a meeting with a doctor
d a doctor who is available at night or at the weekend
e a time when your life is suddenly in danger
f medicines that you can only get with a note from a doctor
g a card that says EU members can see a doctor in EU countries without paying
h a place where a doctor sees people who are ill

4 Read the text again. Answer the questions.

1 Where can you buy standard medicines for a headache or sore throat?
2 Where can you buy medicines for allergies?
3 Where can you buy prescription medicines?
4 What should you do if you need to see a doctor during the day?
5 What should you do if you need to see a doctor at the weekend?
6 What should you do if you have a very bad injury?

5 🔊 042 Listen to three conversations about health problems. Where does each conversation take place? There is one extra answer which you do not need to use.

a at a hotel
b at a pharmacy
c in a GP's waiting room
d at a hospital emergency department

6 🔊 042 Complete the phrases with the correct words. Listen again and check.

| medicines painkillers prescription sore tablets |

PHRASES YOU MIGHT USE

1 I have a _____ from the doctor.
2 I'm not taking any _____ at the moment.
3 I take _____ for my headaches.
4 I have a really bad _____ throat.
5 I just need some _____ .

7 Match the sentences from the listening with the correct definitions.

PHRASES YOU MIGHT HEAR

1 Any other medical conditions?
2 You didn't have any side effects?
3 You must finish the whole course.
4 You can probably claim it back.

a It's important to take all the tablets or medicine.
b You will get back the money you pay.
c Do you have any other problems with your health?
d Did the medicine make you feel ill?

8 🔴 Watch the video. What do you learn about these things? Make notes.

- the city
- pharmacies
- medical centres
- doctors
- A&E departments
- the emergency number

9 🔴 Compare your notes. Watch the video again to check your ideas.

▶ WATCH

LIFE COMPETENCIES

SHARING IDEAS, AND PROBLEM-SOLVING

10 Work in groups. Find information about what visitors can do if they are ill in your city. Discuss the questions.

- Where can you buy medicines such as painkillers?
- Where can you get prescription medicines?
- Do you have to pay to see a doctor?
- How can you see a doctor at night or at the weekend?
- Where should you go in an emergency?

11 Make an information leaflet for visitors to your city. Present it to your classmates.

5 MORE THAN A HOLIDAY

A

TRAVEL

1 Is your country a popular holiday destination? Is it a problem when too many tourists visit some places?

2 Read the quiz and match each question with one of the photos.

3 Work in pairs. Take turns to ask and answer the questions. What kind of traveller are you?

1 Go to page 193 to find the result for your partner.

2 Tell your partner their result. Do they agree?

B

ARE YOU AN ADVENTUROUS TRAVELLER?

1 Before you travel, do you …
a find out as much information about your **destination** as possible and plan everything you can?
b decide one or two places you want to visit and things you want to do?
c not plan too much – you like surprises!

2 Your **accommodation** must be …
a a good hotel room with a bathroom, TV and WiFi.
b with local people – it's the only way to know a place.
c a simple, clean place that's not expensive or a **tent** on a campsite.

3 When you arrive in a new city, do you …
a go out and walk around?
b go to a **tourist information centre** and book your place on a tour with a **tour guide**?
c just visit the most famous and interesting places?

4 Your **luggage** for a two-week holiday is …
a two or three bags and suitcases – you want to be sure you have everything you need.
b one **suitcase** – but it isn't easy to get all your things in it!
c just a **backpack**, you don't like carrying lots of things.

5 You are driving to the airport to catch your flight. There is a lot of traffic on the road, how do you feel?
a Fine. You left your house very early, so you still have lots of time to catch your flight.
b Worried. This **delay** will make you late. You could miss your flight.
c Fine. If you **miss** this flight, you can catch the next one.

C

D

E

3 Complete the sentences with words in pink from the quiz.

1 For me, staying with local people in their houses is the best kind of holiday _____ .

2 The only problem with cheap travel is that if you _____ your flight because of a _____ getting to the airport, you can't just catch the next one.

3 We often go walking and camping in the mountains; We don't take much _____ , just a _____ to sleep in and a _____ with food and water.

4 An interesting city with lots of museums and restaurants is always a good _____ for me!

5 I like to pack a small _____ on Friday night and fly to a city for the weekend.

6 When I visit a city for the first time, I take a proper city tour with a _____ _____ , so I can learn all about its history.

7 I think that asking at the _____ _____ is a good way to find out about what's on.

4 Match the beginnings of the questions (1–6) with the endings (a–f). Then ask and answer with a partner.

1 What's your favourite kind of
2 What kind of holiday accommodation
3 Do you usually take a lot of
4 What do you do if you're camping
5 What do you think you need to know
6 When was the last time you

a and it starts raining?
b missed a flight? What happened?
c to be a good tour guide?
d holiday destination?
e do you like staying in?
f luggage with you when you travel?

LISTENING

1 ● 043 Listen to four people talking about what kind of traveller they are. Match them with their ideal holiday.

Loli   the city
Chloe and Lisa   the beach
Jamie   the mountains

2 ● 043 Listen again. Are the statements true (T) or false (F)? Correct the false statements.

1 Loli likes the beach but she doesn't enjoying swimming.
2 Loli often books her travel and accommodation online.
3 Lisa doesn't like staying in campsites.
4 Chloe and Lisa don't like travelling to places where they can't speak the language.
5 Jamie likes learning about the history of the places he visits.
6 Jamie often goes to the tourist information centre to find out about good restaurants.

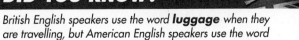

When was the last time you missed a flight?

Last year our train was delayed by an hour and we missed our flight.

DID YOU KNOW?

*British English speakers use the word **luggage** when they are travelling, but American English speakers use the word **baggage**.*

READING

1 Do you know how to ride a horse? Would you like to try riding a camel? Why?/Why not?

2 Read the text about Jon's camel ride.

1 Why did Jon want to ride a camel? Did he enjoy it?
2 Why did he want to get off?

A CAMEL AND ME

Last year when we were visiting Morocco, my friend Ali and I were trying to find something exciting to do, so we booked a three-day tour in the desert – travelling by camel.

We started our tour at 9 o'clock in the morning. Our tour guide's name was Mr Babou and he explained that travelling by camel is a very special experience.

'Camels are very friendly,' he said. 'They love their owners and are strong and brave.'

My camel's name was Aya. She was certainly big and strong but she didn't look very friendly. She was making strange, loud noises when I first saw her. Aya was saying hello to me.

Aya sat down and I got onto her but, as she was standing up, I fell off. This happened the first time – and also the second, third and fourth times! Finally, when Aya stood up for the fifth time, I didn't fall off and we started out across the desert.

After half an hour, I started to feel sick. I realised that riding a camel is a bit like being in a boat and I hate travelling by boat! After another half an hour, I was feeling so bad that I had to stop.

'Stop!' I shouted to Mr Babou. 'I can't do this!'

Aya stopped, and I fell off her again.

As I was lying in the sand, Aya turned her head and looked at me. She had a kind face. I could see that she was a nice animal but it was no good. At two o'clock that afternoon, we were driving to the coast in a rented car. Our camel tour was over.

3 Read the text again and answer the questions.

1 What does Mr Babou think is special about camels?
2 What made Jon feel frightened?
3 Why did Aya make strange noises?
4 Why do camels sit down when you want to ride them?
5 Why did Jon start feeling sick when he was riding Aya?
6 What did Jon think about Aya at the end?

GRAMMAR

PAST CONTINUOUS

 GRAMMAR ON THE MOVE
Watch the video

1 Look at the examples and choose the correct option to complete the rules.

*At two o'clock that afternoon, we **were driving** to the coast in a rented car.*
*Last year when we **were visiting** Morocco, my friend Ali and I **were trying** to find something exciting to do.*

> *1* We use the past continuous to talk about *an action in progress at a time in the past/finished events in the past.*
> *2* We use the past continuous to talk about two things happening *at the same time/at different times* in the past.
>
> **Positive/Negative**
> I/He/She/It **was** (**wasn't**) wait**ing** for you.
> You/We/They **were** (**weren't**) wait**ing** for him.
>
> **Questions and short answers**
> **Were** they wait**ing** for us? Yes, they **were**. / No, they **weren't**.

➡ *GRAMMAR REFERENCE / page 206*

2 Complete the sentences and questions with the correct past continuous form of the verbs in brackets.

1 What _____ they _____ at ten o'clock last night? (do)
2 It _____ yesterday, it _____ ! (not rain/snow)
3 They _____ on the bed in their hotel room and _____ TV at midnight. (lie/watch)
4 Last night she _____ her suitcase and he _____ some work. (pack/do)
5 I _____ in Paris last year. I _____ in Berlin. (not live/study)
6 '_____ he _____ the tour guide yesterday?' 'No, he _____ .' (look for/not be)

3 Use the words to make sentences in the past continuous.

1 Where / you / go / yesterday afternoon?
2 The children / not play / on the beach this morning.
3 She / try / take / a photo?
4 Your friend / not stay / this hotel.
5 'He / look at / her?' 'No / not.'
6 Which / city / they / visiting?

4 **P** ● 044 Listen to the dialogue and note where *was* and *were* are stressed.

A: Where were you last night? Were you at the party?
B: Yes, we were.
A: Was it good?
B: Yes, it was great! Weren't you invited?
A: Yes, we were. But we couldn't go because my mum was cooking us dinner.

5 **P** ● 045 Read the rules and choose the correct options. Then listen and check your answers.

> *Was* and *were* are usually unstressed in sentences. However they are stressed when used in negative contractions (*weren't/wasn't*) and at the end of sentences (Yes, they *were*).

1 A: Was it hot that day? *stressed/unstressed*
  B: No, it wasn't. *stressed/unstressed*
2 A: Was the exam really three hours long? *stressed/unstressed*
  B: Yes, it was. *stressed/unstressed*
3 The actors in the play were really funny. *stressed/unstressed*

6 Work in pairs and ask and answer.

1 Where were you living five years ago?
2 What were you doing before you came to class?
3 What were you doing this time yesterday?

LISTENING

1 Benedict Allen is a British explorer. A few years ago he crossed the Gobi Desert alone. Discuss the following questions with a partner.

1 Which countries is the Gobi Desert in?
2 What sort of problems do you think Benedict Allen had on his journey? (Think about weather, food, water, transport, etc.)

2 ● 046 Listen to part of a talk about Benedict's Allen's journey across the Gobi Desert. What was the weather like during his journey?

3 ● 046 Listen again and choose the correct answers.

1 Benedict Allen started his journey across the Gobi Desert in
  a August 1987. b August 1997.
  c August 1998.
2 It was a journey of
  a 6,000 km. b 1,600 km.
  c 16,000 km.
3 Benedict didn't use … to help him find his way.
  a animals b cars and motorbikes
  c modern technology
4 He needed to cross the desert
  a before the end of the winter.
  b before the beginning of the winter.
  c during the winter months.
5 One of Benedict Allen's camels ran away because it
  a was lost. b didn't want to leave the desert.
  c was afraid.
6 His most difficult problem was
  a not having enough food.
  b the cold.
  c not having enough water.

4 Work in pairs and discuss the questions.

1 What do you think are the good and bad things about being an explorer?
2 Which parts of the world would you like to travel to and explore? Why? Where wouldn't you like to go?

GRAMMAR

PAST SIMPLE AND PAST CONTINUOUS

 GRAMMAR ON THE MOVE
Watch the video

1 Read the examples and then choose the correct options to complete the rules.

*Aya **stopped** and I **fell** off her again.*
*When they **were watching** the news, he **heard** the beginning of a story.*

> **1** We use the **past continuous** with the past simple to talk about one action happening *in the middle of/after* another one.
> **2** We use the **past simple** to talk about finished actions in the past that can happen *at the same time/after each other*.

➡ **GRAMMAR REFERENCE** / page 207

2 Read and underline the actions that happened in the middle of another action in these sentences.

1 We were packing our bags when the dog ran out of the house.
2 When we were driving home, I realised I didn't have my passport.

3 Choose the correct form of the verb – past simple or past continuous.

1 We *were visiting/visited* the city centre when I *was losing/lost* my purse.
2 The bus *stopped/was stopping* and we *got off/were getting off*.
3 This time yesterday, I *had/was having* dinner in a restaurant and *read/reading* a book.
4 He *met/was meeting* his friend when he *walked/was walking* on the beach.

4 Complete the sentences with the correct form of the verb using the past simple or past continuous.

1 Where _____ you _____ (go) when we met you?
2 My friends _____ (sail) down the river when the storm _____ (start).
3 We _____ (drive) home when a dog _____ (run) in front of the car.
4 The sun _____ (shine) when we _____ (come out) of the museum.

GRAMMAR: *WHEN, WHILE* AND *AS*

1 Read about Helen Skelton and look at the sentences with *while, as* and *when*. Choose the best options to complete the rules.

Helen Skelton is a young woman who travelled 3,000 kilometres down the Amazon River alone by boat and, two years later, crossed Antarctica. **While** she was working on children's television in the UK in 2010, the director of the programme asked her to travel down the Amazon to raise money for charity. Some people didn't believe that she could finish such a difficult trip, but she did! A TV crew filmed her **as** she was doing it and lots of people were waiting to welcome her **when** she finished her journey. Two years later, she travelled 800 kilometres across snow and ice in Antarctica on skis and by bike.

> **1** We can use **when** or **while** or **as + past continuous**, to mean 'during the time that' and to connect two things that are happening at *the same time/different times*.
> **2** We can use **when + past simple** to introduce a finished action that happens *in the middle of/after* a longer action.

➡ **GRAMMAR REFERENCE** / page 207

2 Match the beginnings of the sentences 1–6 with the endings a–f.

1 When I was travelling across the desert,
2 As she was running out of the house,
3 While you were swimming in the sea,
4 More people were arriving at the party
5 My parents met
6 I finished packing our suitcases

a while you were looking for your passport.
b when they were working in South America.
c as we were leaving.
d I saw a lot of snakes.
e I was lying on the beach.
f she tripped and fell.

VOCABULARY

EASILY CONFUSED WORDS

1 Read the text. What does Eliza do for her job?
What kind of travelling doesn't she enjoy?

My friend Eliza works for a hotel company in Rome and she has to **travel** a lot. Her company often sends her on **trips** to visit hotels in far-away places, so she sometimes spends hours and hours on planes and trains. On a long **journey**, she reads or listens to music on her tablet. She says that travelling isn't a problem for her if she has a good book to read!

However, she sometimes has to go on quite long **cruises** because her company also offers this kind of holiday. She doesn't enjoy this at all because boats make her very sick. Even the short sea **crossing** between France and England was too long for her when she came to visit me last year. She doesn't mind spending hours on a plane, though, and two 15-hour **flights** in a week is normal for her.

2 Read the text again and match the beginnings and endings of the definitions.

1 To travel
2 If you go on a journey
3 A cruise is when
4 A trip is when
5 A crossing is a journey
6 A flight is when

a across a large area of water, like a sea.
b you travel from one place to another.
c you go somewhere by plane.
d you go on holiday in a ship and stop to visit places.
e is to go from one place to another.
f you visit a place for a short time and come back again.

3 Choose the correct option.

1 The *journey/trip* from Madrid to Barcelona takes about six hours by car.
2 We went on a great camping *trip/crossing* in the mountains last weekend.
3 Did you *travel/trip* to Tijuana for work last week?
4 My aunt went on a *cruise/flight* down the coast of France and Italy last year and visited lots of beautiful places.
5 I got a cheap *flight/crossing* from Paris to London, but I didn't realise that the airport was so far from the city centre.
6 The weather was very stormy during the *crossing/travel*; many of the passengers were ill and it took longer than usual to reach the other side.

READING PART 4 | TRAINING

1 Read the text about Antoine de Saint-Exupéry and the exam tip.

Antoine de Saint-Exupéry

Antoine de Saint-Exupéry was born in France in 1900. He learned to ¹_____ a plane at the age of 12. When he grew up, he became one of the first pilots to deliver mail ²_____ plane. He went on ³_____ over the Sahara Desert and the Andes Mountains, bringing mail to people there.
Once he ⁴_____ lost while travelling over Africa and crashed his plane in the middle of the desert. He wasn't killed but his story was in all the newspapers. When he ⁵_____ to Paris after his adventure, he was very famous.
He later wrote books about his adventures, such as *Night Flight* and *Wind, Sand and Stars*, but people probably know his book called *The Little Prince* best.

> *Look at the first gap in the text and the possible answers below. Which verb do we use with* a plane?
> *We can say* drive a car *and* ride a bike *but the pilot of a plane flies it, so B is the correct answer.*

2 Look at the other gaps. For each question, look at the three possible answers and decide which one fits the gap best.

1 **A** drive   **(B)** fly   **C** ride
2 **A** in   **B** on   **C** by
3 **A** trips   **B** holidays   **C** visits
4 **A** went   **B** got   **C** took
5 **A** stayed   **B** visited   **C** returned

DIFFERENT TYPES OF HOLIDAY

1 Look at the pictures of the different types of holiday and discuss the questions.

1 What can you see in the pictures?

2 Which words in the box would you use to describe each picture?

crowded	fantastic	lovely	noisy	popular
quiet	relaxing	terrible	tiring	

2 🎧 047 Listen to four people talking about their holidays. Match the speakers with the types of holiday in the pictures from Exercise 1. Which picture isn't mentioned?

Pablo ....   Arturo ....

Julia ....   Teresa ....

3 🎧 047 Listen again. Who had a good time and who didn't enjoy their holiday?

4 Complete the sentences with the phrases in the box.

> For me, a holiday is a time to relax
> The weather was fantastic   I didn't have a good time
> I think that the best holidays are   It was lovely

1 .... It was terrible! I hate being out in the rain.

2 .... The place was so quiet – it was really nice.

3 I didn't really enjoy it. ...., but New York is too noisy and crowded for that.

4 We had a great time. .... – really warm and sunny.

5 .... when you are with your friends.

5 Work in pairs. Look at the pictures again. Do you like these different things to do on holiday? Say why or why not.

6 Now ask and answer the questions.

1 Do you think walking in the mountains is good for you?

2 Do you think going to a fun park is exciting? Why?/Why not?

3 Which of these things to do on holiday do you like best?

4 Do you prefer to go on holiday with your friends or your family? Why?/Why not?

5 What did you do on your last holiday? Did you have a good time? Why?/Why not?

7 🎧 048 Now listen to some candidates doing Speaking Part 2. Look at the checklist and tick what the candidates do.

The candidates ask each other questions.	☐
The candidates give longer answers.	☐
The candidates give reasons using *because*.	☐
The candidates use phrases like *I think*, and *In my opinion*.	☐

WRITING

AN EMAIL ABOUT SOMETHING THAT HAPPENED ON HOLIDAY

1 🔊 **049 Listen to Lily calling her friend Carla and answer the questions.**

1 Where is she? What's she doing?
2 Who is she on holiday with?
3 Is she having a good time?

2 **Read Lily's email to Carla later in the week. What changed during the week?**

Hi Carla,

Right now I'm sitting in a café in town to write this email. It's cold and raining outside and I'm drinking coffee and eating cake. But today I'm finally beginning to enjoy the holiday!

Yesterday, we went for a long walk in the mountains. We carried everything with us on our backs. I had to carry a big backpack with all the food and I hated it! In the evening, when we were cooking our dinner we saw lots of sheep. They were coming down the mountain towards our campsite. They damaged the tents so badly that we decided to stay at a hotel.

This morning, when we were eating breakfast my friend Jo said that she wanted to stay at the hotel for the rest of the holidays, so we aren't going back to the campsite! After that, we went shopping and I bought some souvenirs – I'm really enjoying my holiday now!

Love

Lily

---

3 **Look at the time expressions in blue in Lily's email. Match the expressions with the phrases that mean the same thing.**

1	Right now	a	then
2	After that	b	the time just before the night
3	Yesterday	c	at this moment
4	In the evening	d	the day before today
5	This morning	e	before lunch, today
6	Today	f	this day

4 **Choose a time expression from Exercise 3 to complete the sentences. Use each expression once.**

1 We spent the day on the beach; _____ we went home to change and we went out to a club.
2 It's raining today, but _____ the weather was fantastic and we were out all day.
3 I'm sitting in the sunshine, enjoying the view _____ ; I can see across the valley.
4 _____ we got up early and we went for a long walk, so this afternoon, we're going to have a rest.
5 Yesterday morning, we visited lots of interesting places in the old city; _____ we had a fantastic lunch in a restaurant.
6 _____ is the first day of our holidays. I'm so excited.

5 **You are going to write an email to a friend about your holiday. Use the ideas below to help you plan what you are going to say. Write some notes.**

Paragraph 1:
• Where are you on holiday?
• Who are you on holiday with?
• Where are you when you are writing the email?
• What are you doing?
• How are you feeling right now?

Paragraph 2:
Think about something that happened on your holiday.
• When did it happen?
• Where were you and what were you doing when it happened?
• How did you feel about it?

6 **Write your email. When you have finished, exchange emails with a partner and check each other's work.**

READING PART 4

✅ EXAM FACTS

- You read a text which has six gaps in it.
- There are three possible answers for each gap.
- You choose the correct word for each gap.

⚠ EXAM TIPS

- Read the whole text first and think about the words that might go in the gaps.
- Look at the three possible answers and think about the differences between them.
- Check that the answer you choose is correct for the gap in meaning and grammatically.

For each question, choose the correct answer.

The hotel room that's actually an aeroplane

If you're going to Costa Rica, and think that normal hotel rooms are **(1)** _____ , you might like to try staying in an aeroplane at the holiday resort of Costa Verde.

When the plane was too old to **(2)** _____ passengers anymore, it was broken into five **(3)** _____ . These were put on lorries and taken from San Jose airport to the Costa Rican rainforest. Workers put the plane back together and built two bedrooms, two bathrooms, a dining room and a kitchen inside. They put the plane on a platform, fifteen metres above the forest floor and because the plane is so **(4)** _____ people who stay in it have beautiful **(5)** _____ over the Costa Rican rainforest.

The plane is a fantastic place to stay, but it **(6)** _____ $500 a night.

1	**A**	missing	**B**	empty	**C**	boring
2	**A**	carry	**B**	keep	**C**	catch
3	**A**	slices	**B**	areas	**C**	pieces
4	**A**	high	**B**	wide	**C**	large
5	**A**	looks	**B**	views	**C**	pictures
6	**A**	spends	**B**	costs	**C**	pays

SPEAKING PART 2

1 Here are some pictures that show different places to go on holiday.
Do you like these different places to go on holiday? Say why or why not. Talk together.

2 Do you think a holiday on an island is expensive? Why?/Why not?
Do you think a holiday in the mountains is fun? Why?/Why not?
Do you think a holiday in a city is boring? Why?/Why not?
Do you think a holiday in the countryside is interesting? Why?/Why not?
Do you think a holiday in a desert is a good idea? Why?/Why not?

3 Which of these holidays do you like best?

4 When you go on holiday, do you prefer camping or staying in a hotel? Why?
Which country would you like to go to on holiday? Why?

➡ **SPEAKING BANK** / pages 241–242.

HOW WAS IT?

Gave it a go ☐

Getting there ☐

Aced it! ☐

GOING ON A SIGHTSEEING TOUR IN ...
BERLIN

1 Look at the photos (A–D) of Berlin. What tourist activities do they show? Read the text about sightseeing tours in Berlin and match the photos with the paragraphs.

Berlin is a busy place, full of colour and activity – and never boring! To help you discover this wonderful city, you can find information about some of the best sightseeing tours here.

BUS TOURS

First time in Berlin? Then take one of the hop on / hop off bus tours through the city. These double-decker buses will take you past the city's must-see sights, including the Brandenburg Gate, Alexanderplatz, the Reichstag Parliament building, Potsdamer Platz and much, much more. You can buy tickets for one day or more, so you can get on and off the tour buses as you like – giving you time to really explore Berlin. With the Berlin Welcome Card you can save 25% on city sightseeing tours by bus!

BIKE TOURS

You can use Berlin's well-marked cycle routes to cycle around the city and explore it on your own. However, you might prefer an organised bike tour with a guide. These tours are a great way to meet new friends and see another side to the city. Popular bike tour companies like Berlin on Bike offer a discount with the Berlin Welcome Card.

WALKING TOURS

Does the city really have 'ghost stations'? What is a 'Datsche' – and where do you find it? On a walking tour of Berlin, you can hear about the more unusual side of life here and discover hidden places that are off the main tourist track. The guides know a lot about their city and can tell you what life is really like in Berlin.

TRABI SAFARI

The Trabant 601 is the best known car from former East Germany and you now have the chance to drive one through this amazing city. Experience a trip back in time, either on your own or as part of a group of cars on an organised tour.

2 Read the text again. Are these statements true (T) or false (F)? Correct the false statements.

1 You cannot get off the bus until the end of the bus tour.
2 You need a new ticket for the bus tour each day.
3 Bike tours are a good way to meet other tourists.
4 Guides on walking tours can give you information about how people live in the city.
5 On a Trabi tour, someone else drives the car for you.

3 Find the phrases (1–6) in the text and match them with the correct definitions (a–f).

1 hop on / hop off bus
2 double-decker bus
3 the city's must-see sights
4 well-marked cycle routes
5 a discount
6 off the main tourist track

a a lower price
b you can sit upstairs or downstairs on this bus
c paths for bikes that are clear and easy to see
d away from the places that visitors usually see
e you can join and leave this bus as many times as you like
f the famous parts of the city that everyone should see

4 🔊 050 Listen to three conversations about sightseeing tours. What does each person want to do? There is one extra answer which you do not need to use.

a get information about hiring a bike
b book tickets for a walking tour
c buy a Berlin Welcome Card
d get information about a bus tour

5 🔊 050 Complete the phrases with the correct words. Listen again and check.

| can we hire | do you sell | how long |
| how much | some information | |

PHRASES YOU MIGHT USE

1 I'd like _____ about the City Circle sightseeing tour.
2 _____ does the tour take?
3 _____ are the tickets?
4 _____ Berlin Welcome Cards here?
5 _____ some bikes here?

6 Match the sentences (1–6) with the correct definitions (a–f).

PHRASES YOU MIGHT HEAR

1 It's valid all day.
2 It takes in all the main sights.
3 There's free admission.
4 You get up to 30% discount.
5 There's also free public transport.
6 There's a returnable deposit.

a You can go in without paying.
b You can take the bus or train without paying.
c You can use it from the morning till the evening.
d You have to pay an amount of money, but you will get it back if you return the bike safely.
e It visits all the places tourists want to see.
f You can get it for a lower price.

7 ▶ Watch the video. What do you learn about these places? Make notes.

• the Berlin Wall
• the Brandenburg Gate
• Checkpoint Charlie
• ghost stations
• Potsdamer Platz

8 ▶ Compare your notes. Watch the video again to check your ideas.

▶ WATCH

LIFE COMPETENCIES

DECISION-MAKING AND MAKING NOTES

9 Work in groups and imagine that you are visiting a city for three days. Plan your visit. Agree which places you want to visit and which tours you will go on and why. Tell your classmates about your plans.

PROGRESS CHECK 2

UNITS 3–5

1 Match the photos A–F with the sentences, 1–6.

1 He's hurt his leg. ....
2 He's got a headache. ....
3 He's got toothache. ....
4 He's got a stomach ache. ....
5 He broke his arm. ....
6 He's got backache. ....

2 Complete the sentences with the words in the box.

back	brain	fingers	heart
knees	neck	stomach	toes

1 Your .... is inside your head.
2 You hand has five ....
3 Your .... is between your head and your body.
4 Your .... are at the end of your feet.
5 Your .... are in the middle of your legs.
6 The food you eat goes into your ....
7 Your .... makes blood move around your body.
8 Your .... goes from your shoulders to your legs, and is not the front of your body.

3 Complete each sentence using *can*, *can't*, *could* or *couldn't* and a word in the box.

play	ride	sleep	speak	swim

1 I'm so tired. I .... last night.
2 Jack loves travelling. He .... four languages.
3 Kate hurt her arm and .... tennis last week.
4 Stacey never comes to the pool with us because she ....
5 Ben is very good at sport. He .... a bike when he was three!

4 Complete each dialogue with the words in the box above it.

ill	matter	pharmacy	should

1 **A:** What's the ¹............ ?
  B: I feel ²............ . I'm really tired and hot.
  A: If you have a high temperature, you ³............ go to the ⁴............ and buy some medicine.

get up	much	shouldn't	streamed

2 **A:** What did you ¹............ to at the weekend?
  B: Not ²............ . I ³............ a documentary about animals in the rainforest and played some video games.
  A: You ⁴............ spend so much time watching screens! It's not good for you!

comedy	horror	how about	shall

3 **A:** ¹............ going to the cinema at the weekend?
  B: I'm not sure. There's a ²............ film on and I don't like watching scary things! I enjoy funny films.
  A: OK. Well, there's a ³............ on too. ⁴............ we go to see that instead?

crowded	relaxing	should	trip

4 **A:** How was your ¹............ to France?
  B: It was OK, but there were a lot of people on the beach. It was really ²............ .
  A: Oh, I'm sorry to hear that. You ³............ go somewhere quieter next time.
  B: Yes, I think I will. That will be much more ⁴............ .

ache	problem	rest	Why don't you

5 **A:** My legs really ¹............ . It hurts when I walk.
  B: ²............ go to the doctor?
  A: I don't need to. I know what the ³............ is. I did too much exercise yesterday.
  B: Well, you'll just have to ⁴............ today.

5 Complete the sentences with the words in the box. You won't need all of the words.

comedy   crime drama   documentaries
news   quiz shows   science fiction

1 Did you see the _____ this morning? The president is going to visit our town!
2 I really enjoy _____ . I like to see if I can answer the questions.
3 There's a great new _____ programme on TV. It's about people who can travel forwards in time.
4 Did you watch that _____ last night? The police officer in it is so clever!
5 I don't watch much drama on TV. I prefer _____ programmes which make me laugh.
6 I love _____ , especially the ones about animals.

6 Choose the correct option to complete the sentences.

1 When people go out walking they often carry a *backpack/luggage*.
2 The place where you put up a tent is a *campsite/ destination*.
3 There are regular ferry *crossings/travels* from England to Ireland.
4 Before you go on holiday, you have to pack your *accommodation/suitcase*.
5 People often ask how long a *journey/travel* will take.
6 If your plane is late, we say there is a *miss/delay*.
7 If you have a holiday on a boat, it's called a *flight/ cruise*.
8 A *tourist information centre/tour* is a place where you can find out about the city that you are visiting.

7 Students often make mistakes with verbs in the past simple. Correct the mistakes in the sentences.

1 Last night I go to a disco on the beach.
2 We enjoied it when the country's team won.
3 Did you went anywhere for your summer vacation?
4 We play volleyball at the lake last summer.
5 The weather were warm and cloudy.
6 The T-shirt only costed me £5.

8 Put the verbs in brackets into the past simple or past continuous to complete the sentences.

1 I was watching a film when you _____ (call). That's why I _____ (not answer).
2 While I _____ (play) tennis at the weekend I _____ (hurt) my foot.
3 I _____ (go) to a concert last night. It _____ (be) amazing!
4 Sorry, I _____ (not hear) what you said because I _____ (listen) to the radio.
5 What _____ (you do) when I _____ (phone) you last night?
6 It _____ (be) a long journey, so I _____ (read) a book to make the time go quicker.

9 Read these two emails and write a word in each gap. You have been given the first letter of each missing word.

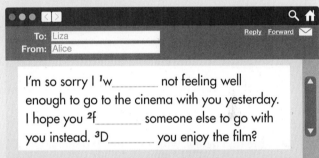

To: Liza
From: Alice

Reply Forward

I'm so sorry I ¹w_____ not feeling well enough to go to the cinema with you yesterday. I hope you ²f_____ someone else to go with you instead. ³D_____ you enjoy the film?

To: Alice
From: Liza

Reply Forward

That's okay. I ⁴c_____ Maya. She didn't ⁵h_____ anything to do yesterday evening, so we ⁶w_____ to the cinema together. The film was great. What a pity you ⁷c_____ not come.

6 TIME FOR FOOD

B

READING

1 Look at the photos (A–C). What is happening in them?

Do you do these activities (A–C)? Why?/Why not?

2 Read the text below. Which activity is popular with most young people?

COOKING? *No, thanks!*

Most people really enjoy food but it seems not many of us want to cook it. In the UK, people spend more time watching cookery programmes and food vlogs or posting food photos on social media than they do cooking their own food. Millions of British people watch cookery programmes with celebrity chefs every week, but over 20% of people in Britain say that they never make a meal from start to finish. They often say that they don't have any time to cook. In contrast, nearly 70% of young people say that they take photos of their food to post online.

We all know friends or family members who love to share photos of everything they eat for breakfast, lunch and dinner – from **cereal** with some **yoghurt** and a **mango** to a **mushroom omelette** or a **chicken** or **beef curry** with **broccoli** and hot **chillies**. For some people, every meal is a photo opportunity and their friends have to wait patiently until they take the perfect food photo. It can be really annoying, and it's not just other diners who get fed up with this. Some top chefs in Paris and New York don't want customers to take any photos in their restaurants. They say they want people to come to their restaurants and enjoy the food without taking photos. But is it too late to change this habit? And is there any way to get more people into the kitchen and cooking?

3 Read the text again. Are these statements true (T) or false (F)? Correct the false statements.

1	Most British people enjoy cooking.	T/F
2	Celebrity chefs are very popular in the UK.	T/F
3	A fifth of people don't make complete meals.	T/F
4	Most young people don't want to share their food photos.	T/F
5	All chefs are happy for customers to take photos of their food.	T/F

4 Look at the two questions at the end of the text. Discuss them with your partner.

C

VOCABULARY

FOOD AND MEALS

1 Complete the definitions with the words in blue in the texts.

1 _____ and _____ are kinds of meat that we get from cows and a type of bird.
2 _____ is a green vegetable that we cook and eat.
3 _____ are small red or green vegetables with a hot taste – we use them to make _____ .
4 We make _____ from milk. It's white but you can buy different types with fruit added.
5 Lots of people eat _____ with milk for breakfast.
6 A _____ has a round top. It's often brown or white.
7 A _____ is a large, sweet fruit which grows in hot countries.
8 An _____ is a food which we can make from eggs.

2 Work in pairs and ask and answer.

1 Do you or your friends take photos of food? Why?/Why not?
2 What are the most popular food programmes in your country? Do you watch them?

VOCABULARY: PREPARING FOOD

 A  B  C

1 🔊 051 **Listen to three people describe how they make their favourite snack. Which photo (A–C) is each speaker talking about?**

Speaker 1 _____   Speaker 2 _____   Speaker 3 _____

2 🔊 051 **Listen again and complete each description with the cooking verbs in the box.**

chop fry peel	First I ¹ _____ the skin off the potatoes and then I use a sharp knife to ² _____ them into small rectangular pieces. After that I put some oil in a frying pan. When the oil is very hot, I put the potatoes in the pan and ³ _____ them until they are brown. I eat them with lots of salt. I love them!
burn grill	The best way to cook the meat is to ⁴ _____ it. I usually cook the steak for about 3–5 minutes on each side. You can cook it for longer if you want to but be careful not to ⁵ _____ it! When it's ready, I put the steak between two pieces of bread with some salad and then it's ready to eat. It's my favourite sandwich.
add steam stir	First, I ⁶ _____ the rice for 15 minutes above a saucepan of boiling water until it's soft. Then I put some coconut milk in another saucepan and ⁷ _____ sugar or honey to make it sweet. I put the rice and the sweet coconut milk together and cook them gently for three minutes. I make sure that I ⁸ _____ the rice and coconut milk every few seconds. When the rice is ready, I eat it with fresh mango. Delicious!

GRAMMAR

GRAMMAR ON THE MOVE
Watch the video

COUNTABLE AND UNCOUNTABLE NOUNS

1 **Look at the examples and complete the rules.**

*… from cereal with **some** yoghurt and **a** mango …*
***Some** top chefs in Paris and New York …*

> There are two kinds of noun in English – **countable** (C) and
> **uncountable** (U).
> **1** Countable (C) nouns are things we can count. They can be
> singular or plural. **¹**_____ **egg / two eggs**
> **2** Uncountable nouns (U) are things we cannot count. They only have
> a singular form. e.g. **milk**, **rice**.

➔ **GRAMMAR REFERENCE** / page 208

2 **Decide if these types of food are countable or
uncountable. Write *U* or *C*.**

1 yoghurt _____

2 bread _____

  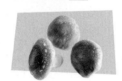

3 apple _____

4 mushroom _____

3 🅿 🔊 052 **Read the rules and then listen and repeat
the examples.**

> The *-s* ending of plural nouns is pronounced in different ways.
> • *-s* is pronounced /ɪz/ when a noun ends with the
>   consonant sound: *s, z, ch, dg, sh, x*
> • *-s* is pronounced /z/ when a noun ends in a voiced
>   consonant sound: *b, d, g, l, m, n, r, v, w, th, ng*
> • *-s* is pronounced /s/ when a verb ends in a vowel
>   sound or an unvoiced consonant sound: *a, e, i, o, u*
>   and *c, k, f, p, t*
> *He **eats** two **eggs** and two **slices** of bread for breakfast every
> morning.*

/s/	/z/	/ɪz/
eats	*eggs*	*slices*

4 🅿 🔊 052 **Listen again and put the words in the
correct column.**

apples	bananas	cakes	cups	fridges
mangos	pieces	sandwiches	snacks	

A/AN, SOME AND ANY

5 **Look at some more examples and choose the best
option to complete the rules.**

*20% of people in Britain say that they never make **a** meal …
They often say they **don't** have **any** time to cook.
Some top chefs … don't want customers to take **any** photos.
And is there **any** way to get people back in the kitchen …?*

> **1** We use **a** or **an** with singular *countable/uncountable* nouns.
> **2** We use *some/any* with uncountable and countable plural nouns
>   in positive sentences.
> **3** We use *some/any* with uncountable and countable plural nouns
>   in negative sentences.
> **4** We use *some/any* with uncountable and countable plural nouns
>   to ask questions.
> **Note:** We also use **some** in questions to ask for and offer things,
> e.g. *Do you want some coffee?*

➔ **GRAMMAR REFERENCE** / page 208

6 **Choose the best answer.**

1 I need to go to the shops because we haven't got
some/any bread.

2 *Is/Are* there any players on the football pitch?
Yes, there *is/are*.

3 I can give you *some/a* help this afternoon.

4 *Is/Are* there any homework for today? No, there *aren't/
isn't*, but there *is/are* some exercises for tomorrow.

5 I'm thirsty. Can I have *any/some* tea?

7 **Complete the text about what the dancer Jake
Winston eats in a day with *some*, *any* or *a/an*.**

> When I first get up in the morning, I drink
> **¹**_____ water but I don't eat **²**_____
> food because I go running for an hour and
> a half. When I come home, I have **³**_____
> cup of tea and **⁴**_____ cereal. Then I go
> to the gym and do **⁵**_____ exercise.
> At lunchtime and for dinner I usually eat
> **⁶**_____ pasta with chicken and lots
> of vegetables. For dessert, I have
> fruit and sometimes **⁷**_____ small
> bar of chocolate. I eat as much as
> I want at meal times, but I don't
> have **⁸**_____ snacks.

8 **Look at the photo on
page 193 and use the
words in the box to
talk about what you
can and can't see in
the photo.**

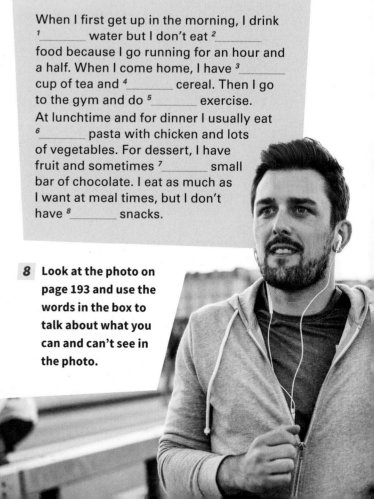

1 Does your fridge look like the one in the photo? Do you leave notes for your family/housemates? What do you leave notes about?

> Hi Katie
> I didn't have any milk for breakfast this morning, so I took some of yours. Sorry! I didn't use all of it. There is still a little in the carton.
> I'll get you some more on the way home from work this evening. ☺
> Bea

2 Read the note that Katie found on the fridge from her housemate Bea. Which statement is correct? Use the questions *in italics* to help you decide.

A Katie took some milk from the fridge.
Who didn't have any milk for breakfast this morning?

B Bea used all of Katie's milk.
What's in the carton in the fridge now?

C Bea will bring Katie some more milk later today.
What is Bea going to do on the way home from work?

3 Now read some other notes and messages carefully and underline the important words. Choose the correct answer.

1

SOFA FOR SALE

Price £500 (cost £600 new) – never used
I can accept a lower price if you collect it!

Phone Kim:
078573451

A Kim has only used the sofa a few times.
B The price is the same as a new sofa.
Ⓒ It might be possible to pay less than £500 for this sofa.

> *A is wrong because the note says 'never used'.*
> *B is wrong because Kim paid £600 for the sofa but only wants £500 for it now.*
> *C is correct because she will accept a price lower than £500 if you collect it.*

2

> Ben
> Your friend Sara called. She can't play squash on Friday but she could play on Saturday or Sunday. Sunday's better for her. Could you let her know when you're free? Mum

A Sara can play squash with Ben on Friday if he can't play on Sunday.
B Sara would prefer to play squash with Ben on Sunday, rather than on Saturday.
C Sara wants to play squash with Ben on both Saturday and Sunday if he's free.

3

I need help with my garden for two hours, twice a week.
Own transport needed.
Monday and Thursday are perfect but we can discuss.

Jane (0744871921)

A The gardener can decide how many hours they want to work for Jane.
B The gardener can call Jane to talk about transport for getting to her garden.
C The gardener can discuss which days of the week are possible for them to work.

GRAMMAR

EXPRESSIONS OF QUANTITY

GRAMMAR ON THE MOVE
Watch the video

1 What sort of things do you know how to cook? Do you ever cook for other people?

2 🔊 053 **Rob is staying with his friend Vanessa in Buenos Aires. He is cooking dinner for her and her friends. Listen and choose the correct answers.**

1 Rob is making
   a vegetable chilli.　　**b** vegetable soup.

2 He thinks Vanessa and her friends don't like
   a food with a lot of salt in it.　**b** spicy food.

3 He needs
   a two packets of rice.　**b** half a packet of rice.

4 To make the dessert, Rob needs
   a two lemons.　　**b** eight lemons.

5 He also asks Vanessa to buy
   a cream.　　　**b** sugar.

3 **Look at the examples and complete the rules.**

*How many lemons are there?　Not **many**.*
*How much rice do we have in the cupboard?　Not **much**.*
*Can you get me **a few** oranges?　I need **a little** cream.*
*I need **a lot of** lemons.*
*I don't like food that has **a lot of** salt in it.*

1 We use **How** _____ and **not** _____ to ask questions and make negative statements about quantity with **countable** nouns.
2 We use **How** _____ and **not** _____ to ask questions and make negative statements about quantity with **uncountable** nouns.
3 We use **a** _____ to talk about small quantities with **countable** nouns.
4 We use **a** _____ to talk about small quantities with **uncountable** nouns.
5 We use **a** _____ to talk about large quantities with **countable** and **uncountable** nouns.

➡ *GRAMMAR REFERENCE* / page 209

4 **Choose the best answer.**

1 This tea is too sweet! You only need to put *a little/a few* sugar in it.

2 Only *a few/a lot of* people in my class know how to cook.

3 How *much/many* yoghurt is in the fridge? Not *much/many*.

4 *How much/How many* sandwiches would you like?

5 There were *a few/a little* students who had problems, so the teacher gave them *a few/a little* help with their homework.

6 I don't know how *much/many* salt to put in the soup.

5 **Complete the dialogues with the words in the boxes.**

an (x2)　any　many (x2)　much (x2)　some

A: How ¹_____ sandwiches do you want for lunch? And do you want ²_____ fruit and chocolate?
B: Just two sandwiches please and I'd love ³_____ fruit and chocolate!
A: How ⁴_____ chocolate do you want?
B: Not ⁵_____ – just two or three squares.
A: And how ⁶_____ pieces of fruit?
B: Can I have ⁷_____ apple and ⁸_____ orange?

a few (x2)　a little　a lot of　many　some

C: Would you like ⁹_____ cake?
D: Just ¹⁰_____ . I'm trying to be more healthy, so I'm not eating so ¹¹_____ sweet things at the moment.
C: Do you usually eat ¹²_____ sweet things?
D: Yes I do. When I have a drink, I always have ¹³_____ biscuits with it, or ¹⁴_____ sweets, too. But I know that sugar isn't good for you.

6 **Complete the sentences so they are true for you. Tell your partner about what you eat.**
In what ways are you the same? In what ways are you different?

- I eat a lot of …
- I don't eat very much … or very many …
- I know that I eat too much …

1 When was the last time you went to a friend's house for a meal or you invited friends to your house? What did you eat? What did you drink?

2 🎧 054 For each question, choose the correct answer. You will hear Katie telling her friend Ben about a dinner party she went to. Read the tip and then listen to the first part of the recording.

> First, read question 1 and the options carefully and underline the important words.
>
> A isn't correct because Ben says he once met Maria at Katie's mum's house. B isn't correct because Katie says she doesn't know if Maria is a good cook, so she wasn't the cook. C is correct because Katie says Maria's husband Dan did the cooking.

1 The person who cooked the meal was
   A Maria's mum.
   B Maria.
   C Maria's husband Dan.

3 🎧 055 Now listen to the whole conversation and choose the correct answers for 2–4.

2 What does Katie say about the main course?
   A It was too spicy for her.
   B She left part of it.
   C The mango was the best bit.

3 What did Katie eat for dessert?
   A strawberries and cake
   B strawberries with yoghurt
   C orange cake with yoghurt

4 Where did Ben get a recipe for a chocolate cake?
   A from a TV programme
   B from a website
   C from a recipe book

SPEAKING

MAKING SUGGESTIONS

1 Look at the three restaurants and discuss the questions with a partner.

1 What type of food can you eat in each restaurant?

2 Which restaurant would/wouldn't you like to go to for lunch? Why?/Why not?

A

B

C

2 Henry and Izzy are arranging to meet for lunch. Number the texts in order.

> .... Hi Henry, **I'd love to**. I have some things to do this morning, but I'm free at 12.30. **Where shall we meet?**

> .... OK. Great. I'll see you in front of the art museum at 12.30.

> .... Hi Izzy, **Would you like to** meet for lunch today? I'm free after 12.00. What about you?

> .... **Shall we meet** in front of the art museum? There are lots of restaurants near there.

3 🔊 056 **Listen to Izzy and Henry talking about where to eat. Answer the questions.**

1 What kind of food doesn't Henry like?

2 Where do they decide to eat?

4 🔊 056 **Who says these phrases, Izzy (I) or Henry (H)? Listen again to check your answers.**

1 .... Sorry I'm late!

2 .... Are you hungry?

3 .... Yes, I am. I didn't have any breakfast!

4 .... I'm afraid I don't eat cheese.

5 .... I know you like curry.

6 .... Do you feel like eating fish?

5 **Complete the expressions Izzy and Henry use to make and respond to suggestions. Use the words in the box.**

about	afraid	feel	idea	Let's
mind	says	shall	sit	What

1 .... find somewhere to eat straightaway then.

2 Where .... we go?

3 I don't ....

4 My sister .... it's very good.

5 I'm .... I don't eat cheese.

6 How .... going for an Indian meal?

7 Do you .... like eating fish?

8 .... about having some sushi?

9 That's a great ....

10 Shall we .... outside?

6 **Answer the questions.**

1 Which expressions in Exercise 5 are for making suggestions/asking questions?

2 Which expressions are for responding to suggestions?

7 **Work in pairs. You are going to decide where to have lunch. Turn to page 193 and follow the instructions. Try to use the phrases in Exercise 5.**

8 **When you have finished, change roles and have the conversation again.**

DID YOU KNOW?

*If you go to a restaurant in the UK, the first course on the menu is called the **starter** but in the US, it is called the **appetiser**.*

*In the UK, the second course – the most important one – is called the **main course** but in the US people often use a French word and call it the **entrée**.*

WRITING

A RECIPE

1 **Work in pairs and discuss the questions.**

1 How often do you cook?
2 Do you use recipe books or recipe websites?
3 What's your favourite recipe?
   What ingredients do you need to make it?

2 🎧 057 **Listen to Sunita explaining how to make a meal. What is she making?**

3 🎧 057 **Complete the instructions with the verbs in the box. Then listen again and check.**

add (x3)	chop (x2)	cook	fry
mix	peel	put	serve	wash

Instructions

1 First _____ the garlic and ginger and _____ them into small pieces.
2 Then _____ the onions and other vegetables.
3 _____ the garlic, ginger and chopped onion lightly in some oil. When they are soft, _____ the curry powder.
4 After that _____ the other chopped vegetables and _____ everything together.
5 _____ for 15–20 minutes until the vegetables are soft.
6 While the curry is cooking, _____ the rice and _____ it into a saucepan.
7 _____ water and a pinch of salt. Cook for 20 minutes.
8 Finally, _____ the curry with the rice.

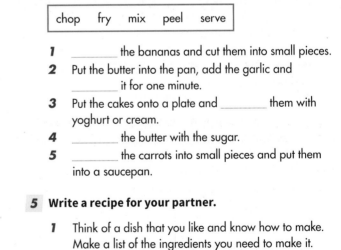

4 **Complete the sentences with the verbs in the box.**

chop	fry	mix	peel	serve

1 _____ the bananas and cut them into small pieces.
2 Put the butter into the pan, add the garlic and _____ it for one minute.
3 Put the cakes onto a plate and _____ them with yoghurt or cream.
4 _____ the butter with the sugar.
5 _____ the carrots into small pieces and put them into a saucepan.

5 **Write a recipe for your partner.**

1 Think of a dish that you like and know how to make. Make a list of the ingredients you need to make it.
2 Write the list of instructions for how to make this dish. Use the verbs from Exercise 3. Write at least one sentence with *when*, *until* and *while*.
3 Exchange recipes with your partner. Do you understand how to make your partner's dish?

READING PART 1

For each question, choose the correct answer.

 EXAM FACTS
- You read six short notices or messages.
- For each notice or message, you read a question or statement and choose the answer A, B or C.
- The notices and messages can be texts, emails, signs, notices on a noticeboard, or a website.

⚠ EXAM TIPS
- Read each notice or message carefully and underline the important words.
- Read the answers A, B and C carefully and find the one which says the same as the notice or message.
- Remember that you might see a word from the notice or message in A, B or C, but this doesn't always mean it is the correct answer.

1

Sami's café
Chef wanted – must be available next week
Ask inside for details

If you'd like to work at the café
A speak to a member of staff.
B come back next week.
C give your details to the chef.

2

Luisa – there's a new restaurant in South Road, I think it's called Poole's. I'm going tomorrow with Michael if you want to join us. Annie.

Why did Annie send the message?
A to ask Luisa where the new restaurant is
B to invite Luisa to go to the restaurant with her
C to ask Luisa's advice about which restaurant to go to

3

Bookshop
Half-price sale on textbooks starts next week.
Extra discount for students.

A You can't buy textbooks until next week.
B Only students get discounts on books here.
C Prices of some books will be lower next week.

4

All those entering the factory must cover their hair. There are hats near the factory entrance for visitors to use. Staff must use their own.

A The hats are to make it easier to find members of staff.
B People who come to visit the factory can borrow a hat.
C The hats for visitors are different from the staff hats.

5

Jon,
I know we planned to meet at 7 pm, but I'm working late. Let's forget about the film and just get something to eat.
Roberto

Roberto wants to
A change a plan that he made with Jon.
B explain why he won't be able to meet Jon today.
C say sorry about something he forgot to do for Jon.

6

Let staff know if we can do anything to improve your stay.

Hotel manager

You should talk to the staff if
A you want to stay longer.
B you like the changes to the hotel.
C you have any problems.

🔊 058 **For each question, choose the correct answer.**

You will hear Lewis talking to his friend Laura about a cooking course.

1 Why didn't Laura go to the cooking class yesterday?
- **A** Her bus didn't come.
- **B** She left college late.
- **C** She forgot.

2 What does Laura say about her cooking?
- **A** She wants to be as good at cooking as a restaurant chef.
- **B** There are some things she doesn't enjoy cooking.
- **C** There isn't enough variety in what she cooks.

3 In yesterday's class Lewis made
- **A** curry.
- **B** a dessert.
- **C** soup.

4 Lewis thinks that the teacher should
- **A** be kinder to the students.
- **B** give the students clearer instructions.
- **C** show the students what they need to do.

5 What time will Lewis pick Laura up for next week's class?
- **A** at 6.30 pm
- **B** at 6.45 pm
- **C** at 7 pm

✅ **EXAM FACTS**
- You listen to two people talking.
- You answer five questions about what you hear. The information for two or three questions will come from one of the speakers, and the rest from the other speaker.
- The answers will be option A, B or C.

❗ **EXAM TIPS**
- Read the questions or statements carefully and underline the important words.
- Look at the names in each question so you know which person will answer each question.
- Remember that the speakers may not use exactly the same words as the questions or statements you read.
- Remember that some questions or statements will ask about a speaker's opinion.

HOW WAS IT?

Gave it a go ☐

Getting there ☐

Aced it! ☐

A

BUYING A COFFEE AND A SNACK IN ...
VIENNA

1 Look at the photos (A–D) of cafés in Vienna. What do you think is special about the cafés in Vienna? Do people often go to cafés in your country?

2 Read the text about coffee houses in Vienna. Are these statements true (T) or false (F)? Correct the false statements.

1 The tradition of coffee houses is very old.
2 You can spend a long time drinking coffee and reading the newspaper in a coffee house.
3 You have to pay if you want a glass of water.
4 The waiters want you to leave quite quickly.

3 Read the reviews of some coffee houses in Vienna. Which café ...

1 serves the customers quickly?
2 looks nice from the outside?
3 is expensive?
4 serves large pieces of cake to the customers?

B

YOU MUST VISIT ...
a coffee house in Vienna

C

Vienna is full of traditional coffee houses (or cafés) where you can enjoy a good cup of coffee, as well as delicious cakes, pastries and small snacks. Visiting one or two of these famous coffee houses is a must for every visitor to Vienna.

Coffee houses first appeared in Vienna in the 17th century and they have remained popular because of their relaxed atmosphere. Friends can stay and chat for as long as they want, and it is completely normal for a customer to stay there alone for hours and read the newspaper. The waiter will always serve a glass of cold tap water with your coffee and, if you stay for a long time, they will bring you more water from time to time. The idea is that you are a guest who should feel welcome and you shouldn't feel that you have to leave quickly.

So, which Viennese coffee house should you visit?

Café Vienna ◉◉◉◉◯
Customer review
We never felt rushed here. The quality of the coffee was excellent and the portions of chocolate cake with whipped cream were generous. There's table service. The waitress was busy, but friendly and still smiling. Better than a big chain.

Café 100 ◉◉◉◉◯
Customer review
Excellent coffee and fast service! They also have all sorts of snacks including gluten free, if you're hungry. Very, very friendly staff. Good location in the Old City. Not cheap, but then if you want great food you don't mind paying a bit extra! Well worth a visit.

Café Schokolade ◉◉◉◯◯
Customer review
Every tourist comes here to take photos and eat. The building is lovely, outside and inside, and there's a nice atmosphere, but the food and cakes here are nothing special. The level of service is not up to standard.

D

4 Find the phrases in the reviews and choose the correct definitions.

1 we never felt rushed
   a We didn't feel that we had to eat quickly.
   b The waiters asked us to leave quickly.
2 a generous portion
   a a big piece
   b a small piece
3 table service
   a There aren't enough tables.
   b The waiter comes to the table to serve you.
4 a big chain
   a a café with a well-known name, that belongs to a big group
   b a very big café
5 well worth a visit
   a you should go here
   b it's nice, but expensive
6 not up to standard
   a not as good as I hoped
   b better than I hoped

5 🔊 059 **Listen to three conversations. Where does each one take place? There is one extra answer which you do not need to use.**

a a sandwich bar   c a traditional café
b a pizza restaurant   d a fast food restaurant

6 🔊 059 **Complete the phrases from the recording with the correct words. Listen again and check.**

| allergic to | do you do | does it have |
| what muffins | what's a | with two forks |

PHRASES YOU MIGHT USE

1 _____ Kardinalschnitte?
2 _____ nuts in it?
3 I'm _____ nuts.
4 Can we have one Kardinalschnitte, _____ , please?
5 _____ decaf coffee?
6 _____ do you have?

7 Sometimes people use difficult words and phrases when you ask about or order food. Choose the correct definitions.

PHRASES YOU MIGHT HEAR

1 We do have gluten-free options.
   a All our cakes have gluten in.
   b We have some cakes with no gluten.
2 Eat in or take away?
   a Do you want just a drink, or food too?
   b Do you want to eat here, or take the food outside?
3 Any fries with that?
   a Would you like chips?
   b We don't have any chips.
4 We're out of chicken sandwiches.
   a We don't have any more chicken sandwiches.
   b We don't serve chicken sandwiches.
5 Have you seen our combos?
   a There's a special offer if you buy some things together.
   b Can you help me look for them?
6 Coming up.
   a Please come here.
   b I will get this for you now.

8 🔊 **Watch the video. What do you learn about these things? Make notes.**

- the city
- coffee shops and cafés
- types of desserts
- Wiener Schnitzel
- three famous cafés

9 🔊 **Compare your notes. Watch the video again to check your ideas.**

▶ WATCH

LIFE COMPETENCIES

EVALUATING OPTIONS AND COMMUNICATION

10 Work in pairs and choose a city that you would like to visit. Find out about a traditional meal or snack in the city. Then look at some reviews and find information about the best place to try it. Tell your classmates.

7
LIVE LIFE!

A

B

C

VOCABULARY

FREE TIME

1 What do you like doing most in your free time? Do you have a hobby? Do you like doing the same things as your friends?

2 Read about some of the world's most popular hobbies. Match the words in orange with the photos (A–H).

1 Almost everyone listens to music! Some people also like going to **gigs** to hear their favourite bands or singers play live. Other people like singing themselves or even **doing Massaoke**!

2 All over the world people enjoy **doing exercise**. Some people play team sports and others enjoy running, cycling or **going to the gym**.

3 Lots of people enjoy cooking, and **baking** is an especially popular hobby at the moment. People love making cakes and posting photos and videos of their creations online.

4 Some people work and study hard, so when they have free time, they enjoy **doing nothing**! They like just hanging out with their friends and talking.

5 Everywhere you go people are taking photos with their phones and **photography** is now really popular with all ages.

6 **Playing board games** is a great way to relax with friends. There are lots of different kinds of games to choose from nowadays, but traditional ones like chess are still popular.

3 Complete the sentences with the correct form of the words in orange in Exercise 2.

1 Wow, those photos that you posted of your holiday are amazing! You're really good at _____ !

2 Did you know that our favourite band is playing on Saturday? We should try to get tickets to the _____ .

3 I'm really tired. I feel like just _____ today.

4 Would you like to help me make a cake for Fran? You're really good at _____ !

5 We could invite Tim and Liz over and just relax. Or we could play some _____ .

6 I don't feel very fit. I think I need to do some _____ .

7 Shall we go to the _____ tomorrow morning, or would you prefer to go for a bike ride?

8 Dan loves singing. He usually _____ at the weekend.

4 Work in pairs and discuss the questions.

1 Which of these hobbies do you do? Tell your partner about the last time you did them.

2 Which hobbies would/wouldn't you like to try? Why?

D

YOUR LOVE IS LIKE A SHADOW

E

F

G

H

LISTENING

1 🅰 060 **Listen to two people talking about their hobbies. Which of the hobbies on the page are they talking about?**

2 🅰 060 **Listen again and complete the information.**

Interview 1
Name: _Declan_   Age: ....
Where from? ....   Hobby: ....
Interview 2
Name: _Kimberley_   Age: ....
Where from? ....   Hobby: ....

3 🅰 060 **Which person does/did these things? Write D for Declan or K for Kimberley. Listen again and check.**

1 started the hobby at secondary school   ....
2 uses expensive equipment to do the hobby   ....
3 feels happy and full of energy while they are doing the hobby   ....
4 says that you can spend your whole life learning to do their hobby   ....
5 forgets his/her problems when he/she is doing the hobby   ....
6 does their hobby at weekends   ....

4 **Would you like to try Massaoke? Is it popular in your country?**

5 **Reorder the words below to make questions from the interviews.**

1 when / start / taking photos / did / you?
2 special / equipment / do / use / lots of / you?
3 good / you / at / are / photography / how
4 like / why / you / it / do?
5 how / make / does / feel / you / singing Massaoke?
6 often / do / do / you / how / it?

6 **Make notes about your favourite hobby then interview your partner about theirs. Use the questions in Exercise 5.**

GRAMMAR

GRAMMAR ON THE MOVE
Watch the video

PRESENT PERFECT: *HAVE YOU EVER ... ?*

1 Read the examples and complete the rules.

*Have you **ever been** to a Massaoke club?*
*No, I **haven't tried** Massaoke.*
*Have you **ever had** lessons? No I **haven't**.*
*I see things I **have never noticed** before.*

---

1 We use the present perfect tense with **never** and **ever** to talk about:
   - general experience
   - unfinished time up to now.
Ever means 'in our life up to now'.
We use **never** to talk about things we have not done in our life.
2 We form the present perfect with the verb _____ + the past participle of the main verb.
3 To form the past participle of regular verbs we add _____ to the end of the verb.

Positive and negative
I/You/We/They **'ve/have / haven't/have never** learn**ed** to draw.
He/She/It **'s/has / hasn't/has never** play**ed** board games.

Questions and short answers
Have I/you/we/they **ever** bak**ed** a cake?
Yes, I/you/we/they **have**. / No, I/you/we/they **haven't**.
Has he/she/it **ever** liv**ed** in a big city?
Yes, he/she/it **has**. / No, he/she/it **hasn't**.

➡️ *GRAMMAR REFERENCE / page 210*

2 Match the verbs with the past participles in the box.

been	eaten	got	spoken
sung	swum	taken	won

1 take   *4* eat   *7* swim
2 win   *5* sing   *8* get
3 be   *6* speak

3 Complete the sentences with the present perfect form of the verb and the words in brackets.

1 I *have never visited* an English-speaking country. (never, visited)
2 _____ you _____ the sunrise? (ever, watch)
3 My parents _____ to a gig. (never, go)
4 She _____ studying English. (always, enjoy)
5 _____ he _____ in the river? (ever, swim)
6 We _____ in this town. (always, live)

4 P 🔊 061 Listen to the three questions. What TWO different sounds can you hear that link the subjects *you* and *they/I* with *ever*?

Have you⌒ever eaten sushi?   Yes, I have.
Have they⌒ever swum in a lake?   Yes, they have.
Have I⌒ever asked you to help me before?   No, you haven't.

5 P 🔊 061 Listen again and repeat.

PRESENT PERFECT WITH *JUST*

6 Look at two more sentences and choose the correct option to complete the rules.

*I**'ve just been** on a weekend course ...*
*... as a new club **has just opened** ...*

---

1 We use the present perfect with **just** to talk about something that *happened a long time ago/a short time ago*.
2 We put **just** *before/after* **have** or **has** and *before/after* the main verb.

➡️ *GRAMMAR REFERENCE / page 211*

7 Complete the sentences. Use the verb in brackets and *just*.

1 Would you like a biscuit?
   No thank you. I'm not hungry. I*'ve just finished* lunch (finish)
2 Where's the teacher?
   She's in the hall. I _____ her. (see)
3 Your living room looks great!
   Thanks. My parents _____ it. (paint)
4 Is that a new cooker?
   Yes it is. We _____ it. (buy)

8 Work in pairs. Tell each other about something new using *just*.

   - a thing you bought
   - a person you met
   - a film/TV programme you saw

1 Look at the photo. What do you think Jerome Claudel's hobby is?

During the day, Jerome Claudel works in an office, but in the evenings he is a member of a drama group and has performed in three plays already this year! He talked to our reporter Jane Field.

Why did you join a drama group?
My first acting experience on **stage** was when I joined this drama group. I always loved going to the theatre, but I had no idea if I could act. One day I decided to try. I was spending too much time at home and I was interested in meeting some new people and doing something different.

What sort of plays does the drama group do?
We've never acted in anything too serious. When people come to the theatre, they want to forget their problems, so most of our plays are comedies.

Tell me about a recent play you've done.
This year, we put on a historical drama for the first time and it was a big success: the **audience** loved the story! But the clothes – the historical **costumes** – cost a lot of money for our costume department to make, so I don't know if we will do another one.

Are you good at acting?
I'm quite good at acting, but I have to work hard at it. About a week before a **performance**, we practise every day. I go straight to a **rehearsal** after work and I don't get back home until ten o'clock at night. I get very tired! But all the actors want the play to be good so we work really hard.

2 For these questions, choose the correct answer. First look at Question 1 and underline the key words.

1 Why did Jerome join a drama group?
  A He tried acting once when he was younger and loved it.
  B He wanted to make new friends and try something new.
  C He had a lot of acting experience and hoped he was good enough.

> *A is wrong because he says the first time he tried acting was when he joined the drama group. C is wrong because he had no experience of acting, he just loved going to the theatre a lot. B is correct because he says 'I was interested in meeting some new people and doing something different.'*

2 Why does Jerome's drama group do a lot of comedies?
  A Comedy acting is easier than serious acting.
  B People come to the theatre to have a good time.
  C The actors are bored with doing so many serious plays.

3 What does Jerome say about the historical drama?
  A The audience loved the costumes.
  B The actors had to make their own costumes.
  C The costumes were very expensive.

VOCABULARY

THE THEATRE

1 Put the words in order to make correct definitions of words related to the theatre.

1 are the people / The audience / a performance. / who watch
2 in front of people. / acting, playing music or dancing / A performance is
3 he or she wears / is the set of clothes / during the performance. / An actor's costume
4 practise the play. / A rehearsal / is when the actors /
5 perform. / The stage / where the actors / is the place

2 Complete the sentences with the words in the box.

audience	costumes	performance	rehearsal	stage

1 We didn't have a big _____ . Only ten people came to see our play.
2 He forgets everything when he's on _____ and performing in front of people.
3 The _____ begins at 7.30 pm. Please arrive on time.
4 All the actors must come to the _____ tomorrow to practise this difficult part of the play.
5 I have six different _____ to wear on stage. I need to change my clothes quickly and often.

3 Work in pairs and discuss the questions.

1 Have you ever been to the theatre? Would you like to go?
2 What is the last play you saw? Which play would you like to see?
3 Have you ever acted on stage? Did you enjoy it? If not would you like to act on stage?

DID YOU KNOW?

*In British English, the spelling is **theatre** but in American English, the spelling is **theater**.*

1 Have you ever been to a classical concert to hear an orchestra play? Would you like to go? What music did you hear/would you like to hear?

THE RECYCLED
ORCHESTRA

The **recycled** orchestra (Orquesta de Reciclados de Cateura) is very special. The musicians are all children from the city of Asunción in Paraguay and the musical instruments that the children play are made of recycled **rubbish**. These recycled instruments sound as good as real instruments and the children play beautiful music with them.

2 Read about the recycled orchestra. Answer the questions.

1 Who are the musicians in the recycled orchestra? Where are they from?

2 What is special about their instruments?

3 Match the words in bold with the definitions.

1 things people don't want and throw away ....

2 used again ....

4 🔊 062 Listen to how the recycled orchestra started. Why did Favio Chavez start trying to make musical instruments?

5 🔊 062 Listen again and choose the best answer.

1 Favio Chavez first came to Asunción to
  a teach music.
  b work on a recycling project.
  c learn about making things out of rubbish.

2 Recycled instruments are better than real instruments for the children because
  a they last for a long time.
  b people don't want to steal them.
  c they don't break.

3 The orchestra started to become famous when
  a the children learned to play their instruments well.
  b they started to give concerts in Asunción.
  c a film about them appeared on the internet.

4 When the orchestra visited Rio de Janeiro, the children were excited because
  a they saw the ocean for the first time.
  b they were in a different country.
  c they met famous people.

6 Work in pairs and discuss the questions.

drum	flute	keyboard
piano	trumpet	violin

1 Can you play any of these musical instruments? Which would you like to play?

2 Which do you think would be the most difficult/easy to learn?

3 Which is your favourite musical instrument? Why?

VOCABULARY

MUSIC PERFORMERS

1 How often do you listen to music? What kind of music do you like?

2 Read these interviews with some people talking about music in their lives and answer the questions.

1 Who performs music? Who listens to music?
2 Who plays an instrument? Which one?

We're in a band – I'm the guitarist but I also play the drums. Diego is the lead singer and we're both songwriters. The musical style of the band is a mix of pop and soul.

Valeria and Diego

I'm not a musician but I'd love to be a drummer. I can't really sing either, but I love music! At the moment I'm listening to a lot of female solo artists, but my favourites are Rihanna and Adele.

Alex

3 Read the interviews again and answer the questions.

1 What sort of music does Valeria and Diego's band play?
2 Who writes Valeria and Diego's music?
3 What kind of music is Alex enjoying at the moment?
4 What would Alex like to learn to play?

4 Complete the definitions with a word in yellow from the texts.

1 A .... is a musician who plays the guitar.
2 .... aren't part of a band, but sing on stage alone.
3 .... write songs – both the words and the music.
4 A .... plays the drums for a band.
5 A .... is the person who sings the most in a band.
6 A .... is a person who plays a musical instrument or sings.

5 Complete the text about a successful British band with the words from Exercise 4.

Clean Bandit is a very successful electronic music band from Cambridge in the UK. The band has won lots of prizes and has also had number-one songs. The three members of the band are Grace Chatto and brothers Jack and Luke Patterson. Grace plays the cello and also sings, but she isn't the
¹ .... Luke is the ² .... – he usually plays the drums. Jack plays lots of different instruments, including the piano, the keyboard and the violin, but usually he is the
³ .... Grace and Jack also help to write lots of the songs, as they are talented
⁴ .... as well. All three of the band members are great ⁵ .... ! Clean Bandit often works together with ⁶ .... such as Zara Larsson, Ellie Goulding and Jess Glynne. This makes the band's music really exciting!

6 Work in pairs and discuss the questions.

1 Who are your favourite bands and solo artists?
2 Do you go to gigs and concerts? What was the last one you went to? Whose gig or concert would you like to go to?

INTERNATIONAL MUSIC FESTIVAL

26–29 JULY
CHARLSBURY PARK, KENT

Buy tickets to your favourite international music festival!

◆ Five stages – amazing music and dance performances all day

◆ World-famous musicians and dancers

◆ International market selling delicious food and drink

◆ Excellent arts area where you can try fun art and painting activities

◆ Dance and music classes – all styles from classical to jazz

◆ Tickets: 4-day ticket £185, 3-day ticket £150, 1-day ticket £70

◆ Children aged 13 years and under – free

◆ Ticket price includes: entry to the festival and all performances and workshops

◆ Camping in pleasant countryside: £10 per tent per night, includes free parking and free WiFi

WRITING

A LEAFLET

1 Have you ever been to a music, dance or arts festival? Which one? Where? What did you see and do?

2 Look at the leaflet for a festival in the UK. Find this information.

1 When and where is the festival?
2 What kind of festival is it?
3 How many days does it last?
4 How much is a ticket for the whole festival?
5 Can you go for one day? How much does this cost?
6 How much does camping cost for the whole festival?
7 What different things can you see and do?

3 Find the adjectives the writer of the leaflet uses to describe these things.

1 the festival
2 the performances and performers
3 the place where you can camp
4 the arts area
5 the arts activities you can do
6 the market
7 the food and drink on sale

4 You are going to design a leaflet for a festival.

1 Think about what kind of festival it is. Use the ideas below.
- arts festival
- film festival
- comic book festival
- computer games festival

2 Make notes about the practical details of the festival.
- Where is it?
- When is it?
- How much does it cost?
- What is included in the ticket price?
- Special information about toilets, parking, wi-fi, etc.

3 Choose the activities at your festival. You can use these examples.
- singing
- dancing
- games
- workshops
- acting
- wearing costumes

4 Choose some adjectives to describe each of the activities and events at the festival.

5 Design your leaflet. Make sure it includes all the information that people need.

1 ⏵ 063 Listen to Carmen and Yannis answer questions about themselves in the speaking exam. Complete the personal information about them.

	YANNIS	CARMEN
Work or studies		
Age		
Nationality		
City		

2 Who do you think gives better answers, Yannis or Carmen? Why?

3 ⏵ 064 Now listen to Carmen and Yannis answer questions about their hobbies and weekend activities.

What do we learn about:

1 Yannis's hobbies and weekends?
2 Carmen's hobbies and weekends?

4 ⏵ 064 Listen again and complete the questions the examiner asks.

1 What's your _____ hobby?
2 How _____ _____ do you have for doing hobbies?
3 Please tell me _____ a new hobby you would like to try.
4 Where do you _____ at weekends?
5 What _____ the _____ thing about last weekend?
6 _____ _____ something about your plans for next weekend.

5 Work in pairs and ask and answer about each other's hobbies and what you do at weekends. Use different question words: *what, who, how, when, how much, where, how often*. Try to ask one question using a past verb, or one question about the future.

VOCABULARY: LINKING WORDS

1 Read about how Michael and Lotti started doing their hobbies. Which person started their hobby:

1 so that they can be alone?
2 because they wanted to help their friends?

> My friends were in a band at school and I only started playing the drums **because of** them. The band's drummer left very suddenly the day before a gig. **Because** it was impossible to find anybody else, I agreed to try to play. I loved it and soon started saving money to buy my own drums.
> *Michael*

> I go running **so that** I can have some time to myself every day. My husband is a serious runner **so** he gets up at 5.30 every morning and goes for a long run before breakfast.
> *Lotti*

2 Look at the expressions in bold that the speakers use to explain and give reasons. Complete the rules with the words in the box.

because   so   so that

1 We use *because of* + noun and _____ + clause to talk about the reason for something.
2 We use _____ + clause to talk about the purpose of an action – what the plan was/is.
3 We use _____ to talk about the effect of an action – what happened or will happen as a result.

3 Complete the sentences with the words in the box.

because   because of   so   so that

1 He started learning Spanish _____ he could talk to his girlfriend's family in Mexico.
2 We couldn't go running today _____ the rain.
3 I was feeling tired and unfit _____ I started going to the gym.
4 _____ he spoke such good Spanish, he soon started to enjoy life in Spain.

READING PART 3

EXAM CHECK

1 **Complete this text about Reading Part 3 by choosing the correct word or phrase.**

In Part 3, you have to read ¹*three short texts/one long text* and answer ²*five/six* questions. There are ³*three/four* possible answers for each question. Some of the questions are actually sentences, and you have to ⁴*write/choose* the option which completes the sentence. Sometimes the last question is about the ⁵*name of the writer/title of the text*.

2 **For each question, choose the correct answer.**

1 How did Jenny's friend Natalia feel when they were on the beach?
- **A** surprised that Jenny knew so much about stars
- **B** amazed that there were so many stars
- **C** pleased that they could see a few stars between the clouds

2 What did Jenny like about going to the planetarium?
- **A** getting some books
- **B** hearing the stories
- **C** seeing the films

3 When she looks at the night sky, Jenny first tries to find
- **A** the North Star.
- **B** the Plough.
- **C** the moon.

4 In the future, Jenny wants to
- **A** help other people to see more stars.
- **B** live in an area with not many lights.
- **C** take a course about stars.

5 What is the best title for this text?
- **A** What everyone should know about stars
- **B** How my hobby changed my life
- **C** Why I prefer the darkest nights

Last year I went on holiday with my friend Natalia. The weather was cloudy – except for one night when we sat on the beach looking at the stars. 'It's a pity we don't know which stars we're looking at, Jenny,' said Natalia. 'I know some of them,' I answered. 'That's amazing!' said Natalia when I finally finished telling her all the names I knew.

My interest in stars began when I was eight. My aunt took me to a planetarium – a building where you can see films of the stars at night. A guide showed us the groups of stars, called constellations, and told us stories about how they got their names. The stories were wonderful – like the ones in the books I had at home.

Since then, I've always looked at the sky at night. Everyone knows you can see the stars better when it's not cloudy, but a lot of people don't realise that a bright moon also stops you seeing very much. I always look for a constellation called the Plough, because once I see that, I can find the North Star and the other constellations.

I wanted to learn more about the stars, so I took a course at college. There are so many lights in the city that we had to go into the countryside to see any stars. I'm planning to make videos about the places you can go to which don't have this problem. I'll post them online for everyone to watch.

1 Work in pairs. One of you is the examiner, and asks these questions. The other person answers the questions.

What's your name?

Where do you live?

2 Work in pairs. One of you is the examiner, and asks these questions about going out with friends. The other person answers the questions. Then swap roles.

When do you usually see your friends?

Do you usually see your friends at weekends?

How long have you known your best friend?

Have you known your best friend since you were at school?

What do you usually do when you go out with friends?

Do you go to the cinema with friends?

What do you do when it's a friend's birthday?

Do you have a party for your friend's birthday?

Now, please tell me something about the friend you spend most time with.

Does this friend live near you?

How did you meet this friend?

Why do you like spending time with this friend?

➡ **SPEAKING BANK** / page 240.

✓ EXAM FACTS

- At the beginning of Part 1, the examiner will ask you a few details about you and where you live.
- After this, the examiner will tell you the topic you are going to talk about, and ask each of you two questions about this topic.
- Finally, the examiner will ask you to give a longer answer, by saying, 'Please tell me something about …' This will be on the same topic as the earlier questions.

❗ EXAM TIPS

- Remember – the questions will always be about you and your life.
- Don't worry if you can't think of an answer – the examiner will help you by asking another question.
- When the examiner says, 'Please tell me something about …', try to give two or three pieces of information.

HOW WAS IT?

Gave it a go ☐

Getting there ☐

Aced it! ☐

REAL WORLD

A

SPENDING YOUR FREE TIME IN ...
LONDON

1 What hobbies can you enjoy in the city? Look at the words and phrases in the box and discuss in pairs.

B

> buying clothes   learning about history   sports
> trying new food   visiting museums   watching films or plays

2 Read the text about three things to do in London. Match the photos (A–C) with the activities. Which activity would you like to do? Why?

3 Read the texts again. Are these statements true (T) or false (F)? Correct the false statements.

1 The Street Art Tour always goes to the same places.
2 Camden Market has always sold clothes.
3 You can eat lots of different foods on the Food Tour.

C

THINGS TO DO IN LONDON

London is a great place to enjoy all kinds of hobbies, and learn something new. There's something for everyone, from water-sports and skateboarding to art, drama and cooking.

Street Art

If you like art, come on a street art tour with us and see some of London's amazing street art. We know where all the best street art is and on one of our tours you will see work by over 40 street artists. Street art in London is changing all the time as older pieces disappear and new ones appear. This means that our tours are always fresh. We take you to different parts of the city each time. We run tours on Tuesdays, Saturdays and Sundays. If you're interested in joining us, please go to the booking page.

Camden Market

Camden Market is a great place for anyone who's interested in clothes and fashion. The first market at Camden started in 1974 as a small arts and crafts market. It then started selling clothes and quickly became popular with people who were looking for 'different' clothes. Everybody who was 'cool' was down at Camden Market on a Sunday afternoon to buy their fashionable clothes. Many young fashion designers began with a stall at Camden Market.

East End Food

Food lovers will love our tour! The East End of London is not like any other part of the city. People from all over the world live there, so it's full of delicious food from different countries. Our four-hour East End Food Tour visits lots of different places like markets, shops, cafés and restaurants and at each one you are offered a tasting. You will also meet some of the people who live and work in this part of the city and you will get to see places that few tourists visit. You will also see ancient Roman ruins, 18th century houses and hidden parks.

4 Find the phrases in the text and choose the correct definitions.

1 street art
  a paintings on walls and buildings
  b works of art inside people's homes
2 arts and crafts market
  a a market that sells things people have made
  b a market where artists can buy things they need for their work
3 stall
  a someone who sells things in a market
  b a place where you buy things in a market
4 a tasting
  a a small amount of food to try
  b a meal
5 ancient ruins
  a ugly new buildings
  b parts of very old buildings
6 hidden parks
  a parks that lots of people visit
  b parks that most people don't know about

5 065 **Listen to three conversations. Who is speaking? There is one extra answer which you do not need to use.**

a a customer and a stallholder at Camden Market
b a guide and a tourist on a tour
c two tourists on a Street Art Tour
d two tourists on an East End Food Tour

6 065 **Complete the phrases with the correct words. Listen again and check. Which phrase can you use to agree with someone?**

| are you | first time | I'm here |
| never seen | true | very busy |

PHRASES YOU MIGHT USE

1 _____ from London?
2 _____ for two weeks.
3 It's _____ .
4 It's my _____ in London.
5 I've _____ a tour like this in my city.
6 That's _____ .

7 Choose the correct definitions for these informal words and phrases.

PHRASES YOU MIGHT HEAR

1 It looks like we're on the move again.
  a Some people are leaving the tour.
  b The tour is going to the next place now.
2 If you nip down here again …
  a If you come here again …
  b If you go to a different market …
3 It's worth the few pounds to get the tour.
  a It's a good idea to pay and go on a tour.
  b The tour is too expensive.
4 You get off the tourist track.
  a You see a lot of tourists.
  b You go to places where not many tourists go.

8 Watch the video. Answer the questions about things to do in London.

1 What is the London Eye?
2 How long does a trip take on the London Eye?
3 What kind of ticket should you buy if you want to get off a boat and then get on again?
4 What is the name of the clock on the Houses of Parliament?
5 Why do tourists visit Abbey Road?
6 How old is Borough Market? What kinds of food can you buy there?

9 Compare your answers. Watch the video again to check your ideas.

▶ WATCH

LIFE COMPETENCIES

DECISION-MAKING AND EMOTIONAL SKILLS

10 Work in groups and choose a city. Find out about tours, sports or courses you can do there and make a list of the five you like best. Discuss and put them in order from 1–5, from the thing that you would most like to do (1) to the thing that you would least like to do (5). Tell your classmates.

8 FEELS LIKE HOME

READING

WHERE I LIVE

1 Look at the photos and discuss the questions with a partner.

1 Which photo is most like where you live?

2 Which places would you like to live in? Which would you not like to live in? Why?

2 Complete the descriptions with the words in the box and match with the photos (A–E).

> cottage   houseboat
> studio apartment/flat
> townhouse   villa

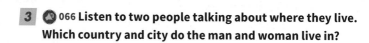
Homes   About   🔍 Search

1 This comfortable, modern .... has a large garden and pool.

2 If you like living on the river, this .... is the home for you!

3 This is a large .... It's in the middle of the country with fields around it.

4 This .... is on a quiet terraced street near the city centre.

5 This .... is ideal for a student or young professional: there is everything you need in one room.

3 🎧 066 Listen to two people talking about where they live. Which country and city do the man and woman live in?

4 🎧 066 Listen again and choose the correct answer.

1 Ling lives
   a alone.   *b* with her family.   *c* with her sister.

2 The part of the city she lives in is
   a expensive.   *b* old and near the river.
   c near the river and very busy.

3 Her house is
   a 43 years old.   *b* 35 years old.   *c* 100 years old.

4 Huan has lived in his home for
   a one week.   *b* one month.   *c* one year.

5 He lives on the
   a 23rd floor.   *b* 33rd floor.   *c* 32nd floor.

6 His home is
   a modern and new, but not near the city centre.
   b new and in the city centre.
   c expensive and in the city centre.

5 What do you think Ling's and Huan's homes are like? Match the photos with the people.

Ling _____   Huan _____

6 Read the descriptions and check your answers to Exercise 5.

My apartment isn't very big but it's very comfortable. There's a kitchen, a living room, a bathroom and one bedroom. I like the kitchen because it's very modern and it has a **balcony** where you can sit outside and enjoy the fantastic **view** of the city. My favourite room is the living room. There's not much **furniture** – only my sofa, a big television and a computer. I think that's all I need to be happy! I keep my car in a **garage**, which is in the **basement** under the apartment **building**.

👤 **Huan**

Our house is small, but it has three floors. On the **ground floor** there is the kitchen and our noodle shop. On the first floor, there is a bathroom and a living room and on the second floor are our two bedrooms. My bedroom is my favourite room because it has a lot of light. From the bedrooms you can go onto the top floor – the **roof** garden. We are friends with all our **neighbours**. We have lived in this house all our lives, but it isn't ours: we rent it. We pay our **rent** to the owner every month.

👤 **Ling**

7 Read the descriptions again. Find this information.

1 Why does Huan like his kitchen?
2 What is great about the balcony in Huan's home?
3 Where does Huan park his car?
4 How many floors does Ling's house have?
5 Where is the garden in Ling's house?
6 What do Ling and her sister have to do every month?

VOCABULARY

HOUSES

1 Complete the sentences with the words in purple from the texts.

1 Don't spend too much money! We need to pay the _____ for our apartment at the end of the month.
2 Our cat climbed on the _____ of the house but then she couldn't get down.
3 We haven't got a _____, so we park the car in the street.
4 I have a good _____ from my bedroom window – I can see the whole street.
5 My office is in a really nice, modern _____ .
6 We don't have a garden, but our apartment has a big _____ where I can grow flowers.
7 He only has a bed and one chair in his room; there isn't any other _____ .
8 In most people's houses, the kitchen and living room are on the _____ _____ and the bedrooms are on the first floor.
9 I can't go to sleep because the _____ in the next apartment are making a lot of noise.
10 We have a _____ under the house where we watch films and play games.

2 Put the words in order to make questions. Then interview your partner about his/her home.

1 is / home? / old / How / your
2 floors / have? / does it / How many
3 favourite room? / your / What's
4 have / a garden / Do / or a balcony? / you

LISTENING

1 Read about the house in the photo. Answer the questions.

1 Where is the house? Who lives there?
2 How long has she lived there?
3 How much does the house cost?

CELEBRITY NEWS

Simone Woodley has just put her Los Angeles house up for sale for $9.5 million.

The actress and singer has lived in her home in Beverly Hills for eight years and has spent three million dollars on the house. In that time she has built a recording studio, games room and movie theatre.

Since she met her husband last year, she has spent less time in the house and has decided to sell it. She is now looking for a new home in New York.

2 🔊 067 Listen to a news reporter who is visiting the house. Tick the rooms she goes into.

☐ bedroom ☐ indoor swimming pool ☐ gym
☐ dining room ☐ kitchen

3 🔊 067 Listen again and choose the best answer.

1 At the beginning of the visit, the reporter is standing
   a in the garden.   *b* in the hall.
2 She goes up the stairs
   a to the first floor.   *b* to the second floor.
3 There are
   a 10 bedrooms and 5 bathrooms.
   b 5 bedrooms and 10 bathrooms.
4 In the kitchen, everything is
   a white and grey.   *b* gold and white.
5 The reporter says she loves
   a the view from the window.
   b the big fridge.

VOCABULARY

KITCHEN ITEMS

1 Match the words (1–6) with the definitions (a–f).

1 sink   4 cupboard
2 cooker   5 tap
3 fridge   6 oven

a a piece of furniture that is used to keep food cold
b the part above a sink that water comes out of
c a piece of kitchen equipment with a door, which is used for cooking food
d a piece of equipment used to cook food
e a piece of furniture with a door that you put things in
f a bowl that is fixed somewhere in a kitchen or bathroom where you can wash dishes or your hands

PREPOSITIONS

2 Label the pictures with the words in the box. Where is the red box?

behind	between	in front of
next to	opposite	under

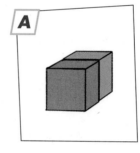 A

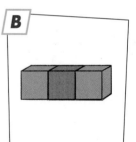 B

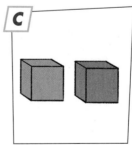 C

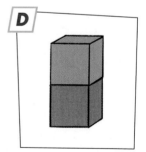 D

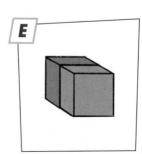 E

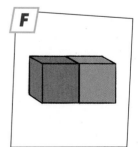 F

3 Do you spend much time in the kitchen of your home?

4 Work in pairs and describe your kitchen using the words in Exercises 1 and 2. Your partner must draw a plan.

5 **P** **068 Listen to these phrases and repeat.**

Under the sink	Next to the tap
Opposite the fridge	Between the cooker and the fridge
Behind the oven	In front of the oven

GRAMMAR

PRESENT PERFECT WITH *FOR* AND *SINCE*

 GRAMMAR ON THE MOVE
Watch the video

1 **Look at these sentences about the celebrity house and answer the questions.**

*The actress and singer **has lived** in her home in Hollywood **for eight years**.*
***Since she met** her husband last year, she **has spent** less time in the house.*

1 When did the actress start living in this house? Is she still living there now?
2 When did she start spending less time at the house? Does she spend less time there now?

2 **Choose the best option to complete the rules.**

We use the present perfect tense with **since** and **for** to talk about an action which started in the past but continues up to and includes the present. We use:

1 *for/since* to talk about a period of time, e.g. *eight years, one week, two minutes.*
2 *for/since* to talk about when a situation started, e.g. *last Christmas, yesterday, five minutes ago.*

***How long** have you lived here?*
*I**'ve lived** here **since** I moved to London. / I**'ve lived** here **for** ten years.*
***How long** has he known his girlfriend?*
*He**'s known** her **since** 2017.*
***How long** have they known each other?*
*They**'ve known** each other **for** 10 or 12 years.*

➡ **GRAMMAR REFERENCE** / *page 212*

3 **Choose the correct option *for* or *since* to complete the sentences.**

1 We've been married *for/since* five years.
2 She's liked the house *since/for* the first time she saw it.
3 Our television is new. We've only had it *since/for* six weeks.
4 My father has worked at the shop *for/since* 2010.
5 I haven't seen my parents *since/for* January.
6 They haven't been to the cinema *for/since* two months.

4 **Work in pairs. Use the words to make questions. Take turns to ask and answer using *for* and *since*.**

- live in your home
- know your best friend
- have your bike/car/that pair of shoes, etc.
- know how to read/ski/drive/cook, etc.
- like (a hobby/film/book/type of music, etc.)

How long have you lived in your house?

I've lived there for five years.

DESCRIBING WHERE YOU LIVE

1 🔊 069 **Listen to Luzia talking about where she lives.**

1 Which country does she come from?
2 Does she live in a house or an apartment?

2 🔊 069 **Put the words in order to make six questions the teacher asks Luzia. Listen again and check.**

1 in the city? / do you live/ And where
2 live with? / Who / do you /
3 lived there? / have you / How long
4 apartment? / like your / Do you
5 favourite room? / What's / your
6 you don't like / apartment? / Is there anything / about your
7 room? / describe your / Can you

3 **Luzia uses adjectives to make her description more interesting. Sort the adjectives in the box into pairs of opposites.**

beautiful	big	cheap	expensive		modern
noisy	old	quiet	small	ugly	

4 **Prepare to tell your partner about where you live and what your house/apartment and your room are like. Use the phrases below and the adjectives from Exercise 3 to help you.**

USEFUL LANGUAGE

It's a large/small city/town/village etc.
It's in the north/south/east/west of my country.
It's on the Atlantic Ocean/the coast etc.
I live in the city centre/the country etc.
I live near the park/the river/the cathedral etc.
The building is old/new. My apartment/bedroom is on the first/second/third floor etc.
It's old/modern/big/small etc.
There is/are … I like/don't like … because …
My favourite room is … because …

5 **Work in pairs and take turns to ask and answer the questions in Exercise 2 using the phrases above.**

> Where do you live in the city?

> I live in the city centre, near the church.

SPEAKING: DESCRIBING A PICTURE

1 🔊 070 **Listen to a man describing the photo. Complete the description with the preposition phrases in the box.**

at the back of	in the middle of	in front of
on the left	on the wall	

This is a photo of a living room. The walls are white and there's a grey rug on the floor. ¹_____ the room there are three big windows, but there aren't any curtains. ²_____ the window there's a round table with a white chair on each side of it. The part of the chair that we sit on – I don't know the name in English – is red. ³_____ the room there's a big glass table and on the table there are some pink flowers in … I don't know what it's called in English but it's a kind of pot for flowers. ⁴_____ there's a grey sofa and above the sofa, ⁵_____ , there's a big picture. On the right of the table there are two black chairs and there's a dog standing in front of them.

2 **In the text the man describes some objects he doesn't know the name of. Underline the phrases he uses.**

3 **Match the objects in the box with their descriptions.**

bookshelf	lamp	rug	seat	vase

1 The part of a chair that we sit on – I don't know the name in English. _____
2 I don't know what it's called but it's a kind of pot. _____
3 I don't know the word for this – it's something we put on the floor to keep our feet warm. _____
4 I've forgotten the English word: we use it for making light. _____
5 I don't know how to say this: we keep books on it. _____

GRAMMAR

PRESENT PERFECT WITH *YET* AND *ALREADY*

 GRAMMAR ON THE MOVE
Watch the video

1 Have you ever moved house? Where and when did you move from and to?

2 🔊 071 **Anthony is moving from London to Helsinki. Listen to a telephone conversation with his friend, Laura.**

1 Why is he moving to Finland?
2 How did he find his new apartment?

3 🔊 071 **Listen again and complete the phrases with two words. Then complete the rules with *yet* and *already*.**

1 Have you _____ anywhere to live _____ ?
2 I've _____ _____ my new apartment.
3 You haven't actually _____ it _____ ?
4 I've _____ _____ the first month's rent.
5 Have you met your new boss _____ ?
6 I've _____ _____ my boss.

---

1 We use _____ in positive sentences.
  • It goes between **have** and the past participle.
  • It means that something happened before now or before we expected.
2 We use _____ to ask questions and in negative sentences.
  • It goes at the end of the sentence or question.
  • We use it to talk about things we plan to do in the future, but which are not done.

➡ **GRAMMAR REFERENCE** / page 213

4 Look at Anthony's list of things to do before he leaves for Helsinki. Complete his conversation with Laura. Use the verbs in brackets in the present perfect with *yet* and *already*.

---

finish packing ✓
say goodbye to the neighbours ✓
text my friends with my new address
and phone number
book a taxi to take me to the airport

Laura: So Anthony are you ready to go?
¹ _____ (finish packing)?

Anthony: Yes, I have. My suitcases are by the door. And I've ² _____ (say goodbye) to the neighbours who live in the apartment next to me.

Laura: And ³ _____ ? (text friends) We can't come to visit you if we don't know your address!

Anthony: No, not yet and I ⁴ _____ . (book taxi) My flight is really early. I'll do that now.

5 Work in pairs. Take turns to ask and answer. Has your partner done any of these things today yet?

• have a cup of tea/coffee
• have lunch
• read something in English
• text a friend
• listen to some music

GRAMMAR

PRESENT PERFECT OR PAST SIMPLE

1 What are important things to do when you move to a new town? How do you make friends and meet people?

2 Read about Paula, who has moved to a new town. Has she met any new people yet?

I've been here **for** one month and haven't done much to my apartment **yet**, but I've met the neighbours – I invited them round for coffee yesterday. They're really nice. I also joined a gym on my first day here and I've been almost every day **since** then. **Last night**, I went out for a meal with some girls from my exercise class and it was great fun. I've just ordered some new furniture and I bought some paint for the living room **two weeks ago** but I haven't had time to start painting yet.

3 Look at the examples and complete the rules with the words in the box.

*I've **been** here **for one month** and **haven't done** much to my apartment **yet**.*
*I **bought** some paint for the living room two weeks **ago**.*

ago	finished	for	unfinished

> **1** We use the **present perfect tense** to talk about ¹ .... events that began in the past but are still happening or are still true now, e.g. *I've been here* ² .... *one month.*
>
> **2** We use the **past simple tense** to talk about ³ .... events that happened at a precise time in the past, e.g. *I arrived here one month* ⁴ ....

4 Complete the sentences with the past simple or present perfect form of the verbs in brackets.

1 My friends .... to Argentina last year. (move)
2 He .... in that house since he was a baby. (live)
3 Don't touch that wall; I .... painting it yet! (not finish)
4 I .... some new curtains at the weekend. (buy)
5 That cup .... in the kitchen sink for a month. (be)
6 She .... her new dress in the wardrobe before she went to bed last night. (put)
7 I .... your umbrella when I was cleaning the house yesterday. (find)
8 How long .... that milk .... in the fridge? (be)

5 Work in pairs and tell your partner about something:

* interesting you did last week
* nice you ate on holiday
* you've never seen
* you haven't finished yet
* you haven't done today yet but plan to do

READING PART 5   TRAINING

Read Ben's email to Lucy. Write ONE word for each gap.

> First read the email and decide what kind of word fits in each gap. It could be a verb, a preposition, a word that joins two ideas, a negative, etc.
>
> Look at the example sentence 0 and look for clues to the missing word in the context. You can see this sentence has no verb at the moment and there is a second person pronoun, you. What phrases do you know which start with How …? The missing word is the verb are.
>
> Now look at gaps 1–4 and think about the words that might fit there. Look at the words around the gaps for clues.

To: Lucy Edwards
From: Ben Evans
Reply Forward

Hi Lucy

How **(0)** .... you? I'm sorry I haven't written sooner. I've been here in Berlin for one month. I really like my job here and I like my new apartment too. It's **(1)** .... the fifth floor so I have a great view of the city from my window. The only problem **(2)** .... I don't have enough furniture. I haven't had time to buy a bed yet. At night, I sleep on my hard sofa in **(3)** .... living room. It's not comfortable at all. I'm planning to **(4)** .... shopping on Saturday!

Why don't you visit me soon!

Ben

1 Fran has received an email from her friend Rose. Read the message. What do you think a 'housewarming party' is?

To: fran.johnson93@hotmail.com
From: rose.pearson@yahoo.com
Subject: Housewarming party

Reply Forward

Hi Fran,

How are you? Did you know I've just moved to a new apartment? It's on Lake Street, near the station and it's great. It's quite large with a beautiful modern kitchen. The apartment is on the ground floor so I even have a garden!

I'm having a housewarming party on Saturday and I'm writing to invite you. I've invited all our friends from the language school and my brother, Harry. It's at 7.30 pm and the address is 21, Lake Street.

I hope you can come!

Best wishes

Rose

2 Read the email again and answer the questions.

1 How does Fran know Rose?
2 What has Rose just done?
3 Where and when is the party?
4 What does Rose tell Fran about the apartment? (three things)
5 Who are the other guests who are coming to the party?

3 Find the following functions in Rose's message.

1 Greeting for the beginning of an email
    Hi + name
2 Friendly phrase for first line of email ....
3 Phrase to say why you are writing ....
4 Phrase to end an email ....

4 For which of the functions 1–4 in Exercise 3 could you use these expressions?

- Hello + name ....
- See you soon! ....
- How are things? ....
- So, I wanted to know if … ....
- I hope you're well ....
- I wanted to ask you … ....
- Dear + name ....
- All the best ....

5 Fran is going to write an email to Harry, a friend of hers and Rose's, and ask if they can go to the party together. Write the questions she needs to ask to find out the following information.

- how Harry is getting to the party (transport)
- if they can go together
- where they can meet (suggest a place)

6 Decide how to begin and end the email and what to put in the subject line. Look at Rose's email in Exercise 1 to help you.

7 Write Fran's email to Harry. Write 25 words or more.

EXAM FOCUS

READING PART 5

For each question, write the correct answer.

Write ONE word for each gap.

Example: **0** are

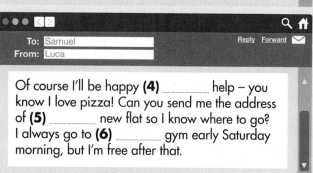

To: Luca
From: Samuel
Reply Forward

How **(0)** _____ you? I've finally found a new flat, and I move into **(1)** _____ on Saturday. There's just one problem – I have lots **(2)** _____ heavy furniture to move. Max is coming to help, but I don't think two people are enough. **(3)** _____ you mind helping too? When we finish I'll buy pizza for everyone.

To: Samuel
From: Luca
Reply Forward

Of course I'll be happy **(4)** _____ help – you know I love pizza! Can you send me the address of **(5)** _____ new flat so I know where to go? I always go to **(6)** _____ gym early Saturday morning, but I'm free after that.

EXAM CHECK

1 **Read the questions (1–5) and match them with the correct answers (A–E).**

1 How many words should I write?
2 Who is my message for?
3 What do I write about?
4 How can I join my ideas together?
5 What should I be careful about?

A There will be an email or some instructions which give information about the person you should write to.
B Use words like *and, because* or *so.*
C Try to use correct grammar and spelling.
D 25 or more.
E There are three questions which you need to answer.

2 **You want your English friend Jamie to stay at your house next weekend.**

Write an email to Jamie:

*   ask Jamie to come
*   tell Jamie what you can do together at your house
*   say what Jamie should bring

Write **25 words** or more.

➡ **WRITING BANK** / *pages 233–234.*

HOW WAS IT?

Gave it a go ☐

Getting there ☐

Aced it! ☐

REAL WORLD

A

B

LIVING AND LEARNING IN ...
MALTA

1 Read the information about language courses in Malta and look at the photos (A–C). Why do you think Malta is a good place to study English?

2 Read the text about studying English in Malta. Are these statements true (T) or false (F)? Correct the false statements.

1 School groups can only come in the Easter and summer holidays.

2 Many schools offer special courses for families that all family members will enjoy.

3 Adult classes are only for people who are already good at English.

4 Host families are a good idea for teenagers.

5 Most hotels are not very far from the language schools.

6 Self-catering apartments are always quite expensive.

WHY STUDY
ENGLISH IN MALTA?

Malta is the perfect place to study English. It has beautiful weather, warm seas, friendly people, and 6,000 years of history. It is also an English-speaking country.

COURSES

School groups

Most language schools welcome school groups all year round. They offer a good range of lessons and an activity programme for all ages. Most schools also offer a summer package so that students can enjoy a language holiday over Easter or summer.

Family courses

Come to Malta with your family and have a great holiday to remember. Many schools offer special courses for families, with lessons, accommodation and activities that all families will enjoy.

Adult courses

Schools also offer adult courses at all levels, from beginners to advanced. Classes are usually small, often with no more than ten students in each class. The adult courses are for people who want to learn how to speak English for their work or to use on holiday.

ACCOMMODATION

Host families

A host family offers you a warm welcome in their home, where you can hear and speak plenty of English. This is the best choice for teenagers aged 13–17. It gives you the chance to experience everyday life in Malta and learn how people live on this beautiful island.

Hotel accommodation

A hotel is the perfect choice for people who want to feel that they are on holiday! Most hotels offer a swimming pool, restaurants and evening entertainment. Many hotels are in St Julian's Bay, where you can be close to your school and the beach!

Self-catering apartments

Self-catering apartments are perfect for families, or people who want to cook for themselves. Most schools offer self-catering apartments at different prices, usually close to the schools.

C

3 Find the phrases in the text and choose the correct definitions.

1 an activity programme
  a a set of different activities you can do
  b a TV programme about different activities
2 package
  a a holiday where you pay for everything together
  b a holiday with no language lessons
3 airport transfers
  a places to stay near the airport
  b journeys to and from the airport
4 host family
  a your family
  b a family you stay with while you are studying
5 evening entertainment
  a meals in the evening
  b things to do in the evening, e.g. films and shows
6 self-catering apartment
  a a flat where you stay and cook your own food
  b a flat where someone comes and cooks for you

4 🔊 072 **Listen to three conversations. Who is speaking? There is one extra answer which you do not need to use.**

a two new students
b a student and a host family member
c a student and the school receptionist
d a new student and a teacher

5 🔊 072 **Complete the phrases with the correct words. Listen again and check.**

don't have	I've got	I've met	like to book
not very keen	there are		

PHRASES YOU MIGHT USE

1 I'd .... some accommodation.
2 .... four people in my family.
3 .... my host family.
4 .... my student card.
5 I .... any allergies. I eat everything.
6 I'm .... on spicy food.

6 Choose the correct definitions for these informal words and phrases.

PHRASES YOU MIGHT HEAR

1 Yes, I've got you here.
2 If you want to go ahead, just let me know.
3 Have you settled in OK?
4 Have you dealt with all the formalities?
5 You can get that up and running.
6 Any particular preferences?

a Have you completed the documents?
b Are there any things you like or don't like?
c I've found your name on the computer.
d Do you feel comfortable with your host family?
e You can start using it.
f Tell me if you want to book it.

7 ⏺ **Watch the video. What do you learn about these things in Malta? Make notes.**

- towns and cities
- history and culture
- language schools
- free-time activities

8 ⏺ **Compare your notes. Watch the video again to check your ideas.**

9 **Work in pairs. Plan a language course for someone who wants to come and live and study in your country. Think about these questions.**

- Where is it?
- Who is it for? (school groups, families, etc.)
- What accommodation is there?
- How long are the lessons?
- What free-time activities are there?

▶ WATCH

LIFE COMPETENCIES

CREATIVITY, INNOVATION AND DECISION-MAKING

10 **Make a leaflet to advertise a language course. Then read all the leaflets in your class. Which language course would you like to do the most? Why?**

UNITS 6–8

1 Complete the sentences about the photo using words in the box. You don't need all of the words.

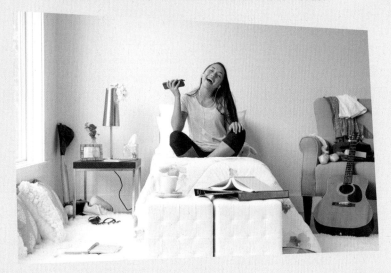

behind	between	in	in front of	next to	under

1 There is a bed, a chair and a table _____ the room.

2 The table is _____ the bed and the window.

3 There is a guitar _____ the chair.

4 On the table, there are some flowers _____ the picture.

5 There are some trainers _____ the table.

6 There is a teddy bear on the bed, _____ the girl.

2 Choose the correct option to complete the sentences.

1 A *solo artist/songwriter* is someone who performs alone.

2 When they're playing on stage, the *drummer/guitarist* usually sits down, but the other people in the group stand up.

3 When the *musicians/artists* started to play, the fans started to sing and clap.

4 A group of people who play pop music together is called a *concert/band*.

3 Add food words to complete this text. You have the first letter of each word to help you.

I think that it's important to look after yourself, so I try to go to the gym two or three times a week and eat healthy food, especially vegetables like ¹b_____ . I'm a vegetarian, so I don't eat ²b_____ , ³c_____ or fish. I eat eggs, cheese and milk, though, so I often like to make an ⁴o_____ for lunch – my favourite is ⁵m_____ . Afterwards I usually have fruit such as ⁶m_____ or maybe a ⁷y_____ .

4 Complete the sentences using the words and expressions in the box.

a	a few	a little	many	much	some

1 Could I have _____ cake, please?

2 I'm not feeling well. I only had _____ soup for my lunch!

3 I'll buy some fruit when I go out – there's not _____ left.

4 Don't forget to take _____ water with you. It's a very hot day.

5 How _____ spoons of sugar do you have in your coffee?

6 Put _____ grapes in this bowl, please. I only need 4 or 5 for my fruit salad.

7 If you're thirsty, there's _____ carton of orange juice in the fridge.

5 Complete the sentences about the people's hobbies using the words in the box.

> playing board games   baking   doing exercise
> doing nothing   going to gigs   going to the gym
> photography

1 I love _____ every day after college. The running machine is my favourite thing.

2 I really love _____ . In fact, I make a cake every time someone in my family has a birthday. I really enjoy _____ too, so I take photos of all my cakes and post them on social media.

3 I love art, and my hobby is really fun. I like making sculptures and giving them to people as presents. I also love listening to music, so when I'm not doing art, I like _____ with friends.

4 My friends and I enjoy getting together and _____ such as Monopoly.

5 When I was younger I didn't like sport. I preferred _____ . Now, though, I really enjoy _____ especially, running in the park.

6 Put the word in brackets in the correct place in each sentence.

1 **A:** Have you travelled somewhere by plane? (ever)
   B: Actually, I've come back from New York. It was fantastic! (just)

2 **A:** Have you finished that book? (yet)
   B: Of course! In fact, I've started a new one. (already)

3 **A:** What game is that you're playing? I have seen it before. (never)
   B: Oh, we've had this years. My dad bought it in China. (for)

7 Students often make mistakes with countable and uncountable nouns, and *some*, *any*, *a*, *many*, etc. Correct the mistakes in the sentences.

1 I bought a jeans and a beautiful trainers.
2 It was a good weather.
3 My favourite meal is the pasta.
4 At the park no-one sells some food.
5 Don't forget to buy a juice.
6 We took much photos.

8 Complete each sentence with the correct form of the past simple or present perfect of the verbs in brackets.

1 I _____ (buy) a new sofa yesterday. The old one wasn't very comfortable.

2 _____ she _____ (have) that clock for a long time?

3 I _____ (leave) my keys at home this morning, and now I can't get into my flat.

4 I _____ (not/see) that desk before. Is it new?

5 Sorry it's so cold in the living room. I _____ (not/put) the heating on yet.

6 I _____ (meet) my new neighbours a few days ago. They're really friendly.

9 Read the text, and choose the correct answer (A, B or C) for each gap.

I love going to my friend Ben's house. He lives in a beautiful modern ¹_____ in the centre of town. It's quite big, and there is a lovely ²_____ that you can sit on when the weather is nice. It's an unusual place to live in, because the kitchen is ³_____ . Ben's a really good cook, so he often ⁴_____ friends to his place for a ⁵_____ at the weekends. We all sit in the kitchen and chat while Ben ⁶_____ the food. Everything is always delicious, but I try not to eat too much at the beginning of the meal, as I love the sweet ⁷_____ that Ben makes.

1	**A**	apartment	**B**	cottage	**C**	houseboat
2	**A**	view	**B**	balcony	**C**	basement
3	**A**	above	**B**	out	**C**	upstairs
4	**A**	meets	**B**	calls	**C**	invites
5	**A**	meal	**B**	dinner	**C**	snack
6	**A**	puts	**B**	prepares	**C**	cuts
7	**A**	desserts	**B**	starters	**C**	main courses

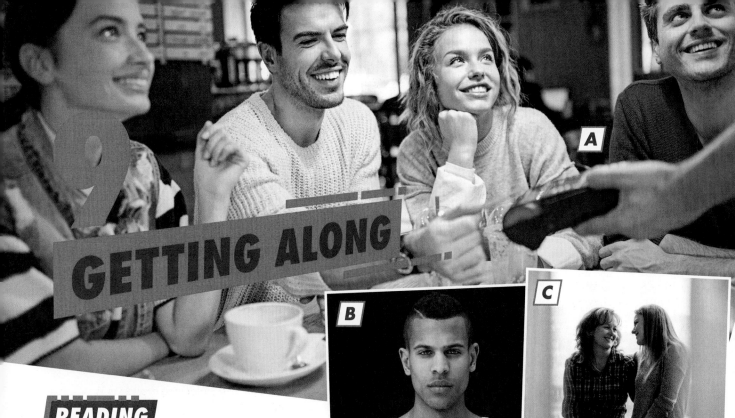

GETTING ALONG

READING

1 Think about one of your friends. Tell your partner about them.

- Where did you meet?
- Why do you like them?
- How long have you known them?
- What do you do together?

2 Match the photos (A–E) with the texts (1–5).

WHAT KIND OF
FRIEND ARE YOU?

1 THE CLEVER FRIEND – You're intelligent and you like reading and learning new things. You're often **busy** because you're interested in so many things. Sometimes you're quiet but this isn't because you're **shy**. It's because you're thinking about something!

2 THE **GENEROUS** FRIEND – If you go to a café with friends, then you're happy to pay for the drinks because you like sharing and giving. You're **friendly** and are usually nice to people.

3 THE FUNNY FRIEND – You know lots of jokes and stories and you enjoy making your friends laugh.

4 THE COOL FRIEND – You dress well, look good and know it. You are very **confident**. Because of this, people often want to know you and be your friend.

5 THE **RELIABLE** FRIEND – You don't forget things and you always help your friends when they need you.

3 Match the words in blue in the text with the definitions.

1 When you are _____ , you have lots of things to do.

2 A _____ person believes that they can do things well, like get good marks or get a good job.

3 It's normal to be quiet and feel a bit _____ when you meet or talk to lots of new people.

4 _____ people like meeting new people and find it easy to talk to them.

5 If you are _____ , you enjoy giving people money and presents or sharing your things with them.

6 When someone is _____ , they always do what they say they will do, like arriving on time and working hard.

4 🎧 073 Listen to four people talking about their best friends. For each speaker note down where and when they met.

1 Chris and John _____
2 Emma and Sonia _____
3 Enrique and Juan _____
4 Helena and Jasmine _____

5 🎧 073 Listen again. What do they like about their friends?

6 What kind of friend do you think you are? Why?

7 Look at the photos of best friends Grace and Matteo. Where do you think they met? What do you think they are like?

8 Now read the texts about Grace and Matteo and find out. Where do they work?

HOW WE MET

Matteo on Grace:
I met Grace when I came to her restaurant in London. The first thing I noticed about her was her smile. I needed to get a job and she agreed to give me some work for the summer. That was ten years ago and I'm still here. Grace is a very friendly, generous person. She never gets **angry** with me, even when I do stupid things! It's also very exciting to work with her. She knows so much about food, and I have learned to cook many great dishes from her. Sometimes when I arrive at work I'm **in a bad mood** or I'm **worried about** something, but then I sit down with Grace to talk and half an hour later, I'm feeling fine. I love working here – with my friend.

Grace on Matteo:
At first, I didn't really want to give Matteo a job because I thought he was too young. But the restaurant is very busy in the summer, so I decided to offer him a job in the kitchen for a few months. That was ten years ago and he's still here! I love working with him. Restaurant kitchens are very noisy, busy places and it's easy to get **stressed** but Matteo is always calm. He's a quiet person, but people never **argue** with him. They listen to what he says and they do what he asks them to do. We **get on very well** because we're interested in the same things.

9 Read the texts again and answer the questions.

1 What did Matteo first notice about Grace when he met her?
2 How long have they worked together?
3 Why didn't Grace want to give Matteo a job?
4 Why does Grace like working in the kitchen with Matteo?

VOCABULARY

FEELINGS AND EMOTIONS

1 Match the beginnings of the definitions of the words in red from the texts with the endings (a–f).

1 You are **angry** when you have a strong feeling
2 You are **worried** when you are unhappy
3 Your **mood** – which can be bad or good – is
4 To **get on well** or **badly** with someone is to have
5 When I get **stressed** in my job I feel that I
6 When people **argue** they disagree about

a a good or bad relationship with them.
b against someone who's behaved badly.
c something, shout and get angry.
d have too much to do and everything is going wrong.
e the way you feel at a particular time.
f about bad things that might happen.

2 Complete the sentences with the words and phrases from Exercise 4.

1 I _____ with my parents. We can talk about anything and we never argue.
2 I felt very _____ when my friend stopped answering her phone and I didn't know where she was.
3 My mum is in a _____ because my dad forgot her birthday.
4 They _____ about money all the time. He thinks she spends too much!
5 I like to arrive at work on time and feel really _____ if there are delays and I think I'm going to be late.
6 The teacher was _____ with us because we didn't do our homework.

3 Work in pairs and ask and answer the questions.

1 Who do you get on well with? Why?
2 When do you feel stressed?
3 When was the last time you got really angry with someone? Why? What did they do?

DID YOU KNOW?

*British English speakers talk about being **angry**, but American English speakers often say that they are **mad**.*

GRAMMAR

VERBS / ADJECTIVES + *TO* + INFINITIVE

 GRAMMAR ON THE MOVE
Watch the video

1 Look at the examples and choose the best answer to complete the rule.

*I **needed to get** a job.*
*I **decided to offer** him a job in the kitchen.*
*It's very **exciting to work** with her.*
*It's **easy to get** stressed.*

> After some adjectives and after some verbs, we use
> **to** + *infinitive/past participle*.
> We use **to** + infinitive after some adjectives:
> *I'm (not) **happy/ready/pleased to do** this.*
> *It's **better/easy/difficult/exciting (not) to do** this.*
> We use **to** + infinitive after some verbs:
> *You can **learn/want/decide/agree to do** something*

➡ **GRAMMAR REFERENCE** / *page 214*

2 Put the words in order to make sentences with a verb or adjective + *to* + infinitive.

1 find out about / in a different country. / to /
It was interesting / life
2 to / next year. / that there's a trip / We were excited /
to America / hear
3 say / to their friends. / They were sad / goodbye / to
4 She promised / to / in the evening. / help him
5 learn / but it was / I tried / how to ski / to /
too difficult.

3 Complete the sentences with the correct form of a verb or adjective in the box + *to* + infinitive.

decide	easy	exciting	happy	learn	want

1 It's _____ learn a new skill if you have a good teacher.
2 Most children have _____ speak before they are three years old.
3 I didn't _____ go to bed because I didn't feel tired.
4 He _____ wait for his friend in front of the school.
5 I was _____ hear that my sister passed all of her exams!
6 It was very _____ be at the match last night.
Both teams scored lots of goals!

4 **P** 🔊 074 Listen to four sentences. Notice which syllables are stressed. How is the word *to* pronounced when it is unstressed?

*It's **easy** to⌒**get** stressed.*
*I **needed** to⌒**get** a job.*
*I **didn't really want** to⌒**give** Matteo a job.*
*He's **happy** to⌒**pay** for the **drinks**.*

5 **P** 🔊 074 Listen again and repeat. Try to link the unstressed *to* with the previous word in the sentence and copy the pronunciation (/tə/ not /tuː/).

6 Complete the sentences so that they are true for you. Tell your partner.

1 Nobody has ever asked me to …
2 I have decided to …
3 I think it would be interesting to …
4 It's difficult for most people to …

1 What kind of problems can people have when they move away from their home and family for the first time?

LIFE CHANGE

MICHAEL

Our family moved from the country to a big city when I was about 12. It was a difficult time for me. My new school was very big. I didn't know anyone and missed my friends. Our apartment in the city was small and I couldn't sleep because of the loud traffic and other sounds in the street. I hated being there, and felt sad, but then I started skateboarding. I was good at it and it was a way to make friends. After that, life got better.

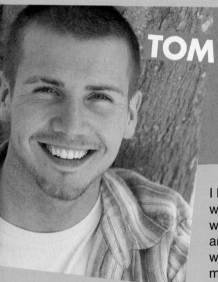

TOM

My parents sent me away to live and study at a school when I was 14. They were worried about me because I didn't study and they thought the new school would make me work more. At first, I was angry with everyone – my parents, the teachers, the whole school! But the teachers were nice. I got interested in nature because the school was in a beautiful place in the country and I began to enjoy science lessons. I also started playing tennis. In the end, I was very happy there.

ERIC

I lived in the same city until I was 20 and then I went away to university. I chose a university a long way from my parents. It was near the mountains and the sea and I couldn't wait to leave home. But when I got there, I missed my family. It was easy to make new friends, but studying was difficult. I also missed my life in the city – the shops, cinemas and cafés. After a year, I moved to a different university nearer home.

2 Read the texts. For these questions, choose the correct answer.

> *Look at question 1 and underline the key words. Who talks about when he was a teenager?*
> *Tom is the only person who talks about when he was a teenager. He says his parents sent him away to school. This means his parents weren't with him.*

		Michael	Tom	Eric
1	Which person went to live in a new place without his family when he was a teenager?	A	(B)	C
2	Which person chose to move to a new place?	A	B	C
3	Which person thought his new home was too noisy?	A	B	C
4	Which person didn't enjoy living away from the city?	A	B	C
5	Which person made friends through sport?	A	B	C

3 Work in pairs and tell your partner about a time when you moved to a new place or started a new school or a new job. Answer the questions.

1 When and why did you move?
2 How did you make friends?
3 What did you enjoy doing in the new place?
4 Who and what did you miss?

GRAMMAR

VERBS + -ING

GRAMMAR ON THE MOVE
Watch the video

1 🔊 075 **Listen to four people talking about how they cheer themselves up (make themselves feel happier) when they are sad or stressed. Number the speakers in the order you hear them.**

Monica

Tima

Paola

Fahad

2 🔊 075 **Listen again and complete the sentences.**

1 When I'm sad, I try to find something that will make me laugh. I love _____ funny films.
Before _____ down to watch, I make some hot chocolate.

2 I always enjoy _____ around, and thinking about the game helps me to forget my problems.

3 When I want to cheer myself up, I phone a friend.
I soon stop _____ about sad things.
I always feel better after _____ to them.

4 I hate _____ in a dirty, untidy place, so washing up and making everything clean and tidy makes me happy.

3 **What cheers you up when you are feeling sad or worried? What do you do? Where do you go? Who do you talk to?**

4 **Look at the examples of verb + -ing from Exercise 2 and choose the correct options to complete the rules.**

*When I'm sad, I **love watching** funny films.*
*Before **sitting** down to watch, I make some hot chocolate.*

We use **verb + -ing**:
1 *Before/After* verbs of preference plus some others, e.g. **start**, **finish**, **stop**, **suggest**.
2 After *adjectives/prepositions*.

➡ **GRAMMAR REFERENCE** / page 214

5 **Complete the sentences with the correct form of the verbs in the box.**

be	go	play	read	revise	visit

1 I really enjoy _____ other countries. I go abroad as often as possible.
2 Thank you for _____ so generous.
3 Have you finished _____ that book? I'd like to borrow it.
4 My parents are talking about _____ to America.
5 He is good at _____ the guitar.
6 I hate _____ for exams. There's always too much to learn.

6 **Complete the sentences using the verbs in the box and either *to* or *-ing*.**

carry	go	help	learn	take	watch

1 **A:** Do you enjoy _____ to the cinema?
   B: Yes, I love _____ films on the big screen!
2 **A:** I really want _____ the piano.
   B: Do you? Well you should start _____ lessons then.
3 **A:** Did you ask James _____ you move house?
   B: Yes, he's agreed _____ some boxes for me.

7 **Work in pairs and ask and answer.**

• Have you ever forgotten to do something important?
• Have you ever decided to learn a new skill?
• Where do you hate/enjoy going on holiday?

1 🔊 076 **Listen to four conversations. How does the main speaker feel? Match the conversations with the feelings.**

Conversation 1: Lisa feels …   sad
Conversation 2: Alison's dad feels …   excited
Conversation 3: Jill feels …   worried
Conversation 4: Lara feels …   angry

2 🔊 076 **Listen again and choose the correct answers.**

> *First look at Question 1 and the options and underline the key words. Then listen.*
>
> *A is wrong because Alfie didn't forget to bring the tablet – he lost it. B is wrong because Lisa says she doesn't care about the present. C is correct because Lisa says she's disappointed because he forgot her party.*

1 You will hear two friends talking. Why is Lisa angry with Alfie?
  A He forgot to bring Lisa's tablet back.
  B He didn't buy Lisa a birthday present.
  C He didn't go to Lisa's birthday party.

2 You will hear a mum and a dad talking about their daughter, Alison. Where's Alison now?
  A at the cinema
  B at a pizza restaurant
  C at a party with friends

3 You will hear Jill and Lenny talking about Jill's holiday. What has Jill never done before?
  A travelled outside her country
  B gone on holiday without her parents
  C been in an aeroplane

4 You will hear Lara saying goodbye to her friend Tom. What's Tom going to do?
  A move to a new town
  B start a new job
  C move to a new house

PUSH YOURSELF B1

GRAMMAR: MORE EXPRESSIONS WITH -ING AND TO

1 **Complete the sentences from four conversations with the phrases in the box.**

> move   coming to the beach   going to the park
> study computing   visiting Paris   getting wet and cold
> go up the Eiffel Tower   getting a good job

1 I **don't mind** _____ or taking a short walk by the river, but I don't like long walks and you know I **can't stand** _____ .

2 **A:** Do you **feel like** _____ this afternoon, it's a beautiful day!
  B: No thanks it's too hot for me. I **can't be bothered to** _____ .

3 **A:** I'm **planning to** _____ at college.
  B: Well, I'm **keen on** _____ with good money – and I think going to university will help me to do this.

4 I'm really **excited about** _____ . **I'm hoping to** _____ and see all the famous places.

2 **Look at the expressions in bold in Exercise 1. Which are followed by to + infinitive and which are followed by the -ing form?**

3 **Match the phrases with the definitions.**

1 If you **don't mind** doing something
2 If you **can't stand** doing something
3 If you **feel like** doing something
4 If you **can't be bothered** to do something
5 If you're **planning** to do something
6 If you're **keen on** doing something
7 If you're **excited about** doing something
8 If you're **hoping** to do something

a you are looking forward to doing it.
b it is your intention to do it.
c you are not in the mood for doing it.
d you think it is OK to do it.
e you would like to do it and you think there is a good chance you can do it.
f you really hate doing it.
g you are in the mood for doing it.
h you think it is a good idea to do it.

4 **Complete the phrases so they are true for you. Tell your partner.**

1 I'm really not keen on …
2 I'm excited about …
3 In the future, I hope to …
4 Sometimes, I really can't be bothered to …

SPEAKING

GIVING ADVICE

1 Who do you talk to when you have a problem? Do your friends often ask you for advice with their problems?

2 🎧 077 Listen to three people telling their friends about a problem they have. Who has a problem:

1 with their friends?
2 with their job?
3 with their studies?

Sara

Mike

Tom

3 🎧 077 Listen again. Answer the questions.

1 What is Sara's friend doing that is making her unhappy?
2 Why is Mike tired?
3 Who doesn't Tom get on with? Why?

4 🎧 078 Now listen to Sara, Mike and Tom's friends giving them advice about their problems and answer the questions.

Which speaker A, B or C ...

1 says that they should stop studying so much.
2 says that they should be polite to the rude person.
3 says that they should say sorry to their friend and stop worrying about it.

5 🎧 078 Listen again and complete each piece of advice with expressions in the box. You will need to use one of the expressions twice.

> it's not a good idea to   tell her   why don't you
> you shouldn't   you should   stop worrying
> what about   try to

A

_____ that you're sorry that you upset her but there's nothing more you can do.

Then _____ about it.

B

_____ stop studying so much and take some time to relax before you go to bed.

_____ work on a computer just before you sleep; _____ do something different.

_____ talk to a friend about it?

C

_____ leave your job if you enjoy it!

_____ ask some other people if they feel the same?

_____ asking your boss very politely to change the way she speaks to you?

6 Do you agree with the advice? Why?/Why not? What other advice would you give?

7 Work in pairs. What advice could you give to these people? Use the expressions in Exercise 5 and the ideas below.

- join a gym
- talk to them about it
- explain why
- ask them why
- try other types of activity
- join some clubs
- find a hobby to do with other people

> I want to be fit and healthy but I hate doing sport.

> I share an office with a really untidy person and it's making me very stressed!

> My friend is always talking about me behind my back.

> I'm shy and I don't have many friends.

> My parents want me to study computers at university, but I want to study languages.

WRITING

GIVING ADVICE

1 Have you ever done a language course or other course and lived away from home? Would you like to? What problems did you/could you have?

2 Felix is doing a language course. Read his email to Alice, his English friend. Why has he written to her?

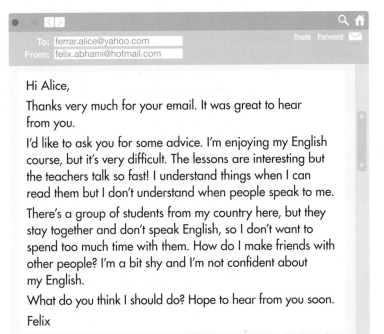

To: ferrar.alice@yahoo.com
From: felix.abhami@hotmail.com

Reply Forward

Hi Alice,

Thanks very much for your email. It was great to hear from you.

I'd like to ask you for some advice. I'm enjoying my English course, but it's very difficult. The lessons are interesting but the teachers talk so fast! I understand things when I can read them but I don't understand when people speak to me.

There's a group of students from my country here, but they stay together and don't speak English, so I don't want to spend too much time with them. How do I make friends with other people? I'm a bit shy and I'm not confident about my English.

What do you think I should do? Hope to hear from you soon.

Felix

3 Read the email again. What problems does Felix have:

1 with his studies?
2 with making friends and meeting people?

4 Read Alice's reply to Felix. What's the best advice that she gives him?

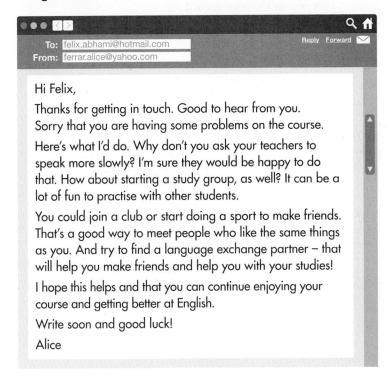

To: felix.abhami@hotmail.com
From: ferrar.alice@yahoo.com

Reply Forward

Hi Felix,

Thanks for getting in touch. Good to hear from you. Sorry that you are having some problems on the course.

Here's what I'd do. Why don't you ask your teachers to speak more slowly? I'm sure they would be happy to do that. How about starting a study group, as well? It can be a lot of fun to practise with other students.

You could join a club or start doing a sport to make friends. That's a good way to meet people who like the same things as you. And try to find a language exchange partner – that will help you make friends and help you with your studies!

I hope this helps and that you can continue enjoying your course and getting better at English.

Write soon and good luck!

Alice

5 Find expressions that Felix and Alice use to:

say thank you for an email	*1*
say they are happy about receiving an email	*2*
ask for advice (Felix); agree to give advice (Alice)	*3*
end an email	*4*

6 Write a plan for an email giving advice to your friend Pete, who is moving to a new town. He wants advice about making friends.

Use Alice's email in Exercise 4 as a model. Think of three pieces of advice.

7 Write your email. Use the expressions in Exercise 5 to help you. Then, check your partner's work. Does your partner …

- begin and end the email with the correct expressions?
- use correct spelling?
- give advice for each problem?
- use correct punctuation?
- use different advice expressions?
- use correct grammar?

EXAM CHECK

1 **Read these sentences about Reading Part 2 and decide if they are true (T) or false (F). Correct the false statements.**

1 You read three texts which are all about the same topic.
2 You answer five questions about the texts.
3 You have to decide which text has the information that correctly answers the question.
4 The questions come after the texts.
5 To answer the questions, you choose A, B or C.

2 **For each question, choose the correct answer.**

	Gabriel	Antonio	Peter
1 Who is surprised about the hours that his boss works?	A	B	C
2 Who likes it when his boss asks for advice?	A	B	C
3 Who thinks that his boss is good at helping new workers?	A	B	C
4 Who thinks his boss works too hard?	A	B	C
5 Who says his boss is popular with customers?	A	B	C
6 Who has a boss who doesn't mind if workers are late?	A	B	C
7 Who helps his boss with something that she finds difficult?	A	B	C

My boss

Gabriel

My company sells computers. When I was new here, I wasn't sure about my boss. I thought she was giving me all the boring jobs! But she soon started giving me more interesting and more difficult work. If someone can't get to work on time she never gets angry. Of course, if you've got a meeting with a customer, you have to let her know. We always decide things as a team, and she asks us what we think the company should do, which is great.

Antonio

I like my boss at the bank. When people first start here, the job is difficult for them, but she's always happy to explain things and give useful advice. Actually, I don't know how she finds the time. There's so much work, and she doesn't start very early, or finish late. It's amazing how she does it. Our customers like her too and they always ask for meetings with her. They're not happy if someone else goes instead. It's a problem sometimes, as she's so busy.

Peter

My company sells furniture. My boss almost never takes time off, and is often in the office until late at night. She should take a break sometimes. Maybe she thinks we won't be able to do the job without her! She's a very nice person, and all the team like her. Sometimes that's a problem, because she's not great at telling people when they're doing something wrong. Usually I offer to do that for her! I don't mind.

LISTENING PART 4

EXAM CHECK

1 Use numbers between 1 and 5 to complete these sentences about Listening Part 4. You can use some numbers twice.

In Part 4, you hear ¹_____ short recordings. In some of the recordings, ²_____ people are speaking, and in others you hear only ³_____ . For each recording, there is ⁴_____ question with ⁵_____ possible answers. You listen to the recordings twice.

2 🔊 079 **For each question, choose the correct answer.**

1 You will hear two friends talking about a restaurant they've been to. What did they like about it?
   A The food was good.
   B The prices were cheap.
   C The staff were nice.

2 You will hear a woman telling a friend about her new colleague. What's her new colleague like?
   A He's lazy.
   B He's funny.
   C He's friendly.

3 You will hear a woman leaving a message for her husband. What does she want him to do?
   A prepare dinner
   B get some shopping
   C collect her from work

4 You will hear two friends talking about an exhibition. How does the man know about it?
   A The artist is a friend of his.
   B He saw posters in the street.
   C His brother works at the museum.

5 You will hear a man giving a message to passengers at a train station. Why is he giving them the message?
   A Their trains are going to arrive late.
   B Some of them can get money back.
   C They need to buy tickets online.

HOW WAS IT?

Gave it a go ☐

Getting there ☐

Aced it! ☐

REAL WORLD

MEETING PEOPLE IN ...
MELBOURNE

1 Look at the photos (A–D) of places in Melbourne. What do you know about Australia and Melbourne? How do you think you can find friends in a new city? Read the text about Melbourne and compare your ideas.

Life in **Melbourne**

Home   About   Profile   Browse groups   🔍 Search

It can be difficult to make friends in a big city. You can be surrounded by thousands of people, but still feel lonely and on your own. Try these ideas to meet new people and if you're lucky, you'll make some good friends.

Parties
Make sure you accept party invitations, but only from people you have met. Remember, there are thousands of other people out there who want to meet people like you! But remember to stay safe and always go to new places with a group of people.

Courses
Enrol on a course you're interested in – like an evening class at the college near you. You'll learn something new and it's a good way to meet people you have a lot in common with.

Take up a hobby
There are thousands of hobbies to choose, from yoga and art to an aerobics exercise class or volleyball. The main thing is to choose something you are really into.

Volunteer work
This can be a great way to meet people. Choose work that interests you. Volunteering at the local zoo won't be much fun if you don't like animals!

Travel
You might think it's strange, but leaving the city can be a good way to make friends. Tours and backpacker's hostels can be great places to meet people because people who are travelling are often more interested in meeting new people.

The internet
There are lots of groups on the internet where you can find friends, for example people who go to the cinema together, or people who are interested in a sport. Remember it takes time to meet people and find out if you get on well with them, and of course, remember to stay safe when you're meeting people online.

2 Read the text again. Are the statements true (T) or false (F)? Correct the false statements.

1 The writer says you should always accept invitations to parties.
2 If you choose a course you are interested in, you might meet people who like the same things as you.
3 It is more difficult to find friends outside the city.
4 You can often find friends quickly online.

3 Complete the sentences with the words in the box.

enrol   get on well   get to
have a lot   make   take up

1 When you _____ friends, you meet people and become friends.
2 When you _____ on a course, you start to do it.
3 If you _____ in common with someone, you like the same things.
4 If you _____ a new hobby, you start doing it.
5 If you _____ know someone, you meet them and start to know them.
6 If you _____ with someone, you like them and are friends with them.

4 🔘 080 Listen to three conversations. What are the people doing? There is one extra answer which you do not need to use.

a getting information about joining a club
b asking about volunteering
c organising a party together
d enrolling on a course

5 🔘 080 Complete the phrases with the correct words. Listen again and check.

as a volunteer   book   give me   have to be
interested in   OK if   to enrol

PHRASES YOU MIGHT USE

1 Is it possible to work here _____?
2 Is it _____ I come to the centre this afternoon?
3 I'm _____ the photography course. Can you _____ some information about it, please?
4 I'd like _____ on the course, please.
5 Do you _____ a member of the club?
6 How can I _____ a court?

6 Choose the correct definitions for these informal words and phrases.

PHRASES YOU MIGHT HEAR

1 You'd need to drop in here.
2 Then we can take it from there.
3 I'll just have to take some details from you.
4 That's all in order.
5 You'd be better off joining.
6 It doesn't make sense for you to pay to become a member.

a We will decide what to do next.
b I need to write down your name, address, etc.
c It isn't a good idea for you to join the club.
d It would be cheaper for you to become a member of the club.
e That's fine.
f You must come into the office.

7 ▶ Watch the video. What do you learn about these things in Melbourne? Make notes.

- the city
- beaches and surfing
- sport
- Phillip Island

8 ▶ Compare your notes. Watch the video again to check your ideas.

▶ WATCH

LIFE COMPETENCIES

EMOTIONAL SKILLS AND DESCRIBING YOUR OWN CULTURE

9 Work in groups. Imagine that someone your age has just arrived in your town or city. Think about what their interests might be, then make an information pack for them. Suggest three ways that they can meet people and make friends. Share your ideas with another group.

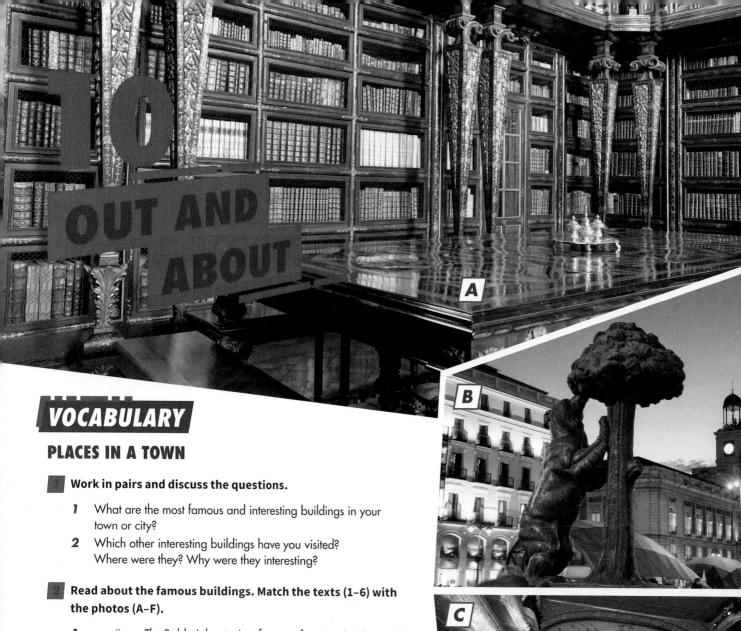

10 OUT AND ABOUT

VOCABULARY

PLACES IN A TOWN

1 Work in pairs and discuss the questions.

1 What are the most famous and interesting buildings in your town or city?
2 Which other interesting buildings have you visited? Where were they? Why were they interesting?

2 Read about the famous buildings. Match the texts (1–6) with the photos (A–F).

1 ___C___ *The Bolshoi theatre* is a famous **theatre** in Moscow in Russia. You can see ballet and opera performances there.

2 _____ *The Joanina Library* is part of the **library** of the University of Coimbra in Portugal. It's 300 years old and has more than 250,000 books.

3 _____ *Puerta del Sol* is a busy square in the centre of Madrid in Spain. There's a famous **statue** there of a bear under a tree and this is a popular meeting point.

4 _____ *The Tivoli* **Fountains** are in the gardens of the Villa d'Este in Rome in Italy. 875 metres of canals bring water to its 51 fountains.

5 _____ *Wembley Stadium* is very big, modern football **stadium** in London, England. You can see football matches there and also concerts. Lots of famous bands have performed there.

6 _____ *Chapultepec* **Castle** is in the middle of Chapultepec Park in Mexico City. The building is more than 300 years old and is the home of the Mexican National History Museum.

3 Work in pairs and discuss the questions.

1 Think of examples of the following in your country.
   a a famous castle
   b a museum
   c a big department store
   d a beautiful fountain
   e a famous theatre
   f a big statue

2 Where are they?
3 What is special about them?
4 How would you describe them to a visitor?

E

F

LISTENING PART 1 — TRAINING

1 ⚐ 081 **You are going to hear four conversations about places in town. First look at question 1 and the pictures and underline the key words. Then listen.**

> At first Emma thinks the play starts at 7.00. Then she checks the tickets and sees it begins at 7.30. They discuss meeting at 7.15, but then they decide it's better to meet at 7.00 (to give them more time), so the correct answer is C.

1 What time does the play begin tonight?

2 ⚐ 082 **Now listen to the other three conversations and choose the correct answers.**

2 How far away is the best sports centre?

3 What are Carl and Jack going to see at the stadium?

4 Where will the friends meet?

READING

1 What famous parks are there in your country?
Where are they? Have you visited them?
What can you see and do in them?

2 Read about the High Line and the Lowline.

1 Which part of New York are they in?
2 What are they and what is unusual about them?

THE HIGH LINE

The High Line was a **railway line** that ran above the streets of the **district** of Manhattan in New York. The line closed in 1980 and nobody used the land for a long time. Grass and other plants started growing there and in 2004, the City of New York decided to turn this space into a park. They planted flowers and trees and put in **benches** for people to sit on. Today, the High Line is a 2.33-kilometre-long green **path** across the city. Because it's high up in the air, there's a great view. It's a place where you can see the sky and enjoy the **fresh air** right in the **middle** of Manhattan.

THE LOWLINE

The Lowline is a project for another park in Manhattan that may happen in the future. At the moment, it's a big, empty **space** under the city, which might become the world's first underground park! The space used to be the Williamsburg bus station, which closed in 1948. Scientists have found a special way to use technology to bring **sunlight** underground so plants and flowers can grow there. The project will be very expensive but the City of New York hopes it will be popular with New Yorkers.

3 Read the texts again and answer the questions.

1 What was the High Line before it became a park?
2 What happened in 1980?
3 How long is the High Line park?
4 What can you see when you walk along the High Line?
5 What is the Lowline like right now?
6 How will scientists grow plants and flowers underground?

4 Complete the sentences with the **pink** words from the text.

1 A ＿＿＿＿ ＿＿＿＿ is a place for trains to run on.
2 There are ＿＿＿＿ in the garden where people can sit down.
3 A ＿＿＿＿ is an area of a city.
4 There is more ＿＿＿＿ in the country and by the sea than in the city because the air is cleaner.
5 A ＿＿＿＿ is a place for people to walk along.
6 The ＿＿＿＿ is in the centre of something.
7 A ＿＿＿＿ is an empty area that can be used.
8 Plants and trees need water and ＿＿＿＿ to grow.

5 Work in pairs and discuss the questions.

1 Have you ever been to New York? Would you like to go?
2 What kind of park would you like there to be in your town?
3 Where would be a good place for a new park in your town?

DID YOU KNOW?

In the USA, the part of the street where there are no cars and people can walk is called the **sidewalk** and an underground train system is called a **subway**.

In the UK, people walk on a **pavement** and if they want to catch an underground train they take the **underground** or in London, it's called the **Tube**.

GRAMMAR

WILL/MAY/MIGHT

GRAMMAR ON THE MOVE
Watch the video

1 Look at the examples from the text and choose the correct options to complete the rules.

*The Lowline is a project that **may happen** in the future.
It **might become** the world's first underground park!
The project **will be** very expensive.*

> **1** We use **will/won't**, **may/may not** and **might/mightn't** to talk about *the future/the past/the present*.
> **2** We use **will** when we are *not sure/sure* about something.
> **3** We use **may** and **might** when we are *not sure/sure* about something.
> **4** We use the *infinitive/present tense* of the verb after **will**, **may** and **might**.
>
> **Positive and negative**
>
> | | will/'ll | will not/won't |
> |------------|----------|------------------------|
> | subject + | may | may not |
> | | might | might not/mightn't |
>
> **Questions and short answers**
> **Will/May/Might** + subject … ?
> subject + **will/may/might**.
> subject + **won't/may not/might not**.

➡ **GRAMMAR REFERENCE** / page 216

2 Choose the correct options to complete the sentences.

1 The park *might/will* open in January, but I think it will be delayed.

2 If you post the letter today, I'm certain it *will/might* arrive by Thursday.

3 It *may/will* be the tallest statue in world, but I'm not sure.

4 Don't invite him to the gig: I know he *won't/mightn't* come. He hates that kind of music.

3 Complete the sentences with the correct form of **will**, **may** or **might** and the verb in brackets.

1 He _____ to the park with us this afternoon. He hasn't decided yet. (come)

2 There's not enough light here. Those plants _____ . It's just not possible. (not grow)

3 We don't know what to do with this space. We _____ it into a park. (turn)

4 We're not sure how much money we have. There _____ enough. (not be)

4 Read the newspaper article and answer the questions.

1 What was this place in the past?

2 What is it now?

3 What do you think might happen to it?

THE FUTURE OF
THE SHOE FACTORY

The old shoe factory in the city centre closed 20 years ago. Nobody has used the building since then and the area has become a green space. Now that Mr Smith, the owner, has died, the city owns the factory and needs to decide what to do with it.

What will happen to this big space in our city centre?

5 Read about two people. How do you think they might use the land?

Mr Jones is a businessman.
He wants to buy the land.
Mr Jones might …

Mrs Greene works for the city.
She wants to keep the land.
Mrs Greene may …

6 ● 083 Listen to the people talking and find out if you were right. For each person:

1 Write one sentence about what they say **will** and **won't** happen.

2 Write one or two sentences about what they say **may/might** happen.

7 Work in pairs and compare your sentences.

1 Did you write the same things? Which do you think is the best idea?

2 Imagine you have bought the land. What ideas do you have for what you will/may/might do with it?

VOCABULARY

DIRECTIONS

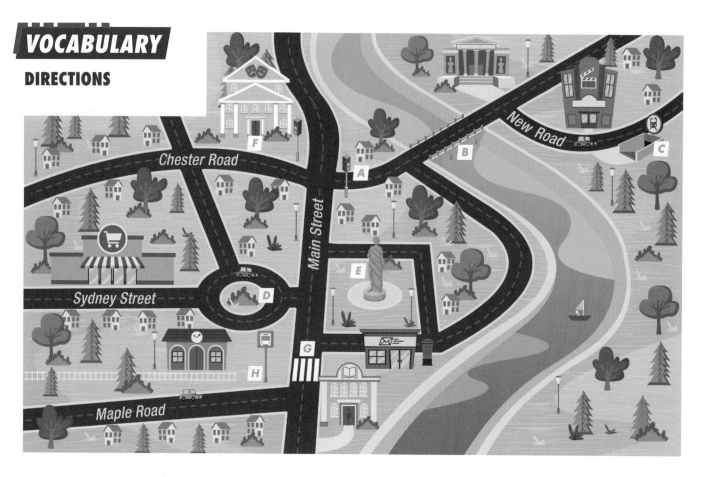

1 Read the sentences then look at the town map and match the letters (A–H) with the words in bold.

1 The statue is in the middle of the **square**.
2 There are **traffic lights** on Chester Road.
3 There's a **crossing** on Main Street.
4 There's a **roundabout** at the end of Sydney Street in front of the square.
5 You have to go over the **bridge** to get to the museum.
6 There's a **bus stop** on Maple Road near the station.
7 There's an **underground station** outside the cinema.
8 The theatre is on the **corner** between Chester Road and Main Street.

2 ● 084 Matias has just arrived in town and has asked for directions. He's at the library. Listen and number the sentences below in the order you hear them.

☐ Go **over the bridge** and **go straight on**.
☐ Come out of the library and **turn right**.
☐ Go **straight on down** the main street.
☐ **Take the first turning** on the right into New Road.
☐ You'll see it **on your left**.
☐ **Turn right at the traffic lights** into Chester Road.

3 ● 084 Listen again and follow the directions on the map. Where is he at the end?

4 ● 085 Matias is now at the railway station. Listen, look at the map and follow the directions. Where is he?

1 .... *2* ....

5 ● 086 Match the beginnings of these phrases for asking for directions with the correct endings (a–d). Listen and check your answers.

1 Excuse me. Do you know where
2 Can you tell me how to
3 Excuse me. Could you give me
4 Could you tell

a me where the museum is?
b directions to the town square?
c the station is?
d get to the library?

6 P ● 086 Listen to the sentences in Exercise 5 again. Notice the intonation. Add arrows to show if the phrases have:

a a rising intonation – does the speaker's voice go up? ↗
b a falling intonation – does the speaker's voice go down? ↘
c a rising, then falling intonation – does the speaker's voice go up, ↗ then down? ↘

7 P ● 086 Listen and repeat.

8 Work in pairs. Take turns to ask for and give directions to these places using the correct intonation.

Start from the underground station on the map.

• the cinema
• the library
• the main square
• the park

1   **Think about these questions.**

- What's your home town or village?
- Where is it?
- What's interesting or special about it?

2   **Match the examiner's questions (1–6) about a candidate's home town with their answers (a–f).**

1   Where is your town?

2   What do you think is the most interesting building in your town?

3   Where is the best place to go shopping in your town?

4   What do you like doing in your town in your free time?

5   How often do you go to the park in your town?

6   How do people travel around in your town?

a   There's a big mall by the station, but I actually prefer the shops in the town centre.

b   Maybe about once a week. I go there with my friends to go skateboarding.

c   Most students take the bus or travel by bike, but there are also a lot of cars in my town.

d   It's in the north of the country, by the sea.

e   There's a very good sports centre, and I like going there to do a gym class or go swimming.

f   The theatre is the most interesting building. It's probably about 500 years old.

3   **Work in pairs and take turns to ask and answer about your home town using the questions above.**

4   087 **The examiner will also ask you some questions like the ones below. Listen to a candidate answering the questions and decide which order she is answering the questions.**

1   Please tell me something about where you would like to live in the future.

2   Please tell me something about the street where you live.

3   Please tell me something about the last time you went out in your town with your friends.

5   **Make notes for your answers to the questions in Exercise 4. Then ask and answer.**

VOCABULARY: CITY WORDS

1   **Read the texts about two famous cities. Which city would you prefer to live in? Why?**

Hong Kong is famous for its **skyscrapers** – especially the tall office buildings in the **historic** Central district. Seven million people live there, so it's good that there's an excellent **public transport** system with lots of trams, buses, ferries and a great subway. It's a very busy city but there are some **traffic-free** areas like Victoria Peak – a tree-covered mountain that's fun to climb.

There are 3.9 million people living in Los Angeles and most of them have a car! It isn't a good city for **pedestrians** because there are places where there are no **pavements** for them to walk on. So you need to have a car if you live here. Unfortunately, because there are so many cars, there are a lot of **traffic jams** and the air can get very **polluted**.

2   **Complete the sentences with the words in purple from the text.**

1   If _____ in the city becomes cheaper, people will use the buses more and there won't be so many cars.

2   The water in the river is very _____ and all the fish are dead.

3   Next year, people won't be able to drive in the city centre on foot: it will be _____ .

4   I don't think I would like to live high up in a _____ . I don't like lifts!

5   I was late for work because I spent an hour sitting in my car in a _____ .

6   A _____ stepped in front of my bike and I hit him. Luckily, he wasn't hurt.

7   Tell the children to stay on the _____ and not to walk in the road.

8   We must look after _____ buildings because they help us remember the past.

A _____

B _____

GRAMMAR

WILL/SHALL FOR OFFERS AND PROMISES

 GRAMMAR ON THE MOVE
Watch the video

1 Label the photos with the words in the box.

| bank   police station   post office   restaurant |

C _____

D _____

2 🔊 088 Listen to three conversations. Where are the speakers?

conversation 1 _____
conversation 2 _____
conversation 3 _____

3 🔊 088 Answer the questions. Listen again to check.

1 How much money does the woman want to change?
2 Does the woman in the restaurant want a dessert? What does she order?
3 Where does the man want to send the letter?

4 Look at the examples and choose the best options to complete the rules about *will* and *shall*.

Shall I bring the dessert menu?
I'll put the letter straight in the post bag.

---

1 We use *will/shall* to make a promise or to announce that we have decided to do something.
2 We use *will/shall* to make suggestions and offers.

Will
subject +   **'ll help** them with their bags./
            'll get you a drink.
            won't ever tell anyone./
            won't do that again.

Shall
Shall I/We carry that for you?/start now?
Note: We only use **shall** in the first person.

➡ *GRAMMAR REFERENCE / page 216*

5 Choose the correct options to complete the sentences.

1 *Shall I/Will I* wait for you after the lesson?
2 Your suitcase looks heavy. *I shall/'ll* carry it.
3 It's late. *Shall/Will* we go to bed?
4 Sit down and I *'ll/shall* make you a cup of tea.

6 Complete the sentences with the correct form of *will/ shall* and the verbs given.

1 It's nearly two o clock; _____ lunch now? (have)
2 He _____ us the exam results as soon as he knows them. (tell)
3 _____ I _____ you some money for your train ticket? (give)
4 I _____ you this evening before eight. (phone)

7 Work in pairs. Take turns to make offers and promises in these situations.

• The two bags your friend is carrying look very heavy. (offers with *I*)
• It's a hot day and your friend has arrived at your house. (offers with *I*)
• Your friend has given you an important message to give to her teacher. (promise)
• You are at a party with your friend; it's late and you're tired. (suggestions with *we*)

WRITING

A THANK YOU EMAIL

1 Look at the photo. Have you ever visited Paris? What did you see and do? What would you like to see and do if you visit Paris in the future?

2 Read the email and answer the questions.

1 Why has Aylin written to Julie?
2 Find three things Aylin did in Paris.
3 What was her favourite moment and why?
4 What does Aylin hope Julie will do?
5 What is Aylin looking forward to?
6 Who does Aylin want Julie to say 'hi' to?

To: julie.durand@yahoo.fr
From: vardar.aylin@gmail.com
Subject: My visit

Reply Forward

Hi Julie

I just wanted to thank you for taking me to visit Paris last week. I had a great time!

I loved visiting the Louvre, as it's the biggest museum I've ever visited. I also really enjoyed the boat trip on the river Seine. But my favourite moment was when we went up the Eiffel Tower. I'll never forget seeing that fantastic view of Paris! I hope you can come to visit me in Istanbul soon. I'm looking forward to showing you my favourite places.

Say hello to your friends Marie and Lilou from me. It was great to meet them.

Lots of love,

Aylin

---

3 Find seven phrases Aylin uses to talk about her experiences in Paris in a positive way.

I had a great time!

4 Now use the phrases in Exercise 3 to complete the sentences below.

1 Say hello to your parents. It was .... them.
2 I .... visiting the old town. It was lovely.
3 I think that was my .... of the trip so far!
4 It was the best water park ....
5 I'll .... seeing the mountains for the first time.
6 Thank you for our trip to the beach last week. I ....
7 I .... the Empire State Building in New York.

5 You are going to write an email to a friend to thank them for a visit to their town. Plan what to write. Use the model in Exercise 2 to help you.

Paragraph 1: Explain why you are writing. Mention something you did and why you liked it.
Paragraph 2: Say what your favourite moment of the trip was.
Paragraph 3: Write about something you did on the trip that you will never forget. Write about something you visited that was the best/biggest you've ever visited.
Paragraph 4: End the message. Talk about when you hope to see your friend again.

6 Write your email. When you have finished, exchange with a partner and check each other's writing.

• Make sure that they haven't forgotten any of the information in Exercise 5.
• Check they've begun and ended the email in the correct way.
• Check their grammar, spelling and punctuation.

LISTENING PART 1

EXAM CHECK

1 **Read these sentences about Listening Part 1, and decide if they are true (T) or false (F). Correct the false statements.**

1 You hear five long recordings in Listening Part 1.
2 To answer a question, you choose one answer from four options.
3 You hear each recording twice.
4 Numbers are sometimes tested in this part of the test.
5 In some of the recordings there is only one person speaking.

2 🔊 089 **For each question, choose the correct answer.**

1 Where did Chris go yesterday?

2 What is the woman looking for?

3 What is broken in the woman's house?

4 Why will the man stay at home this evening?

5 How did the woman find out about the job?

SPEAKING PART 1

EXAM CHECK

1 Complete this information about Speaking Part 1, using some of the words in the box.

four	know	live	tell	three	two	understand

At the beginning of Speaking Part 1, the examiner will ask you your name, age, and where you
¹_____ . Then the examiner will say which topic you are going to talk about, for example,
shopping, or music. The examiner will ask each candidate ²_____ questions about this topic.
After this, the examiner will ask candidate A an extended question, starting with the words
'Please ³_____ me something about …' After this, they will do the same again with a new
topic. This time, candidate B will answer the extended question. If you don't ⁴_____ a
question, the examiner will help by asking the question in another way. For the extended
question, you should try to give ⁵_____ pieces of information.

2 Work in pairs. One of you is the examiner, and asks these questions. The other person answers the questions.

What's your name?
Where do you live?

3 Work in pairs. One of you is the examiner, and asks these questions about the place where you live. The other person answers the questions.

1 Who do you live with? (Do you live with your family?)
2 What type of building do you live in? (Do you live in an apartment building?)

4 Change roles. The person who answered the questions before is now the examiner.

1 How long have you lived in your home? (Have you lived in your home for two years?)
2 What can you see from your windows? (Can you see houses from your windows?)

5 Change roles again. The person who answered the questions before is now the examiner.

Now, please tell me something about the street where you live.
1 Are there shops on your street?
2 Is there a lot of traffic on your street?
3 Do you know other people who live on your street?

➡ *SPEAKING BANK* / page 240.

HOW WAS IT?

Gave it a go ☐

Getting there ☐

Aced it! ☐

REAL WORLD

VISITING TOURIST SITES IN ... ROME

A

1 What's your favourite city? Which other cities would you like to visit? Why?

2 Work in pairs. Look at the photos (A–C) of Rome. Do you know these places? Discuss the questions, then read the text about Rome and check your answers.

1 What do you think happened in the Colosseum?
2 What do you think visitors throw in the fountain?
3 What kind of things did Leonardo da Vinci design?

3 Find the phrases in the text and choose the correct definitions.

1 open-air theatre
  a a free theatre
  b a theatre with no roof
2 a must for any visitor
  a something that all visitors should see
  b a place where not many visitors go
3 top tourist attractions
  a places that not many tourists visit
  b places that are most popular with tourists
4 well worth a visit
  a you should go here
  b you shouldn't go here

4 Read the reviews of the Colosseum. Are the statements true (T) or false (F)? Correct the false statements.

1 You should buy your tickets before your visit.
2 It's better to go in the mornings.
3 The weather is often cold.
4 You can't visit the site when it's dark.
5 It's better not to visit at popular times of the year.

• Home   • Travel   • Food   • Lastest news

WHEN IN ROME

There are hundreds of places to visit in Rome. Here are a few that you should definitely see.

The Colosseum is on everyone's list of sites to see in Rome. In this open-air theatre in ancient Rome, gladiators and other people fought wild animals or other fighters, while crowds watched and cheered. It is a must for any visitor to Rome.

The Trevi Fountain is one of Rome's top tourist attractions. It is covered with wonderful statues of ancient stories and strange creatures and is a lovely place to enjoy a coffee. Tourists throw money into the water, because they believe that if they do this they will come back to Rome one day.

The Leonardo da Vinci Museum is a fantastic, small museum and well worth a visit. Learn all about the life of the famous artist and look at some of his ideas, including his plans for flying machines. Although Leonardo da Vinci lived and worked over 500 years ago, the ideas of this amazing artist and scientist have changed all our lives.

Visit the Colosseum, Rome

◎◎◎◎◎ **A wonderful place to visit!**
Buy your tickets online before you go. Arrive early to beat the queues. Get a video guide – it explains everything!

◎◎◎◎○ **Visit Rome to learn about ancient Roman civilisation.**
If you go in summer, remember to wear comfortable clothes because it can get very hot. Take plenty of water with you.

◎◎◎◎◎ **It's a good idea to take a tour.**
We had a guide who told us all about the history of the site. Visit during the day and also at night – it's beautiful!

◎◎◎◎◎ **Everyone should see this amazing monument!**
Visit out of season if possible. We visited in December and it was very quiet – and no lines at the ticket office.

◎◎◎◎○ **So interesting!**
We spent two hours here and still didn't see everything. This is definitely a must when you visit Rome!

B MUSEO LEONARDO DA VINCI *experience* 50 MACHINES 22 PAINTINGS

5 Read the reviews again. Complete the phrases with the correct words.

> early   queues   take   video guide
> visit   your tickets

1   Buy _____ online.
2   Arrive _____ .
3   Beat the _____ .
4   Get a _____ .
5   _____ a tour.
6   _____ out of season.

6 🔊 090 Listen to three conversations. What are the people doing? There is one extra answer which you do not need to use.

a   going into a museum
b   watching a video guide
c   taking a tour of the Colosseum
d   visiting the Trevi Fountain

7 🔊 090 Complete the phrases with the correct words. Listen again and check.

> are you   everyone says   is it OK
> is there   what time

PHRASES YOU MIGHT USE

1   _____ travelling?
2   _____ it's beautiful.
3   _____ a discount for students?
4   _____ to take photos?
5   _____ does the museum close?

8 Choose the correct definitions for these informal words and phrases.

PHRASES YOU MIGHT HEAR

1   They reckon between 50,000 and 80,000.
   a   They think there were …
   b   They know for certain that there were …
2   There's no flash photography.
   a   You can't take photos that use a bright light from your camera.
   b   Please use the bright light on your camera to take photos.
3   You're holding other people up.
   a   You are waiting for other people to move.
   b   Other people are waiting for you to move.
4   We ask you to leave promptly.
   a   You must leave quickly when the museum closes.
   b   When the museum closes, someone will ask you to leave.
5   You can't miss it.
   a   You must go there.   b   You can see it easily.

9 ⚫ Watch the video. What do you learn about these things in Rome? Make notes.

• the Colosseum   • the Trevi Fountain
• the Circus Maximus   • the Piazza Navona

10 ⬡ Compare your notes. Watch the video again to check your ideas.

▶ WATCH

C

LIFE COMPETENCIES

STUDY SKILLS AND LEARNING TO LEARN

11 Work in pairs and choose an important site you would like to visit in another city. Read some reviews by people who visited the site. Write a booklet with some information about it and some advice for tourists who want to visit it. Share your ideas with the class.

11 SAVING AND SPENDING

READING

MONEY AND ME

1 Work in pairs and discuss the questions. Match the questions (1–4) with the photos (A–D).

1 What do you like **spending** money on?
2 Are you **saving** money at the moment to buy or do something special?
3 Do you ever **lend** money to friends? Why?/Why not?
4 Have you ever **wasted** money on anything?

Rani

1 The saver

I love saving money and I think I'm very good at it! When I'm shopping, I always look for **reduced items** – things that the shop is selling for a lower price. If it's possible to get a **discount** on something, for example, 10% off, I always try to do this. The only thing I <u>spend</u> a lot of money on is tech – my pc, smartphone, tablet, etc. I always have a good computer and a new phone: I work from home and I need good equipment. I don't like <u>lending</u> money to people and I never <u>borrow</u> any, not even from the bank!

Carola

2 The upcycler

Money isn't important to me, but I also don't <u>earn</u> much in my job, so I have to be careful how I spend it! I go everywhere by bike or public transport as this <u>costs</u> less than having a car. I buy most of my clothes in **sales** and I still get lots of nice things, but for better prices! I love upcycling because I hate <u>wasting</u> things, so I often go to fleamarkets at weekends to see if I can find old things to make into something new. It's fun and it <u>saves</u> money.

David

3 The spender

I earn a good **salary** but I spend it all. I'm not very good at saving money. I enjoy being generous and buying people presents. If I go for a coffee or dinner with a friend, I often <u>pay</u> the **bill**. I also love buying clothes and shoes, especially trainers. I have 15 pairs! If I want something, I don't check the price, I just buy it. Because I never keep the **receipts** for things I've bought, I'm never sure how much money I've spent!

2 Read the texts. Which person:

1 doesn't have much money? ....
2 spends money on technology? ....
3 earns quite a lot of money? ....

3 Read the texts again and find the answers to these questions.

1 Find two ways in which Rani saves money.
2 What does Carola like doing, which saves money?
3 Why does David never know how much money he has spent?

VOCABULARY

SPENDING AND SAVING

1 **Look at the words in blue in the texts. Match the definitions with a word.**

1 This is money you get every month for doing your job.
....

2 This is when a shop lowers the price of something, e.g. by 10%. ....

3 This is a piece of paper you get when you pay for something in a shop. ....

4 This is a special time when a shop sells some things at a lower price. ....

5 This is a piece of paper you get at the end of a meal in a restaurant. ....

6 These are things that cost less than they did before.
....

2 **Now look at the underlined words in the text. These verbs are all about money. Read the sentences and choose the correct answer.**

1 The price of an item is how much it *costs/pays*.

2 Jack would like to go to New York, so he's *lending/saving* all his money for the trip.

3 They *lend/waste* a lot of money buying expensive clothes that they never wear.

4 My brother *spent/saved* all his money on a really expensive computer.

5 I asked my friend to *borrow/lend* me two euros so I could buy a coffee.

6 I don't *earn/pay* as much as my sister – she has a really big salary.

3 **Complete the dialogues using the correct form of some of the words from Exercises 1 and 2.**

1 **A:** Can I ¹ _____ fifty euros? There's a jacket I want in the ² _____ . There's a 50% ³ _____ , so the price is really good. I'll give it back to you tomorrow.

   B: That's what you always say! I ⁴ _____ you money all the time, but you never pay me back.

2 **A:** I went to the new Mexican restaurant today.

   B: Really? That's expensive. How much did that ⁵ _____ ?

   A: I don't know. The waiter brought the ⁶ _____ and my friend ⁷ _____ for it all.

3 **A:** How much money do you ⁸ _____ , Sandra?

   B: Not very much. I don't have a big ⁹ _____ . I'd like to buy a new car, but it's difficult for me to ¹⁰ _____ the money.

4 **Work in pairs. Ask and answer the questions below.**

1 Have you ever saved up for anything?

2 Have you ever bought anything at a discount or in a sale?

3 Do you usually pay the bill in a restaurant?

> I bought some great trainers in a sale. Unfortunately, they're a bit too small for me.

DID YOU KNOW?

*In the UK, people use **coins** and **notes** to pay for things in cash. In the US, people use **coins** and **bills**.*

*In the UK, people ask for the **bill** when they want to pay in a restaurant, but in the US they ask for the **check**.*

LISTENING

MAKING PLANS

1 Do you use a calendar? What kind of things do you use it for?

Marta's calendar

11.30 am:
- meet Cara at department store – go shopping for summer clothes
- Look for birthday present for Mum! (garden centre)

7.00 pm:
- dinner Milo's restaurant

Josh's calendar

2.00 pm:
- bus to town – buy food and drink for the party

2.30 pm:
- meet Jez at the supermarket – collect drums from music shop after shopping (take taxi?)

7.00 pm:
- party starts!

2 Look at the two calendars and read about Marta's and Josh's plans for Saturday.

1 Which two shops is each person going to?
2 What do they plan to buy?
3 What are their plans for Saturday evening?

3 🎧 091 Listen to Marta and Josh talking about their plans.

1 Why is Marta going to the garden centre?
2 What kind of party is Josh going to?

4 🎧 091 Listen again and choose the correct answers to complete the sentences.

1 Marta wants to go to the department store to
   a buy a dress.   *b* try on a dress.
2 She hopes that the dress she likes will be
   a the right colour.   *b* the right size.
3 She doesn't like
   a the changing rooms at Darby's.
   b the shop assistants at Darby's.
4 Josh is going to pay for his shopping
   a by card.   *b* in cash.
5 He mustn't forget to ask for
   a cash from Alfie's friends to pay for the shopping.
   b a receipt for the shopping.
6 He needs to give Alfie's dad
   a his change from £50.
   b £50 to pay for a taxi.

VOCABULARY

SHOPPING

1 🎧 091 Listen again to Marta and Josh and complete the sentences from the audio using the words below.

> by card   change   changing room   in cash
> shop assistants   size   till   try (it) on

1 I'm going to _____ in the shop if they have it in my _____ .
2 I don't like the _____ there because it's always busy, but the _____ are really nice.
3 I'm going to pay for everything _____ and I mustn't forget to ask for a receipt at the _____ .
4 Alfie's dad gave me £50 _____ to pay for a taxi.
5 I must remember to give him the _____ .

2 Complete the texts about shopping with the words in Exercise 1.

When you shop for clothes, even online, it's always a good idea to **¹**_____ the item you like before you buy it. You can go to the company's high street shop, try on the item, then go home and buy it online. This means you can be sure it's the right **²**_____ and that it suits you before you buy it. If there are lots of people in the shop, the **³**_____ can be busy and you may have to wait, but be patient! If you are not sure what looks good on you, ask a **⁴**_____ for advice. They are usually happy to help.

These days, most people don't carry a lot of money with them and pay **⁵**_____ for everything. I prefer to pay **⁶**_____ at the supermarket because it helps me not to buy too much. However, paying by contactless card is still the quickest way to pay – you don't have to wait for your **⁷**_____ when you get to the **⁸**_____ !

3 Work in pairs and discuss the questions.

1 Do you usually pay for things by card or in cash? Why?
2 Do you sometimes buy clothes without trying them on? Why?/Why not?
3 Do you like shop assistants talking to you when you are shopping? Why?/Why not?

GRAMMAR

THE PRESENT CONTINUOUS FOR FIXED PLANS

 GRAMMAR ON THE MOVE
Watch the video

1 **Look at the examples. Do they talk about the present or the future? Complete the rule.**

We're meeting in front of Darby's, the big department store.
I'm taking the 2 o'clock bus into town.

> We use the present continuous to talk about *fixed/less certain* plans for the future.

→ **GRAMMAR REFERENCE** / **page 219**

2 **Complete the dialogue about Laura's holiday plans using the verbs in brackets.**

Laura:	My friend Jenny and I ¹ _____ (go) on a tour of Italy in the middle of July. I can't wait! We ² _____ (visit) Rome, Florence and Venice in the first week, but we aren't going to spend all our time in cities. In the second week, we ³ _____ (travel) to the coast and we ⁴ _____ (stay) in a hotel near the beach.
Lily:	When ⁵ _____ you _____ ? (leave)
Laura:	We ⁶ _____ (fly) to Rome on 15th July and we ⁷ _____ (come) back on the 30th. We ⁸ _____ (not stay) in a hotel in Rome, though. Our friend Giacomo ⁹ _____ (meet) us at the airport and we ¹⁰ _____ (go) to his parents' house for the weekend. They ¹¹ _____ (take) us to the theatre on Saturday evening.
Lily:	That all sounds great.

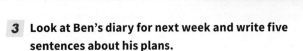

Monday
12.30 – meet Sam for lunch (Reno's café)
Tuesday
7.00 pm – football practice leisure centre
Wednesday
9.00 am – dentist appointment
Thursday
Guitar lesson 6.30 pm
Friday
Day off! No work. Go running in the park with Liz in the morning
Saturday
afternoon – shopping with Pete

3 **Look at Ben's diary for next week and write five sentences about his plans.**

On Monday he's meeting Sam for lunch. They're going to Reno's café.

4 **Work in pairs and tell your partner about some fixed plans you have for:**

- this evening
- your next holiday
- next weekend
- tomorrow

THE PRESENT SIMPLE FOR SCHEDULES AND TIMETABLES

5 **Look at the examples and complete the rule.**

*The restaurant **opens** at 7.00 pm.*
*The bus to town **leaves** at 2.00 pm.*
*Football practice **begins** at 7.00 pm.*

> We use the present simple to talk about something that will happen in the future according to *a schedule or timetable/fixed personal plans*.

→ **GRAMMAR REFERENCE** / **page 219**

6 **Look at these sentences about fixed plans and schedules and choose the correct answer.**

1 The sports centre *closes/is closing* at 9 pm on Saturdays.
2 She *has/is having* dinner in town with friends this evening.
3 The last train *is leaving/leaves* the station at midnight.
4 He *is visiting/visits* his brother next weekend.
5 We're *meeting/meet* in front of the theatre at six. The play *starts/is starting* at 6.15, so don't be late!

7 **Complete the sentences with the present simple or present continuous.**

1 The flight _____ at 12.30 from terminal B. (leave)
2 They _____ on holiday next week. (go)
3 The band's tour _____ in Berlin in February. (end)
4 Emily _____ Dan outside the cinema this evening at half past seven. (meet)

1 What kind of clothes do you think you can buy in these shops?

| clothes shop | department store | market | supermarket |

2 🔊 092 For each question, choose the correct answer.

You will hear Paula asking her friend Maria for advice about shopping for clothes. What clothes does Maria say Paula should buy from each place?

Listen to the first part of the audio.

Example: supermarket **E** swimsuit

> *Paula says there weren't any sun hats at the supermarket, but there are lots of swimsuits.*

3 🔊 093 For each question (1–4), choose the correct answer.

	Places to shop		**Clothes**
1	clothes shop	**A**	dress
2	department store	**B**	pair of shorts
3	market	**C**	socks
4	clothes website	**D**	sun hat
		E	swimsuit
		F	T-shirt
		G	trainers

GRAMMAR

GOING TO

GRAMMAR ON THE MOVE
Watch the video

1 Look at the examples. Do the sentences talk about the present or future? Complete the rule.

I'm going to buy some new clothes for my holiday.
I'm going to get one for myself.

> We use **be going to** + verb to talk about *definite plans/our intentions.*

⇒ **GRAMMAR REFERENCE** / page 218

2 Complete the sentences and questions with *going to* and the verbs in brackets.

1 After lunch, he _____ (go shopping).
2 Gemma can't drive. When _____ (learn)?
3 How _____ you _____ (get) to the party tomorrow?
4 I _____ (not/walk). It's too far.
5 _____ you _____ (buy) a new phone soon?

3 What are you going to do today or tomorrow? Write five sentences, then tell your partner.

4 **P** 🔊 094 Listen to the dialogue. How is *going to* pronounced?

A: **What** ⌢ are you **go**ing to **do** this week**end**? Do you **have** any **plans**?

B: Not **rea**lly. I'm **go**ing to **stay** at **home** and **watch** TV this **eve**ning.

A: **Yes**, so ⌢ am ⌢ **I**! And I'm **go**ing to **go** to **bed** ear**ly** for **on**ce.

5 **P** 🔊 094 Listen to the dialogue again and repeat. Try to reproduce the stress pattern and pronunciation in *going to*.

6 Complete the sentences with the correct form of the present continuous, *going to* or the present simple.

1 I _____ late at the office on Friday. I have a meeting with a customer. (work)
2 She _____ to the gym after college today. (go)
3 The concert _____ at 8.00 pm. (start)
4 We _____ TV later. (watch)
5 The train _____ at 8.30 pm. (leave)
6 She _____ the 8.30 pm train to London. (take)

For these questions, choose the correct answer.

> First, look at text 1, the question, the options and the correct answer, A. Which phrase in the text tells you that A is correct? A is correct because Claire says, 'Shall I get a pair for you?' B is wrong because Claire already knows Lisa's shoe size. C is wrong because Claire says that the trainers are on sale, not that there is a sale.

1

> Hi Lisa, There are trainers on sale in Brown's for €20! Shall I get a pair for you? They're black, size 38, just like you wanted. Claire

Why did Claire write this message?

(A) to offer to buy Lisa some trainers
B to find out what Lisa's shoe size is
C to tell Lisa that there's a sale in Brown's

Now choose the correct answers for the other texts. Think about why the other answers are not correct.

2

Special offer in book department!
THREE for the price of **TWO!**
(the cheapest is free)

A You can buy three books and only pay for the cheapest one.
B If you buy three books, one of them is free.
C Customers who buy two books can get a third book for a lower price.

3

> Jake, we've got no food in the fridge! Can you meet me at the supermarket after work? Bring the car so we can take the shopping home. Katie

A Katie is asking Jake when he is going shopping.
B Katie wants Jake to drive her to the supermarket.
C Katie wants Jake to go shopping with her after work.

4

Gina's Shoe Shop
50% off!
Hurry – offer ends Monday
Some sizes nearly gone

A You can buy shoes at a cheaper price than usual.
B Only some sizes of shoes are half price.
C You can buy shoes for half price from Monday.

VOCABULARY: MONEY AND SHOPPING

Shona Evans is a songwriter. Sometimes she earns a lot of money but at other times she doesn't have a lot of work and her **bank account** is almost empty. Shona always tries to get **good value for money** when she goes shopping and she's good at finding **bargains**. Her new Gibson 334 guitar **is worth** about €2,000, but she bought it online for only €900! Because she never knows how much money she's going to have, Shona prefers not to buy anything **on credit** in case she can't pay it back. This means she can't **afford** to buy a new car. The **second-hand** car she drives is 15 years old now, but she doesn't mind. 'I don't want to **owe** money to the bank,' she says, 'and as long as I have a good guitar, I'm happy.'

1 Read the text and match the beginnings of the definitions (1–8) with the endings (a–h).

1 You can afford something
2 If something is second-hand
3 How much something is worth
4 A bank account is
5 A bargain is something
6 When you buy things on credit
7 You get good value for money
8 You owe money when

a you have borrowed it and haven't given it back.
b where people keep their money.
c that you buy for less than its usual price.
d when you have enough money to pay for it.
e it is not new; somebody else had it before you.
f is how much money people will pay for it.
g when you pay less than usual for high quality.
h you can have them now and pay for them later.

2 Work in pairs and discuss the questions.

1 How old were you when you opened your first bank account?
2 What kind of things do people often buy on credit?
3 What have you bought that was a bargain or good value for money?

WRITING

REVIEW OF A DEPARTMENT STORE

1 What's the most famous department store in your country? Why is it famous? Have you ever visited it?

2 Read this review of a department store and answer the questions.

1 What did the reviewer like most about the store?

2 What did the reviewer think about the sales assistants?

3 What didn't the reviewer like?

4 Is the reviewer's overall opinion of the store good or bad?

I love shopping so I was excited about my visit to Bryson's Department Store. It's 200 years old and it's in the city centre.

It's an amazing place full of fantastic things on six floors. One of the best things about it is the food department, where you can buy all sorts of delicious food and taste things for free. There is also an excellent café with a great view of the city. For me, the high point of Bryson's is the clothes department, as the clothes are so on trend. Even the changing rooms are stylish – I stayed in there for ages!

The worst thing about Bryson's is that it's so crowded. It's also easy to get lost inside because it's so big and it's difficult to find any store plans. The friendly shop assistants helped me, but there weren't many of them and I had to wait a long time to pay. Another negative point for me is the high prices. Don't go there if you are looking for discounts, although they do have a great winter sale in January!

Overall, I would recommend Bryson's and I'm definitely going to go back there next time I'm in the city.

3 What expressions does the reviewer use to introduce the following:

a	good points	*One of the best things about it is*
b	bad points	
c	a final opinion	*................................., I would/ wouldn't recommend*

4 You are going to write a review of a department store you have visited. Include information about:

- the building
- the shop assistants
- the different products
- places to eat
- the changing rooms
- prices

5 Plan your review. Use the table to help you.

Paragraph 1 Where is the store What is the building like	*It's in … It's near …* *The building is …* *It has … floors,*
Paragraph 2 Bad points	*A bad/The worst thing about …* *is …* *It is/They are …*
Paragraph 3 Good points	*The high point/best thing about … is …* *There is/are …*
Paragraph 4 Conclusion	*All in all* *I would/wouldn't recommend I'm (not) going to go back*

6 Write your review. When you have finished, exchange your review with a partner and check his/her work. Can you make at least one suggestion to improve it?

SPEAKING

SHOPPING HABITS

1 Put the words in order to make questions about shopping.

1 enjoy / shopping? / you / Do
2 What sort / things / buying? / like / do / of / you
3 do / go / shopping? / Where / you
4 favourite / shop? / What's / your
5 bought / Have / you / recently? / anything
6 and / you / buy them? / when / Where / did

2 🔊 095 **You are going to hear two people talking about shopping. Listen and complete the table.**

	INES	LUCA
Enjoy shopping?		
Where shop?		
Favourite shop?		
Bought recently?		
When and where?		

3 Who do you think gave the best answers? Think about who:

- gave full answers.
- used adjectives.
- gave examples and reasons.

4 🔊 096 **Listen to Luca again and complete his answers to the questions using the words below.**

as   because   so (x2)   That's why

Interviewer: Do you enjoy shopping?
Luca: Yes, I do. I like shopping a lot. I especially like clothes shopping. **1** .... I love going to cities on holiday.

Interviewer: And what sort of things do you like buying? Where do you go shopping?
Luca: I really like wearing fashionable things,**2** .... when I have money, I like buying clothes and shoes a lot. There's a big shopping centre in my town and I go there. It's very crowded, but I really like it **3** .... it has a lot of shops!

Interviewer: And what's your favourite shop?
Luca: There's a clothes shop called *Place* that I like a lot. That's probably my favourite shop **4** .... the shop assistants are really helpful and I always see things I want to buy.

Interviewer: Have you bought anything recently?
Luca: Yes, I bought some boots – some really nice black boots. Unfortunately, they weren't in the sale, **5** .... they were quite expensive, but they look great.

5 What do we use the words in Exercise 4 for?

A to give reasons
B to order information
C to introduce a new clause

6 You are going to talk about shopping with your partner.

- Make notes for your answers to the questions in Exercise 1.
- Try to add as much detail as possible. Use the correct tense.

7 Work in pairs and take turns to ask and answer your questions. Add some more questions, for example:

1 What do you like spending your money on?
2 Do you do much shopping online?
3 What are your favourite shopping websites?
4 Do you buy expensive clothes? Why?/Why not?
5 Do you buy anything second hand?

EXAM FOCUS

EXAM CHECK

1 In Reading Part 1 you read six texts. Some of them will be longer than others. In the box you can see all of the types of texts you might read. Decide if each one is a shorter text (up to 14 words) or a longer text (up to 25 words).

> email   label on a product   notice on a work/school/club noticeboard   post-it note
> shop notice   sign on a wall   text message   web message

Shorter text

label on a product

_____

_____

_____

Longer text

email

_____

_____

_____

2 For each question, choose the correct answer.

1

> **CINEMA**
> Discounts Sunday – Friday
> when you pay online.
> Collect tickets from the
> information desk.

If you want cheaper cinema tickets
- **A** ask at the information desk.
- **B** go on a Saturday.
- **C** visit the website.

2

> Kelly, I tried to make a dentist
> appointment for you, but they
> told me I have to call before
> 9 am. I was too late. Sam

Why did Sam leave this message?
- **A** to explain to Kelly why he didn't do something
- **B** to let Kelly know how to do something
- **C** to ask Kelly to do something for him

3

> ●●● ◀ ▶   🔍 🏠
> **From:** Len Grainger   Reply Forward ✉
> **To:** All staff
>
> A set of keys was left in the café
> earlier. The receptionist has them in
> her desk at the main entrance.

- **A** The entrance keys are now kept in a different place.
- **B** Let a member of staff know if you find these keys.
- **C** Talk to the receptionist if you've lost your keys.

4

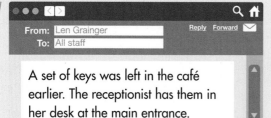

> Tina, are you still at the restaurant?
> I left my jacket there. Could you
> get it and bring it to the party
> tomorrow? Anna

Anna wants Tina to
- **A** pick up something Anna forgot.
- **B** go somewhere with her.
- **C** buy something for her.

5

Supermarket
Our bread oven is broken.
No fresh bread today.
Buy yesterday's bread half-price.

A This supermarket doesn't sell fresh bread anymore.
B You can get the bread cheaper because it wasn't baked today.
C If there's a problem with your bread you should return it to the supermarket.

6

Meg, Frankie says you're coming cycling with us tomorrow. Bring a jacket – it's going to rain. Do you know the theatre? We're meeting there. Petra

Why did Petra write this message?
A to invite Meg to go on a cycling trip
B to give Meg advice about a cycling trip
C to check the meeting place for a cycling trip

LISTENING PART 5

EXAM CHECK

1 **Read these sentences about Listening Part 5, and choose the correct options.**

1 You will hear *one person speaking/a conversation between two people*.
2 There are *five/six* questions to answer, and an example which has already been completed.
3 There are two lists. In the first list you will see the names of people, days, things or places. *You hear these in the order you read them/You may hear these in any order.*
4 In the second list there are *seven/eight* options. You will not hear these in the order you read them.
5 You have to choose one option from the second list for each option in the first list. You *will/will not* need to use all of the options in the second list.

2 🔊 097 **For each question, choose the correct answer.**

You will hear Alicia talking to a friend about her party. What job will Alicia do each day?

Example:

0 Monday   Ⓒ

Days		Jobs	
1	Tuesday ☐	**A**	buy a dress
2	Wednesday ☐	**B**	buy food
3	Thursday ☐	**C**	buy plates and glasses
4	Friday ☐	**D**	clean the house
5	Saturday ☐	**E**	cook the food
		F	cut her hair
		G	download music
		H	invite the neighbours

HOW WAS IT?

Gave it a go ☐

Getting there ☐

Aced it! ☐

REAL WORLD

DEALING WITH MONEY IN ... STOCKHOLM

1 Look at the photos (A–D) of ways of paying for things in Stockholm. Match them with 1–4. How do you usually pay for things when you go shopping?

1 cash
2 a contactless card
3 a smartphone
4 a credit card or debit card

2 Read the fact box about currencies. Then read the blog about how to pay for things in Stockholm. How do most Swedish people pay for things?

Different countries use different currencies.

United Kingdom: £ pound
USA: $ dollar
Europe: € Euro
China: ¥ Yen
Sweden: Kr krona

Home   **Latest posts**   **Subscribe**   🔍 **Search**

Although Sweden is an EU country, it does not use the euro. The currency is the Swedish krona (the plural form is kronor). Most stores in Stockholm only accept kronor, but some shops in tourist areas also accept euros. However, remember that if you pay in euros, the exchange rate might not be very good for you. No shops or restaurants accept dollars.

You can pay by credit card and debit card almost everywhere in Sweden, from big, expensive shops to taxis and hamburger stalls. You can also use contactless cards or pay with your smartphone for most things. People in Sweden don't usually carry much cash with them, but use cards or their phones for most payments. In fact, some museums and other places in the city don't accept cash at all, so you have to use a card or your phone to pay.

There are lots of currency exchange shops in the city, where you can change your own currency into kronor. But the exchange rate is often not very good, and they don't accept coins, only banknotes. There are also cash machines all over the city. They are blue, and are called Bankomats. Remember, the machines don't accept contactless cards, so you need to know your pin number.

3 Read the blog again. Are the statements true (T) or false (F)? Correct the false statements.

1 All shops in Stockholm accept Swedish kronor and euros.
2 You can't use dollars to pay for things.
3 You can only use credit cards to pay for expensive things.
4 You can't pay by cash in some museums.
5 There aren't many cash machines in the city.
6 You can use contactless cards at the cash machines.

4 Match the words from the blog with the correct definitions.

1 currency
2 exchange rate
3 credit card
4 debit card
5 payments
6 banknotes
7 coins
8 pin number

a small, round pieces of metal money
b the kind of money that people use in a particular country
c the set of four numbers that you use with a credit card or debit card
d a card that takes money from your bank account immediately
e a card that takes money from your account at a later time.
f situations when you pay for things
g pieces of paper money
h how much money you get when you change one currency into another

5 🔊 098 Listen to three conversations. What are the people doing? There is one extra answer which you do not need to use.

a asking about a cash machine
b asking about the exchange rate in a currency exchange shop
c buying some things in a shop
d going into a museum

6 🔊 098 Complete the phrases with the correct words. Listen again and check.

| cash machine | discount | far |
| pin number | take | use |

PHRASES YOU MIGHT USE

1 Is there a student _____ ?
2 Can I _____ contactless?
3 Is there a _____ near here?
4 How _____ is it?
5 Do you _____ cards?
6 I need to use my _____ .

7 Choose the correct definitions for these informal words and phrases.

PHRASES YOU MIGHT HEAR

1 There you go.
   a There's a problem with the card machine.
   b The card machine is ready for you.
2 That's gone through.
   a The payment was OK.
   b There was a problem with the payment.
3 Any one will do.
   a You can choose any road to go along.
   b Someone will tell you which road to choose.
4 Problem solved.
   a That is a problem for us.
   b There's no problem now.
5 The other way round.
   a Turn your card around, please.
   b Don't put your card in yet.

8 ▶ Watch the video. What do you learn about these things in Stockholm? Make notes.

- the old town
- the currency
- paying for things

9 ▶ Compare your notes. Watch the video again to check your ideas.

▶ WATCH

LIFE COMPETENCIES

CRITICAL THINKING AND UNDERSTANDING YOUR OWN CULTURE

10 Work in pairs and think about tourists who visit your town or city. Talk about:

- the currency
- banknotes and coins
- how most people pay for things
- need for cash
- where to find cash machines

11 Make an information pack about shopping and spending for visitors. Present it to your classmates.

PROGRESS CHECK 4

UNITS 9–11

1 Match the things in the pictures (A–F) with the places where you can get them (1–6).

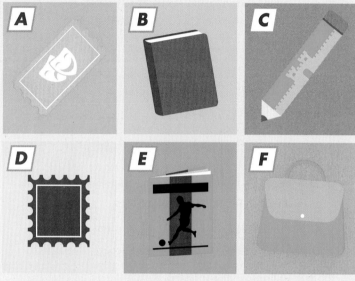

1 post office ....
2 department store ....
3 library ....
4 castle ....
5 theatre ....
6 stadium ....

2 Complete the sentences with the words in the box. You don't need all of the words.

borrow	cost	earn	lend	pay	save	spend	waste

1 How much do you .... in your job?
2 I don't have enough money for the bus. Can you .... me some?
3 Those shoes look expensive! How much did they ....?
4 I'm trying to .... money at the moment because I want to go on holiday.
5 How much did you .... for that phone? I'd like one like it.
6 Keep your money for things you need. Don't .... it on clothes that you don't wear.

3 Match the beginnings and endings of the sentences.

1 My friend is really generous
2 Jane is very shy
3 The little boy was very shy
4 My sister is very reliable
5 Sara is worried
6 My boss is so busy at the moment
7 That politician seems very confident
8 My mother gets angry

a so she will remember to do what you ask her.
b because she has her driving test tomorrow.
c when people don't tell her the truth.
d that she will win the election.
e so she doesn't talk to people she doesn't know.
f when he started school.
g that she often doesn't eat lunch.
h and she often buys presents for people.

4 Choose the correct option to complete the sentences.

1 I'm *happy to/easy to* see the film on Sunday if you're not free tonight.
2 I've *agreed to/learned to* study French at university.
3 I don't usually watch films at home. I *prefer to/want to* go to the cinema.
4 Why didn't you *tell/ask* someone to help you carry that shopping? It's so heavy!

5 Complete the conversations in shops using the words in the box. You don't need all of the words.

> bill   by card   change   changing room
> customer   in cash   receipt   sale   size   till

1   **A:** I'm not sure if these jeans are the right _____ for me. Can I try them on, please?
    B: Of course. The _____ is over there.
2   **A:** Would you like to pay in cash or _____ ?
    B: Cash, please.
    A: Thank you. So, that's fifteen pounds, and you gave me twenty. Here's your _____ .
    B: Thanks.
3   **A:** Excuse me. I'd like to return these sunglasses. They're broken.
    B: Have you got a _____ for them?
    A: Yes, I have.
    B: Great. If you go over there to the _____ , my colleague will help you.
    A: Thank you.

6 Find the place or thing which is different in each group.

1   crossing   corner   bridge
2   bus stop   underground station   roundabout
3   main square   fresh air   sunlight
4   roundabout   district   traffic lights

7 Students often make mistakes with the form of verbs when one verb follows another. Correct the mistakes in the sentences.

1   My mum cooks it for me because I don't like cook.
2   I want invited you to my house.
3   You need buy some food and water.
4   After that it stopped to rain and it was sunny.
5   We have study hard for the test.
6   I'd like know which restaurant you went to last night.

8 Choose the correct options to complete the sentences.

1   *I go/I'm going* to the supermarket. Is there anything you need?
2   I've booked the flight. It *leaves/is leaving* at eight o'clock in the morning.
3   I can't go swimming with you. *I have/I'm having* a doctor's appointment.
4   Do you think the shops *are/will be* busy if we go about 2 pm?
5   *I buy/I'm going to buy* some tickets for the football final. Would you like to come?
6   *Will you go/Are you going* to the library? Can you return this book for me, please?
7   I'm not sure, but I *might/will* go to the cinema this evening.
8   It *can/may* rain later, so I don't think a barbecue is a good idea.

9 Read the two emails and complete each gap with a verb.

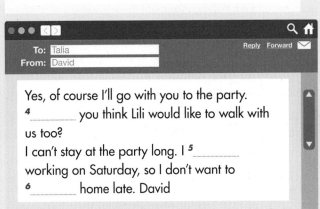

To: David
From: Talia

Hi. ¹_____ you going to Rex's party on Friday? What time do you think you ²_____ go? I don't know any of the other people Rex has invited, so ³_____ we go together?

To: Talia
From: David

Yes, of course I'll go with you to the party. ⁴_____ you think Lili would like to walk with us too?
I can't stay at the party long. I ⁵_____ working on Saturday, so I don't want to ⁶_____ home late. David

12 THROUGH LIFE

VOCABULARY

SCHOOL SUBJECTS

1 **Work in pairs and discuss the questions.**

  1 How old are people when they start school, go to university and get their first job in your country?
  2 What can you see in the photos? Which school subjects do they show?

2 **Read these descriptions of people's favourite school subjects. Match the descriptions with the subjects.**

biology   chemistry   drama   geography   history   maths   modern languages   physics

1 Some people think this subject is boring, but I love numbers: I'm the best in the class at **doing equations**. _____

2 For me, learning how to speak to people from other countries is very exciting. _____

3 I enjoy **doing research** and **writing essays** about the past. I think it helps us understand the present. _____

4 Studying living things is so interesting! I especially love **finding out** about the human body. _____

5 I enjoy finding out about the Earth and how mountains and rivers are made. _____

6 I love **doing experiments** in this class, but my favourite topic is atoms. _____

7 I like this subject because it helps us to understand how light, energy and objects work together. _____

8 I like learning about the theatre and I love **taking part in performances**. _____

3 **Complete the sentences with the correct form of the expressions in bold from Exercise 2.**

  1 His homework is to w_____ an e_____ about education in Britain and the USA.
  2 I don't know much about Chinese history – I'm going to the library to d_____ some r_____ .
  3 My friend is very good with numbers. He can d_____ e_____ very fast in his head!
  4 In our science lesson, we are going to d_____ an e_____ with water and electricity.
  5 Next year, I am going to t_____ p_____ in a p_____ of *Romeo and Juliet*.
  6 I am trying to f_____ o_____ about how I can study in an English-speaking country.

4 **Work in pairs and take turns to ask and answer the questions.**

  1 What is/was your favourite school subject? Why?
  2 What is/was your least favourite subject? Why?
  3 When was the last time you wrote an essay? What did you write about?
  4 When and where was it? What did you do?

READING

MY EDUCATION

1 Read about three people at different stages in their lives and their education. What job does each person want to do in the future? Who already has a job?

2 Read the texts again and answer the questions.

1 Why did Fung move to her grandparents' home?
2 What exam is she going to take soon? What does she hope will happen if she passes it?
3 Why is Angeles studying at the Monterrey Instituto Tecnológico?
4 Angeles didn't pass an exam recently. Which subject was it in?
5 Why is Massimo studying in the evenings?
6 When will Massimo start earning more money?

3 Match the beginnings of the sentences (1–6) with the endings (a–f) to make definitions.

1 Children go to **primary school**
2 You go to **secondary school**
3 A **qualification** is what you get
4 To **graduate** is
5 A **degree** is what a university
6 You get **good marks**

a when you give lots of correct answers.
b when you finish a course and pass an exam at the end.
c to complete your university education successfully.
d gives you at the end of your course, if you pass.
e when you finish primary school.
f from age 4–5 to age 11–12.

4 Look at the texts again to find five different verbs we can use with *exam*.

5 Complete the sentences with a verb from Exercise 4 in the correct form. Use each verb once.

1 Of course you won't pass your exam if you haven't _____ it.
2 I find this subject very difficult: I'm worried that I will _____ the exam.
3 'What mark do I need to get in order to _____ the exam?' 'You need at least 50%.'
4 She's working very hard at the moment. She's _____ for her final exams at university.
5 It's a very difficult exam. He's _____ it four times and he still hasn't passed.

Fung, China

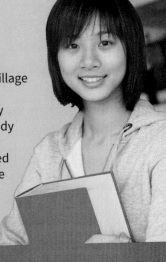

I'm 18 years old and in my last year at **secondary school**. I'm from a small village in the mountains and after I finished **primary school** I came to live with my grandparents in the city so I could study here. If you want to go to university in China, you need to pass an exam called the *gaokao*. I'm studying for this at the moment. If I **get good marks** in the exam, maybe I'll get a place at university.

Angeles, Mexico

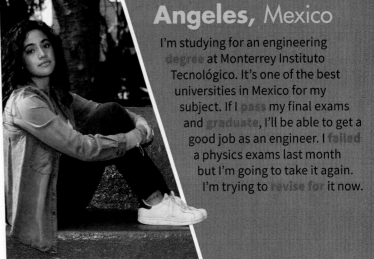

I'm studying for an engineering degree at Monterrey Instituto Tecnológico. It's one of the best universities in Mexico for my subject. If I pass my final exams and graduate, I'll be able to get a good job as an engineer. I failed a physics exams last month but I'm going to take it again. I'm trying to revise for it now.

Massimo, Italy

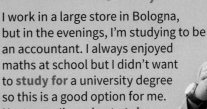

I work in a large store in Bologna, but in the evenings, I'm studying to be an accountant. I always enjoyed maths at school but I didn't want to **study for** a university degree so this is a good option for me. Next year, I'm going to **take** my final exam. If I **pass** it I'll be so happy. It's easier to change jobs if you've got a good **qualification**!

6 Work in pairs and discuss the questions.

1 Where did/do you go to secondary school?
2 What important exams have you taken so far? Did you find them difficult or easy? Why?
3 What qualifications would you like to get in the future? What do you need to study to do this?

DID YOU KNOW?

In the US, **primary school** is called **elementary school**.
After elementary school, students in the US go to **high school** (junior high school (12–15), then senior high school (15–18))

ZERO CONDITIONAL

GRAMMAR ON THE MOVE
Watch the video

1 Read these sentences from the texts and then choose the best options to complete the rules.

*If you **want to** go to university in China, you **need to** pass an exam called the gaokao.*
*It's easier to change jobs if you **have** a good qualification.*

> **1** We use the zero conditional to talk about *facts that are generally true/the future*.
> **2** We use the *present/future* in zero conditionals.
>
> | *If* clause (condition) | Main clause (result) |
> |---|---|
> | **If** + present simple | present simple |

➡ **GRAMMAR REFERENCE** / page 220

2 Complete these zero conditional sentences with the correct form of the verbs in brackets.

1 If he *doesn't get* enough sleep, he ___*is*___ too tired to study the next day. (not get/be)
2 If she _____ something, she _____ the teacher. (not understand/ask)
3 I _____ better if the weather _____ warm and sunny. (feel/be)
4 They can _____ the exam again if they _____ it the first time. (take/fail)

FIRST CONDITIONAL

3 Read these sentences from the texts and choose the best options to complete the rules.

*If I **pass** it, I**'ll be** happy.*
*If I **pass** my final exams and graduate, I**'ll be** able to get a good job.*

> **1** We use the first conditional to talk about a possible condition and its result *in the future/now*.
> **2** The 'if' clause is in the *present/future* tense, and the main clause is in the *present/future* tense.
>
> | *If* clause (condition) | Main clause (result) |
> |---|---|
> | **If** + present simple | (future) **will** + verb |

➡ **GRAMMAR REFERENCE** / page 220

4 Complete these first conditional sentences with the correct form of the verbs in brackets.

1 If I ___*have*___ enough time tomorrow, I ___*'ll help*___ you with your essay. (have/help)
2 My dad _____ angry if I _____ the test. (be/not pass)
3 If you _____ good marks in the test, I _____ you any homework. (get/not give)
4 He _____ his exams if he _____ harder. (fail/not work)

5 Use the words given to write zero or first conditional sentences and questions.

1 What happen if / I not pass exam?
2 If / students arrive late for class / teacher / never / let them in.
3 If / he study / late tonight / he / be / tired in the morning.
4 What / you / give me / if help you / with / your essay tomorrow?

PUSH YOURSELF / B1

GRAMMAR: *UNLESS* AND *WHEN*

1 We can also use the first conditional with *when* and *unless*. Compare these examples and complete the sentences.

a > I'll tell him **if** I see him.

b > I'll tell him **when** I see him.

1 In a, the speaker is *not sure/sure* he or she will see the person.
2 In b, the speaker is *not sure/sure* that he or she will see the person.

a > I'll pass the exam **if** I revise for it.

b > He won't pass the exam **unless** he revises for it.

3 Look at sentence b. Which word means *except if*?

2 Complete the sentences with the correct options.

1 He won't finish on time *unless/if/when* he works a bit faster.
2 *If/Unless/When* he works a bit faster this morning, he'll finish on time.
3 You won't get a job with a big salary *unless/if/when* you have good qualifications.
4 You're tired now, but you'll feel much better *when/if/unless* you wake up tomorrow.
5 We'll be late *unless/when/if* we leave soon.
6 *If/Unless/When* you don't have something to eat now, you'll be hungry later.

READING PART 4 — TRAINING

1 Look at these 'life events'. Which have you experienced? When/where? Which haven't you experienced yet? Tell your partner. Give as much information as possible.

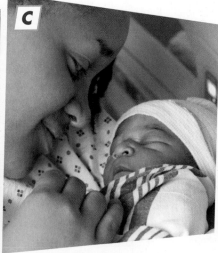

- be born
- start primary school
- finish secondary school

- graduate from university
- move away from home
- learn to drive

- get your first job
- get married
- have children

> I was born on the 24th September 1998 in a small town near Bilbao in Spain.

> I started primary school when I was six years old. My first teacher was Señora Vasquez.

2 What do you know about the actor Rebel Wilson and her life? Tell your partner.

3 Read the text about Rebel Wilson's life. For these questions, choose the correct answer for each gap.

Rebel Wilson

The comedy actor Rebel Wilson was born in 1980. She **¹**_____ up in Sydney, Australia with her two sisters and her brother. As a child, Rebel was always really **²**_____ at sums, and she hoped to have a successful **³**_____ in mathematics. But after leaving school, she was educated at the University of New South Wales, where she decided to do Theatre and Performance Studies. Rebel's first big acting job was on TV and she became **⁴**_____ for playing Toula in the Australian comedy series *Pizza*. She later **⁵**_____ to the USA where she has starred in the movie *Bridesmaids* and the musical comedy film *Pitch Perfect*. She has also written her own TV comedy series *Super Fun Night*.

Read the first two sentences with the (1) gap and think about what type of word is missing (a verb). A is wrong because get up means to stand up or to get out of bed. B is wrong because go up means to go to a higher place. C is correct because the sentence tells us where Rebel spent her years as a child.

	A		**B**		**C**	
1	got		went		grew (C circled)	
2	nice		good		easy	
3	work		occupation		career	
4	famous		funny		favourite	
5	chose		moved		arrived	

GRAMMAR

THE PASSIVE

GRAMMAR ON THE MOVE
Watch the video

1 Read the examples. Do we know: what makes mountains and rivers, who educated Rebel Wilson, who asked the students to bring their dictionaries? Complete the rules.

I enjoy finding out about how … mountains and rivers ***are made****.*
*She **was educated** at the University of New South Wales.*
*The students **were asked** to bring their dictionaries **by** the German teacher.*

> **1** We use the passive when we *know/don't know* who or what did the action or it is *important/not important* who did the action.
> **2** To form the passive, we use the correct form of the verb _____ + past participle.
> **3** To say who does or did the action, we use the word _____ .
>
> **Present:** *is/are* **+ past participle**
> *At the moment, the computers **are kept** in the science classroom.*
>
> **Past:** *was/were* **+ past participle**
> *Last year, the computers **were kept** in the science classroom.*

➡ **GRAMMAR REFERENCE** / *page 221*

2 Match the beginnings of the sentences (1–5) with the endings (a–e).

1 English is
2 That photo was
3 The students are
4 I'm sorry, all the cake was
5 That book was

a not taught how to use computers.
b written 50 years ago.
c spoken all over the world.
d eaten during the party.
e taken by a friend when I was much younger!

3 Complete the sentences with the correct present or past passive form of the verbs in brackets.

1 I _____ (ask) to teach a maths lesson last week.
2 French _____ (not teach) at our school at the moment.
3 This photo _____ (taken) in Spain two weeks ago.
4 The exercise books _____ (collected) after every lesson, so the teacher can mark them.
5 He _____ (give) some money for his birthday yesterday.

Andrea – farmer

Amir – engineer

LISTENING

1 Work in pairs and discuss the questions.

1 What jobs have you done in your life? What job would you like to do? Why?
2 What is important for you in a job? Put the following in order from 5 (most important) to 1 (least important).
   • a good salary
   • interesting work
   • a boss/company who is good to work for
   • learning new things
   • having enough time off (holidays, weekends etc.)

2 🔊 099 Listen to the people in the photos talking about their jobs. Number the photos in the order you hear about them.

3 🔊 099 Listen again and choose the correct option to complete each sentence.

1 Andrea says that she enjoys her work because she likes
   a being outside.
   b working with animals.
2 Joe would like to
   a have more breaks during the day.
   b talk to people more.
3 Lee says that people are often
   a afraid of their dentist.
   b good friends with their dentist.
4 Amir finds it difficult that he has to
   a speak English a lot.
   b travel a lot.
5 Mai works for
   a a big international company.
   b herself.
6 Carmen doesn't like
   a trying to find new stories.
   b her boss.

Joe – receptionist

Lee – dentist

Mai – businesswoman

Carmen – journalist

VOCABULARY

JOBS AND WORK

1 Match the beginnings of the sentences (1–6) with the endings (a–f) to make definitions.

1 The **staff** of a company
2 **Long hours** means that
3 A **break** is a period of time when you
4 The **boss** is the person whose job is to
5 A **diploma** is a piece of paper that shows
6 A **day off** is time when

a tell other people how to work and what to do.
b people work later than workers normally do.
c that a person has passed an exam.
d can stop work and rest.
e are the people that work there.
f you are on holiday and not at work.

2 Complete the phrases from the listening with the correct form of the words in Exercise 1.

1 The problem is that I never have any holidays or _____ _____ – it's too difficult to find someone to look after the animals.

2 We don't get many _____ during the day. One of us has to be at the front desk all the time.

3 In my country it takes eight years to be a dentist. I have a couple of degrees and _____ !

4 I have my own company with a _____ of 500 people.

5 I work _____ _____ and my diary is full every week.

6 The only thing I don't like about my job is my _____ . I hate people telling me what to do!

3 Would you prefer to work for a company or work for yourself? What are the advantages and disadvantages of each?

LISTENING PART 3 [TRAINING]

🔊 100 **You will hear Annie talking to her friend Mick about her new job. For each question, choose the correct answer.**

1 Why did Annie leave her old job?
   A She wanted to work in computer programming.
   B She didn't enjoy the travelling she had to do.
   C She didn't like it because the work changed.

Before you listen, read the questions and options and underline the key words. Look at question 1 and listen.

Annie says she had to spend so much time away from home, and staying in hotels was lonely and boring, so B is the correct answer.

2 Mick is surprised to hear that Annie
   A hated her old job.
   B wanted to work at home.
   C enjoys cooking.

3 Where does Annie sell most of her cakes?
   A online
   B in the baker's shop
   C at the market

4 What does Annie say is the most difficult thing about her new business?
   A She has no colleagues.
   B She has less money.
   C She has fewer holidays.

A   B

WRITING

A JOB APPLICATION

1 Have you ever been to a circus or an aquarium? What do you think it would be like to work in these places?

2 Match the photos (A and B) with the job adverts (1 and 2). What are the good and the bad points of each job?

3 Read the two job advertisements and complete the information.

   1 **Place of work**
      Where is the job?
      Job 1: _____   Job 2: _____

   2 **Tasks**
      What do you do in this job?
      Job 1: _____   Job 2: _____

   3 **Salary**
      How much money can you earn?
      Job 1: _____   Job 2: _____

   4 **Hours**
      When/How often do you have to work?
      Job 1: _____   Job 2: _____

   5 **Qualifications**
      What kind of qualification do you need?
      Job 1: _____   Job 2: _____

   6 **Things to send**
      What do you need to send if you want the job?
      Job 1: _____   Job 2: _____

4 Look at the application email for the first job and the expressions in bold. Which expressions does the writer use to ...?

   a explain why she is writing
   b talk about what you can see in her videos
   c talk about what she sent with the email
   d say where she saw the job advertised
   e describe herself in a good way
   f begin the message
   g end the message
   h talk about next contact

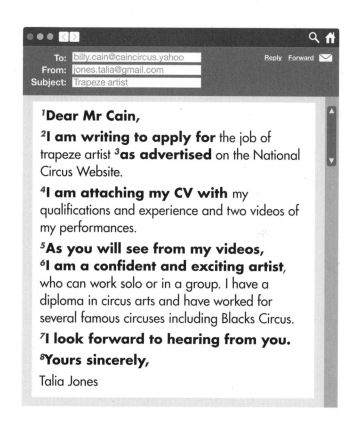

To: billy.cain@caincircus.yahoo   Reply Forward
From: jones.talia@gmail.com
Subject: Trapeze artist

¹Dear Mr Cain,

²I am writing to apply for the job of trapeze artist **³as advertised** on the National Circus Website.

⁴I am attaching my CV with my qualifications and experience and two videos of my performances.

⁵As you will see from my videos,
⁶I am a confident and exciting artist, who can work solo or in a group. I have a diploma in circus arts and have worked for several famous circuses including Blacks Circus.

⁷I look forward to hearing from you.

⁸Yours sincerely,

Talia Jones

5 Put the words in order to make sentences from another job application.

   1 your website. / the job of / I am writing to / as advertised on / apply for / English teacher

   2 my CV / and a copy of my teaching diploma. / I am attaching

   3 teacher. / I am / a patient, friendly

   4 in Granada. / I have worked / As you will see / for several schools / from my CV,

   5 from / I / hearing / you. / look / forward to

6 Write an email to apply for job B in Exercise 1. Use the email in Exercise 4 and the notes below to help you.

   • You have five years' diving experience
   • You are brave, calm and not afraid of sharks
   • You have a diving certificate and experience of swimming with sharks

1 CAIN'S CIRCUS

WANTED:

Trapeze Artist for exciting new show to tour in Europe

- Hotel accommodation is provided during tour
- You must be over 18 and be athletic and not afraid of heights
- Send photos and videos of your performance

billy.cain@caincircus.yahoo

Salary
€25–€35,000 per year
(6–8 performances a week)

2 SEA WORLD
AQUARIUM

We are looking for a cleaner for our shark tank.
You must have:
- 🐟 a diving qualification
- 🐟 two year's diving experience
- 🐟 a degree in marine biology

We give you special lessons to learn about working with sharks.

Send your CV and a letter telling us why you want the job
ken.timmins@seaworld.com

Salary:
€40–€45,000
per year
Hours:
35 hours a week

SPEAKING

JOB INTERVIEW

1 What kind of questions are usually asked at job interviews? What questions should you ask in a job interview? Why?

2 🎧 101 **Talia has an interview for the trapeze artist job. Listen and complete the information.**

Name: Talia Jones
¹Age: ....
Qualifications: A diploma in ² ....
³Amount of experience: ....

3 🎧 101 **Listen again and match the beginnings of Billy Cain's questions (1–5) with the endings (a–e).**

1 So, you're 21 years old,
2 **Can you tell us about**
3 **How many years' experience of**
4 **Can you tell us**
5 **Which other languages**

a trapeze work do you have?
b something about your other skills?
c do you speak?
d **your qualifications** and experience?
e **is that right**?

4 **Put the words in the correct order to complete Talia's questions to Mr Cain.**

1 are you / What / offering / salary?
2 costumes / Are / provided? / the
3 my / get / hotel room? / Will I / own
4 going to / Am I / perform / people? / with / other
5 be / Who / boss? / will / my
6 we / hours / practise? / How many / will
7 will I / per week? / time off / get / How much

5 **Match the answers a–g with the questions in Exercise 4.**

a You'll perform with five other artists.
b We can offer you €33,000 a year.
c My wife Ania trains the artists and will be your boss.
d There are 10 hours of practice a week.
e Mondays and Tuesdays are your days off.
f No, you'll share a room with another artist.
g Yes, we provide the costumes.

6 **P** 🎧 102 **Listen to these pairs of questions. For each pair, does the speaker's voice:**

a go up?   b go down?   c go up, then down?

Wh- questions
1 *What time do we start in the mornings?*
Where is the photocopier?

Yes/no questions
2 *Can I park here?   Is this my chair?*

7 **P** 🎧 102 **Listen again and repeat. Try to reproduce the intonation.**

8 **Work in pairs. You are going to role-play the interview for the shark tank cleaner's job.**

1 Think what extra information you would like to ask at your interview and prepare at least six questions. Think about:
- salary
- working hours during the day
- breaks
- boss
- other people you will work with
- sharks – dangerous? friendly?
- training
2 Think about how the interviewer will answer these questions.

9 **When you are ready, role-play the interview with your partner. Then swap roles.**

READING PART 4

EXAM CHECK

1 Match the beginnings and endings of these sentences to complete the information about Reading Part 4.

1	In Reading Part 4, you have to	**a**	vocabulary.
2	There are six gaps	**b**	is correct grammatically.
3	To complete each gap	**c**	you choose from three options.
4	Reading Part 4 tests your	**d**	in the text.
5	You also need to make sure your answer	**e**	read quite a long text.

2 For each question, choose the correct answer.

What is a Curriculum Vitae?

A CV, or Curriculum Vitae, is a short, one or two-page document that you send to companies when you're looking for a job. The first part of your CV should give your contact **(1)** _____ – your name, address and phone number. Don't forget to **(2)** _____ your email address too. After that, you should write about what and where you have studied. The next part is about your work **(3)** _____ – any jobs you have done. It's **(4)** _____ to write about the job that you have now, first. It's also good to give information about languages you can speak and computer programs you can **(5)** _____ . Some people write about their hobbies on a CV, too. When you finish writing your CV, check that you haven't made any **(6)** _____ in the spelling or grammar.

1	**A**	facts	**B**	instructions	**C**	details
2	**A**	keep	**B**	include	**C**	join
3	**A**	experience	**B**	activity	**C**	practice
4	**A**	normal	**B**	popular	**C**	comfortable
5	**A**	pass	**B**	take	**C**	use
6	**A**	problems	**B**	mistakes	**C**	accidents

EXAM CHECK

1 Answer these questions about Listening Part 3, using words in the box.
You don't need to use all of the words.

one   two   three   four   five   yes   no

1 How many people will you hear? ....

2 How many questions are there? ....

3 Is there an example at the beginning? ....

4 How many options are there for each question? ....

5 Are there questions about the speaker's opinions and feelings? ....

2 🔊 103 **For each question, choose the correct answer.**

You will hear Lena and Max talking about a course which Max has done.

1 When Max's boss told him to do the course, Max felt
   A worried.
   B excited.
   C angry.

2 Max thought the teacher was good at
   A including everyone in the lessons.
   B giving students interesting work to do.
   C explaining anything that was difficult.

3 What didn't Max like about the course?
   A The breaks weren't long enough.
   B There were too many students.
   C The classes began too early.

4 Lena is going to do the course because
   A her job has changed since she started it.
   B she would like to earn more money.
   C she wants a new job.

5 When is Lena going to do the course?
   A next week
   B next month
   C next year

HOW WAS IT?

Gave it a go ☐

Getting there ☐

Aced it! ☐

PLANNING TO STUDY IN ...
GENEVA

1 Would you like to study in another country for a short time? Why?

2 Look at the photos (A–D) of Geneva. Then read the text and match the photos with the paragraphs.

3 Read the text again. Are the statements true (T) or false (F)? Correct the false statements.

1 A lot of university classes are in English.
2 You can only study science or business in Geneva.
3 You can go skiing all year near Geneva.
4 Geneva is a very big city.

| Home | About | Q Search |

STUDYING IN GENEVA

1 Nowadays lots of students at school or university have plans to study abroad, as it's so easy to arrange. Universities are happy to accept students from all over the world. Many universities offer student exchanges for undergraduates, so students can study in another country for a few months or a year. Some universities also offer scholarships, which give students money to help them pay for their studies. Many classes are in English, so you don't need to learn the language of the country where you want to study.

2 Geneva has one of the best universities in the world. You can study any subject in Geneva, but it's especially good if you want to study science subjects because it's an important centre for scientific research. A lot of postgraduates choose to study in Geneva for this reason. There are also many international businesses in the city, so it's a very good place to study international business and maybe work for a multi-national company to get some work experience.

3 Geneva is also in a beautiful part of the world. It's in the Swiss Alps, so there are mountains all around where you can go skiing in the winter, or hiking in the summer. Lake Geneva is great for boat trips, and of course there is the famous tall fountain, the *Jet d'Eau*.

4 Life in Geneva is relaxed and enjoyable. The old city has some lovely buildings and there are lots of cafés and restaurants where you can meet friends and enjoy good food. It's quite a small city, so it's easy to get around, and you don't have to spend a lot of time travelling.

4 Read the text again. Match the words and phrases with the correct definitions.

1 student exchange
2 undergraduate
3 scholarship
4 postgraduate
5 international
6 work experience

a a student who has finished one course at a university and is studying more
b the chance to work at a business for a short time
c a student who is studying their first course at university
d when students from two schools or universities in different countries can each go to the other school or university for a short time
e money that a student is given by a university to pay for their course
f about lots of different countries

5 🎧 104 Listen to three conversations. Who is talking and what are they doing? There is one extra answer which you do not need to use.

a Two new students are arranging to go to a welcome event together.
b Two teachers are preparing for a welcome event for new students.
c Two new students are meeting for the first time at a welcome event.
d A new student is asking for information about a welcome event.

6 🎧 104 Complete the phrases with the correct words. Listen again and check.

> can you give me   do I need to   is there
> what time   which room   about you

PHRASES YOU MIGHT USE

1 _____ some information about the welcome event?
2 _____ does it start?
3 _____ is it in?
4 _____ take anything with me?
5 _____ food at the event?
6 What _____ ?

7 Choose the correct definitions for these informal words and phrases.

PHRASES YOU MIGHT HEAR

1 You might want to get there nice and early.
   a It's a good idea to get there early.
   b It's nice that it starts early.
2 You can't miss it.
   a It's difficult to find.
   b It's easy to find.
3 I think that's it.
   a I think that's all you have to take.
   b I think that's very important.
4 There are a few snacks.
   a There will be a lot to eat.
   b There will be some small things to eat.

8 🎦 Watch the video. What do you learn about these things in Geneva? Make notes.

- the city
- organisations in the city
- the university
- life in the city

9 🎦 Compare your notes. Watch the video again to check your ideas.

▶ WATCH

D

LIFE COMPETENCIES

SOCIAL RESPONSIBILITIES

10 Work in groups. Plan a welcome event in your town or city for students from other countries. Think about:

- where to have the event
- what kind of event it is
- what food and drinks to serve
- who to invite

11 Make an event plan and present it to the class.

13

ABOUT ME

A

READING

FAMILY RELATIONSHIPS

1 **Work in pairs and discuss the questions.**

1 Do you come from a big family or a small family?
2 What are the good and bad things about:
   a having lots of brothers and sisters?
   b being an only child?

2 **Look at the photos and read about Aidan and Jasmine. Which photo is Aidan's family and which photo is Jasmine's?**

JASMINE

My family is very small as I'm an **only child**. My family is just my mother, my father and me! We get on really well. My only other **relative** is my aunt Linda, who's **an important person in my life**. She's **single** – she's never **married** – and I've always spent lots of time with her. She's an artist and taught me to draw and paint. She's really interested in fashion and I like the lovely jewellery and colourful clothes that she wears. The other very important person in my life is my **fiancé**, Tom. We've just got **engaged** and we're getting **married** next year.

AIDAN

I'm from a large family. My two brothers and I live with our father and Katie, our **stepmother**. She has two daughters and we all live together in one house. It's often quite crowded and noisy, but I love my family! I've got two little **stepsisters**, Minnie and Lulu. They love animals and sports. They're quite funny and I actually get on better with them than my brothers! I live at home but I'm hoping to get my own flat soon.

3 **Read the texts again and answer the questions.**

1 How many brothers or sisters has Jasmine got?
2 What has Jasmine learned from her aunt?
3 What is Jasmine doing next year?
4 How many people does Aidan live with?
5 Are Aidan's stepsisters older or younger than him?
6 What is Aidan planning to do soon?

4 **Use the blue words in the text to complete the sentences.**

1 Lauren likes being an _____ because she says her parents always have time to talk to her.
2 Pablo is _____ again; he doesn't have a girlfriend at the moment.
3 My sister got _____ last month but I haven't met her _____ yet. They've decided to get married in September.
4 My mum met John last year and now they're married so he's my _____ .
5 I get on really well with my _____ . We're the same age and I've known her since our parents met five years ago.
6 I don't see my _____ very often because most of them live in Australia.
7 My granny is a very _____ ; I can talk to her about any problems.

5 **Work in pairs and tell your partner about:**

- people you have lived with/live with now.
- a person in your family you get on well with.
- a relative who is an important person in your life.

B

VOCABULARY

PERSONALITY ADJECTIVES

1 Work in pairs and describe the people in the photos.

A _____   B _____

2 🔊 105 Listen to Aidan describing his two brothers. Label the photos with the correct name, *Harry* or *Leo*.

3 🔊 105 Listen again and complete the sentences with the words in box.

> annoying   brilliant   confident   kind
> lazy   quiet   sociable   sweet

1 That's Minnie on the right and Lulu on the left. Aren't they _____ ?
2 He's much cleverer than I am – he's really _____ .
3 He's just very _____ ! To start with he's a bit _____ .
4 He's also not very _____ to Harry.
5 He's much more _____ and _____ . He has lots of friends.
6 Harry is _____ and shy.

4 Choose the correct options to complete the definitions.

1 A *brilliant/confident* person is very clever and understands and learns new things easily.
2 A person who is *sweet/annoying* is pleasant and attractive – we usually say this about children.
3 *Sociable/Kind* people enjoy talking to people and making new friends.
4 A *lazy/quiet* person doesn't talk much or make a lot of noise.

5 Which brother do you think you would get on with best? Why?

LOOK LIKE AND *BE LIKE*

6 Look at the questions and answers A and B. Which question:

1 asks for information about hair/eye colour, clothes, etc.?
2 asks for information about what kind of person they are, e.g. *funny*?
3 uses *do* or *does*?
4 uses *am/is/are*?

A

What does your brother look like?

He's not very tall but he's very good looking.

B

What's he like?

He's very annoying! To start with he's a bit lazy.

7 Look at the sentences below. Are they the answers to question A or B? Circle the correct option.

1 He's very friendly and sociable.   A/B
2 He's quiet and shy.   A/B
3 He's tall and good looking.   A/B
4 He's lazy and not very kind.   A/B
5 He's short and thin with straight fair hair.   A/B

8 Work in pairs. Take turns to describe a person you both know or a famous person. Can your partner guess who it is?

• Say two things about what he/she looks like.
• Say two things about what he/she is like.

She's got big brown eyes and curly hair.

She's funny and clever but she often forgets things.

Is it Rachel?

GRAMMAR

COMPARATIVE ADJECTIVES

GRAMMAR ON THE MOVE
Watch the video

1 Read the examples from Aidan's conversation and the rules and answer the questions.

*Harry is tall**er** and thi**nner than** me.*
*Leo is **more** confident and **more** sociable **than** Harry.*
*He is **better**-looking **than** both me and Harry! And he's funni**er**.*

1 What do we add to the end of short adjectives to make comparatives?

2 Which word do we put before long adjectives?

3 Which word do we use after the adjective, before the second thing we are comparing?

4 What is the comparative form of **good**?

Comparing adjectives
Short adjectives + -er
If the adjective ends in consonant + vowel + consonant, we double the consonant.
e.g. *thin* – *thinner*   *big* – *bigger*   *wet* – *wetter*   *than*
If the adjective ends in consonant + 'y', we change the 'y' to 'i'.
funny – *funnier*   *pretty* – *prettier*   *lazy* – *lazier*   *than*
Long adjectives – more in front of the adjective
more expensive   *more* interesting   *more* important   *than*
Irregular adjectives
good – *better*   *bad* – *worse*   *far* – *further*   *than*

➡ **GRAMMAR REFERENCE** / page 222

2 Read and complete the text about Alistair and Jonny Brownlee. Use the correct comparative form of the adjectives in brackets.

CHAMPIONS in the family

Alistair and Jonny Brownlee are two of the best triathletes in the world, and won gold and silver medals at the Olympic Games in Rio de Janeiro in 2016. They are also brothers. Alistair is two years
¹_____ (old) than Jonny and he is also a bit
²_____ (tall).

They work well together in races and are both very strong but is one Brownlee brother ³_____ (successful) than the other one? Is Alistair a
⁴_____ (strong) swimmer than Jonny? Is Jonny a
⁵_____ (fast) runner than Alistair? And is one brother a ⁶_____ (quick) cyclist than the other? Well, sometimes Alistair wins and sometimes Jonny wins, but in the end they are still brothers, and when Jonny couldn't run any further near the finish line in a race in Mexico in 2016, it was Alistair who stopped running to help his brother across the finish line.

3 Work in pairs and take turns to compare you and your family or friends.

> My sister is younger than me, but she's taller.

PUSH YOURSELF B1

GRAMMAR: EQUAL COMPARISONS WITH (NOT) AS ... AS

> She is just **as intelligent as** her sister.

> His hair is**n't as long as** your hair.

> Her sister is**n't as friendly as** she is.

> He's **as lazy as** you are!

1 Look at the examples and choose the correct answer to complete the summary.

a We use **as** + adjective + **as** when we want to talk about things being *different/the same*.

b We use (**not**) **as** + adjective + **as** when we want to talk about things being *different/the same*.

2 Complete the sentences with an expression *(not) as ... as* and the adjectives in brackets.

1 He's very quiet, but he's _not as shy as_ your friend Sam. (not shy)

2 'I'm really bad at dancing!' 'No, you aren't. You're just _____ me!' (good)

3 It costs a lot to live in Milan, but it's still _____ Tokyo. (not expensive)

4 Driving a car is _____ riding a motorbike. (not dangerous)

5 'I didn't enjoy the book. Perhaps the film will be better?' 'No, the film is just _____ the book! (boring)

6 You can stay with us _____ you like. (long).

1 Work in pairs and discuss the questions.

1 Are clothes and shoes important to you?

2 Do clothes say something about a person?

2 Turn to page 195 to find out what kind of dresser you are.

3 106 For each question, write the correct answer in each gap. Write one word or a number, or a date or a time.

You will hear some information about a new shop.

LILY'S Fashion Boutique

Address:	*149 High Street*
Date opens:	**(1)** ....
Will sell:	clothes for **(2)** ....
Time shop closes:	**(3)** .... pm
For jobs, contact:	Mr **(4)** ....

READING PART 5 TRAINING

Read a woman's email to her brother. For these questions, write the correct answer in each gap. Write ONE word for each gap.

Example: *0* *am*

> Look at the example and the sentence around it. Ellie is talking about a new job starting next week.
>
> We use the present continuous to describe future plans. The verb you need before -ing is to be. So '*I **am** starting*' is the correct answer.
>
> Read the text and look at questions 1–5. Try to decide what kind of grammar word is needed.

To: ben.baker@aol.com   Reply Forward ✉

From: ellie.diazt@gmail.com

Hi Ben

I __*am*__ starting my new job next week, and I feel really excited about it.

Yesterday, I **1** .... shopping with my friend Owen. He's better **2** .... me at choosing clothes.

At first, I decided **3** .... buy a jacket and trousers. But then I saw a grey suit with a skirt and I really liked it a **4** .... It was **5** .... expensive than the jacket and trousers, but I bought it.

I'll look good on my first day!

Write soon,

Love

Ellie

DID YOU KNOW?

In the UK, some people wear **trainers** on their feet. Women put their money in a **purse**, which they often carry in a **handbag**.

However, in the US, people wear **sneakers** on their feet, women carry **purses** and keep their money in a **wallet**.

1 Are you interested in the clothes that celebrities wear? Why?/Why not? Which celebrities do you think dress well?

2 Read about some of the people on the list of the world's best-dressed celebrities. Match the texts with the photos (A–C).

A

B

C

3 Read the texts again. Who:

1 might wear boots and sunglasses with a designer dress at a party?

2 wears very interesting clothes?

3 makes fashion writers feel excited?

4 has an unusual style?

5 is always on the best-dressed list?

4 Complete the sentences with words in red from the texts.

1 Do you have a piece of _____ , like a ring or necklace, that is special to you?

2 Sam always buys clothes and shoes from famous _____ .

3 Joe never wears _____ or _____ to job interviews, but he still looks smart.

4 Cara reads a lot of fashion magazines to see what _____ are in.

5 Do you only wear _____ when you do sport, or do you wear them all the time to be fashionable?

6 Oh, no! I've forgotten my _____ . It's got my money, keys and phone in it.

7 Emma, do you only wear _____ when it's sunny or do you wear them to look cool too?

8 It's too hot to wear shoes. I think I'll put on my _____ today.

5 Work in pairs. Which celebrities are the best dressed in your country? What is their style like?

BEST-DRESSED CELEBRITIES

1 Actress Lupita Nyong'o is one of the most successful stars in Hollywood at the moment. She is also famous for the way she dresses. **Fashion** magazine writers and photographers always get excited when she arrives at film premieres and parties. Her dress is usually the prettiest and she wears the coolest shoes or **sandals** from the best new **designers**.

2 Actor Eddie Redmayne was a model before he started acting. Perhaps this is why he has been on the best-dressed list every year since he became famous. He often wears the smartest and most interesting **suits** and **ties** from the world's hottest designer **brands** – and he looks fantastic!

3 Everybody talks about what the singer Rihanna wears. At celebrity parties, her clothes and **handbag** are often the most unusual. She wears beautiful designer dresses with cool hats, **jewellery** or **sunglasses** and big boots or **trainers**.

GRAMMAR

SUPERLATIVE ADJECTIVES

 GRAMMAR ON THE MOVE
Watch the video

1 **Read the rules and answer the questions.**

1 What do we add to the end of short adjectives to make superlatives?
2 What do we put before long adjectives?
3 Which word do we use before the superlative words?
4 Which word is the superlative form of **good**?

Superlative adjectives

Short adjectives + -est
If the adjective ends in consonant + vowel + consonant, we double the consonant.
*hot – hotter – **the hottest***   *big – bigger – **the biggest***
*thin – thinner – **the thinnest***
If the adjective ends in 'y', we change the 'y' to 'i'.
*pretty – prettier – **the prettiest***   *funny – funnier – **the funniest***
*ugly – uglier – **the ugliest***

Long adjectives – *most* in front of the adjective
the most expensive   *the most interesting*
the most colourful

Irregular adjectives
*good – better – **the best***   *bad – worse – **the worst***
*far – further – **the furthest***

➡ **GRAMMAR REFERENCE / page 222**

2 **Complete the sentences with the superlative form of the adjectives in brackets.**

1 It's _____ film I've ever watched. (boring)
2 That's _____ pair of trainers in the shop. (cheap)
3 I'm sorry, but that's _____ car I have ever seen. I'm not going to buy it! (ugly)
4 She's one of _____ actors in Mexico. (famous)
5 That's _____ hotel in the city (good). It's also _____ (expensive).
6 It was _____ day of the year. (hot)

3 **Complete the article with comparative and superlative forms of the adjectives in brackets.**

What's new in clothes?

Most people just want to look good and feel comfortable when they buy clothes, but for some people, the clothes they buy are ¹_____ (important) than that. At the moment one of ²_____ (interesting) things in the shops are clothes made from upcycled or recycled materials like old plastic bottles or glass. Making these clothes is ³_____ (difficult) and ⁴_____ (expensive) than making normal clothes. However, a lot of people now think we should make more upcycled or recycled clothes to help our planet and they are ⁵_____ (happy) to buy them than in the past.

4 **107 Listen to some superlative adjectives. How is the -est ending pronounced?**

5 **P** **107 Listen again and repeat.**

hottest	thinnest	funniest
biggest	prettiest	ugliest

6 **Work in pairs and talk about:**

• the smartest clothes you've ever worn
• the best-dressed, most fashionable person you know
• the most interesting film you've ever seen/book you've ever read
• hottest and/or coldest place you have ever visited

7 **Have you got any upcycled or recycled clothes? Are they becoming popular in your country?**

WRITING

A PRODUCT REVIEW

1 Work in pairs and discuss the questions.

1 Do you follow any fashion bloggers or other bloggers on the internet?
2 What other kinds of products do you watch/read reviews about?
3 How much do reviews and blogs help you decide what to do or buy?

2 Read the review from a fashion blogger's website and answer the questions.

1 Where and when can people buy the trainers?
2 What does the reviewer like about the trainers?
3 What negative things does he say about them?
4 What advice does he give about buying the trainers?

I'm so happy that the new trainers from my favourite brand are on sale at last! I bought mine online, but you can find them in sports shops, too.

I fell in love with the colours of the trainers immediately. **They are the best-looking trainers I've seen for a long time** – and they are also very light and comfortable to wear. But **for me, the best thing about them is** that they are so cool! You can wear them with anything – they'll make all your other clothes look good.

On the less positive side is the price (€109.99). The trainers look great, but they are not very practical or good value for money. When I wore them in the rain, my feet got wet in five minutes. There are lots of cheaper, stronger trainers available.

So do I recommend the trainers? **It depends on what you want**. If you are looking for a pair of trainers to wear every day, then they aren't **a good buy**. But if you need a pair of great-looking trainers, these are the best. Buy them quickly before they sell out!

3 Look at the phrases in bold in the text. Which phrase(s) does the writer use:

1 to say what he likes about the product? ....
2 to introduce a negative point about the product? ....
3 to talk about whether or not it's a good idea to spend money on the product? ....

4 Look at the end of the review. What do you think 'sell out' means?

5 Look at the plan of the review. Match the paragraph numbers with the topics.

Paragraph 1   a   the bad things about the product
Paragraph 2   b   conclusion: overall opinion of the product recommendation
Paragraph 3   c   the good things about the product
Paragraph 4   d   introduction where/when you bought the product

6 In which part of a review could you use these phrases?

USEFUL LANGUAGE

1 The great thing about X is …
2 All in all, I would/wouldn't recommend …
3 The biggest disadvantage of X is …
4 What I liked best about X is …
5 They would/wouldn't be a good buy for …
6 I'm not so happy about …

7 You are going to write a review of a product you have bought recently. Choose the product and use the structure in Exercise 5 to help you plan your review.

- Think of some interesting adjectives to describe the product.
- Think of how you feel about the product and why.
- Think of two advantages and two disadvantages of the product.
- Decide what you recommend overall.

8 Write your review. When you have finished, exchange your review with a partner and check each other's work. Make sure they have included an introduction, the advantages and disadvantages of the product, and a conclusion. Check the grammar, spelling and punctuation.

SPEAKING

APPEARANCE AND PERSONALITY

1 **Look at the photos. Work in pairs and answer the questions.**

    1 Where do you think the photos were taken?
    2 Who do you think the people are?
    3 What are they doing?

2 **Work in pairs and take turns to describe each person in the photos. What do the people look like? What are they wearing?**

He/she is …   He/she's got …
He/she's wearing …   He/she looks …

3 **Read the comments. Which photos could they match with? Do you agree with them?**

1 They look quite serious.

2 It could be in Britain.

3 The woman has got red hair.

4 It might be face paint.

5 They're having a really good time.

6 They look very happy!

4 🔊 108 **Listen to two people talking about the photos. Which photo is each person talking about?**

5 🔊 108 **Look at the opinion words the speakers use and complete the sentences below. Listen again and check.**

I'm sure   I (don't) think   could be   it might be
maybe   perhaps   probably

1 _____ the people in the middle of the photo are friends.
2 _____ they're having a really good time.
3 … she's got something on her face – _____ face paint.
4 _____ they are at a music festival or gig.
5 It's a sunny day, but _____ it's very hot.
6 There are trees with lots of green, so I think it's _____ summer.
7 It _____ in Britain.
8 They look quite serious – _____ they're thinking about work.

6 **Work in pairs. Turn to page 194 and talk about the photo. Describe the people, where they are and what they're doing. Use the language in Exercises 2 and 5 to help you.**

READING PART 5

EXAM CHECK

1 **Read these sentences about Part 5 and decide if they are true (T) or false (F).**
Correct the false statements.

1 Reading Part 5 tests your vocabulary.
2 You complete an email or postcard by choosing words from three options.
3 There will only be one text for you to read.
4 There are words missing from the text.
5 There is an example which has been done for you.

2 **For each question, write the correct answer.**

Write ONE word for each gap.

Example: **0** VERY

From: Gina
To: Mary

Reply   Forward

Thank you **(0)** .... much for sending me the photos you took at my sister's wedding last week. Your photos are much better **(1)** ....
mine! You took some fantastic photos **(2)** .... my sister – her dress looks beautiful. **(3)** .... you enjoy the wedding?

(4) .... the hotel that I booked for you alright? I've never stayed
(5) ...., but my friend says it's good. That's why I chose it.

I'm going to visit your town next week for work. **(6)** .... you like to meet for dinner?

I'll call you when I get there.

LISTENING PART 2

EXAM CHECK

1 Match each question about Listening Part 2 with the correct answer.

1	How many people will I hear?		*a*	maybe
2	What will I read?		*b*	No. Some are numbers.
3	How many answers do I write?		*c*	one
4	Are all of the answers words?		*d*	a form or some notes
5	Will I have to listen for the spelling of a name?		*e*	Five. There's also an example.

2 ◆ 109 **For each question, write the correct answer in the gap.**

Write one word or a number or a date or a time.

You will hear a woman talking at the start of a course on fashion.

Fashion – short course

Name of room for lessons: *North*

Time lessons start: **(1)** _____ am

Day for drawing lesson: **(2)** _____

Name of photographer: **(3)** Peter _____

Bring: **(4)** _____

We'll make: a **(5)** _____

HOW WAS IT?

Gave it a go   ☐

Getting there   ☐

Aced it!   ☐

REAL WORLD

SHOPPING FOR CLOTHES IN ...
DUBAI

1 Look at the photos (A–C) of Dubai. Which place would you prefer to go shopping in? Why?

2 Read the introduction to the text about shopping in Dubai. Are prices generally higher or lower in Dubai than in other countries?

Dubai is a great place to go shopping for clothes and other things. There are lots of big, modern shopping malls with shops selling all kinds of items. Many of the things you can buy are tax free, so they are cheaper than in other countries.

1 The malls are a great place to buy clothes. There are lots of shops that sell designer clothes with top brand names at great prices. The shops open at 10 am and the mornings are a good time to shop because the malls are quite quiet. Evenings are busier, but it's cooler then, so shopping is easier and more fun than in the afternoon.

2 The traditional markets, called souks, are also a good place to go shopping for clothes. A lot of things are cheaper in the souks, so these are the places to find bargains. But, the prices aren't fixed, so you have to know how much you are happy to pay for something. Go to the souk to find colourful scarves and dresses. You can also find second-hand clothes at very low prices in some souks. There are also lots of interesting souvenirs to take home with you.

3 Every year, there is a month-long shopping festival in Dubai. The shops in the malls all have sales, with some great price reductions. At the Dubai Global Village, there are stalls selling things from all around the world, so it's a great place to find clothes that are a bit different. There is also music and dancing in the streets, a big wheel to ride on and fireworks in the evenings. It's like one big shopping party!

3 Read the rest of the text. Match the photos (A–C) with the paragraphs.

4 Read the text again. Are the statements true (T) or false (F)? Correct the false statements.

1 There are only a few shopping malls in Dubai.
2 The afternoon is the best time to visit shopping malls in Dubai.
3 You can often buy things for less money in the souks.
4 The prices in the souks are always the same.
5 There is entertainment in the streets during the shopping festival.
6 You can buy things from lots of different countries at the Dubai Global Village.

5 Find the words and phrases in the text and choose the correct definitions.

1 tax free
  a without paying extra money to the country
  b without knowing where things come from
2 designer clothes
  a clothes with well-known names
  b clothes that are made specially for you
3 bargain
  a something that is cheaper than usual
  b something that is more expensive than usual
4 souvenir
  a a present
  b something you buy to help you remember a place
5 price reduction
  a a higher price
  b a lower price
6 special offer
  a a lower price for a short time
  b something you can only buy at some times of the year

6 ● 110 Listen to three conversations about shopping for clothes. What are the speakers doing? There is one extra answer which you do not need to use.

a buying clothes in a market
b asking a friend for advice about clothes
c asking a shop assistant about the price of some clothes
d asking a shop assistant for a different size

7 ● 110 Complete the questions with the correct words. Listen again and check.

bigger	colours	discount	fit
how much	look	sale	suits

PHRASES YOU MIGHT USE

1 Do you have a _____ size?
2 Do you have it in other _____ ?
3 Are these shoes in the _____ ?
4 _____ are they?
5 Is there a _____ for students?
6 How do they _____ ?
7 That colour really _____ you.
8 They _____ me perfectly.

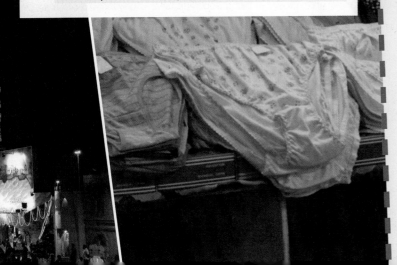

8 Choose the correct definitions for these informal words and phrases.

PHRASES YOU MIGHT HEAR

1 We usually have all sizes in stock.
  a We don't usually sell all sizes.
  b There are usually all sizes in the shop.
2 I'm afraid not.
  a No, I'm sorry.
  b I think it's possible they aren't.
3 If you come this way …
  a You wear them like this.
  b Please follow me.
4 It's worth taking a look.
  a You might find something you like here.
  b Don't look at these.

9 ● Watch the video. What do you learn about these things in Dubai? Make notes.

- the city
- shopping malls
- the souks
- the shopping festival

▶ WATCH

LIFE COMPETENCIES

CREATIVITY AND INNOVATION

10 ● Compare your notes. Watch the video again to check your ideas.

1 Work in pairs. Imagine you are going shopping in Dubai to buy some new clothes. You have 300 Emirati Dirham to spend and want to find some bargains.
  - Find out how much this amount is worth in your country's money.
  - Find some information about what you can buy in Dubai.
  - Look at some websites for shops and souks in Dubai.
  - Decide what to buy.
2 Compare with your classmates. Who found the best bargains?

14 PLAY IT, WATCH IT, LOVE IT

B

VOCABULARY

SPORTS

1 Work in pairs and discuss the questions.

1 Which sports do/don't you enjoy playing or watching?
2 How much time do you spend playing or watching sport a week?
3 Do you have a favourite sports team?

2 Look at the photos of the six most popular sports in the world. Match the photos with the sports and then do the quiz.

athletics   basketball   cricket
football   rugby   tennis

C

D

E

F

3 111 Put the sports in order 1–6 from the most to the least popular. Compare your ideas with a partner. Listen and check your answers.

4 Write the most popular sports in your country. Compare your answers with a partner.

5 Choose the correct words to complete the sentences.

1 Football players mustn't touch the ball with their hands; they have to *kick/hit/play* it with their feet.

2 She is going to *push/throw/score* the ball to another player in her *group/team/set*, who will try to catch it.

3 Our team are *losing/winning/succeeding* the match; we have already *made/scored/hit* three goals and the other team only one.

4 Please lend me your tennis *bat/racket/stick* to use in this match. I've broken mine!

5 There are different running *sports/races/games* in the Olympic Games, for example 100 metres, 400 metres and 800 metres.

6 If a tennis player hits the ball into the *goal/net/bat*, he/she doesn't win a point.

7 A cricket *goal/net/bat* is quite big and heavy so your arms can get tired during a long *sport/match/race*.

Which sport ...

1 is a game for two or four people? You can play it indoors or outdoors by **hitting** a ball over a **net** with a **racket**.

2 is a game in which two **teams** of 11 players **kick** a ball and try to **score goals**?

3 is a competition with lots of different sports where people run **races**, jump and **throw** things?

4 needs two teams of 15 players for a **match**? The ball isn't round and the goal is the shape of a letter H.

5 is popular in countries like Australia and India? The players try to hit a ball with a long, square **bat**.

6 is a game which often has a lot of very tall players? Two teams try to **win points** by throwing a ball through a high **net**.

READING

'Football is a team sport and not an individual sport. We win as a team, and every individual is better if we are part of the team.'

Fernando Torres

1 Work in pairs. Read the quote about football and answer the questions.

1 What do you think it means?
2 Do you think it is also true for other sports?
3 Are you a football fan? Why?/Why not?

2 Read the text about football. Which facts are new for you? Which facts do you find the most interesting?

The changing face of
FOOTBALL

Football is a very old sport, which some people say began in China in 500 BCE! When people started playing it in England in the 13th Century, the game was called 'football' because rich people rode horses for all their sports but this was a game ordinary people could play on foot. People were banned from playing it because the games sometimes lasted for days, there were no rules and players were often badly hurt or even killed! For hundreds of years, people couldn't play football in the street or other public places.

At this time, women played football too. Women's teams in Britain were also very popular and successful in the 1800s. But in 1921, the British Football Association decided that women's teams couldn't use their football pitches to play matches. Amazingly, this didn't change until 1971 when the Women's Football Association started.

Italy had the first professional women players in the 1970s and women's football has continued to grow globally since then. At the next FIFA Women's World Cup, teams from 24 countries will take part and millions of fans will experience the highs and lows of watching their teams score amazing goals or lose exciting matches against tough opponents. And with more and more girls taking up football, the future of the women's game looks good.

FOOTBALL RULES – IN A NUTSHELL!

Teams can't have more than 11 players on the pitch.
Players can use their feet, head or chest to play the ball.
Players mustn't touch the ball with their hands during play.
The ball needs to cross the goal line to be a goal.
Referees can show players a red card and send the player off the pitch.
Referees have to add any injury time at the end of each half.

3 Read the text again. Are these statements true (T) or false (F)? Correct the false statements.

1 The game of football is more than 1,000 years old.
2 It's called football because you use your feet to play the game.
3 For hundreds of years, people could play football anywhere in England.
4 Before 1971, women's teams couldn't use the same pitches as men to play matches.
5 Women's football is becoming less popular.

4 Complete the description with the words in the box.

goal	loses	match	off	pitch	red card
referee	rules	score	send	teams	

In modern football, there are two **1**_____ of 11 players. They play the game outdoors on a big field called a football **2**_____ .

The players can't touch the ball with their hands. The aim of the game is to kick the ball into the other team's **3**_____ . Each time a player does this, they **4**_____ a goal. The team which **5**_____ is the one which has the least goals. A football game is called a **6**_____ and it is 90 minutes long, with a break of 15 minutes in the middle. Modern football has lots of **7**_____ that say what players can and can't do. A **8**_____ controls the game. If a player doesn't follow the rules, the referee can give him or her a **9**_____ and **10**_____ him or her **11**_____ .

DID YOU KNOW?

The game British people call football is called **soccer** in the USA.

British people play **football** on a **pitch** and Americans play **soccer** on a **field**.

GRAMMAR

GRAMMAR ON THE MOVE
Watch the video

CAN, MUST, HAVE TO, NEED TO

1 Read the sentences and complete the rules with the verbs in the box.

*Teams **can't** have more than 11 players.*
*Players **can** use their feet, head or chest.*
*Players **mustn't** touch the ball.*
*Players **must** be fit to play.*
*The ball **needs to** cross the goal line.*
*Goalkeepers **don't need to** stay in their goal.*
*Referees **have to** add any injury time.*
*They **don't have to** wear a black top anymore.*

| can   don't need to   have to   mustn't |

We use …
¹_____ to talk about things we are allowed to do.
can't / ²_____ to talk about things we aren't allowed to do.
must / ³_____ to talk about things that are necessary.
don't have to / ⁴_____ to talk about things that aren't necessary.

Be careful not to confuse **mustn't** and **don't have to**.
*You **mustn't** touch the ball with your hand. (It's the rule.)*
*You **don't have to** go to the party. (You can if you want but it's not a necessity.)*

➡ **GRAMMAR REFERENCE** / page 224

2 Match the beginnings of the sentences (1–6) with the correct endings (a–f).

1   If you aren't coming to football practice
2   You can't wear trainers for the match;
3   We don't need to hurry,
4   You mustn't say bad things
5   She needs to try harder
6   We must all work together

a   to be a good team.
b   about the players in the other team.
c   you have to tell the team captain.
d   if she really wants to improve.
e   we've got lots of time.
f   you need proper football boots.

3 Complete the sentences with the correct forms of *can, must, have to* and *need to*. Sometimes more than one answer is possible.

1   I _____ to wear glasses when I'm reading or I _____ see the words on the page.
2   On Sundays, I _____ get up as early as I do on the other days of the week. I _____ stay in bed.
3   '_____ you run as fast as Jake?' 'No, I _____ .'
4   You _____ eat a lot of fruit and vegetables if you want to be healthy.
5   My English is getting better and I _____ look in the dictionary so much when I'm reading something.
6   They _____ listen when the teacher is explaining something.
7   All of you _____ come to football practice next week. It's important because the team _____ learn to work together better.
8   '_____ I _____ wear these white shorts?' 'Yes you do. Everyone in the team has to wear them.'

4 Complete the sentences so they are true for you. Then compare your ideas with a partner.

1   People don't have to …
2   Sometimes, we all need to …
3   If you want to do well in English, you must …

LISTENING

1 **Work in pairs and discuss the questions.**

1 Do you like running? Why?/Why not?

2 How far can you run?

3 What clothes and equipment do you need to be a runner?

2 **Read the text about Kenyan runners, then answer the questions.**

1 What sort of races do Kenyans often win?

2 Which part of Kenya do many of the runners come from?

3 112 **Listen to a journalist talking to Florence Kipoge, a teacher at a running school. Why does she think there are so many good runners in this part of Kenya?**

4 112 **Listen again and choose the best answers to complete the sentences.**

1 Before talking to Florence Kipoge, the journalist
   a went running.
   b watched some of the students running.

2 Many of the students run to school every day
   a because their families don't have any transport.
   b because they want to practise running.

3 When Florence was a teenager she ran
   a five kilometres every day.
   b ten kilometres every day.

4 People in this part of Kenya get strong legs and breathe well
   a because they run uphill a lot.
   b because they work hard.

5 Students at the school have a good running style because they don't
   a eat too much.
   b usually wear shoes.

6 Students buy running shoes
   a when they win money in competitions.
   b when they hurt their feet.

7 Florence says the students at the school
   a dream about being rich.
   b work and train very hard.

5 **Work in pairs and discuss the questions.**

1 Have you ever done a lot of training for a sports competition or event? When? How many hours? What did you do?

2 Would you like to be a professional sports person? Why?/Why not?

KENYA'S
AMAZING YOUNG RUNNERS

There are Kenyan athletes at all the big running competitions in the world and often they are the winners. Some of them have won lots of races, so they are real champions! At the last Olympic Games, Kenyan athletes won the gold and silver medals for many of the long-distance races including the men's and the women's marathon. Many of these athletes are from the same part of Kenya – the mountains above the Rift Valley. The mountain air helps train them to breathe well when they are running. There are special schools in the Rift Valley which help train young people to become professional runners. We went to visit one of them.

VOCABULARY

DO, PLAY AND GO WITH SPORTS

1 **Read the sentences and complete the rules with *do*, *play* and *go*.**

*They're **playing** hockey.*
*My friend Catrina loves **doing** karate.*
*He **goes** running on Saturday mornings.*

1	We use _____ with non-team sports and activities.
2	We use _____ for ball games.
3	We use _____ with sports ending in *-ing*.

2 **Put the sports and activities on the correct line.**

aerobics   baseball   cycling   fishing   gymnastics
handball   horse riding   judo   rock climbing
sailing   skiing   snowboarding   surfing
volleyball   windsurfing   yoga

1 do: _____   *2* play: _____   *3* go: _____

3 **Work in pairs and ask and answer about the sports you and your friends do. Ask how often, when and where they do them. How do they make them feel?**

I go swimming once or twice a week at the sports centre. I go late in the evening. Swimming helps me feel relaxed.

1 Look at the words and pictures and match each picture (1–3) with a set of words (A–C). What do you think is happening in the story?

A

| bare feet | have idea | take off | win |

B

| dog | sit down | track | trainers |

C

| begin | race | run away | take |

2 Work in pairs. Write one or two sentences for each picture. Use the words in the boxes to help you. Then put the sentences together to make a story.

3 Read the story below. How is it similar to yours? How is it different? Which tenses are used?

> As Joe was sitting down on the track to put on his trainers, a dog arrived. The dog took a trainer and ran away.
>
> Joe didn't know what to do. He didn't have time to catch the dog before the start of the race.
>
> Suddenly, he had an idea. He took off his other trainer and ran barefoot. He won the race!

4 Read another longer version of the story about Joe. Answer the questions.

1 How is it different from the one in Exercise 3? Is it more interesting? Why?

2 What kind of words are in blue?

> As Joe was sitting down on the hard, red track to put on his new trainers, a big, friendly dog arrived. The dog took one of Joe's expensive trainers and ran away.
>
> Joe didn't know what to do. The race was going to start so he didn't have time to catch the silly dog.
>
> Suddenly, he had a brilliant idea. He took off his other trainer and ran barefoot. He won the race!

5 Rewrite the beginnings of these stories. Make them more interesting by adding adjectives in front of the nouns. Use the adjectives in the box to help you.

angry	beautiful	big	busy	colourful
crowded	expensive	fantastic	fresh	hard
large	modern	new	quiet	round	small
shiny	strange	terrible	ugly	

1 One day I was sitting in a **café** when I noticed that there was a **bag** on the **table** next to me.

2 A **woman** was walking through the **park** when suddenly she saw an **object** on the **path** in front of her.

3 One afternoon, as I was crossing the **road** to my house, a **car** stopped in the street next to me and a **man** put his **head** out of the window to speak to me.

6 Look at the three pictures on page 194. Write the story shown in the pictures. Write 35 words or more.

GRAMMAR

TENSES REVIEW

1 Complete the text with the verbs in the box in the correct tense.

begin	be born	stop	study
take part	win (x2)	work (x2)	

Trischa Zorn is an American para-athlete. She was blind when she ¹_____ in California in 1964 and she ²_____ swimming when she was 10 years old. She started training for the Olympics while she ³_____ still _____ at high school and she ⁴_____ seven gold medals at the Olympic Games in Arnhem in 1980. Since then she ⁵_____ in six more Olympics Games and ⁶_____ a total of 55 medals! When she ⁷_____ swimming, she worked as a teacher for five years, but she now ⁸_____ for the US government. At the moment she ⁹_____ on a project to help disabled soldiers do sports and train for the Olympic Games.

2 Work in pairs. Which tenses are used in the gaps? Why are they used?

3 🔊 113 Listen to the words. What do you notice about the vowel sounds in the words? Listen again and repeat.

b<u>ou</u>ght   th<u>ou</u>ght   t<u>au</u>ght   s<u>a</u>w

VOCABULARY: ADVERBS

1 They worked **slowly** but they finished the job. **Afterwards** they sat down and had a rest.

2 We put the bags down **carefully** on the ground and lay down on top of them. **Surprisingly** we didn't feel tired.

3 I **quickly** climbed into the room through the open window. Then I closed it. **Luckily** there was no one in the room to see me.

1 Read the information about adverbs and complete the gaps with one of the phrases in the box.

how something happened
how the speaker or writer feels about something
when something happened

Adverbs of time: show us ¹_____ , e.g. *before, afterwards, next, finally.*
Adverbs of manner: show us ²_____ , e.g. *suddenly* (quickly and unexpectedly)
Sentence adverbs: show us ³_____ , e.g. *fortunately* (it's a good thing), *unfortunately* (it's a bad thing). They go at the beginning of the phrase.

2 Look at the example sentences above and match the adverbs in bold with the three types of adverbs below.

adverbs of time _____   adverbs of manner _____
sentence adverbs _____

3 Choose the best option to complete the sentences.

1 We had dinner and *afterwards/before/suddenly* we went to bed.

2 I forgot my purse and couldn't pay for my coffee, but *fortunately/unfortunately/sadly* my friend paid for me.

3 I was getting ready to go out when *finally/suddenly/before* the telephone rang.

4 She was sad because her friend forgot to say goodbye *after/before/next* he left.

5 *Finally/Unfortunately/Suddenly* it was already dark when we arrived at the house, so I couldn't see the beautiful garden.

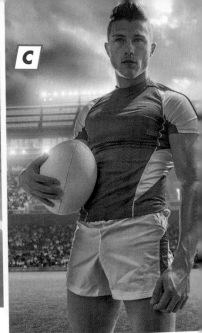

LISTENING

A

B

C

Loli, Monterrey
Basketball fan ....

Sandra, Cardiff
Rugby fan ....

Arno, Milan
Formula 1 fan ....

1 Look at the photos of three sports. Match the photos with the names of the people and the sports they like. Are these sports popular in your country? What do you know about them?

2 ▲ 114 Listen to the three speakers talking about why they became sports fans. Write the names of the speakers in the order you hear them in the first row of the table below.

3 ▲ 114 Listen again and complete the rest of the table.

	1	2	3 ....
Age when he/she started watching the sport			
Why he/she started watching the sport			
Where the sport is played/ practised			*(basketball) court*
What the person likes about the sport/feels when watching a match	*It's exciting – she likes the singing during matches and the atmosphere*		

4 Match the words with the definitions.

1 away match
2 home match
3 live
4 season ticket

a a sports game that a team plays in the town where they come from
b a piece of paper that you can use to go and watch all the matches of one team in one year
c a sports game that a team plays in a different town
d seen or heard at the same time as it is happening

5 Read what Sandra says about rugby and complete the gaps with the words below.

| away matches   home matches   live   season ticket |

Now I'm a serious fan and I have a ¹ .... to watch the Cardiff Blues, the team I support. I go to all the Blues' ² .... and I sometimes follow them to ³ .... I really love watching rugby ⁴ ....

6 Work in pairs and discuss the questions.

1 What are the advantages and disadvantages of watching a sport live and watching it on television or online?
2 Why do you think sports teams win home matches more often than away matches?
3 How much do tickets to sports matches cost in your country? Do you ever go? Why?/Why not?

1 Look at these pictures. Which of these sports have you tried? Which did you enjoy or not enjoy? Why?

2 🔊 115 Listen to two exam candidates, Mei and Luca, discussing the pictures. Complete the table. Put a tick if he/she likes the sport or cross if he/she doesn't like it. Make notes about any other information you hear.

	MEI	LUCA
Basketball	X *very fast game* *She's not very good*	
Running		
Swimming		
Tennis		

3 Do Mei and Luca do this task well? Give reasons.

4 🔊 116 Now listen to the examiner asking questions about the sports in the pictures and write down three questions the examiner asks.

5 In phase 1 of Part 2 of the speaking exam you have to discuss some pictures with your partner. Look at the pictures on page 195 and follow the instructions.

6 🔊 117 Now listen to Mei and Luca doing phase 2 of Speaking Part 2. Which sport would Luca like to learn? Does Mei prefer watching sports or playing sports?

7 🔊 117 Listen again. Complete the gaps in the phrases that Mei and Luca use to give positive opinions about sports.

> it's good for you   I think it's amazing
> my favourite thing is   I'd like to go
> it looks awesome

1 'Which new sport would you like to learn, Mei?'
'I'm interested in learning how to water-ski.'
'Why?'
'Because _____ . Some people say it's a dangerous sport, but _____ '

2 'And what about you, Luca?'
'I'd like to try snowboarding. My cousins are very good snowboarders and _____ snowboarding with them.'

3 'Which do you prefer, watching sports or playing sports, Luca?'
'I don't know really. It's different for different sports. But probably playing sports, because it's fun and _____ '

4 'And you, Mei?'
'Definitely watching sports. _____ to go to a football match to watch my team.'

8 Work in pairs. Ask and answer the following questions.

1 Which new sport would you like to learn?
2 Which do you prefer, watching sports or playing sports?

WRITING PART 7

EXAM CHECK

1 **Complete this information about Writing Part 7 with words in the box.**

| write | tell | pictures | words | decide |

In Writing Part 7 you see three **1**_____ . Together, they **2**_____ a story.
You have to **3**_____ what the story is, and then **4**_____ it. Your story needs to be at
least 35 **5**_____ long.

2 **Look at the three pictures.**

Write the story shown in the pictures.

Write 35 words or more.

➡ **WRITING BANK** / *pages 235–236.*

EXAM CHECK

1 The sentences below tell you what happens in Speaking Part 2, in the order that it happens. Match the beginning of each sentence with the correct ending.

1 At the beginning of Speaking Part 2, the examiner will

2 Next, the examiner will

3 Then the examiner will

4 After this, the examiner will

5 Finally, the examiner will

a stop you and ask each of you a few questions about the pictures.

b give you and your partner five pictures to look at.

c take the pictures away, and ask you two more questions about the same topic.

d give you one or two minutes to talk about the pictures with your partner.

e ask if you like the things you can see in the pictures.

2 In this part of the test you are going to talk together.

Here are some pictures that show different sports you can do in the sea.

Do you like these different sports you can do in the sea? Say why or why not. Talk together.

➡ **SPEAKING BANK** / pages 241–242.

3 Now one of you is the examiner and the other is a candidate. The examiner should ask these questions, and the candidate should answer.

- Do you think swimming in the sea is dangerous? Why?/Why not?
- Do you think sailing in the sea is difficult? Why?/Why not?
- Do you think surfing in the sea is fun? Why?/Why not?

4 Now change. The person who was the candidate before is now the examiner. The examiner should ask these questions, and the candidate should answer.

- Do you think windsurfing in the sea is easy? Why?/Why not?
- Do you think fishing in the sea is interesting? Why?/Why not?

5 For each question below, take turns to ask and answer.

- Which sport do you do most often? Why?
- Do you prefer to do sports alone, or in a team? Why?

HOW WAS IT?

Gave it a go ☐

Getting there ☐

Aced it! ☐

REAL WORLD

GOING TO A SPORTS EVENT IN ...
MADRID

1 Look at the photos (A–D) of football in Madrid. What can you see in the photos? Do you ever go to football matches or watch them on TV? Which team do you support?

2 Read the webpage about a tour of the Bernabéu Stadium. Which part of the tour would you enjoy the most? Why?

VISIT THE STADIUM

Tour length: 1 hour and 30 minutes

Best time to visit: early in the morning

TOUR HIGHLIGHTS

⚽ Enter the rooms where the home team and away team get changed. Look at the shirts of famous players who have played for Real Madrid.

⚽ Walk through the tunnel onto the pitch and imagine hearing thousands of fans cheering for you.

⚽ Walk around the pitch.

⚽ See the different stands where fans sit to watch the game.

⚽ Imagine what it's like to kick a ball into one of the famous goals.

⚽ Visit the stadium museum and learn the history of the club and the stadium.

⚽ Look at the trophies Real Madrid has won.

⚽ On match days, why not buy a ticket and stay on to see the game?

3 Read the webpage again. Match the words and phrases with the correct definitions.

1	home team	*a*	the team that is playing a game at its own stadium
2	away team	*b*	an area of grass where people play football
3	tunnel	*c*	large silver or gold cups that teams get if they win competitions
4	pitch	*d*	the part of a stadium that players walk through to start the game
5	stands	*e*	the parts of a stadium where the people who are watching the game sit
6	trophies	*f*	the team that is playing a game at another team's stadium

4 Read three reviews of a stadium tour in the UK. Which person didn't enjoy it?

ClareM

I'm not a supporter of this team, and I'm not very keen on football, but this was a great way to spend a morning. You can go right to the top of the stadium and get a great view of the pitch. I loved the shop, too – I bought a team scarf as a souvenir!

TomR44

There's lots of information about the club. We also bought audio guides, which told us all about the history of the club. We loved seeing all the trophies. You can go right down to the pitch side and sit where the manager sits. Great fun!

KizziGrand

I usually love stadium tours, but this one wasn't great! It was really busy, and they make you move around so quickly you don't get a chance to see anything. The changing rooms were really disappointing, and there was no time for photos. The tour ended at the shop, where everything was really expensive!

5 Read the reviews again. Which person …

1 thinks that there were too many people on the tour?
2 bought something as a reminder of their visit?
3 learned a lot from listening to something?
4 thinks there wasn't enough time for the tour?
5 enjoyed being somewhere where an important person usually goes?
6 doesn't like football?

6 🔊 118 Listen to three conversations. Who are the people? There is one extra answer which you do not need to use.

a two tourists talking during a stadium tour
b a fan buying tickets to watch a match
c a guide showing people around a stadium
d two tourists talking after a match

7 🔊 118 Complete the phrases with the correct words. Listen again and check.

| chance | great | referee | support | too | what |

PHRASES YOU MIGHT USE

1 Which team do you _____ ?
2 _____ about you?
3 That was a _____ game!
4 Me _____ !
5 The goalkeeper had no _____ !
6 I think the _____ got that wrong.

8 Choose the correct definitions for these informal words and phrases.

PHRASES YOU MIGHT HEAR

1 Let's see what we've got.
   a I will check which tickets we have.
   b I can't see any free tickets.
2 Which part of the stadium did you have in mind?
   a Do you mind where you sit?
   b Where would you like to sit?
3 It's hard to say.
   a It will be difficult for you to see.
   b I'm not sure.
4 If the action's all at your end, …
   a If the game all happens close to you, …
   b If the game finishes very quickly, …
5 You should get a better view from there.
   a You should choose a different seat.
   b I think you will see better from there.

9 🔘 Watch the video. What do you learn about these things? Make notes.

- Madrid
- football teams in the city
- stadium tours
- buying tickets for matches

10 🔘 Compare your notes. Watch the video again to check your ideas.

▶ WATCH

LIFE COMPETENCIES

SHARING IDEAS AND RESPECTING OTHERS' CONTRIBUTIONS

11 Work in pairs. Choose another famous sports event you are interested in. Find out about tickets and tours. Compare your ideas in groups. Agree which event you would all like to go to the most.

PROGRESS CHECK 5

UNITS 12–14

1 Match each photo with what the person says about their clothes.

1 I love well-known brands, and I always try to look fashionable. I love dark colours. ....

2 I like to wear casual clothes when I go on holiday, and I always make sure I pack my sunglasses and sandals. ....

3 I wear trainers and sports clothes a lot as I'm quite sporty, but it's important to me to look cool too. ....

4 I have to look smart for my job so I always wear a suit and tie at work. ....

2 Match each person described in the sentences with a word in the box. There are two words which you don't need to use.

| annoying clever fit funny |
| kind lazy quiet sociable |

1 My sister loves spending time with her friends and meeting new people. ....

2 My best friend tells lots of jokes and makes me laugh a lot. ....

3 My cousin spends a lot of time reading, and never says very much. ....

4 My teacher is always happy to help people and is nice to everyone. ....

5 My brother spends all his time lying in bed – he never does anything! ....

6 My dad knows the answer to any question I ask him.

....

3 Complete the text with words in the box.

| fiancé   important person in my life   married |
| only child   relatives   small family |

Most of my friends have lots of brothers and sisters, cousins, and aunts and uncles, but I don't have many ¹............ . I come from a ²............ . My mum has one sister, but my dad is an ³............ . My parents are very happy together – they have been ⁴............ for twenty-one years. I think the most ⁵............ is my sister, Jenny. She's older than me, and it's her wedding in a few months. Her ⁶............ is called Rob, and he's really nice.

4 Choose the correct option to complete the sentences.

1 You *can/have to* wear a special hat when you go horse riding. It's dangerous if you don't.

2 Do we *must/need to* wear football boots for the match on Saturday?

3 You *don't have to/mustn't* wear white clothes to play cricket, but people usually do.

4 Do you know if we *can/shall* go fishing in this lake?

5 We have a new team kit. All players *could/must* wear it for the next match.

6 You *mustn't/don't have to* go climbing in those shoes! It's dangerous. Wear trainers.

5 Choose the correct option to complete the sentences.

1 **A:** Are you *going/doing* swimming on Friday?

  B: Yes. I need to *train/race* as much as possible – I've got a *champion/competition* next month, and I really want to win.

2 **A:** Have you ever *done/played* cricket before?

  B: No, but I can *catch/play* a ball, and I know how to hold the *net/bat*, so I'm sure I'll be fine.

3 **A:** Why didn't you *play/do* football on Saturday?

  B: I got a *red card/own goal* the week before, so I was sent off. I have to miss the next three *pitches/matches*.

4 **A:** I'm not very good at *season/team* games like volleyball, so I *go/do* athletics after work one day a week.

  B: Which sport? Running?

  A: Yes, I'm a long-distance runner. I run 10,000 metre *races/medals*.

5 **A:** Have you tried any new sports recently?

  B: Yes. When I was on holiday, I *played/went* surfing every day.

  A: That sounds great. I'm going to *go/do* karate for the first time on Wednesday. I've seen it on TV, but I don't know anything about the *points/rules*.

6 Put the adjectives into the comparative or superlative form to complete the sentences.

1 The new college library is much _____ (big) than the old one.

2 My science course at college is _____ (interesting) than the science classes I had at school.

3 I really like meeting customers. It's the _____ (good) part of the job.

4 The new girl in my class at university is the _____ (friendly) person I've ever met.

5 I don't understand why my mark for the history project was _____ (bad) than yours.

6 I'm much _____ (busy) at work now that two of my colleagues have left.

7 Students often make mistakes with comparative and superlative adjectives. Correct the mistakes in these sentences.

1 I liked the tennis competition because it was between the better players in the world.

2 I want to go by car because it's more fast.

3 Football is the sport more popular in the world.

4 Tennis is one of my most favourite games.

5 We're going to the sports centre by car because that's more safer.

8 Match the beginnings and endings of the sentences to make conditional sentences.

1 When it rains

2 If you see Charlie

3 I'll wear this dress to the party

4 Do you ever look at your phone

5 You won't get the job

6 If he arrives late,

a if it's hot.

b when you're in class?

c if you dress like that!

d will you tell him about the meeting?

e what shall we do?

f we play tennis in the sports hall.

9 Read the text about cricket. Choose the correct word, A, B or C, for each gap.

I started ¹_____ cricket when I was at school, and I really enjoyed it. I'm at university now, and I'm a member of the university cricket team. We ²_____ twice a week to get ready for our matches. In a game of cricket there are two teams of eleven players. You need a large area to play in, a long ³_____ made of wood, and a ball. The ball is very hard. In the past, some players got hurt when a ball ⁴_____ them on the head, so now players ⁵_____ wear a type of hat called a helmet. This has made the game much ⁶_____ than it was before.

1 **A** doing **B** playing **C** going

2 **A** train **B** race **C** throw

3 **A** net **B** racket **C** bat

4 **A** throw **B** kick **C** hit

5 **A** must **B** shall **C** would

6 **A** safe **B** safer **C** safest

10 Complete the sentences by choosing the correct words, then match each person with the school subject or job in the box.

chemistry   drama   farmer   history   journalist   maths

1 When I was at primary school, I loved working with numbers and *doing/taking* equations.

2 I've just graduated from university. I spent a lot of time on stage, *taking/getting* part in performances.

3 At secondary school there are special classrooms called labs where we can *pass/do* experiments.

4 I'm *revising/passing* for an exam at the moment. I've got to remember lots of important events that happened in the past.

5 I'm good at *doing/finding out* research, and writing essays, and I've just got a job on a local newspaper.

6 I work with animals, and then one day a week I go to college because I want to get some *degrees/qualifications*.

11 Change the passive sentences into active sentences.

1 My tooth was pulled out by the dentist.

2 That bridge was built by a really famous engineer.

3 We were asked to find out about rivers by our geography teacher.

4 I was given really good marks by my modern languages teacher.

COMMUNICATION ACTIVITIES

UNIT 1, PAGE 17, EXERCISE 7: STUDENT A

1 Read about Karen and ask your partner questions to complete the missing information. Use the words to help you.

> Karen always gets up early because she starts work at
> ¹_____. She works in the gardens of a ²_____
> and she walks to work. She doesn't have breakfast
> before she leaves, but she buys ³_____ in a café.
> When she arrives at work, she sits down and
> ⁴_____. After breakfast, ⁵_____. She goes
> home for lunch at 12.00 pm and comes back to work
> ⁶_____. After lunch, she sometimes has a meeting
> with ⁷_____ to talk about what she needs to do
> next. She finishes work at ⁸_____ and walks home.

1	What time …	**5**	What …
2	Where …	**6**	When …
3	What …	**7**	Who …
4	What …	**8**	When …

2 Read about Roman and answer your partner's questions about him.

> Roman works on an oil rig in the Gulf of Mexico.
> He works on the rig for two weeks and then he goes
> home for a week. When he's on the rig, he works very
> hard. Sometimes he works at night. When he does this,
> he starts work at 10.00 pm and finishes at 7.00 am.
> When he works nights, he gets up at 3.00 pm in the
> afternoon and goes to the gym. He has a big meal in
> the cafeteria and then he often plays table tennis with
> his friend Pepe. Roman has to wear special clothes for
> his work because it's very cold on the oil rig. He gets
> dressed and is ready for work at 9.45 pm.

UNIT 2, PAGE 33, EXERCISE 7: SPEAKING, DESCRIBING A PHOTO

Student A

Student B

UNIT 3, PAGE 41, EXERCISE 6

QUIZ: MY SCREEN LIFE

8–16: You're not a fan of screens and you never will be. You probably aren't into computers but you do know how to use the internet for useful things.

17–27: You sometimes use the internet to help you but you don't spend hours and hours on it. You can live without your screens.

28–34: You're a screen fan. You spend a lot of time in front of screens. Go out and speak to your friends a bit more often.

35–40: You love your screens! You spend a lot of time on your phone or tablet. Don't forget that there are other things to do too!

UNIT 5, PAGE 64, EXERCISE 3: VOCABULARY, TRAVEL

Quiz: Are you an adventurous traveller?

1 a = 1 point, b = 2 points, c = 3 points
2 a = 1 point, b = 3 points, c = 2 points
3 a = 3 points, b = 2 points, c = 1 point

4 a = 1 point, b = 2 points, c = 3 points
5 a = 2 points, b = 1 point, c = 3 points

5–8 points: You like to feel safe and comfortable when you travel. That isn't a bad thing, but you don't get many surprises. Maybe you could try to be a little more adventurous on your next trip.

9–12 points: You enjoy travelling. You don't like to take big risks, but you still have a good sense of adventure.

13–15 points: You are an adventurous traveller! You love trying new things and meeting new people. For you the world is one big adventure.

UNIT 6, PAGE 80, EXERCISE 8: GRAMMAR, *A/AN*, *SOME* AND *ANY*

| biscuits | bread | cheese | chicken | eggs | fruit | jam | juice |
| melon | milk | salami | sausage | tomatoes | yoghurt |

There's some fruit.

There aren't any eggs.

UNIT 6, PAGE 84, EXERCISE 7: SPEAKING, MAKING SUGGESTIONS

Work with a partner and decide where to have lunch.

A: Apologise for arriving late.
B: Reply. Ask if A is hungry.
A: Reply. Suggest a restaurant.
B: Suggest an alternative.
A: Give a negative response.
B: Suggest an alternative.
A: Give a positive response and suggest where to sit.

UNIT 1, PAGE 17, EXERCISE 7: STUDENT B

1 Read about Karen and answer your partner's questions about her.

> Karen always gets up early because she starts work at 7.00 am. She works in the gardens of a big, old house in her village and she walks to work. She doesn't have breakfast before she leaves, but she buys a cup of tea and a sandwich in a café. When she arrives at work, she sits down and eats her breakfast. After breakfast, she works in the garden. She goes home for lunch at 12.00 pm and comes back to work at 2.00 pm. After lunch, she sometimes has a meeting with the owner of the garden to talk about what she needs to do next. She finishes work at 5.00 pm and walks home.

2 Read about Roman and ask your partner questions to find the missing information. Use the words to help you.

> Roman works on an oil rig ¹_____ . He works on the rig for two weeks and then he goes home ²_____ . When he's on the rig, he works very hard. Sometimes he works at night. When he does this, he starts work at ³_____ and finishes at 7.00 am. When he works nights, he gets up at 3.00 pm in the afternoon and goes to⁴_____ . He has a big meal in the cafeteria and then he often plays ⁵_____ with ⁶_____ . Roman has to wear special clothes for his work because ⁷_____ . He gets dressed and is ready for work at ⁸_____ .

1	Where …	**5**	What …
2	How long … for?	**6**	Who …
3	When …	**7**	Why …
4	Where …	**8**	When …

UNIT 13, PAGE 173, EXERCISE 6: SPEAKING, APPEARANCE AND PERSONALITY

UNIT 14, PAGE 183, EXERCISE 6: WRITING PART 7

UNIT 13, PAGE 169, EXERCISE 2: LISTENING PART 2

Read the texts and match them to the styles in the photos (A–E). What kind of a dresser are you?

1 .... You aren't interested in fashion and you don't like wearing special clothes when you go out to parties. You want to be comfortable, so your favourite clothes are jeans and T-shirts.

2 .... Because you move a lot you like comfortable clothes. You like shorts and T-shirts that make it easy to do exercise. You prefer **trainers** to shoes and you like wearing **sandals** in summer.

3 .... You like **suits** or jackets. If you are a man, you often wear a **tie** and if you are a woman you probably wear expensive shoes and have a **handbag** to match. You want to look good enough to walk into an expensive restaurant or an important meeting at any time.

4 .... Clothes are important to you and you like to follow people on social media to see the colours and **styles** that are in. If you are a woman, you like to buy new **jewellery** too sometimes.

5 .... The important thing for you is to look good. You always have the most fashionable **brand** of jeans and trainers, and you like **sunglasses** with a brand name, too!

A Cool

B Smart

C Sporty

D Casual

E Fashionable

UNIT 14, PAGE 185, EXERCISE 5: SPEAKING PART 2

Work in pairs and talk about the four pictures.
Think about:

- the name of the sport
- any famous sportspeople or teams you know
- where/when you have done this sport
- why you do it and who you do it with
- your opinion of it – do you like it? Why?/why not?
- words you could use to talk about it

Remember to ask your partner for his/her opinion.
Use the expressions in the box below.

| What do you think?   What about you?   Do you play … ? |

Now take it in turns to ask and answer the examiner's questions about the sports above.

Student A

Do you think learning judo is difficult?
Do you think rock climbing is dangerous?
Which of these sports do you like best?

Student B

Do you think cycling is expensive?
Do you think volleyball is fun?
Which of these sports do you like best?

GRAMMAR REFERENCE

STARTER UNIT

BE

POSITIVE AND NEGATIVE SENTENCES

I	am/'m	
	am not/'m not	20 years old.
You/We/They	are/'re	Spanish.
	are not/aren't	happy.
He/She/It	is/'s	
	is not/isn't	

QUESTIONS

Am	I	
Are	you/we/they	20 years old?
Is	he/she/it	Spanish?

SHORT ANSWERS

Yes,	I	am.
	he/she/it	is.
	you/we/they	are.
No,	I	am not.
	he/she/it	isn't.
	you/we/they	aren't.

We use *be* to talk about:
- nationality   *I'm French.*
- age   *She's 20.*
- jobs   *My mum and dad are teachers.*
- feelings   *Are you happy?*
- time   *It's 10 o'clock.*
- where things are   *The plates are on the table.*

PRACTICE

1   **Rewrite these sentences with the short forms of the underlined words.**

1   <u>You are</u> 20 years old.   ....
2   My brother <u>is not</u> very funny.   ....
3   **A:** Are you French?
    B: No, <u>I am not</u>.   ....
4   We <u>are not</u> teachers. <u>We are</u> students.   ....
5   <u>She is</u> Australian.   ....

2   **Complete the sentences with the correct form of *be*.**

1   My sister .... 19.
2   I .... not very happy this morning.
3   Two of my friends .... American.
4   **A:** .... your mother a doctor?
    B: No, she .... She .... a teacher.
5   **A:** .... you 18 years old?
    B: Yes, I ....

HAVE GOT

POSITIVE AND NEGATIVE SENTENCES

I/You/We/They	have/'ve	
	have not/haven't	got a phone.
He/She/It	has/'s	
	has not/hasn't	

QUESTIONS

Have	I/you/we/they	got a phone?
Has	he/she/it	

SHORT ANSWERS

Yes,	I/you/we/they	have.
	he/she/it	has.
No,	I/you/we/they	haven't.
	he/she/it	hasn't.

In short answers, we do not use *got*.
Yes, I **have**. ~~Yes, I have got.~~
Use *have got* to talk about:
- things we own   *I've got a new top.*
- how people look   *She's got blue eyes.*
- people in our families   *I have got two brothers and a sister.*

PRACTICE

3   **Choose the correct words to complete the sentences.**

1   Kelly *hasn't/haven't* got a new dress to wear for the party.
2   Paul and Liza *has/have* got two children.
3   My brother and I *has/have* got black hair.
4   **A:** *Has/Have* we got any homework tonight?
    B: No, we *haven't got/haven't*.
5   All my friends *has/have* got smartphones.

4 Complete these sentences with the correct form of *have got.*

1 My family is very large. I _____ three brothers and two sisters.
2 We don't know what the time is because we _____ a watch.
3 My older brother Ben _____ a new car.
4 **A:** I don't know where my phone is. _____ you _____ it?
   B: No, I _____ .
5 I'm sorry, but we _____ any coffee.

CAN/CAN'T/LIKE/DON'T LIKE

We use *can/can't* + verb (without *to*) to talk about ability:
I **can swim**.
He **can't speak** Japanese.
We use *like* + noun to say what we think of things or people:
I **like** chocolate.
He **doesn't like** cats.
We **like** American films.

PRACTICE

5 Correct the mistakes or tick the correct sentences.

1 She can't to paint very well.
2 We don't liking dogs.
3 He likes going on holiday.
4 They don't like fast food.
5 I like watch films on TV.
6 She can read Chinese.

WH- QUESTION WORDS

* We use question words to ask certain types of questions.
* We call these words *Wh- words* because they contain the letters *wh* (*WHy, WHat, HoW*).

QUESTION WORD	USE	EXAMPLE
What	asking for information	*What is your name?*
When	asking about time	*When is the party?*
Where	asking what place	*Where do you live?*
Who	asking which person	*Who is that?*
Whose	asking about ownership	*Whose is this pen?*
How old	asking about age	*How old is he?*

PRACTICE

6 Write the correct question words for each question.

1 _____ does he live?   He lives in London.
2 _____ is that woman?   She's my mother.
3 _____ old are they?   They're only eight.
4 _____ does the bank open? At nine o'clock.
5 _____ is that coat?   It's mine.

7 Complete the questions about the words in bold.

1 He drinks **coffee** for breakfast. _____ does he drink for breakfast?
2 He's in **London**. _____ is he?
3 She's only **twenty years** old. _____ old is she?
4 It's hers. _____ **bike** is this?
5 At six o'clock. _____ does the **film** start?

THE APOSTROPHE 'S

* We use the apostrophe *'s* to show possession:
  The man's car.   My teacher's wife.   Mr Smith's flat.
* If the word ends in *s* use an apostrophe without another *s*:
  Mrs Stephens' book.
* We show possession with nouns that form their plurals by adding -s or -es by putting an apostrophe after the plural *s*:
  The waitresses' uniforms.
* We also use an apostrophe with contractions. The apostrophe replaces a letter or letters that have been removed.
  does not – doesn't   it is – it's
  cannot – can't   you would – you'd

PRACTICE

8 Write the apostrophes in the sentences.

1 This is my best friends car.
2 Steve Browns in my class.
3 The childrens books are on the teachers desk.
4 The new pilots uniforms are dark blue.
5 Its very noisy here.
6 Peters so friendly, hes always helping me.

3RD PERSON *S* IN THE PRESENT TENSE

The *he/she/it* form of most verbs use the infinitive + -s:
He like**s** biscuits.   She love**s** pop music.
He live**s** in London.   It come**s** from Mexico.

PRACTICE

9 Complete the sentences with the correct form of the verbs in the present simple.

1 They _____ (like) fast cars.
2 Steve _____ (eat) too much fast food.
3 She _____ (love) her new job.
4 They _____ (come) from South Africa.
5 He _____ (walk) to college every day.

UNIT 1

PRESENT SIMPLE

We use present simple verbs to talk about:

* things that happen regularly.
  *We **go** to college every day.*
* things that are always true.
  *Summer **comes** after spring.*
  *We **live** in Moscow.*

POSITIVE AND NEGATIVE SENTENCES

I/You/We/They	eat	chocolate.
	don't eat	
He/She/It	eats	
	doesn't eat	

QUESTIONS

Do	I/you/we/they	eat chocolate?
Does	he/she/it	

SHORT ANSWERS

Yes,	I/you/we/they	do.
	he/she/it	does.
No,	I/you/we/they	don't.
	he/she/it	doesn't.

The *he/she/it* form of most verbs uses the infinitive + *-s*.
Sometimes we add *-es* (*do* ➔ *does*; *go* ➔ *goes*).
If the verb ends in a consonant + *-y*, we add *-ies* (*carry* ➔ *carries*).

PRACTICE

1 **Complete the sentences with the correct form of the verb in brackets.**

1 Paul .... the piano every evening. (play)
2 I .... at 6 o'clock every day. (get up)
3 My brother .... football. (like)
4 My friends .... near me. (live)
5 Hannah .... to work by bus. (go)

2 **Write the negative form of the sentences in Exercise 1.**

1 Paul ....
2 I ....
3 My brother ....
4 My friends ....
5 Hannah ....

3 **Underline and correct the mistakes in these sentences.**

1 My brother work in Moscow.
....
2 Tom don't play the piano.
....
3 I plays football every weekend.
....
4 Does she starts work at 9 o'clock every morning?
....
5 My parents doesn't watch TV in the afternoon.
....

ADVERBS OF FREQUENCY

Frequency adverbs tell us how often something happens.

always		I **always** go to bed at night.
usually		I **usually** go to bed at 10.00.
often		I **often** go to bed at 11.00.
sometimes		I **sometimes** go to bed at midnight.
never		I **never** go to bed at lunchtime.

- We use frequency adverbs after the verb *be*.
  They **are always** happy at the weekend.
- We usually put frequency adverbs before other verbs.
  I **often get** home at 5 o'clock.
- In negative sentences, frequency adverbs come between *don't/doesn't* and the verb.
  We **don't always get up** early at the weekend.
- We can also use expressions like *every day, twice a week, once a year* to say how often something happens. We put these at the beginning or the end of sentences.
  Every year, we go on holiday to Italy.
  I have piano lessons **once a week**.

PRACTICE

4 **Put the words in order to make sentences.**

1 evening / go / I / in / never / work / the / to

2 help / homework / his / I / help / my brother / sometimes / with

3 and / I / sister / day / every / My / college / to / walk

4 am / for / I / late / work / sometimes

5 always / at / hard / I / college / work

5 **Make these sentences true for you. Add adverbs or other frequency expressions.**

1 get up at 7 o'clock in the morning

2 have lunch at work

3 go out in the evening

4 go to bed at 10 o'clock

5 sleep for 8 hours

LIKE/LOVE/HATE

We use *like/love/hate* + infinitive to say how we feel about doing things.
I **like to swim**.
He **doesn't like to do** his homework.
We can also use *like/love/hate* + verb *-ing* to say how we feel about doing things.
I **like swimming**.
He **doesn't like doing** his homework.

WANT TO

We use *want to* + infinitive to express a wish or desire.
He **wants to go** swimming.
She **doesn't want to go out** tonight.
They **don't want to watch** that film.

PRACTICE

6 **Put the words in order to make sentences.**

1 camping / He / doesn't / go / like / to

2 early / like / getting up / don't / They

3 coffee / He / loves / iced / drink / to

4 don't / want / We / shopping / to / go / morning / this

5 She / to / her / top / party / wants / wear / new / to / the

PRESENT CONTINUOUS

POSITIVE AND NEGATIVE SENTENCES

I	am/'m	
	am not/'m not	
You/We/They	are/'re	eating.
	are not/aren't	
He/She/It	is/'s	
	is not/isn't	

QUESTIONS

Am	I	
Are	you/we/they	eating?
Is	he/she/it	

SHORT ANSWERS

Yes,	I	am.
	he/she/it	is.
	you/we/they	are.
No,	I	am not.
	he/she/it	isn't.
	you/we/they	aren't.

We use present continuous verbs to talk about things that are happening now.

I'm watching sport on TV.

SPELLING

Most verbs	add *-ing* to the infinitive	*watch* → **watching** *find* → **finding**
Verbs ending in *-e*	take off *-e*, then add *-ing*	*like* → **liking** *write* → **writing**
Verbs with one syllable, ending in consonant plus vowel plus consonant	repeat the last consonant and add *-ing*	*put* → **putting** *run* → **running**

PRACTICE

1 **Complete the sentences with the present continuous form of the verbs in brackets.**

1 My parents _____ (not watch) TV. They _____ (listen) to music.

2 I _____ (write) an email to my cousin in France.

3 **A:** _____ (you, do) your homework?
   B: No, I _____ (not). I _____ (play) a computer game.

4 Tom _____ (run) to work because he's late.

5 Maria _____ (not wash) her hair.

2 **Underline and correct the spelling mistakes in the sentences.**

1 Ben is readding one of his books.
   ....

2 Emma and Anna are puting their clothes away.
   ....

3 Are you cookeing our lunch?
   ....

4 I'm siting in the kitchen.
   ....

5 My brother and sister are danceing in the garden.
   ....

PRESENT SIMPLE OR PRESENT CONTINUOUS?

We use the present continuous to talk about things that are happening now.

We're watching television at the moment.

We use the present simple:

- to talk about things we do regularly.

  I usually **watch** television in the evening.

  I **walk** to work.

- with verbs that describe states (things that don't change) e.g. *be, like, hate, have, want, love, know, understand.*

  I **like** tea but I **hate** coffee.

  I **have** three brothers, and I **love** them all.

We do not usually use state verbs in the present continuous.

I understand German and Spanish.

~~I am understanding~~ German and Spanish.

The verb *have* is a state verb when we talk about things that don't change.

I **have** two brothers.

We can use the continuous form of *have* when we talk about actions.

We'**re having** breakfast.

He'**s having** a wash.

PRACTICE

3 Choose the correct words to complete the sentences.

1 My brother and I *go/are going* to college by bus every day.

2 Dan can't come out. He *does/'s doing* his homework.

3 I *love/am loving* the holidays.

4 Oh no! It *starts/'s starting* to rain.

5 My sister and I *play/are playing* tennis every Saturday.

6 In our family, we *have/are having* a dog and three cats.

4 Underline and correct the mistakes in these sentences.

1 After school, we are usually getting home at five o'clock.

2 Ssh! I listen to the news on the radio.

3 Everyone in my family is hating cold weather.

4 Mateo is having a son and a daughter.

5 Jon has a shower at the moment.

6 Am I talking too quickly? Are you understanding me?

PAST SIMPLE

BE – POSITIVE AND NEGATIVE SENTENCES

I/He/She/It	was	at home yesterday.
	was not/ wasn't	
You/We/They	were	
	were not/ weren't	

BE – QUESTIONS

Was	I/he/she/it	at home yesterday?
Were	you/we/they	

BE – SHORT ANSWERS

Yes,	I/he/she/it	was.
	you/we/they	were.
No,	I/he/she/it	wasn't.
	you/we/they	weren't.

We use *was/were* to talk about the past.
We **were** at college yesterday.
Our new teacher **was** very interesting.

OTHER VERBS

POSITIVE AND NEGATIVE SENTENCES

I/You/He/She/It/ We/They	enjoyed	the film last night.
	did not/didn't enjoy	

QUESTIONS

Did	I/you/he/she/it/ we/they	enjoy the film?

SHORT ANSWERS

Yes,	I/you/he/she/it/ we/they	did.
No,		didn't.

We use the past simple to talk about finished events in the past.
We **studied** a lot today.
I **watched** TV last night.
We often use time expressions with past simple verbs, for example, *last year, yesterday, a week ago.*

SPELLING OF PAST SIMPLE REGULAR VERBS

Most verbs	add -ed	watch → **watched**
Verbs ending in -e	add -d	like → **liked**
Verbs with one syllable, ending in consonant plus vowel plus consonant	repeat the last consonant and add -ed	stop → **stopped**
Verb ending in a consonant + -y	change -y to -i and add -ed	study → **studied**

We **texted** our friends about the party.

IRREGULAR VERBS

There are many irregular past simple verbs* in English. Here are some common ones.

PRESENT SIMPLE	PAST SIMPLE
break	broke
come	came
do	did
drink	drank
eat	ate
get	got
give	gave
go	went
have	had
leave	left
see	saw
take	took

We **left** home at 8.30.
We **went** on holiday to France last year.
*There is a list of irregular verbs on page 226.

PRACTICE

1 **Complete the short conversations with the past simple form of the verbs in brackets.**

1 **A:** Why _____ (be) you late for work yesterday?

     B: Our bus _____ (break) down, so we _____ (walk).

2 **A:** What _____ you _____ (have) for breakfast this morning?

     B: I _____ (eat) toast and eggs and I _____ (drink) orange juice.

3 **A:** What _____ you _____ (get) for your birthday?

     B: I _____ (get) a new phone from my brother, and my sister _____ (give) me a T-shirt.

4 **A:** _____ you _____ (go) out yesterday?

     B: Yes, we _____ . We _____ (go) to a club.

5 **A:** _____ you _____ (watch) the football match on TV?

     B: No, I _____ . My dad _____ (take) me to the game. It _____ (be) great!

6 **A:** I _____ (come) to see you this morning, but you _____ (not be) in.

     B: Sorry I _____ (be) at the dentist.

2 **Complete these sentences with the past simple form of the irregular verbs in the box.**

begin	buy	feel	leave	make	meet	win

1 We _____ home this morning at 7.30.

2 I _____ two races at the weekend but I _____ very tired afterwards.

3 My brother and I _____ lunch for the whole family yesterday.

4 I _____ my friends in town on Saturday. We _____ some new clothes.

5 I _____ to do my homework at seven o'clock. That's three hours ago.

CAN/CAN'T, COULD/COULDN'T + INFINITIVE WITHOUT TO

We use *can/can't* to talk about present abilities.
I **can play** the piano.
I **can't play** the guitar.
Can you **speak** French?
Yes, I **can**. / No, I **can't**.

We use *could/couldn't* to talk about past abilities.
My sister **could talk** before she **could walk**.
I **couldn't sleep** last night.
Could you hear what I said?
Yes, I **could**. / No, I **couldn't**.

The infinitive without *to* follows *can/can't* and *could/couldn't*.
The forms of *can, can't, could, couldn't* do not change.
He **can** (not ~~cans~~) cook.

PRACTICE

1 Complete these sentences with *can/can't* or *could/couldn't*.

1 I've broken my arm so I _____ play tennis at the moment.
2 Some babies _____ swim before they _____ walk.
3 I _____ hear what you're saying. The music is too loud.
4 My mother says I _____ walk when I was one year old, but I _____ when I was two.
5 **A:** _____ you cook?
  B: No, I _____ .

2 Write questions starting with *can* or *could* and then give short answers that are true for you.

1 ride a bike when you were five?
   Could you ride a bike when you were five?
   Yes, I could.

2 swim when you were three?
   _____

3 speak more than two languages?
   _____

4 skateboard?
   _____

5 both of your parents drive?
   _____

SHOULD/SHOULDN'T

We use *should/shouldn't* + infinitive to give someone advice.
You **should do** more exercise.
You **shouldn't eat** too much before you go to bed.

POSITIVE AND NEGATIVE SENTENCES

I/He/She/It/You/We/They	**should eat** more fruit and vegetables.
	shouldn't eat a lot of fast food.

QUESTION FORMS AND SHORT ANSWERS

Should	I/you/we/they he/she/it	ask someone to help me?
Yes,	I/you/we/they he/she/it	**should**.
No,	I/you/we/they he/she/it	**shouldn't**.

PRACTICE

3 **Complete the table with this advice to students before an exam.**

> Go to bed early.

> Work late the day before.

> Spend too much time alone.

> Ask parents or friends to help you.

> Worry.

YOU SHOULD ...	*YOU SHOULDN'T ...*

4 **Complete the sentences with *should/shouldn't* and the verbs in the box.**

arrive   drink   eat   get   ride   wear

1 If it's very hot, you _____ lots of water.
2 If it's cold, you _____ your hat and coat.
3 You _____ too much sugar. It's bad for your teeth.
4 You _____ that bike. There's a problem with it.
5 If you're always tired you _____ more sleep.
6 Students _____ late for school.

PAST CONTINUOUS

POSITIVE AND NEGATIVE SENTENCES

I/He/She/It	was	**listening** to music.
	was not/wasn't	
You/We/They	were	
	were not/weren't	

QUESTIONS

Was	I/he/she/it	**listening** to music?
Were	you/we/they	

SHORT ANSWERS

Yes,	I/he/she/it	**was**.
	you/we/they	**were**.
No,	I/he/she/it	**wasn't**.
	you/we/they	**weren't**.

We use the past continuous:
* to talk about something happening over a period of time in the past.
  *We **were watching** a film at 8 o'clock last night.*
* to talk about two things happening at the same time.
  *They **were watching** the film while I **was doing** the housework.*
* with the past simple to talk about one thing happening in the middle of another.
  *When I left home, my brother **was eating** his breakfast.*
  *While I **was walking** into town, it started to rain.*

PRACTICE

1 **Choose the correct verbs to complete the sentences.**

1 We *listened/were listening* to the news while we *had/were having* lunch.
2 I *slept/was sleeping* when you *phoned/were phoning* this morning.
3 At 3 o'clock this afternoon I *did/was doing* a maths test at college.
4 When I *woke up/was waking up* this morning, it *rained/was raining*.
5 What *are you doing/were you doing* at 10 o'clock last night?

2 **Complete the story with past forms of verbs from the box. You need seven past continuous and three past simple verbs.**

| be | come | drive | listen | pass | read | see | stand | tell | travel |

It was a sunny morning and my parents, my sister and I ¹_____ along a busy motorway.
We ²_____ to Scotland to spend the weekend with some family friends. My sister and I ³_____
magazines and Mum and Dad ⁴_____ to music on the car radio. Suddenly we ⁵_____ bright blue
lights on the road in front of us. A policeman in a yellow jacket ⁶_____ in the middle of the road.
He ⁷_____ everyone to drive more slowly. After a few minutes we ⁸_____ a burning car.
Smoke ⁹_____ out of its engine. There were two fire engines at the side of the road near to it.
Luckily, no-one ¹⁰_____ hurt.

PAST CONTINUOUS AND PAST SIMPLE

WITH *WHEN*, *WHILE* AND *AS*

We can use these words with the past continuous and the past simple to introduce an action happening at the same
time as another.
*Matt was walking home **when** it started to snow.*
*The doorbell rang **while** I was having dinner.*
*They came **as** we were leaving.*

PRACTICE

3 **Choose the correct options to complete the sentences.**

1 While I *watched/was watching* TV, my sister was doing her homework.
2 My friends *often phoned/were often phoning* me when my parents were out.
3 While I was talking to my friend, I *realised/was realising* that something was wrong.
4 It was a lovely day. The sun *shone/was shining* and the birds *sang/were singing*.
5 Paul Pogba *won/was winning* the World Cup with France in Moscow.

4 **Complete the sentences with the past simple or past continuous form of the verbs in brackets.**

1 While I _____ (tidy) my room, I _____ (find) some old photos.
2 As I _____ (leave) the cinema, I _____ (realise) that I'd left my phone behind.
3 While Simon _____ (watch) television, his brother _____ (cook) dinner.
4 When we _____ (hear) the fire alarm, we all _____ (stop) what we _____ (do) and _____ (walk)
out of the building.
5 My computer _____ (crash) while I _____ (update) my web page.

UNIT 6

COUNTABLE AND UNCOUNTABLE NOUNS

COUNTABLE NOUNS	UNCOUNTABLE NOUNS
• are things we can count. *a* **school**, *two* **teachers**, *three* **students**	• are things we cannot count. **air, milk, money**
• can be singular or plural. *one* **student**, *two* **students**	• can't be plural. ~~airs, milks~~ or ~~informations~~
• take *a, an* or numbers. *I am* **a student**. *I have* **three teachers**.	• do not go after *a, an* or numbers. *I like* **water**. *I like* ~~a water~~.

Note:

We use *a* or *an*:

• with singular, countable nouns mentioned for the first time.

A *young child needs a lot of sleep.*

• to talk about jobs.

I want to be **a** *teacher.*

We do not use *a* or *an* with uncountable nouns.

If you have information, you have power.

We use *an* before words which begin with a vowel sound. (including words with a silent 'h').

I've bought **an** *app.*

Let's go there in **an** *hour.*

SOME AND ANY

USE *SOME*	USE *ANY*
• with plural countable nouns. **Some students** *are taking an exam today.* • with uncountable nouns in affirmative sentences. *I've got* **some money** *in my pocket.* • in offers or requests. *Would you like* **some** *coffee? Can you lend me* **some** *money, please?*	• with plural nouns in negative sentences and questions. *We haven't got* **any books** *with us. Have you got* **any questions**? • with uncountable nouns in negative sentences and questions. *She hasn't got* **any money**. *Do we have* **any coffee**?

PLURAL FORMS

For most nouns, add -s	*student* → **students** *banana* → **bananas**
For nouns which end in -s, -ch, -sh, -x, add -es	*bus* → **buses** *match* → **matches** *dish* → **dishes** *box* → **boxes**
For some nouns which end in -f or -fe, change -f to -v and add -es	*half* → **halves** *knife* → **knives** *wife* → **wives**
For nouns which end in consonant + -y, change the -y to -ies	*family* → **families** *city* → **cities**
Some nouns are irregular.	*child* → **children** *man* → **men** *woman* → **women** *person* → **people**

PRACTICE

1 **Complete the table with the nouns in the box.**

baby	box	bread	child	coffee	juice	knife
man	milk	money	person	rice	school	
strawberry	student	tea	teacher	water		

COUNTABLE NOUNS	UNCOUNTABLE NOUNS
baby	

2 **Write the plural forms of the countable nouns in Exercise 1.**

baby babies

3 **Complete the sentences with** *a, an, some* **or** *any*.

1 Would you like _____ apple?

2 Do we need _____ vegetables?

3 _____ students are not at college today.

4 Please can I have _____ water?

5 We haven't got _____ coffee.

6 There's _____ mobile phone on the floor.

EXPRESSIONS OF QUANTITY

We use these words and phrases to talk about quantity.

- Use *How much* with uncountable nouns.
  How much money have you got?
  How much food do we need for our party?
- Use *How many* with plural countable nouns.
  How many students are in your class?
  How many people are coming to our party?
- Use *a little* (= not much) with uncountable nouns.
  Can I borrow **a little sugar**, please?
  There's still **a little time** left.
- Use *a few* (= not many) with plural countable nouns.
  Can I borrow **a few cups**, please?
  There are **a few good films** on TV tonight.
- Use *a lot of* (= a large number) with plural countable nouns and uncountable nouns.
  There are **a lot of people** in the supermarket.
  We've got **a lot of money** in the bank.
- Use *no* (= not any) with plural countable nouns and uncountable nouns.
  There are **no vegetables** in the kitchen.
  There's **no milk** in the fridge.

PRACTICE

4 Choose the correct words to complete the conversation.

A: ¹*How much/How many* food do we need for the party?

B: I'm not sure. ²*How much/How many* people are coming?

A: ³*A lot of/A little* adults and ⁴*a little/a few* children.

B: OK, so we need ⁵*a lot of/a few* food. And drinks?

A: We have ⁶*no/a little* drinks at the moment.

B: OK. Let's get ⁷*a few/a little* orange juice for the children and ⁸*a few/a little* other things for the adults.

IMPERATIVES

We use the imperative form when we tell someone to do something or not to do something.

- Positive sentences
  Turn to page 50.
  Be quick!

- Negative sentences
  Don't be late!
  Don't eat so quickly.

We can make imperatives sound more polite by adding *please*.
Turn to page 50, **please**.
Please don't eat so quickly.
We do not use subject pronouns with imperatives.
Get up! (not ~~You get up!~~)
Don't be late! (not ~~Don't you be late!~~)

We also use imperatives for:

- instructions or directions.
  Boil a litre of water.
  Turn left at the end of the road.
- advice.
  Rest as much as possible.
  Don't worry!

- orders or warnings.
  Be quiet!
  Don't touch that!
- requests.
  Please **close** the door quietly.
- invitations.
  Come to my party!

PRACTICE

5 Complete the sentences with the correct form of the verbs in brackets.

1 _____ your phone here. (use)

2 _____ here. (shout) _____ quietly. (talk)

3 _____ here. (run) _____ slowly. (walk)

4 _____ in here. (come) _____ the other door. (use)

6 Write sentences with imperatives for these situations. Use one of the verbs in the box and the words in brackets.

| ~~buy~~ | forget | go | wash | watch |

1 These jeans are too small for me. (some new ones)
  Buy some new ones.

2 My hands are very dirty. (them)

3 It's Mum's birthday at the weekend. (to buy her a present)

4 The radio is really loud. (it off)

5 I'm really tired. (to bed)

UNIT 7

PRESENT PERFECT

POSITIVE AND NEGATIVE SENTENCES

I/You/We/They	**have/'ve** **have not/haven't**	**been** to Australia. learned to cook.
He/She/It	**has/'s** **has not/hasn't**	

QUESTION FORMS AND SHORT ANSWERS

Have	I/you/we/they	**been** to Australia?
Has	he/she/it	
Yes,	I/you/we/they	**have**.
	he/she/it	**has**.
No,	I/you/we/they	**haven't**.
	he/she/it	**hasn't**.

- The past participle form of regular verbs is the same as the past simple.
  *walk – **walked***
  *smile – **smiled***
- You will need to learn the past participle form of irregular verbs*. Here are some common examples.

be	been
break	broken
come	come
do	done
eat	eaten
find	found
get	got
have	had
meet	met
see	seen
speak	spoken

*There is a list of irregular verbs on page 226.
- We can use the present perfect to talk about our experiences.
  ***I've seen** all the Lord of the Rings films, but **I haven't read** the books.*
- We do not say when something happened with the present perfect.
  ***I've been** to India. (not ~~I've been to India last year.~~)*
- Use the past simple to say when something happened.
  *I **went** to India **last year**.*
- We often use *ever* in present perfect questions (*ever* = in your life).
  *Have you **ever** been to India?*
  *Have you **ever** met someone famous?*
- We can use *never* to talk about things we have not done in our life.
  *She's **never** been to India.*
  *He's **never** met anyone famous.*

PRACTICE

1 Complete the sentences with the present perfect of the verb in brackets.

1. My father ________ (meet) the president of our country.
2. I ________ (never be) in a plane.
3. ________ you ever ________ (travel) to another country?
4. My brother ________ (win) a prize at college.
5. My sister ________ (never swim) in the sea.

2 Choose the correct verbs to complete the conversation.

Ben: Hi, Tim. I [1]*didn't see/haven't seen* you last week. Where were you?
Tim: On holiday in the US. [2]*Did you ever go/Have you ever been* there?
Ben: No, I [3]*didn't/haven't.* But my parents [4]*went/have been* there three or four times.
Tim: You should go. I [5]*went/have been* twice.

PRESENT PERFECT WITH *JUST*

We use *just* to talk about something that happened a short time ago. We put *just* between *have/has* and the past participle.
*I've **just spoken** to my friend Paul.*
*My dad **has just got** home from work.*

PRACTICE

3 Put *just* in the correct position in these sentences.

1. I'm really hot. I've run home from college.
2. We've finished eating.
3. I've texted my brother.
4. He's told me he passed his exam.
5. They've arrived back from India.

UNIT 8

PRESENT PERFECT WITH FOR AND SINCE

We can use the present perfect with *for* and *since* to talk about something that started in the past and continues up to the present.

I've known my best friend **for** a long time.

I've known my best friend **since** I was six.   (= I still know my best friend now.)

FOR

Use the present perfect with *for* to talk about a period of time.

I've studied English **for six years**.

We've lived in Berlin **for three months**.

SINCE

Use the present perfect with *since* to talk about when a situation started.

I've studied English **since 2015**.

We've lived in Berlin **since June**.

PRACTICE

1 **Complete the table with the time phrases in the box.**

24 hours   6 o'clock   400 years   last November   my birthday   October 12th
ten minutes   the end of May   three weeks   12 months   yesterday

FOR	SINCE

2 **Choose the correct options to complete the sentences.**

1 I haven't seen my sister for *last weekend/two weeks*.

2 My parents have been married for *1993/25 years*.

3 I haven't done any cooking since *last weekend/two weeks*.

4 I've had my car since *January/six months*.

5 My father has worked as a doctor for *1994/23 years*.

6 Juan has played the piano since *the age of nine/nine years*.

PRESENT PERFECT WITH YET AND ALREADY

We use *already* and *yet* with present perfect verbs to talk about things that have happened before now but have a connection with now.

ALREADY

- We use *already* to talk about something that happened before now or before we expected.
  *I've **already had** my lunch.* (I'm not hungry now.)
  *We've **already told** Mike where the match is.* (Mike knows, so you don't need to tell him.)
  ***Have** you **already finished** your homework? That was quick!* (The speaker did not expect this.)
- We put *already* between *have/has* and the past participle or at the end of a sentence.
  *I've **already** seen him. / I've seen him **already**.*

YET

- We use *yet* (= until now) in negative sentences and questions to talk about things we plan to do in the future, but which are not done. *Yet* is placed at the end of a sentence.
  ***Have** you **finished** your homework **yet**?*
  *I **haven't read** your email **yet**.*

PRACTICE

3 Put the words in brackets in the correct position in these sentences.

1 Have you _____ tidied your bedroom _____ ? (yet)
2 They've _____ finished _____ their college project. (already)
3 I don't want to watch that programme. I've _____ seen it _____ twice. (already)
4 Tania doesn't want _____ to go to bed _____ . She isn't tired. (yet)

4 Put the words in order to make sentences.

1 I / haven't / my / new / shoes / worn / yet

   ....

2 eating / finished / already / We've

   ....

3 already / all / friends / I've / my / texted

   ....

4 book / finished / Have / reading / that / yet / you / ?

   ....

5 sister / I've / already / my / older / phoned

   ....

UNIT 9

-ING OR TO INFINITIVE AFTER VERBS, ADJECTIVES AND PREPOSITIONS

WE USE *TO* + INFINITIVE AFTER:		
some verbs	choose, help, hope, learn, offer, want	I **hope to go** to university next year. He **wants to help** me. I'm **learning to speak** Italian.
adjectives	happy, difficult, etc.	They were **happy to see** me. This exercise isn't **difficult to do**. She was **surprised to hear** I was ill.
other phrases	would like/love/hate, can't be bothered, planning, hoping	We'**d like to come** and see you later. I **can't be bothered to do** that now. He's **planning to go** to university next year. She's **hoping to get** a new job.

WE USE THE *-ING* FORM AFTER:		
some verbs	enjoy, finish, keep, mind, miss	I **enjoy watching** all sports. We **finished doing** our homework. I **miss seeing** my friends.
prepositions	for, of, about, etc.	Thanks **for helping** me.
other phrases	can't stand feel like, keen on, excited about	I **can't stand waiting** in long queues. She **feels like doing** something special at the weekend. They **are keen on** fishing. I'm **excited about going** to Thailand.

PRACTICE

1 **Choose the correct words to complete these sentences.**

1 I'm pleased *to tell/telling* you the job is yours.
2 My dad offered *to help/helping* me with the shopping.
3 I enjoy *to play/playing* the piano.
4 Let's finish *to watch/watching* the film before we go to bed.
5 My brother and I enjoy *to play/playing* video games.
6 Thank you for *to help/helping* me.

2 **Underline the mistakes and correct them.**

1 My friends and always enjoy to meet in town on Saturdays.
....
2 I hope visiting Brazil one day.
....
3 I'm sorry hearing you're ill.
....
4 All my friends enjoy watch football.
....
5 Do you mind to wait a little longer?
....

3 **Complete the sentences with the correct form of the verbs in brackets.**

1 My friends would love .... (visit) you in your new flat.
2 He's very keen on .... (play) chess.
3 I really feel like .... (have) a barbecue tonight.
4 He can't be bothered .... (finish) his project.
5 He's planning .... (spend) more time with his family.
6 She's hoping .... (pass) her exams.
7 They can't stand .... (be) late.
8 She feels like .... (go) out with her friends.

THE FUTURE WITH WILL

We can use *will/won't* + infinitive without *to* when we talk about the future.

POSITIVE AND NEGATIVE SENTENCES

I/You/He/She/It/ We/They	**will/'ll** **will not/won't**	**see** them tomorrow.

QUESTIONS

Will	I/you/he/she/it/ we/they	**see** Ben tomorrow?

SHORT ANSWERS

Yes,	I/you/he/she/it/ we/they	**will**.
No,		**won't**.

We can use *will/won't* with these words and phrases:
*   *I think/I don't think*
    I **think** Brazil **will** win the match.
*   *sure*
    I'm **sure** you**'ll** pass the English test.
*   *maybe/probably/perhaps*
    Maybe they**'ll** be late for the party.
    I**'ll probably** go to bed quite late tonight.
    Perhaps we**'ll** have a picnic at the weekend.

We can use *will/won't*:
*   to talk about things in the future.
    I think **it will be** warm and sunny tomorrow.
    I'm sure **it won't be** cold and rainy.
*   for something we decide at the time of speaking.
    A: The phone's ringing.
    B: I**'ll** answer it.

WILL AND SHALL FOR OFFERS AND PROMISES

Will and *Shall* are used to express intentions that you decide instantly when you are speaking, such as offers and promises.
Those bags look really heavy. **I'll** *carry them to the car for you.* (offer)
I will *always be your best friend.* (promise)
There are lots of dirty dishes. **Shall I** *do the washing up?* (offer)

PRACTICE

1 **Complete the sentences with *will* or *won't* and the verbs in brackets.**

1   We _____ (not have) time to go shopping before we leave.
2   There's someone at the door. I _____ (go) and see who it is.
3   **A:** _____ you _____ (be) away long?
    B: No, I _____ .
4   I probably _____ (not pass) the maths test. I think it _____ (be) really difficult.
5   I'm sure we _____ (meet) again soon.

2 Put the words in order to make sentences.

1 for / go / holiday / next / our / probably / Spain / to / We'll / year.

....

2 be / colder / I / it / think / tomorrow. / will

....

3 a / have / new / next / Perhaps / teacher / term. / we'll

....

4 Are / be / OK / sure / you / you'll / ?

....

5 come / He / our / party. / probably / to / won't

....

3 Choose the correct options to complete the sentences.

1 *Shall/Will* I make you a cup of tea?
2 Don't worry! *I'll/I shall* help you with your project.
3 *Will/Shall* you love me forever?
4 We *shall not/won't* go by car tonight.
5 Both of the specials sound good, but I think I *will/shall* have the fish pie.
6 Oh no, you've spilled soup on your dress. *I'll/I shall* get you something to clean it.

4 Match sentences 1–6 with sentences a–f.

1 Thank you for lending me the money!
2 I can't hear the TV.
3 We haven't got any sugar.
4 I've got a bad headache.
5 I'm starving.
6 It's hot in here.

a Shall I get you some aspirin?
b I'll pay you back next month.
c Shall I turn up the volume?
d I'll open the window.
e Shall I buy some?
f I'll make you a sandwich.

MAY/MIGHT

Use *may* and *might* (*not*) + infinitive when we are not sure about something in the present or the future.
Jenny **might** be too busy to help us at the moment.
It **may be** sunny tomorrow.
My parents **might buy** a new car next week.
It **may not rain** this evening.
We **might not go** to Jack's party at the weekend.

PRACTICE

5 Ben asks six of his friends if they are coming to his party. Here are their replies. Who is going to the party?

1 I might come. I'll tell you tomorrow. (Suzie)
2 Not sure, I may have to check with my brother. (Hannah)
3 Yes, I'll be there. (Tom)
4 Probably not. I may have to go out with my brother. (Mike)
5 Of course. What time does it start? (Julie)
6 I hope so, but I may have to work. (Ryan)

6 Match sentences 1–6 with sentences a–f.

1 I'm feeling really tired.
2 I'm really hungry.
3 I may phone my brother.
4 I might not go to work.
5 My dad has a new job.
6 Don't call me tonight.

a He might know where my books are.
b I'm not feeling very well.
c We might move house.
d I might be busy.
e I might go to bed early.
f I might have something to eat.

UNIT 11

BE GOING TO

POSITIVE AND NEGATIVE SENTENCES

I	am/'m am not/'m not	
He/She/It	is/'s is not/isn't	going to watch TV all evening.
You/We/They	are/'re are not/aren't	

QUESTIONS AND SHORT ANSWERS

Am	I	
Is	he/she/it	going to stay in tonight?
Are	you/we/they	

SHORT ANSWERS

Yes,	I	am.
	he/she/it	is.
	you/we/they	are.
No,	I	'm not.
	he/she/it	isn't.
	you/we/they	aren't.

Use *going to* + infinitive to talk about:

* future plans.
  I'm going to spend all evening on my studies.
  I'm not going to fall asleep.
* things we predict because of something we can see or because of information we have now.
  It's going to rain. Look at those dark clouds.
  My older sister **is going to have** a baby.

PRACTICE

1 Complete the sentences with *going to* and a verb from the box. There is one verb you do not need to use.

do   miss   (not) need   talk   ride   visit

1 It nearly 8 o'clock. You _____ your bus.
2 Tomorrow morning we _____ our bikes to work.
3 I _____ more exercise in future.
4 We _____ our coats. The sun is coming out.
5 My sister and I _____ our grandparents at the weekend.

2 Complete the conversations with *going to*.

1 **A:** You / have coffee for breakfast?
   Are you going to have coffee for breakfast?
   B: No / tea.
   No, I'm going to have tea.

2 **A:** What you / do this evening?

   B: I / play a video game.

3 **A:** It rain tomorrow?

   B: No, Look at the red sky. It / sunny all day.

4 **A:** What you / do when you leave college?

   B: I / look for a good job.

5 **A:** your team / win the match?

   B: No, the other team is much better. We / lose.

PRESENT CONTINUOUS FOR THE FUTURE

We can use the present continuous to talk about things happening now. We can also use it to talk about future arrangements.

*My sister **is picking** me **up** from the station tomorrow afternoon.*

*We're **having** a holiday in Florida next year.*

*I'm **seeing** the doctor later this morning.*

We use *going to* and the present continuous to talk about the future in different ways. We use *going to* when we talk about something we have decided.

*I'm **going to** have a shower tonight.*

We use the present continuous when we have an arrangement, often with other people.

*I'm **meeting** my friends at the cinema tonight.*

PRACTICE

3 **Choose the best options to complete the sentences.**

1 From now on, I'm *going to eat/eating* less fast food.
2 We're *going to catch/catching* the 8.40 train tomorrow. I have the tickets.
3 I've got toothache, so I'm *going to see/seeing* the dentist at 9.00 tomorrow.
4 **A:** What are you *going to do/doing* when you get home?
  B: I'm *going to phone/phoning* my friend.
5 We're *going to have/having* a party on Sunday. It starts at 7.30.

PRESENT SIMPLE TO TALK ABOUT THE FUTURE

We use the present simple to talk about something that is scheduled or arranged.

*I **have** a driving lesson next Friday.*

*The **plane arrives** at 7.30 this evening.*

*The **school holidays start** at the end of July.*

It's my dad's birthday tomorrow.

PRACTICE

4 **Choose the correct options to complete the sentences.**

1 The last train tonight *leaves/is leaving* at midnight.
2 He's *having/has* dinner with some friends today. They want to show him their holiday photos.
3 I think everyone *comes/is coming* to the party on Saturday.
4 The film *starts/is starting* at eight, so I'll meet you outside the cinema at ten to eight.
5 What are you going to do when you *finish/are finishing* college?

UNIT 12

ZERO CONDITIONAL

- We use the zero conditional to talk about things which are always true.

conditional clause:	main clause/result clause:
if + present verb	present simple verb
If the sun **is** too hot,	it **burns** you.

FIRST CONDITIONAL

- We use the first conditional to talk about likely situations/actions.

conditional clause:	main clause/result:
if + present simple	will + infinitive
If we **run**,	we**'ll catch** the bus.
If we **don't run**,	we **won't catch** the bus.

- The conditional clause can start or finish the sentence.
  If you work hard, you'll pass your exam. (There is a comma after the conditional clause.)
  You'll pass your exam **if** you work hard. (There is no comma after the main clause.)
- We can use the first conditional to talk about the future, but we use a present tense verb after if.
  If you **work** hard, you'll pass your exam. (not ~~If you will work hard, you'll pass your exam.~~)

PRACTICE

1 **Match the sentence beginnings (1–6) with the correct endings (a–f) to make zero and first conditional sentences.**

1	If I have time,	**a**	you get green.
2	If you mix blue and yellow	**b**	she never answers the call.
3	If he phones her,	**c**	I'll go to university.
4	If my computer breaks down again	**d**	I'll phone you.
5	If I pass all my exams,	**e**	I'll buy a new one.
6	If it gets colder than zero	**f**	the water in our pond freezes.

2 **Complete the first conditional sentences with the correct form of the verbs in brackets.**

1 If I _____ (see) my brother, I _____ (tell) him to text you.

2 You _____ (hurt) yourself if you _____ (fall) over on the ice.

3 If we _____ (not catch) the 10 o'clock bus, we _____ (have) to wait for an hour.

4 You _____ (be) late for work if you _____ (not leave) soon.

5 If the music _____ (be) loud, it _____ (wake) the baby.

3 **Put the words in order to make first conditional sentences. Don't forget to add commas to some sentences.**

1 earn / get / a new job / I / I'll / If / more money.
   If _____

2 a car / buy / enough money. / have / I / I'll / if
   I'll _____

3 a / car / to go / buy / I / I'll / If / use / to work. / it
   If _____

4 my bike / fit / get / I / I'll / if / ride / to work.
   I'll _____

5 by bus. / fit / get / go / I / I / if / to work / won't
   I _____

CONJUNCTIONS: WHEN, IF, UNLESS + PRESENT, FUTURE

WHEN

- Use *when* to talk about things that will happen at a particular time.
  When *I get home this evening, I'll have a shower.*

IF

- Use *if* for things that may or may not happen, or to say what happens if something else happens.
  If *I finish work early, I'll go swimming.*

UNLESS

- *unless* means the same as 'if not'.
  Unless *I get home early, I won't go swimming.* (= If I do not get home early, I won't go swimming.)

PRACTICE

4 **Complete these sentences with *if, when* or *unless*.**

1 .... you take me to the station, I'll have to walk.
2 We'll fail the exam .... we revise.
3 .... we hurry, we'll get there in time.
4 Let's watch the late film .... you are not too tired.
5 In some countries, you can't drive .... you are over 18.
6 .... I'm sad, I usually talk to my friends.
7 .... you're not feeling better tomorrow, you should go to the doctor.
8 I'll watch some TV .... I get home tonight.

THE PASSIVE

We form the passive by using the correct form of *be* followed by the past participle.

ACTIVE	PASSIVE
We feed our cat twice a day.	Our cat **is fed** twice a day.
They built our college in 2012.	Our college **was built** in 2012.

We use passive verbs rather than active verbs when:
- we don't know who did the action.
  *My bike **was stolen last week**.*
  (I don't know who stole it.)
- we are more interested in who or what is affected by the action of the verb than who or what does the action.
  *My trainers **were made** in China.* (The focus is on my trainers rather than where someone made them.)
  *We **were given** a lot of homework to do in the holidays.* (Here, *we* are the focus, not the homework or the teachers who gave the homework.)

To say who did something, we use the passive + *by* + the person or thing.
*My stolen bike **was found by the police**.*
*These shoes **were made by my grandfather**.*

PRACTICE

5 **Complete the sentences with the present simple passive form of the verbs in brackets.**

1 A lot of tea .... (grow) in China.
2 Millions of bottles of water .... (sell) every day.
3 Interesting films .... (show) at the cinema in my town.
4 Our furniture .... (make) out of wood.
5 The road .... (close) today because of the storm.

6 **Complete the sentences with the past simple passive form of the verbs in the box.**

build	close	give	send	take	tell

1 Our house .... five years ago.
2 We .... how to get out if there was a fire in the building.
3 The factory in our town .... two years ago. Nobody works there now.
4 I .... a new watch for my birthday.
5 These photos .... on my phone.
6 I .... this email yesterday.

UNIT 13

COMPARATIVES AND SUPERLATIVES

We use comparative adjectives to talk about the difference between two people or things.

*Hannah is **younger** than her sister.*

*I am **taller** than my friend.*

Use superlative adjectives to talk about the difference between three or more people or things.

*Hannah is the **youngest** child in the family.*

*I am **the tallest** student in the class.*

- We often use *than* after comparative adjectives: *I am **younger than** her.*
- We use *the* before superlative adjectives: *She is **the youngest** person in the family.*
- We often use phrases like these after superlative adjectives: *in the family, in the world, in the class* (NOT ~~of the family, of the world, of the class~~).

SPELLING

ADJECTIVE	COMPARATIVE	SUPERLATIVE
one syllable (e.g. *small*), add *-er* or *-est*	**smaller, colder** than	the **smallest**, the **coldest**
one syllable ending in *-e* (e.g. *large, nice*), add *-r* or *-est*	**larger, nicer** than	the **largest**, the **nicest**
short adjectives ending in consonant + vowel + consonant (e.g. *big, thin*), double the consonant and add *-er* or *-est*	**bigger, thinner** than	the **biggest**, the **thinnest**
ending in consonant + *-y* (e.g. *heavy, pretty*), take off the *-y* and add *-ier* or *-iest*	**heavier, prettier** than	the **heaviest**, the **prettiest**
with three syllables or more (e.g. *difficult, important*), add *more* or *most*	**more difficult** **more important** than	the **most difficult** the **most important**
irregular adjectives (e.g. *good, bad*)	**better, worse** than	the **best**, the **worst**

PRACTICE

1 **Complete the sentences with the comparative form of the adjectives in brackets.**

1 My class is _____ than my brother's class. (big)

2 Today's meeting is _____ than yesterday's meeting. (interesting)

3 My new bike is _____ than my old one. (heavy)

4 The sea is _____ than it was last week. (warm)

5 The weather today is _____ than it was yesterday. (bad)

6 These shoes are too small. I need _____ ones. (large)

2 **Underline the mistakes and correct them.**

1 I am the better footballer at my college.

_____

2 Anna is happyer than she was this morning.

_____

3 I want to be fiter so I do lots of exercise.

_____

4 What is the more expensive thing you have?

_____

5 Ben's apartment is largerer than mine.

_____

6 Tom is taller his father.

_____

TO BE LIKE AND TO LOOK LIKE

We use *like* as a preposition in questions, with the verbs *be* and *look* to ask about appearance and character.

We use *be like* to ask about a person's character.

*What **is** she **like**?*

She is very friendly and helpful.

We use *look like* to ask about physical appearance.

*What does she **look like**?*

She's quite tall with blond hair.

PRACTICE

3   Write questions to match the answers.

1   .... ? He's short and wears glasses.
2   .... ? Our new neighbours aren't very helpful.
3   .... ? Their new baby is always happy and never cries.
4   .... ? She is very slim and has long brown hair.

AS ... AS, NOT AS ... AS

We use *as* + adjective/adverb + *as* to compare things or people that are equal in some way.

*The world's biggest mouse is **as big as** a rat.*

*The weather this winter is **as cold as** last year.*

We use *not as ... as* to compare things or people that aren't equal.

*The furniture was **not as beautiful as** I thought it would be.*

*My son isn't **as tall as** his father.*

We can modify *not as ... as* by using *not quite as* or *not nearly as*.

*The last question on the exam was **not quite as easy as** the first one.*

(The last question was easy but the first one was easier.)

*These new trainers are **not nearly as comfortable as** my old ones.*

(My old trainers are a lot more comfortable than these new ones.)

4   Underline the mistakes and correct them.

1   He is tall as his father now.
    ....

2   The climate in England is as pleasant the climate in Ireland.
    ....

3   You must play hard you can if you want to win the match.
    ....

4   This ice cream's not tasty as the one we bought yesterday.
    ....

5   I'm making as many mistakes I did yesterday.
    ....

UNIT 14

MUST/MUSTN'T

Use *must/mustn't* + infinitive without *to*:

* to talk about something that is important and there is no choice.
  I **must be** at work by 8.30 every morning.
  We **mustn't be** late.
* to give strong advice.
  You **must be** careful when you cross the road.
  You **mustn't cross** without looking.

must does not change its form.

| I/You/He/She/It/ We/They | **must wear** a uniform for school. |
| | **mustn't be** late for work. |

We do not usually use *must* in questions. We use *have to*.

What time **do we have to** be at work?

Do you have to wear a uniform for work?

To talk about the past, use *had to*.

We **had to be** at work at 7.30 yesterday.

We **had to take** an exam.

PRACTICE

1 Complete the sentences with *must/mustn't* and verbs in the box.

be   finish   run   talk   use   wear

1 Be quick! We _____ late or we'll miss the start of the film.
2 You _____ trainers when you play tennis.
3 You _____ across the road. It's very dangerous.
4 Shh. You _____ in the library!
5 Put your phone away. You _____ it in the cinema.
6 I _____ my project by tomorrow.

2 Complete the advice to tourists. Use *must* or *mustn't* and a verb.

1 _____ the museum. It's really interesting!
2 _____ the taxis. They're very expensive. Use the metro.
3 _____ the pizza restaurant. They have fantastic food.
4 _____ your passport. Keep it somewhere safe!
5 _____ the cathedral. It's a beautiful building.

HAVE TO

We use *have, has to* + infinitive to talk about things that are necessary.
We have to go to work five days a week.
We use *don't have, doesn't have to* + infinitive to talk about things that are not necessary.
We don't have to go to work at the weekend.

POSITIVE AND NEGATIVE SENTENCES

I/You/We/They	have to	go to work tomorrow.
	don't have to	
He/She/It	has to	
	doesn't have to	

QUESTIONS

Do	I/you/we/they	have to go to work tomorrow?
Does	he/she/it	

SHORT ANSWERS

Yes,	I/you/we/they	do.
	he/she/it	does.
No,	I/you/we/they	don't.
	he/she/it	doesn't.

3 Complete the conversation with the correct form of *have to* and the verbs in brackets.

A: Hi. Do you want to go swimming?
B: No, I can't. My sister and I ¹＿＿＿＿ (help) our flatmate.
A: What ²＿＿＿＿ (you do)?
B: To start with I ³＿＿＿＿ (tidy) the house.
A: And your sister? ⁴＿＿＿＿ (tidy) the house, too?
B: Yes, ⁵＿＿＿＿ , and then she ⁶＿＿＿＿ (wash) the car. And you?
A: I ⁷＿＿＿＿ (not do) anything!

4 Choose the correct verb to complete the sentences.

1 Teachers *have to/don't have to* work in schools.
2 Students *have to/don't have to* go to college in the holidays.
3 Young children *have to/don't have to* go to work every day.
4 Farmers *have to/don't have to* work outside.
5 Police officers *have to/don't have to* wear uniforms.

NEED TO

We use *need to* + verb to express that it is important for us to do something.
She **needs to go** to London at the weekend.
I **need to get up** early tomorrow for my doctor's appointment.
You **need to spend** more time with your family.
We **need to study** harder or we'll fail the exam.

DON'T NEED TO

We use *don't need to* to express that something isn't necessary, but possible. We can use *don't need to* to express that we don't expect someone to do something.
You **don't need to come** early tomorrow.
He **doesn't need to worry** about passing the exam. He's a great student.
I **don't need to work** next Monday.

5 Put the words in order to make sentences with modals.

1 by Friday. / need to / You don't / finish the project
2 everything is OK. / I / home / need to phone / to check that
3 harder or / very good marks. / I really / I won't get / need to work
4 dinner tonight. / needs to / some food for / She / buy

CAN/CAN'T

We use the modal *can* to show that something is possible:
It **can be** very hot in summer. (= It is sometimes very hot in summer.)
You **can** easily get lost in that part of town. (= People often get lost in that part of town.)
We use the negative *can't* or *cannot* to show that something is impossible.
You **can't be** 43. You look so young.
You **cannot be** serious!

6 Put the words in order to make sentences.

1 Anyone / become / famous. / rich and / can

2 very hard. / Learning / can be / a foreign language

3 fifty pounds. / A room / can't cost / in a small hotel / more than

4 around the house. / small children / When you have / you can't leave objects

IRREGULAR VERB LIST

VERB	PAST SIMPLE	PAST PARTICIPLE
be	was/were	been
beat	beat	beaten
become	became	become
begin	began	begun
bend	bent	bent
bite	bit	bitten
bleed	bled	bled
blow	blew	blown
break	broke	broken
bring	brought	brought
build	built	built
burn	burnt/burned	burnt/burned
buy	bought	bought
catch	caught	caught
choose	chose	chosen
come	came	come
cost	cost	cost
cut	cut	cut
deal	dealt	dealt
dig	dug	dug
do	did	done
draw	drew	drawn
dream	dreamt/dreamed	dreamt/dreamed
drink	drank	drunk
drive	drove	driven
eat	ate	eaten
fall	fell	fallen
feed	fed	fed
feel	felt	felt
fight	fought	fought
find	found	found
fly	flew	flown
forbid	forbade	forbidden
forget	forgot	forgotten
forgive	forgave	forgiven
freeze	froze	frozen
get	got	got
give	gave	given
go	went	gone
grow	grew	grown
hang	hung	hung
have	had	had
hear	heard	heard
hide	hid	hidden
hit	hit	hit
hold	held	held
hurt	hurt	hurt
keep	kept	kept
kneel	knelt	knelt
know	knew	known
lay	laid	laid
lead	led	led
learn	learnt/learned	learnt/learned
leave	left	left

VERB	PAST SIMPLE	PAST PARTICIPLE
lend	lent	lent
let	let	let
lie	lay	lain
light	lit	lit
lose	lost	lost
make	made	made
mean	meant	meant
meet	met	met
pay	paid	paid
put	put	put
read	read	read
ride	rode	ridden
ring	rang	rung
rise	rose	risen
run	ran	run
say	said	said
see	saw	seen
sell	sold	sold
send	sent	sent
set	set	set
sew	sewed	sewn
shake	shook	shaken
shine	shone	shone
shoot	shot	shot
show	showed	shown
shut	shut	shut
sing	sang	sung
sink	sank	sunk
sit	sat	sat
sleep	slept	slept
smell	smelt/smelled	smelt/smelled
speak	spoke	spoken
spell	spelt/spelled	spelt/spelled
spend	spent	spent
spill	spilt/spilled	spilt/spilled
spoil	spoilt/spoiled	spoilt/spoiled
stand	stood	stood
steal	stole	stolen
stick	stuck	stuck
strike	struck	struck
sweep	swept	swept
swim	swam	swum
swing	swung	swung
take	took	taken
teach	taught	taught
tear	tore	torn
tell	told	told
think	thought	thought
throw	threw	thrown
understand	understood	understood
wake	woke	woken
wear	wore	worn
win	won	won
write	wrote	written

PHRASAL VERB BANK

A phrasal verb is a verb with two or three parts. The meaning of the verb is sometimes different from the meaning of its separate parts. Phrasal verbs can combine verbs with prepositions or adverbs.

This section focuses on phrasal verbs related to four topics: **getting about**, **in the morning**, **people and communication** and **other phrasal verbs**.

GETTING ABOUT

1 **Match the phrasal verbs to the definitions below.**

> come in   get back   come round
> pick (someone) up   take off

.... = return
.... = leave the ground (a plane)
.... = visit someone's house
.... = enter a place
.... = collect someone from somewhere

PRACTICE

2 **Complete the sentences with the correct form of the phrasal verbs from Exercise 1.**

1 Our plane .... at three tomorrow afternoon.
2 We're away for a few days, but I'll call you when we ....
3 Yesterday evening my dad .... from school in his car.
4 You look tired. Why don't you .... and sit down.
5 I .... to your house yesterday but you were out.

3 **Write a sentence using each of the phrasal verbs.**

IN THE MORNING

1 **Match the phrasal verbs to the definitions below.**

> get up   go out   put something on
> take something off   wake up

.... = stop wearing
.... = stop sleeping
.... = get out of bed
.... = leave
.... = start wearing

PRACTICE

2 **Complete the sentences with the correct form of the phrasal verbs from Exercise 1.**

1 I usually .... at 6.30 and then listen to music for 20 minutes.
2 My mother calls me at 6.50 and I ....
3 Next I .... my night clothes and have a shower.
4 Then I .... my school uniform .... and have breakfast.
5 I usually .... at about 7.45 to catch the bus to school.

3 **Write a sentence using each of the phrasal verbs.**

PEOPLE AND COMMUNICATION

1 **Match the phrasal verbs to the definitions below.**

> call someone back   find out   get on with someone
> grow up   look after

.... = become an adult
.... = return a phone call
.... = get information about
.... = take care of
.... = be friendly with someone

OTHER PHRASAL VERBS

1 **Match the phrasal verbs to the definitions below.**

> fill in   give back   lie down
> try on   turn off

.... = usually something you do before you go
          to sleep
.... = stop a machine or light from working
.... = write information on a form
.... = give something to the person who gave it
          to you
.... = put on clothes to see if they fit

PRACTICE

2 **Complete the sentences with the correct form of the phrasal verbs from Exercise 1.**

1 I need to .... my little sister while my parents are out.

2 I .... very well with all my brothers and sisters.

3 There's a car outside our house. I want to .... who it belongs to.

4 Sorry, I have to hurry. I'll .... you .... tomorrow.

5 We live in the city now, but my parents .... in a small village.

3 **Write a sentence using each of the phrasal verbs.**

PRACTICE

2 **Complete the sentences with the correct form of the phrasal verbs from Exercise 1.**

1 I've got a bad headache so I'm going to ....

2 Don't forget to .... the lights when you leave the building.

3 I always .... shoes .... before I buy them.

4 To get a passport you have to .... a lot of forms.

5 When are you going to .... the book I lent you?

3 **Write a sentence using each of the phrasal verbs.**

WRITING BANK

HOW TO MAKE YOUR WRITING BETTER: ADJECTIVES

To make a sentence more interesting, we can use adjectives.

1 Look at the pairs of sentences. Underline the adjectives in each b sentence.

1 a There was a chair in the corner of the room.
  b There was a <u>comfortable</u> chair in the corner of the room.
2 a We had lunch in a restaurant.
  b We had lunch in a small, friendly restaurant.
3 a A woman showed me the way home.
  b A kind woman showed me the way home.
4 a I knew I had made a mistake.
  b I knew I had made a big mistake.

2 Look at Exercise 1 again. Decide if the sentences are true or false.

Adjectives …
1 describe people or things.
2 usually come after the person or thing they describe.
3 can make sentences more interesting because they add more information.

3 Complete the sentences with an adjective from the box.

expensive	heavy	important	lovely	modern

1 He was carrying a _____ suitcase.
2 I have an _____ message for you.
3 She lives in a _____ apartment.
4 We had a _____ day in the park.
5 She was wearing an _____ jacket.

4 We often use adjectives to talk about good or nice things. Choose the two adjectives which can replace *good* or *nice* in each sentence.

1 It was a very good film. (*exciting/friendly/funny*)
2 She was wearing a nice dress. (*beautiful/lovely/clever*)
3 That's a good idea. (*brilliant/famous/great*)
4 A nice doctor helped me. (*friendly/favourite/kind*)
5 The weather was nice. (*sunny/clever/pleasant*)
6 We had some good food. (*great/hungry/excellent*)

5 We often use adjectives to talk about very good or very bad things. <u>Underline</u> the adjectives which mean 'very good' or 'very bad' in each sentence. Then add them to the table.

1 It was a nice day. We had a <u>wonderful</u> meal.
2 We didn't play tennis because the weather was terrible.
3 I loved the film. It was amazing!
4 I didn't like the food. It was horrible.
5 We watched a film, but it was awful!
6 I think she's a fantastic singer. I love her songs.

VERY GOOD	VERY BAD
wonderful	

HOW TO MAKE YOUR WRITING BETTER: ADVERBS AND INTERESTING VERBS

1 **Look at the pairs of sentences. <u>Underline</u> the adverbs in each b sentence.**

1 *a* I ran home.
   b I <u>quickly</u> ran home.
2 *a* The children were playing in the garden.
   b The children were playing happily in the garden.
3 *a* I read the invitation.
   b I read the invitation carefully.
4 *a* She opened the letter.
   b She opened the letter slowly.
5 *a* I couldn't see because it was cloudy.
   b I couldn't see well because it was cloudy.

2 **Look at Exercise 1 again. Decide if the sentences are true or false.**

1 Adverbs can describe how someone does something.
2 Most adverbs end in -ly.
3 Adverbs always come before the verb.
4 Adverbs can make sentences more interesting, because they describe actions.

3 **Choose the best adverb in each sentence.**

1 A man called my name *loudly/terribly*.
2 The children ate their pizzas *kindly/hungrily*.
3 He spoke *clearly/cheaply*.
4 My friend was driving very *noisily/fast*.
5 She *carefully/busily* picked up the young bird.
6 We found the boat *easily/loudly*.
7 Everyone in the team played *quickly/well*, and we won the game!
8 She sang the song *beautifully/highly*.

4 **Complete the sentences with the adverb in brackets. Choose the correct place to put the adverb.**

1 The _____ police officer spoke to me _____ . (angrily)
   The police officer spoke to me angrily.
2 I _____ read the _____ letter. (quickly)
3 She closed _____ the door _____ . (quietly)
4 He _____ carried the hot drinks into the _____ sitting room. (carefully)
5 We walked _____ through _____ the park. (slowly)
6 Mark didn't _____ sleep _____ last night. (well)

5 **Sometimes we can use a more interesting verb instead of a verb and an adverb. <u>Underline</u> the verb in each b sentence which matches the verb + adverb in the first sentence.**

1 *a* I <u>went</u> to the bus stop <u>quickly</u>.
   b I hurried to the bus stop.
2 *a* Everyone was <u>speaking loudly</u> at the same time.
   b Everyone was shouting at the same time.
3 *a* They <u>were</u> <u>sitting quietly</u> in the garden.
   b They were relaxing in the garden.
4 *a* We <u>got into</u> the water <u>quickly</u>.
   b We jumped into the water.
5 *a* I <u>put</u> the letter <u>quickly</u> into the bin.
   b I threw the letter into the bin.
6 *a* 'I'm lost,' she <u>said sadly</u>.
   b 'I'm lost,' she cried.

6 **Complete the sentences with the verbs in the box.**

| jumped | ran | relaxed | shouted | threw |

1 She _____ into the room and picked up the phone.
2 'Go away!' he _____ .
3 We sat down and _____ for a few minutes.
4 The cat _____ into the man's arms.
5 He _____ the map onto the fire.

USE VERB FORMS CORRECTLY TO TALK ABOUT THE PAST, PRESENT AND FUTURE

1 Read the email. Underline six mistakes with verb forms.

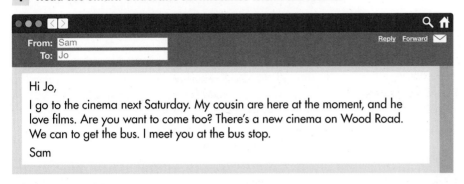

Hi Jo,
I go to the cinema next Saturday. My cousin are here at the moment, and he love films. Are you want to come too? There's a new cinema on Wood Road. We can to get the bus. I meet you at the bus stop.
Sam

2 Write the email from Exercise 1 correctly.

....

....

....

....

3 This email has more information. Read it and choose the correct options.

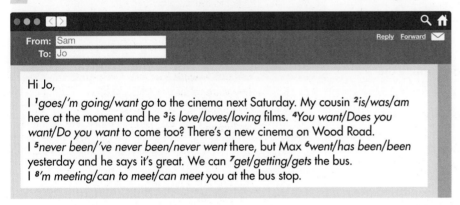

Hi Jo,
I ¹*goes/'m going/want go* to the cinema next Saturday. My cousin ²*is/was/am* here at the moment and he ³*is love/loves/loving* films. ⁴*You want/Does you want/Do you want* to come too? There's a new cinema on Wood Road. I ⁵*never been/'ve never been/never went* there, but Max ⁶*went/has been/been* yesterday and he says it's great. We can ⁷*get/getting/gets* the bus. I ⁸*'m meeting/can to meet/can meet* you at the bus stop.

4 Look at Exercise 3 again. Find an example of these things.

1 the present continuous for future plans ....
2 the past simple for an action in the past ....
3 the present perfect for an experience at some time in the past ....
4 a modal verb ....

5 Complete the email below with the correct form of the verbs in brackets.

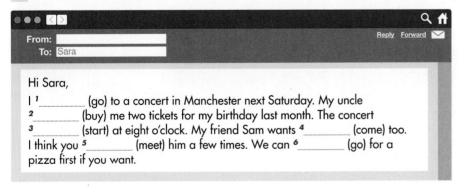

Hi Sara,
I ¹............... (go) to a concert in Manchester next Saturday. My uncle ²............... (buy) me two tickets for my birthday last month. The concert ³............... (start) at eight o'clock. My friend Sam wants ⁴............... (come) too. I think you ⁵............... (meet) him a few times. We can ⁶............... (go) for a pizza first if you want.

6 Use these notes to write an email. Try to use different verb forms correctly.

- ask a friend to come to a water park with you next Saturday
- say where it is
- say how you can get there

USE LINKING WORDS AND RELATIVE PRONOUNS TO MAKE LONGER SENTENCES

1 Read the story. How many sentences are there?

> Dan woke up. He got out of bed. He didn't look at his clock. He opened the fridge. It was almost empty. He was hungry. He decided to go out for some food. He went to a café. It was closed. It was only 6.30 in the morning!

2 Read the same story. This time, the sentences are linked with linking words. <u>Underline</u> the linking words.

> Dan woke up <u>and</u> got out of bed. He didn't look at his clock. He opened the fridge, but it was almost empty. He was hungry, so he decided to go out for some food. He went to a café, but it was closed because it was only 6.30 in the morning!

3 Choose the correct linking words to complete the sentences.

1 I wanted to go to the cinema, *but/so* I didn't have any money.
2 It was late *and/because* I was very tired.
3 It was cold, *but/so* I put on my coat.
4 We couldn't play tennis *but/because* it was raining.
5 I invited Sam, *because/but* he didn't want to come.
6 It was sunny, *but/so* we decided to have a barbecue.

4 Look at the a and b sentences. <u>Underline</u> the linking words that join the sentences in b.

1 **a** He showed me a photo. It wasn't very clear.
  b He showed me a photo which wasn't very clear.
2 **a** I saw a girl. She looked scared.
  b I saw a girl who looked scared.
3 **a** I saw a man in the street. He was singing.
  b I saw a man in the street who was singing.
4 **a** The man was carrying a bag. It looked heavy.
  b The man was carrying a bag that looked heavy.

5 Look at Exercise 4 again. Choose the correct options to complete the rules.

1 We can use *who/which* and *that* to write about people.
2 We can use *who/which* and *that* to write about things.

6 Choose the correct options to complete the stories.

> Emma was on holiday with her friends in a new city, and they wanted to go to a museum. They were lost. Then they saw a girl ¹*which/who* was holding a map. The girl showed Emma her map. But she gave Emma some directions ²*which/who* were wrong! Emma and her family found the museum, but it was closed when they arrived!

> Martin was in the city centre with his mum. He wanted to buy some new shoes, so he went to a shoe shop. He saw some black shoes ³*which/who* he liked. They were very expensive. His mum didn't have much money. She spoke to an assistant ⁴*which/who* worked in the shop. The assistant showed Martin some cheaper shoes. Martin liked these ones, too, so he got them.

WRITING PART 6: A SHORT MESSAGE

1 Read the exam task. How many things must you write about in your email? How many words should you write?

You want to borrow a bike from your English friend, Mike.
Write an email to Mike.
In your email:

- **ask** Mike if **you can borrow** his bike
- explain **why** you need it
- say when you will **give it back**

Write **25 words** or more.

MODEL ANSWER

an informal phrase to start the email   *answer the first point in the task*

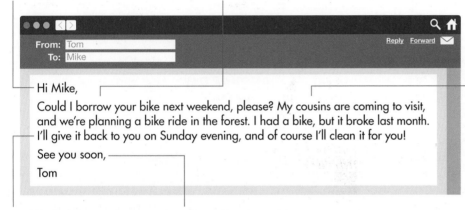

answer the second point in the task

Hi Mike,

Could I borrow your bike next weekend, please? My cousins are coming to visit, and we're planning a bike ride in the forest. I had a bike, but it broke last month. I'll give it back to you on Sunday evening, and of course I'll clean it for you!

See you soon,

Tom

answer the third point in the task   *an informal phrase to end the email*

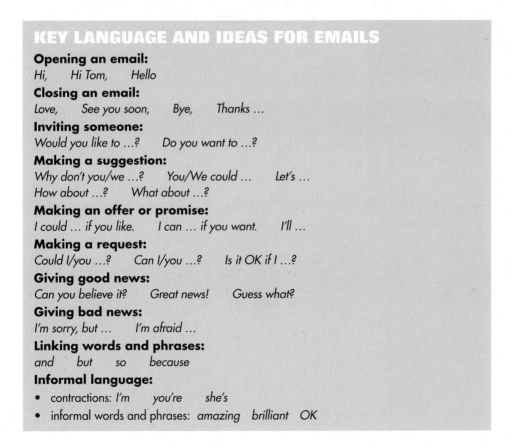

KEY LANGUAGE AND IDEAS FOR EMAILS

Opening an email:
Hi,   Hi Tom,   Hello

Closing an email:
Love,   See you soon,   Bye,   Thanks …

Inviting someone:
Would you like to …?   Do you want to …?

Making a suggestion:
Why don't you/we …?   You/We could …   Let's …
How about …?   What about …?

Making an offer or promise:
I could … if you like.   I can … if you want.   I'll …

Making a request:
Could I/you …?   Can I/you …?   Is it OK if I …?

Giving good news:
Can you believe it?   Great news!   Guess what?

Giving bad news:
I'm sorry, but …   I'm afraid …

Linking words and phrases:
and   but   so   because

Informal language:
- contractions: I'm   you're   she's
- informal words and phrases: amazing   brilliant   OK

2 Complete the suggestions with the words in the box.

could	don't	Let's	Shall	Why

1 Why _____ we get the bus together?
2 We _____ meet outside the cinema.
3 _____ we buy the tickets online?
4 _____ get the train.
5 _____ don't we go for a pizza after the show?

3 Match sentence beginnings 1–5 with endings a–e.

1	Could I borrow	*a*	with my work?
2	Can you help me	*b*	laptop?
3	Is it OK	*c*	your bike?
4	Could I stay	*d*	if I bring my friend Jack?
5	Can you bring your	*e*	at your house on Saturday night?

4 Write sentences about good or bad news. Use the word in brackets.

1 I've passed all my exams. (believe)
Can you believe it? I've passed all my exams!

2 I can't come to your party. (afraid)
_____

3 I'll be a bit late. (sorry)
_____

4 I won the competition! (guess)
_____

5 Read the email. Underline six verbs where you can use contractions.

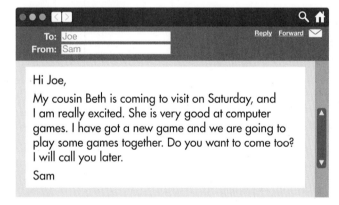

Hi Joe,

My cousin Beth is coming to visit on Saturday, and I am really excited. She is very good at computer games. I have got a new game and we are going to play some games together. Do you want to come too? I will call you later.

Sam

6 Read the exam task. What information should you include in your email?

Your English friend Laura has invited you to go to a concert with her on Saturday, but you can't go. Write an email to Laura.

In your email:
• **say** that you **can't go** on Saturday
• explain **why** you can't go
• suggest **another day** to meet

Write **25 words** or more.

7 Before you write your email, complete the table with ideas.

YOU CAN'T GO ON SATURDAY	I'm sorry, but …
WHY?	… because …
ANOTHER DAY TO MEET	Why don't we …?

8 Write your email, using your notes from Exercise 7.

9 Check your email and make changes if necessary.

☐ Have you answered all the points in Laura's email?
☐ Have you used a suitable phrase to open and close your email?
☐ Have you used a range of language?
☐ Have you used linking words to make longer sentences?
☐ Have you used contractions and informal language?
☐ Have you counted your words?

1 **Read the exam task. How many words should you write?**

Look at the three pictures.
Write the story shown in the pictures.
Write **35 words** or more.

MODEL ANSWER

this tells the first part of the story

past simple verbs for the main events in the story

adjectives and adverbs make the story more interesting

this tells the second part of the story

Mark got up and looked outside. He was happy because it was a sunny day. He decided to play football. He then found his football and hurried outside. Next, he called his friends. Later, his friends arrived, and they played together. They had a wonderful time!

this tells the third part of the story

KEY LANGUAGE AND IDEAS FOR STORIES

Give the story an interesting title:
The robbery   A day out

Use past simple and past continuous verbs:
Mark got up.   It was raining.

Use time expressions:
first   then   later   the next day

Use adjectives to describe people, places and feelings:
friendly   kind   busy   excited   angry

Use adverbs:
quickly   slowly   carefully

Use interesting verbs:
hurried   ran   shouted

2 Complete the story with the past simple or past continuous form of the verbs in brackets.

A surprise visit

Mary was at home one afternoon. She ¹_____ (feel) bored because it ²_____ (rain). Suddenly, Mary's friend Sara ³_____ (arrive) at the house. She ⁴_____ (carry) a pizza in a box, and a video game. Mary was very happy! Mary and Sara ⁵_____ (eat) the pizza together and ⁶_____ (play) the game.

3 Choose the correct time expressions to complete the stories.

Max decided to make a cake. ¹*First/Next*, he went to the supermarket to buy some eggs and butter. ²*Suddenly/Next* he mixed everything together quickly and put the cake in the oven. ³*Finally/First*, the cake was ready! Max ate a big slice, and it was fantastic!

Paula was cycling home. ⁴*First/Suddenly*, she saw a puppy in the road. It was on its own, and it looked sad. It was her friend Sam's dog. Paula called the dog to her. ⁵*Then/Finally*, she phoned Sam. ⁶*Finally/Next*, Sam arrived. He was very pleased, and the dog was so excited!

4 Cross out the adjective that is not possible in each sentence.

1 I was feeling *angry/happy/tired/tall*.
2 The waiter was very *polite/empty/kind/friendly*.
3 The town was quite *busy/quiet/pleased/old*.
4 She was wearing a *blue/big/quick/pretty* hat.
5 It was a *boring/great/high/brilliant* film.
6 He was carrying a *small/black/ready/new* suitcase.

5 Read the exam task. Before you write your story, make notes on your ideas in the table.

Look at the pictures.
Write the story shown in the pictures.
Write **35 words** or more.

PICTURE 1	
PICTURE 2	
PICTURE 3	

6 Write your story, using your notes from Exercise 5.

7 Check your story and make changes if necessary.

☐ Have you written about all three pictures?
☐ Have you used past simple verbs?
☐ Have you used adjectives and adverbs to make your story interesting?
☐ Have you counted your words?

SPEAKING BANK

GIVING PERSONAL INFORMATION

1 🎧 119 **Listen to two students giving personal information. Complete the table.**

	PABLO	**LUCIA**
AGE		
FROM		

KEY LANGUAGE AND IDEAS FOR GIVING PERSONAL INFORMATION

Saying your name:
My name is / My name's …

Saying your age:
I'm … years old.

Saying where you come from:
I come from …

Saying where you live:
I live in …

2 🎧 119 **Match the sentence beginnings 1–4 with endings a–d. Listen again and check.**

1	My	*a*	in Milan.
2	I come	*b*	name's Pablo.
3	I'm eighteen	*c*	from Madrid.
4	I live	*d*	years old.

TALKING ABOUT HABITS, LIKES AND DISLIKES

1 🎧 120 **Listen to Sophie talking about her habits. Which activities does she talk about?**

> doing homework going to the cinema
> meeting friends playing football
> playing tennis watching TV

KEY LANGUAGE AND IDEAS FOR TALKING ABOUT HABITS

I sometimes …
I often …
I usually …
I always …
I never …
I … every day/every weekend/on Saturdays.

Use words like *sometimes, often,* etc. with the present simple form of verbs:
*I **sometimes meet** my friends.*
*I **often go** to the cinema.*
*I **go out** with friends **every weekend**.*

Notice that *sometimes, often, usually,* etc. come before the main verb, but after the verb *be*. Phrases such as *every day, every weekend, on Saturdays* come at the end:
*I **never play** football.*
*I'**m never** late.*
*I **often play** video games.*
*I play video games **every day**.*

2 🎧 120 **Choose the correct options to complete the sentences. Listen again and check.**

1 I *always get up/get up always* early.
2 I *never am/am never* late for school.
3 I *usually do/do usually* my homework when I get home from school.
4 I don't *often watch/watch often* TV.
5 I usually play tennis *in Saturdays/on Saturdays.*
6 I *meet sometimes/sometimes meet* my friends at the weekend.

3 🔊 121 **Listen to Sam talking about his likes and dislikes. What's his favourite sport?**

4 🔊 121 **Complete the sentences with the words in the box. Listen again and check.**

don't	favourite	like	listening	prefer

1 I _____ maths and science.
2 I _____ like art.
3 I enjoy _____ to music.
4 I _____ football to tennis.
5 Basketball is my _____ sport.

GIVING OPINIONS AND REASONS

1 🔊 122 **Listen to a conversation about different activities. Which activity do both people like?**

2 🔊 122 **Complete the conversation with words from the box. Listen again and check.**

about	do	do	don't	fun
going	love	prefer	think	what

Lily: ¹ _____ you like swimming?
Rob: Yes, I ² _____ . It's fun. What ³ _____ you?
Lily: No, I ⁴ _____ like swimming. I ⁵ _____ it's boring. But I love ⁶ _____ to the cinema. It's really interesting. ⁷ _____ do you think?
Rob: No, I think going to the cinema is expensive. I ⁸ _____ to watch films at home. My favourite activity is cycling. Do you think cycling is ⁹ _____ ?
Lily: Yes, I do. I ¹⁰ _____ cycling!

3 🔊 123 **We often give reasons to explain our opinions. Listen to three people giving reasons for their opinions. Choose the reason that each person gives.**

1 I like travelling because
   a you meet interesting people.
   b you learn about different countries.
2 I don't like skateboarding because
   a it's dangerous.
   b it's boring.
3 I love this computer game because
   a it's exciting.
   b I'm very good at it.

4 🔊 124 **Complete the sentences with your own opinions and reasons. Listen and compare your ideas.**

1 I *like/don't like* reading because …
2 I *love/hate* football because …
3 I *like/don't like* shopping because …

DEALING WITH PROBLEMS

1 🎧 126 **Listen to three conversations. Complete the sentences with the words you hear.**

1 _____ that please?
2 _____ the question, please?
3 Could you _____ , please?

2 🎧 126 **Find and <u>underline</u> the mistake in each question. Listen again and check.**

1 Could you repeat again that, please?
2 Can you repeat me the question, please?
3 Could you say again, please?

3 🎧 127 **Listen to two people talking. What are they trying to describe?**

Item 1   *a*   a piece of clothing
Item 2   *b*   a kind of food
Item 3   *c*   a game

AGREEING AND DISAGREEING

1 🎧 125 **Listen to a conversation about playing a musical instrument. What do the people agree about?**

1 It's important to practise.
2 It's very difficult.
3 Lessons are always very expensive.

KEY LANGUAGE AND IDEAS FOR AGREEING AND DISAGREEING

Agreeing:
Yes, I agree with you.
I agree with you that …
Exactly!
That's true.

Disagreeing:
I'm not sure about that. I think …
I don't know. I think …
Yes, but …

KEY LANGUAGE AND IDEAS FOR DEALING WITH PROBLEMS

Asking someone to repeat:
Can/Could you repeat that, please?
Can/Could you repeat the question, please?
Can/Could you say that again, please?

When you don't know the word for something:
I'm not sure what the word is, but it's … (a sport, a kind of food)
It's something you use when you … (play football, cook)
I don't know the word, but it's something you … (wear, eat)
I'm not sure what this is called, but it's a kind of … (animal, plant, game)

4 🎧 127 **Complete what the people say with one word in each gap. Listen again and check.**

1 I'm _____ sure what the _____ is, but you often play this on the beach.
2 I'm not sure _____ this is _____ , but it's something you wear around your neck.
3 I don't _____ what the word _____ , but it's something you eat.

2 🎧 125 **Complete part of the conversation with the phrases in the box. Listen again and check.**

agree with you   not sure about   that's true   yes, but

A: I think it's very difficult to learn an instrument.
B: I'm ¹ _____ that. The guitar isn't very difficult, but it's important to practise every day.
A: ² _____ . I ³ _____ that it's important to practise so that you can get better. I think that lessons are very expensive, too.
B: ⁴ _____ you can watch lessons online and teach yourself.

SPEAKING PART 1

1 🔊 **128 Listen to Ana answering three questions. Does she use full sentences in her answers?**

2 🔊 **128 Listen again. Notice how she adds extra information.**

1 What do you do at weekends?
2 Who do you like spending your weekends with?
3 Where do you like going shopping?
4 What do you like buying?

3 🔊 **128 Complete Ana's answers with *or* or *because*. Listen again and check.**

1 I often go shopping, _____ I sometimes go to the cinema.
2 I like going shopping in London _____ there are lots of good shops.
3 I like buying clothes and shoes _____ I'm interested in fashion.

4 🔊 **129 Read Ana's answer to a longer question. Choose the correct options. Listen and check.**

Examiner: Now, please tell me something about presents that you buy for other people.

Ana: Well, I ¹*love/loved* buying presents for people. I usually ²*buy/am buying* presents for people when it's their birthday. For example, last month I ³*buy/bought* a T-shirt for my brother and he really ⁴*like/liked* it. It's my friend's birthday next week, and I ⁵*take/'m going to take* her to the cinema as a present.

5 **Choose the best answers to the questions.**

1 Where do you usually meet your friends?
   a I usually meet my friends at the weekend.
   b I often meet them at the cinema, or we go for a meal together.
2 Who do you live with?
   a I share a flat with three friends.
   b I live in a small apartment in the city centre.
3 What sports can you do in your area?
   a I play tennis once a week, but I can't play very well.
   b You can play tennis and football at the sports centre near my house.
4 What time do you usually have lunch?
   a I usually have lunch at about one o'clock.
   b I usually have a sandwich and some fruit.
5 What did you eat for breakfast this morning?
   a I don't usually have breakfast, but sometimes I have some cereal.
   b I had some eggs and some orange juice.
6 How many rooms are there in your house or flat?
   a I like my bedroom because it's quite big, and you can see the park from my window.
   b There are two bedrooms, a kitchen, a living room and a bathroom, so five rooms.

6 **Choose the correct options. Then decide if each sentence is about the present, past or future.**

1 I usually *have/had* dinner with my family.
2 I *meet/'m going to meet* my friends tomorrow, because it's the weekend.
3 I sometimes *watch/'m going to watch* films on my laptop because I love watching films.
4 I *cook/cooked* a meal for some friends last night, and it was very good.
5 I *play/'m going to play* tennis next weekend with my friends.
6 I *buy/bought* some new shoes yesterday, and some new jeans too.

7 🔊 **130 Match one piece of extra information (a–e) with each question and answer (1–5). Listen and check.**

1 **A:** Tell me something about what you like doing at home.
   B: I like watching films, and I enjoy playing video games.
2 **A:** Tell me something about what you like to eat with friends.
   B: I sometimes go to restaurants with my friends, and I prefer Italian food.
3 **A:** Tell me something about the clothes you like to buy.
   B: My favourite thing to buy is jeans, because I like wearing them.
4 **A:** Tell me something about the places you like to visit.
   B: I like visiting places that are near the sea.
5 **A:** Tell me something about the sports you like to do.
   B: I like playing football. I play for a team, and we have a game every Saturday.

a My team doesn't often win.
b I love swimming when the weather's hot.
c I've just got a new game.
d We went to a pizza restaurant last weekend.
e I bought some really nice jeans last week.

8 **Practise answering the questions.**

• What's your name?
• How old are you?
• What do you usually do at the weekend?
• Who do you like going shopping with?
• Where do you usually meet your friends?
• What did you eat for breakfast this morning?
• Tell me something about the clothes you like to buy.
• Tell me something about the sports you like to do.

1 🎧 131 **Listen to two students doing the task. Do they talk about all the pictures?**

Do you like these different hobbies? Say why or why not.

2 🎧 132 **Listen to one of the students answering a follow-up question. Does she give reasons for her answers?**

3 🔊 **133 Complete the sentences with the words in the box. Listen and check.**

> | about | agree | do | like | sure | think |

A: I think video games are exciting. What do you ¹_____?

B: I'm not ²_____ about that.

A: What about taking photos? Do you ³_____ taking photos?

B: I often take photos when I'm with my friends. I take photos on my phone. What ⁴_____ you?

A: I like taking photos, too. I've got a camera.

B: I always go cycling at weekends. What ⁵_____ you think about it?

A: I ⁶_____ with you that it's fun.

4 **Match the opinions (1–5) with the reasons (a–e).**

1 I prefer to go on holiday with friends because

2 I prefer to play team sports because

3 I don't like doing outdoor activities when the weather's bad

4 I prefer to watch films at home because

5 I prefer staying in hotels to camping because

a exercising on your own is boring.

b you can have food while you watch.

c it's more comfortable, and you don't get cold at night.

d you can have more fun with people of the same age.

e because nothing is fun when it's raining.

5 🔊 **134 Work in pairs. Look at the pictures and complete the task. Then listen and compare your ideas. Did you discuss the same things?**

Do you like these different summer activities?

6 🔊 **135 Practise answering the follow-up questions. Then listen and compare your ideas.**

- Which of these activities do you like the best?
- Do you prefer to go on holiday to the beach or the countryside?
- Do you prefer swimming in the sea or in a swimming pool?

A2 KEY EXAM INFORMATION

PART/TIMING	CONTENT	EXAM FOCUS
1 **Reading and Writing** 45 minutes	**Part 1:** Discrete three-option multiple choice questions on six short texts. **Part 2:** Matching. There are three short texts with seven items. Candidates are asked to decide which text an item refers to. **Part 3:** Three-option multiple choice. Candidates read a text and are asked to choose the correct answer from five multiple-choice questions. **Part 4:** Three-option multiple-choice cloze. A text is followed by six questions. Candidates select the correct word from each question to complete the text. **Part 5:** Open cloze. Candidates complete gaps in one or two short texts. **Part 6:** Writing – short message **Part 7:** Writing – story	**Part 1:** Candidates focus on overall understanding of emails, notices and messages. **Part 2:** Candidates read for specific information and detailed comprehension. **Part 3:** Candidates read for detailed understanding and main ideas. **Part 4:** Candidates read and identify the appropriate word. **Part 5:** Candidates read and identify the appropriate word with the focus on grammar. **Part 6:** Candidates write a communicative note or email of at least 25 words. **Part 7:** Candidates write a narrative of at least 35 words describing the people, events and locations that are shown in three pictures.
2 **Listening** approximately 30 minutes	**Part 1:** Five short dialogues with three-option multiple-choice questions with pictures. **Part 2:** Longer dialogue. Five gaps to fill with words or numbers. **Part 3:** Longer informal dialogue with five three-option multiple-choice items. **Part 4:** Five three-option multiple choice questions on five short dialogues or monologues. **Part 5:** Matching. There is a longer informal dialogue. Candidates match five items with eight options.	**Part 1:** Candidates are expected to listen and identify key information. **Part 2:** Candidates are expected to identify and write down key information. **Part 3:** Candidates listen to identify specific information, feelings and opinions. **Part 4:** Candidates listen to identify the main idea, message, gist, topic or point. **Part 5:** Candidates listen to identify specific information.
3 **Speaking** 8–10 minutes per pair of candidates	**Part 1 Phase 1:** Each candidate interacts with the interlocutor, giving factual information of a personal nature. **Part 1 Phase 2:** A topic-based interview where the interlocutor asks each candidate two questions about their daily life. **Part 2 Phase 1:** A discussion based on topic-based artwork prompts. Candidates discuss the objects and activities in the artwork with each other. **Part 2 Phase 2:** The interlocutor leads follow-up discussion on same topic as Phase 1. Each candidate is asked two questions.	**Part 1:** Candidates focus on interactional and social language. **Part 2:** Candidates focus on organising a larger unit of discourse.

ANSWERS AND AUDIOSCRIPTS

STARTER

Page 8

VOCABULARY

Exercise 1

Students' own answers.

Exercise 2

A at a sports centre, photo 1
B on holiday, photo 3
C in an English class, photo 2

🔊 Track 002

A

Ben: Hi, I'm Ben. What's your name?
Jim: Hello, Ben. My name's Jim. Nice to meet you.
Ben: Nice to meet you, too, Jim. Is this the basketball club?
Jim: No, it isn't. It's five-a-side football.

B

Man: Are you British?
Woman: No, we aren't. We're Canadian.
Man: Oh, that's interesting. Where are you from in Canada?

C

Girl 1: Is he our English teacher?
Girl 2: Yes, he is. His name is Mr Robinson. He's very nice. Are you a new student?
Girl 1: Yes, I am. This is my first lesson.
Girl 2: Where are you from?

Exercise 3

1 'm
2 's
3 Is
4 isn't, 's
5 Are
6 aren't, 're
7 's, are
8 Is
9 is, 's, Are
10 am
11 are

VOCABULARY

1 Italian, American
2 Spanish, Mexican
3 French, Chinese

Page 9

READING

Exercise 1

1 Karl
2 Robert
3 Adam
4 Zadie
5 Adi

6 Lily
7 Marco
8 Leroy

Exercise 2

1 b   3 a   5 d
2 c   4 f   6 e

Exercise 3

1 who
2 where
3 what
4 how old
5 whose
6 how many

Page 10

VOCABULARY

Exercise 1

1 grandparents
2 nephew
3 uncle
4 nieces
5 aunt
6 cousins
7 granddaughter, grandson

Exercise 2

1 Mum
2 Dad
3 Grandma / Granny
4 Grandad / Grandpa

GRAMMAR

Exercise 1

1 's
2 haven't
3 Have, I have
4 Has, has

Exercise 2

1 Have … got
2 Has … got
3 has … got
4 Has … got

Page 11

READING

Exercise 1

Students' own answers.

Exercise 2

He works at a dance school; He can speak English and Portuguese.

Exercise 3

1 Porto
2 two languages
3 a dance teacher

4 two sisters
5 dance

GRAMMAR

Exercise 1

1 can
2 can't
3 Can
4 can't

Exercise 2

Suggested answers

Can your parents speak English?
Can your dad dance?
Can your teacher swim?
Can your brother/sister play tennis?
Can you cook?

Exercise 3

1 likes
2 doesn't like
3 Does
4 like
5 does
6 doesn't

Exercise 4

1 lives
2 comes
3 likes
4 works

Exercise 5

1 c   2 a   3 b

Exercise 6

1 doesn't live
2 Can … speak Yes, she can.
3 Has … got Yes, she has.
4 does … work? She works at a pizza restaurant.
5 Does … like Yes, she does.
6 doesn't like

Page 12

LISTENING

Exercises 1 & 2

Students' own answers.

🔊 Track 003

A, B, C, D, E, F, G, H, I, J, K, L, M, N, O, P, Q, R, S, T, U, V, W, X, Y, Z

Exercise 3

UK (United Kingdom)
USA (United States of America)
EU (European Union)
DOB (date of birth)
LOL (laugh out loud)

Track 004

1 UK – United Kingdom
2 USA – United States of America
3 EU – European Union
4 DOB – date of birth
5 LOL – laugh out loud

Exercise 4

Suggested answer

Your first name, surname, address and date of birth

Exercise 5

at a sports club

Track 005

George: Hello, I'd like to become a member please.
Woman: OK, that's no problem, which sports are you interested in?
George: Tennis and swimming – and I'd also like to use the gym.
Woman: That's fine. Can I take some personal information? What's your name, please?
George: George Smithson.
Woman: How do you spell that?
George: George G-E-O-R-G-E and my surname is Smithson – S-M-I-T-H-S-O-N.
Woman: Could you spell your surname again, please?
George: Yes, it's Smithson – S-M-I-T-H-S-O-N.
Woman: Thank you, Mr Smithson.

Exercise 6

First name: George
Surname: Smithson

Exercise 7

Date of birth: 17th June. 1995
Address: 16 Redwood Road, New Town, NW4 8JG
Phone number: 06819 772 3451

Track 006

Woman: OK, Could you tell me your date of birth, please?
George: Oh, yes. It's the 17th June, 1995.
Woman: The 17th June … 1995.
George: Yes, that's right.
Woman: Thank you. And now I just need your contact details. What's your address please?
George: It's sixteen – that's one six, Redwood Road R-E-D-W-O-O-D Road, New Town and the postcode is NW4 8JG.
Woman: NW4 8JG.
George: Yes, that's right.
Woman: OK and finally, what's your phone number?
George: It's 06819 772 3451.

Exercise 8

1 name
2 spell
3 old
4 date of birth
5 address
6 phone number

Exercise 9

Students' own answers.

Page 13

SPEAKING

Exercise 1

Beyoncé, famous singer and songwriter. USA
Diego Boneta, famous actor and singer. Mexican-American
Millie Bobby Brown, actress, England

Exercise 2

1 Beyoncé: 4 September, 1981
2 Diego Boneta: 29 November, 1990
3 Millie Bobby Brown: February 19, 2004

Track 007

Beyoncé is a very famous American singer. She was born on the 4th September 1981 in Houston. Beyoncé has got 2 daughters and a son.
Diego Boneta is Mexican-American. He's an actor, but he can also sing. He was born in Mexico City on 29 November 1990. He's got a brother and a sister.
Millie Bobby Brown is a young British actress. She was born on the 19th February 2004 in Marbella. She's got a brother and two sisters.

Exercise 3

Students' own answers.

WRITING

Exercise 1

Name: Miguel, Likes: New York and his job, Lives: New York, Age: 30, Family: his parents and two sisters, Is from: Porto, Languages: English and Portuguese, Things he can do: dance, speak English and Portuguese

Exercises 2 & 3

Students' own answers.

UNIT 1

Page 14

VOCABULARY

Exercise 1

Students' own answers.

Exercise 2

A spend time alone
B spend time with friends
C play video games
D relax at home
E go shopping
F play or watch sport

Exercise 3

Speaker 1 B
Speaker 2 F
Speaker 3 A
Speaker 4 C

Track 008

Narrator: Speaker 1
Woman 1: My perfect day …? Well, on my perfect day, I spend time with my friends. We go to the beach and swim, talk and have fun. We probably go home at about half past seven.
Narrator: Speaker 2
Boy: For me, a perfect day is about sport. I meet my friends at the park when it opens at quarter past eight and we play basketball. When we get tired, we watch sport on TV and eat ice cream.
Narrator: Speaker 3
Man: My perfect day is when I can spend time alone. I like getting up early and going for a long walk in the countryside. I can walk for 15 or 20 kilometres in the fresh air. Perfect!
Narrator: Speaker 4
Woman 2: For me, a perfect day is playing video games for hours with my friends. We play all day and stop at about half past nine in the evening to go for a pizza.

Exercise 4

1 at the beach
2 They watch sport on TV and eat ice cream.
3 going for a long walk alone
4 go out for a pizza

Exercise 5

Students' own answers.

Page 15

LISTENING

Exercise 1

1 one o'clock
2 half past nine
3 quarter past eight
4 quarter to six

Exercise 2

Students' own answers.

Track 009

at half past six
at half past two
at quarter to four
at quarter to seven
at quarter past nine
at quarter past eleven

Exercise 3

1 at **half** past **six**
  at **half** past **two**
  at **qua**rter to **four**
  at **qua**rter to **sev**en
  at **qua**rter past **nine**
  at **qua**rter past e**lev**en
2 the/l/ is silent
3 They are both pronounced /ə/ (like the final sound in *America* or *teacher*)

Exercise 4

Students' own answers.

Exercise 5

1 She's a teacher.
2 She's a police officer.
3 They live in a small village

🔊 **Track 010**

Interviewer: So, Amy, what job do you do?
Amy: I'm a teacher.
Interviewer: Can you tell me about your day? What time do you get up?
Amy: I usually wake up at quarter past seven, but I don't get up! I always stay in bed until half past seven and then I get up! Then I have breakfast with my sister, Olivia. She's a police officer, and we live together.
Interviewer: What do you have for breakfast?
Amy: I usually have toast and Olivia has cereal. We both drink coffee for breakfast. We don't like tea. After breakfast, I have a shower and get dressed. Then I get my bag, put on my coat and leave the house to go to work.
Interviewer: How do you get to work?
Amy: By bus. We live in a small village and it's the quickest way to get into town.
Interviewer: How does Olivia get to work? Does she go by bus, too?
Amy: No, she doesn't catch the bus. She goes by car.

Exercise 6

1 F She wakes up at 7.15.
2 T
3 T
4 F Lessons start at 9 o'clock.
5 T
6 T
7 F She sometimes watches TV.

🔊 **Track 011**

Interviewer: So, Amy, what job do you do?
Amy: I'm a teacher.
Interviewer: Can you tell me about your day? What time do you get up?
Amy: I usually wake up at quarter past seven, but I don't get up! I always stay in bed until half past seven and then I get up!

Then I have breakfast with my sister, Olivia. She's a police officer, and we live together.
Interviewer: What do you have for breakfast?
Amy: I usually have toast and Olivia has cereal. We both drink coffee for breakfast. We don't like tea. After breakfast, I have a shower and get dressed. Then I get my bag, put on my coat and leave the house to go to work.
Interviewer: How do you get to work?
Amy: By bus. We live in a small village and it's the quickest way to get into town.
Interviewer: How does Olivia get to work? Does she go by bus, too?
Amy: No, she doesn't catch the bus. She goes by car.
Interviewer: So, Amy, can you tell me about your day at work?
Amy: I arrive at work at quarter to nine. Lessons start at nine o'clock and lunch is at half past twelve.
Interviewer: Where do you have lunch? Do you have lunch at college?
Amy: No, I don't. I have lunch in a café. Sometimes, if it's a nice day, we buy sandwiches and go to the park.
Interviewer: Who do you have lunch with?
Amy: I often have lunch with some of the other teachers from college, but I like having lunch alone sometimes. In the afternoon, lessons finish at half past three. I do some work and get the bus back. I usually get home at about quarter past five.
Interviewer: What do you do when you get home?
Amy: I take off my work clothes and put on my jeans and go outside for some fresh air! I take my dog for a walk and when we get home, I have dinner. Then I sometimes watch TV.
Interviewer: And when do you go to bed?
Amy: I usually go to bed at about half past ten.

Exercise 7

1 get dressed
2 take off
3 get on
4 wake up
5 put on
6 get up

Page 16

GRAMMAR

Exercise 1

1 regularly
2 always true

Exercise 2

1 don't
2 get up

3 meet
4 doesn't
5 feels
6 have
7 go
8 don't

Exercise 3

1 doesn't get dressed
2 has, doesn't eat
3 walks
4 Do … go, catch
5 don't write

Exercise 4

Students' own answers.

Exercise 5

1 does
2 How, What

Exercise 6

| 1 e | 3 b | 5 c |
| 2 f | 4 a | 6 d |

Page 17

Exercise 7

1 What (job) does he do?
2 Where does he study?
3 Where does he live?
4 Who does he live with?
5 How does he get to work?
6 What time does he start and finish work?
7 What does he do in the evening?
8 Why does he like his job?

SPEAKING

Exercise 1

1 watching, listening
2 studying, walking

🔊 **Track 012**

Interviewer: So, Sergio, what do you like doing in the evening?
Sergio: I like watching TV and I love listening to music.
Interviewer: And what don't you like doing?
Sergio: I don't like studying for my job in the evenings. And I hate walking.

Exercise 2

-ing

Exercise 3

1 staying
2 listening to
3 having
4 meeting
5 dancing
6 playing
7 watching
8 shopping

Exercises 4 & 5

Students' own answers.

Exercise 6

A in a garden, a gardener
B on an oil rig, a mechanic

Exercise 7

Karen

1 7.00 am
2 big, old house in her village
3 a cup of tea and a sandwich
4 eats her breakfast
5 she works in the garden
6 2.00 pm
7 the owner of the garden
8 5.00 pm

Roman

1 in the Gulf of Mexico
2 for a week
3 10.00 pm
4 the gym
5 table tennis
6 his friend Pepe
7 it's very cold on the oil rig
8 9.45 pm

Page 18

READING PART 2: TRAINING

Exercise 1

Students' own answers.

Exercise 2

A the nurse
B the nightclub DJ
C the security guard

Exercise 3

1 C Pablo
2 B Tobi
3 B Tobi
4 A Bridget
5 C Pablo
6 A Bridget

Exercise 4

Students' own answers.

Page 19

GRAMMAR

Exercise 1

1 before
2 after
3 between

Exercise 2

1 sometimes
2 never
3 always
4 usually/often
5 often/usually

Exercise 3

Students' own answers.

Exercise 4

1 once
2 twice

Exercise 5

Students' own answers.

VOCABULARY

Exercise 1

1 photographer D
2 police officer C
3 mechanic A
4 pilot B

Track 013

1

Man 1: I'm a photographer. My job is taking interesting photographs of things, places and people.

2

Man 2: I'm a police officer. My job is to keep people safe. I work in a police station.

3

Woman 1: In my job, I repair machines, like cars, when they go wrong – or I try to! I'm a mechanic.

4

Woman 2: I'm a pilot. My job is to fly planes. I work for an airline.

Exercise 2

1 mechanic
2 photographer
3 pilot
4 police officer

Page 20

PUSH YOURSELF B1

1 f   3 a   5 c
2 d   4 b   6 e

LISTENING PART 1: TRAINING

Exercise 1

Students' own answers.

Exercise 2

Students' own answers.

Track 014

Narrator: One. What job does the woman want to do when she finishes her studies?

Interviewer: You're studying to be a nurse, aren't you?

Student: Yes, but I've decided that's not the job I want. After my course ends, I want to become a DJ.

Interviewer: Wow! Are your parents OK about that?

Student: Well, they're a bit worried but I've told them I'll become a teacher if I can't make any money as a DJ, and they're happy with that.

Exercise 3

2 B   3 C

Track 015

Narrator: Two. What does the police officer do first when he gets home from work?

Interviewer: Now, you're a police officer. What do you do when you get home from work? Do you have something to eat?

Police officer: I usually have a sandwich in my afternoon break, so I'm not hungry when I get home. I go and read in the garden.

Interviewer: Don't you eat any dinner?

Police officer: Yes, but I cook dinner later. And then I watch TV for a while before I go to bed.

Narrator: Three. What time does the man get up in the morning?

Interviewer: You're a DJ on an early morning radio programme, aren't you? What time do you have to get up in the morning?

DJ: Well, I wake up at quarter to four most days.

Interviewer: That IS early. Is that difficult?

DJ: Yes, but I then have a coffee in bed at 4 and I don't usually get out of bed until quarter past four. Then I have a shower and get dressed.

Page 21

WRITING

Exercise 1

Students' own answers.

Exercise 2

She's a waitress. She likes talking to customers.

Exercise 3

Expressions for beginning an email:
Hi, How are you?
Expressions for ending an email:
Love, Write soon!

Exercises 4 & 5

Students' own answers.

Page 22

EXAM FOCUS
READING PART 2

1 C   4 C   7 C
2 A   5 B
3 B   6 A

Page 23

LISTENING PART 1

1 B   4 C
2 A   5 C
3 A

Narrator: For each question, choose the correct answer. One. What time does the man start work?

Woman: How's your new job, Luca? Do you have to start at seven in the morning, as you did before?

Man: That's one of the things I like about this job – the shop opens at half past nine.

Woman: Great! But you have to arrive before then, don't you?

Man: Oh yes. I'm there from nine, but that's much better than seven!

Narrator: Two. Where did the woman go with her friend?

Man: Did you see that film you wanted to see yesterday, with your friend Sara?

Woman: There weren't any seats left when we got to the cinema. Sara works in a restaurant, and she finished work late.

Man: Oh, that's a pity. So what did you do?

Woman: We just walked around the centre of town, chatting, until it was time to come home.

Narrator: Three. How should the man contact Eva?

Man: Do you know how I can contact Eva? I've called her several times this morning, but she never answers.

Woman: She's not good at answering calls. I send her emails. She checks those on her phone when she's working.

Man: OK, I'll try that. I thought about going to her office.

Woman: She's not always there. Sometimes she goes out to meet customers.

Narrator: Four. What does the man need to buy?

Man: I'm going to the supermarket later. Shall I get some bread? I don't think we've got much.

Woman: I got that this morning at the shop on the corner. I wanted some fruit as well, but they didn't have any.

Man: I'll get some then. And what about some fish, for dinner?

Woman: We're going out for dinner tonight. Have you forgotten?

Narrator: Five. Why was the woman late for work?

Woman: I'm really sorry I'm late.

Man: Don't worry, it's only a few minutes. Was the traffic bad this morning?

Woman: Actually, it was fine, but I couldn't start my car. I tried to get a taxi, but there weren't any, so I had to wait for a bus.

Man: Oh, well let me know if you need a lift tomorrow.

Page 24

REAL WORLD

Exercises 1 & 2

Students' own answers.

Exercise 3

1	D	3	B
2	C	4	A

Page 25

Exercise 4

1	b	3	b	5	a
2	a	4	a	6	b

Exercise 5

1	b	2	d	3	a

1

Official: Passport, please. Thank you. What's the purpose of your visit?

Student: I'm here for a holiday and also to learn Spanish.

Official: How long are you planning to be in the country?

Student: I'll be here for five weeks.

Official: OK. When do you fly back?

Student: I'm flying home on the 28th of August.

Official: And where are you staying?

Student: I'm staying with a family in Mexico City.

2

Maria: Hello. You must be Charlie. Welcome to Mexico City.

Student: Thanks.

Maria: Come in. I'm Maria, and this is my husband, Raul.

Student: Pleased to meet you.

Maria: And you. You'll meet our children later, but they're at school at the moment.

Raul: Here, let me take your bags for you. So, how was your flight?

Student: Fine, thanks. No delays.

Maria: Good. Come in and sit down.

Student: Thanks.

Maria: So, you're from the UK?

Student: Yes. I live in Harrow.

Maria: And do you come from a big family?

Student: No. I've got one brother. I'm the oldest.

Raul: That's nice. And is this your first time in Mexico?

Student: Yes. I'm very excited to be here.

Maria: That's perfect. Now, before I show you your room, I'd just like to ask you a few questions. First, about food. Is there anything you don't eat?

Student: No, I like everything.

Maria: Good. Do you have any food allergies? Any foods that make you ill?

Student: No, I'm not allergic to anything.

Maria: That's nice and easy. We usually eat at around 8 o'clock in the evening. Is that convenient for you?

Student: Yes, that's fine for me.

3

Girl: Hi. I'm Eva.

Student: Hi, Eva. I'm Charlie. Nice to meet you.

Girl: Nice to meet you too. Where are you from?

Student: I'm from Harrow, in the UK. I'm staying with Maria and Raul for a few weeks.

Girl: Cool. I'd love to visit the UK one day. What do you do?

Student: I'm a student. I'm studying Spanish and business at university.

Girl: Wow. That's great. And what do you think of Mexico City?

Student: I really like the city. It's very lively and there's lots to do.

Girl: Great. And what about Mexican food?

Student: I love spicy food, so I really like the food here.

Girl: That's good. So, maybe we should go and get some food, then?

Student: Yes, good idea!

Exercise 6

1 I'll
2 I'm staying
3 I've got
4 very excited
5 allergic
6 from
7 student
8 really like

Exercise 7

1	a	3	a
2	b	4	b

Exercises 8 & 9

Mexico City: capital of Mexico; first buildings there in 1300s; Spanish explorers built a new city when they arrived in 1500s; lots of old colonial buildings in the city centre.

Family life: In the past, Mexican families were large, and grandparents, parents and children all lived together; most modern families now just parents and children; family life and traditions still important, for example, a quinceañera is a celebration when a girl becomes 15 and has a big party with family and friends.

Homestays: a good way to learn about family life and culture and learn the language; there are official websites.

Exercise 10

Students' own answers.

UNIT 2

Page 26

VOCABULARY

Exercise 1

Students' own answers.

Exercise 2

1 A   3 B
2 D   4 C

🎧 Track 018

1

Sonia: My friends love to share photos of their trips on social media. These photos are from their holidays at different times of the year. Sam's photo is this winter one with all the snow. It's from his trip to New York and it shows the view from the window of his hotel. I think it's December or January – it's definitely winter!

2

Sonia: My Japanese friend Keiko posts photos every day. That one is from her trip to Kyoto with her family in spring – in April or May, I think. They're walking through a park in the rain, but you can see from the flowers on the trees that it's spring.

3

Sonia: My friend Nathalie visits her grandparents in the forest of Orléans every autumn, so I think this photo is from October or November. This is what a French forest looks like on a foggy day in autumn!

4

Sonia: The last one is from our summer holidays in Ireland. Look at the clear, green sea. Isn't it beautiful? It's a perfect summer day at the end of July.

Exercise 3

1 winter
2 spring
3 autumn
4 summer

Exercises 4 & 5

1 January
2 April
3 May
4 July
5 October
6 November
7 December

🎧 Track 019

January, February, March, April, May, June, July, August, September, October, November, December

Exercise 6

Students' own answers.

Page 27

VOCABULARY

Exercise 1

Students' own answers.

Exercise 2

1 B   2 C   3 A

Exercise 3

1 T
2 F It's wet and often cloudy and foggy.
3 F At night it can be cool.

Exercise 4

1 sunshine
2 storm
3 freezing
4 wet
5 thunder
6 snows
7 foggy
8 temperature
9 cloudy

Exercise 5

-y

Exercise 6

Students' own answers.

Page 28

GRAMMAR

Exercise 1

1 b   2 a

Exercise 2

1 are you
2 It's raining
3 watching
4 is coming
5 're all getting
6 isn't sitting
7 Is
8 isn't
9 's working
10 is

Exercise 3

1 're having
2 'm sitting
3 looking
4 is taking
5 'm messaging
6 're enjoying
7 're walking
8 isn't raining
9 aren't having
10 'm enjoying

Exercise 4

1 are … doing
2 is … wearing
3 are … learning
4 are … doing

Page 29

LISTENING PART 2: TRAINING

Exercises 1 & 2

Students' own answers.

🎧 Track 020

Woman: Hello, everyone. As you know, we're going on a trip to Long Beach soon. It's on the 6th of May – that's one week after the trip to the Science Museum on the 29th of April.

Exercise 3

2 coach
3 towel
4 9.45
5 Burrell

🎧 Track 021

Woman: Hello, everyone. As you know, we're going on a trip to Long Beach soon. It's on the 6th of May – that's one week after the trip to the Science Museum on the 29th of April.

We usually travel by train on our trips. But we're taking a coach this time, because there isn't a station near Long Beach. If you want, you can bring beach balls or games to play. It's possible to rent sunbeds at the beach, but you will need to take a towel. The journey from college to Long Beach takes only one hour. We're going at 9.45 but can everybody be outside school at 9.15? We'll be back at 4.30. If you'd like to join this trip, please pay Sally Burrell in the college office. If Sally's not there, put the money in an envelope and leave it for her. Sally's surname is spelt B-U-double R-E-double-L. Now, any questions?

PUSH YOURSELF B1

Exercise 1

1 C   3 D
2 A   4 B

Exercise 2

heavy storms
strong winds
bright sunshine
clear skies
heavy snow
thick fog
hard frost

Exercise 3

1 thick fog
2 hard frost
3 heavy snow
4 heavy storms, clear skies
5 bright sunshine
6 strong winds

Exercise 4

Students' own answers.

READING

Exercise 1

Students' own answers.

Exercise 2

1 Koon-Sung usually lives in Singapore. Now he's living in Turin, Italy.
Carla usually lives in Mexico City. Now she's living in the United Arab Emirates and on holiday.

2 Koon-Sung is in Turin for his job. He is working on a big engineering project/ making a road in the mountains.
Carla is in the United Arab Emirates because she is on a student exchange programme.

Exercise 3

1 c   3 b
2 b   4 a

VOCABULARY

Exercise 1

1 mountains
2 Islands
3 valley
4 coast
5 hill
6 forest
7 lake
8 waterfall

Page 31

Exercises 2 & 3

Students' own answers.

GRAMMAR

Exercise 1

a 2   c 1
b 4   d 3

Exercise 2

1 rains
2 'm staying
3 's snowing
4 live

Exercise 3

1 plays
2 travels
3 's staying
4 's practising
5 're learning
6 goes
7 doesn't like
8 's wearing

Exercise 4

Students' own answers.

Page 32

WRITING PART 6: TRAINING

Exercise 1

Students' own answers.

Exercise 2

	1	2	3
to do what	go out for pizza	go to the beach and go camping	go to a football match
meet where	in the Arum cafe	in the supermarket car park	at Rose's house
meet when	at 6 pm	at 10 am	at 4.30

Exercise 3

1 *Hi* + name
Hey + name
Dear + name
name only

2 name only
Love + name
with a question
Let me know.
Hope you can make it!

Exercise 4

a 3   b 2   c 1

Exercise 5

Phrases for saying 'yes'	Phrases for saying 'no'
I'd love to come Thanks, that sounds great.	Thanks for asking but … I'd love to come, but I'm afraid …

Exercise 6

1 interested
2 about
3 like
4 afraid
5 sounds
6 come

Exercise 7

Yes, it does.

Exercise 8

Students' own answers.

Page 33

SPEAKING

Exercises 1 & 2

Students' own answers.

Exercise 3

Photo B – the man by the waterfall

🔊 Track 022

Irina: In this photo I can see a man who is standing next to a big, beautiful waterfall. He is quite young and he's got dark hair and a beard. He's wearing a black T-shirt and jeans and he's holding his phone on a selfie stick and he's taking a photo. He's smiling and he looks happy.

The man is in the middle of the photo and he is alone. Maybe he is visiting the waterfall with friends but we can't see them. Behind him, at the bottom of the photo we can see a fence. I think it is to stop people from falling into the river. Behind the fence is the river with the waterfall. It's very big. On the left, at the top of the photo we can see the trees of a big forest.

Exercise 4

1 dark hair … beard
2 a black T-shirt and jeans … happy
3 taking a photo
4 waterfall … friends
5 into … water

Exercise 5

1 He (She/It) looks …
2 Maybe he's visiting …
3 I think the fence is to stop …

Exercise 6

1 next
2 middle
3 bottom
4 Behind
5 top

Exercise 7

Students' own answers.

Page 34

EXAM FOCUS
LISTENING PART 2

1 8 / eight
2 6 / six
3 (the) office
4 75 / seventy-five
5 Albury

🔊 Track 023

Narrator: For each question, write the correct answer in the gap. Write one word or a number or a date or a time.
You will hear a woman giving information about a cycle ride.

Woman: Welcome to the visitor centre at Redhill Forest. I hope you're all ready for your thirty kilometre cycle ride! It's now seven thirty, and we'll be on our bikes and away at eight. We ask everyone to arrive well before the ride starts because someone's always late – but not me! I was here at six! As you're all early, you've got time to visit the shop! For £3 you can buy a hat, or if you prefer a T-shirt, they're £6 each. I hope you've all brought water, but if you haven't it's £1 per bottle.
We did send everyone maps, but if you've forgotten or lost yours, go to the office, which is just behind me, opposite the café. As you know, this forest does have some hills. The highest is three hundred metres!

Don't worry – we won't be cycling up that one today! The highest we'll go is seventy-five metres, which isn't too bad. The ride ends at Albury village. You spell that A-L-B-U-R-Y. Albury. Right any questions …

Page 35

WRITING PART 6
Model answer
Hi Harley,
Good to hear from you. The best place to go walking is in the mountains. There arelots of hotels that you can stay in. The weather is hot at this time of year.
(36 words)

Page 36

REAL WORLD
Exercise 1
A spring
B summer
C autumn
D winter

Exercise 2
1 summer
2 spring
3 winter
4 summer
5 summer and autumn
6 winter

Page 37
Exercise 3
1	a	3	b	5	b
2	b	4	a		

Exercise 4
1	a	2	b	3	b

🔊 **Track 024**
1
Guest: Good morning. Do you know the weather forecast for today? We want to go skiing.
Receptionist: Oh, I don't think you'll have much luck with that today. They're forecasting a big storm coming in from the north about mid-afternoon, with gale-force winds and a lot of snow.
Guest: Oh. So, is it OK to go skiing this morning?
Receptionist: No, I think they'll be closing the slopes all day because you never quite know when the storm will hit, and you don't want to get caught out there once the storm comes.
2
Receptionist 2: Good morning. Not such a good day today.
Guest 2: No. Do you think it will rain all day?

Receptionist 2: No. The forecast is for rain till lunch time, then it should clear and we should get some sun later on.
Guest 2: Oh, that's good. We want to go to the beach after lunch.
Receptionist 2: Yeah, well they reckon from about midday onwards it should dry up, and once the sun comes out, it'll soon warm up.
3
Receptionist 3: Hi. Good morning. Can I help you?
Guest 3: Yes. Do you know if there's rain forecast today?
Receptionist 3: Yes. The morning's going to be fine, quite bright and sunny, but then it's gonna cloud over this afternoon, and there may be a few showers, so you might want to take an umbrella with you.
Guest 3: OK. Thank you.
Receptionist 3: Yeah. The weather's a bit unpredictable at this time of year, so you never know what's going to happen.

Exercise 5
1 forecast
2 OK
3 all
4 want
5 there's

Exercise 6
1	e	3	d	5	b
2	a	4	c		

Exercises 7 & 8
spring: kayaking and whale watching
summer: beaches and swimming
autumn: jogging and film festival
winter: sledge rides and Chinese New Year

Exercise 9
Students' own answers.

Page 38

PROGRESS CHECK 1
Exercise 1
1 wakes up … quarter past seven
2 gets up … half past seven
3 gets dressed … quarter to seven
4 puts on … eight o'clock
5 gets on … quarter to nine
6 takes off … four o'clock

Exercise 2
1 grandmother
2 niece
3 uncle
4 nephew
5 cousin
6 grandfather

Exercise 3
1 has got
2 have got
3 is
4 are
5 hasn't got
6 Has … got

Exercise 4
1 **A** mountain
  B winter
2 **A** coast
  B summer
3 **A** forest
  B autumn
4 **A** spring
  B lake

Exercise 5
1 island
2 west
3 valley, hills
4 waterfall
5 north
6 desert

Exercise 6
1 France
2 Italian
3 Mexico
4 Spanish

Page 39
Exercise 7
1 Nurses often have to work at night.
2 Musicians need to practise every day.
3 Teachers never go to school at the weekend.
4 Some school children always wear a uniform.
5 Is your shop usually busy at weekends?
6 Business people sometimes travel to other countries.

Exercise 8
1 I drink
2 it's raining
3 I wake up
4 it never snows
5 Is he playing
6 We go

Exercise 9
1 ~~coming~~ come
2 She ~~have~~ has (got) green eyes
3 The people there ~~is~~ are very friendly
4 I usually ~~can~~ write
5 The club is always open ~~always~~.
6 ~~I sell~~ I'm selling a bike

Exercise 10
1	C	3	A	5	B	7	B
2	B	4	C	6	A	8	C

UNIT 3
Page 40
VOCABULARY
Exercise 1
Students' own answers.

Exercises 2 & 3
54% watching TV
20% using social media
12% watching videos online
8% playing video games
6% playing sports and doing exercise

🌐 Track 025
Woman: So, how do we spend our leisure time? Well on average, we spend fifty-four per cent of it watching TV. That's still everybody's favourite free-time activity. We spend twenty per cent of our time using social media and twelve per cent watching videos online. On average we spend eight per cent of our free time playing video games, but some people probably spend more. In total we only spend six per cent of our time outdoors playing sports or doing exercise.

Exercise 4
1 chat online – 5; messaging friends – 5; upload photos – 3; download films – 3; watch an episode/series – 4; write or follow a blog – 3; stream music – 5.
2 Her final score is 28. She's a screen fan.

🌐 Track 026
Susie: So, how often do you chat online, Roz?
Roz: Er, that's number five – several times a day. You know that! I chat online with you every evening!
Susie: Yeah, that's true! So what about messaging? Is that five, too?
Roz: Well, I message my friends all day: that's how we talk to each other if we aren't together. So I think the score should be five here.
Susie: OK and how often do you upload photos?
Roz: Mm, I like uploading photos to social media sites to share them with my friends, so that's probably number three. And It's also three for 'how often do you download films. I watch most films online.
Susie: And what about series? How often do you watch them online?
Roz: I usually watch an episode from my favourite series every day, so that's four.
Susie: And blogs and vlogs. Do you have any time to watch those?
Roz: I probably look at them … once or twice a week. So that's three.
Susie: OK, and finally what about streaming music?

Roz: I stream music all the time. It's how I listen to music – so that's another score of five.
Susie: So, let's see that gives you a total score of … 28. So, you spend a lot of time in front of screens. It's the way you like to spend free time and talk to people.

Page 41
Exercise 5
1 chat online
2 message … friends
3 uploading photos
4 watch … episode
5 stream

Exercises 6 & 7
Students' own answers.

PUSH YOURSELF B1
Exercise 1
1 Science-fiction film = 3; horror film = 2; comedy = 1
2 The writer enjoyed the comedy and the scientce fiction film but not the horror film.

Exercise 2
1 d	5 h	9 a
2 b	6 c	10 g
3 j	7 e	
4 i	8 f	

Page 42
GRAMMAR
Exercise 1
1 was
2 were

Exercise 2
1 wasn't
2 Were
3 were
4 Was
5 wasn't
6 weren't

Exercise 3
Students' own answers.

LISTENING PART 5: TRAINING
Exercise 1
Students' own answers.

Exercise 2
Abby was at a barbecue and Sophie was visiting her cousin.

🌐 Track 027
Abby: Hi, Sophie. You didn't come to the barbecue on Saturday. Were you ill?
Sophie: No, I went to see my cousin. She's just had a baby. She's got an apartment near the football stadium.

Exercise 3
1 D		3 E
2 C		4 A

🌐 Track 028
Abby: Hi Sophie. You didn't come to the barbecue on Saturday. Were you ill?
Sophie: No, I went to see my cousin. She's just had a baby. She's got an apartment near the football stadium. Was the barbecue fun?
Abby: Yes, but a few people couldn't come.
Sophie: I suppose Alice was at work.
Abby: Actually, she had to go and buy a present for her older brother. He's getting married next week.
Sophie: Wow! Was Meg at the barbecue?
Abby: No, she phoned me to say she was feeling sick. She didn't get up at all on Saturday. I hope she's better soon – she starts her new job as a games designer in two weeks.
Sophie: Oh dear. Did you see Ben?
Abby: No. He was at home. He had some important homework to do and he didn't even have time to play his favourite video game.
Sophie: Really?
Abby: And James was missing too. He went to see his favourite team play – he just loves football. But it was a shame I didn't see him. I want to ask him which is the best sports shop in town.
Sophie: Send him a text.

Page 43
GRAMMAR
Exercise 1
2 -ed
4 didn't, did

Exercise 2
1 saw
2 got up
3 came
4 went
5 said
6 had

Exercise 3
1 She said 'good morning' when she saw us.
2 I didn't see her there.
3 They had a really good time.
4 Did she stay with you last week?
5 No she didn't.
6 He played video games until midnight.

Exercise 4
1 visited
2 didn't stay
3 got
4 worked

5 helped
6 didn't stop
7 came
8 made
9 cleaned
10 didn't finish

Exercise 5

Students' own answers.

🎧 Track 029

1 I phoned my friend. We loved the film.
2 She cooked lunch. I helped my grandmother.
3 She invited my cousins. We downloaded a film.

Exercise 6

Students' own answers.

🎧 Track 030

1 I uploaded lots of photos.
2 We cooked lunch.
3 They started early.
4 He streamed some music.
5 I liked the film.
6 We enjoyed the party.

Exercise 7

1 What did you do last weekend?
2 Where did you go on your last holiday?
3 How did you come to class today?
4 What was the last really good film you saw?

Page 44

VOCABULARY

Exercise 1

1 When was the last time you downloaded a great song?
2 When was the last time you phoned a friend?
3 When was the last time you watched a film that made you cry?
4 When was the last time you walked more than 5 km?

Exercise 2

1 a new song by a Turkish singer.
2 She wanted to speak to him because it's his birthday and birthdays are special.
3 sad films
4 walk

Exercise 3

2 five minutes ago
3 two years ago
3 last year

Exercise 4

1 yesterday afternoon
2 an hour ago
3 last year

4 last month
5 the day before yesterday

Exercises 5 & 6

Students' own answers.

Page 45

READING PART 3: TRAINING

Exercises 1 & 2

Students' own answers.

Exercise 3

a competition – a situation in which someone is trying to win something or be more successful than someone else

prize – something valuable, such as an amount of money, that is given to someone who succeeds in a competition or game or that is given to someone as a reward for doing very good work

professional – used to describe someone who does something as their job

win – to achieve first position and/or get first prize in a competition, election, fight, etc.

Exercise 4

World of Warcraft, Hearthstone

Exercise 5

2 C   3 B

Exercise 6

Students' own answers.

Page 46

WRITING

Exercise 1

Students' own answers.

Exercise 2

The characters because they are like real people.

Exercise 3

a plot
b dialogue
c character
d scene
e setting

Exercise 4

1 The Originals
2 Madrid
3 science students
4 science fiction comedy
5 Valeria – she's clever and funny but does silly things
6 when valeria finds out that she can fly
7 It's funny and exciting.
8 The characters say interesting things that make the writer think and laugh at the same time.

Exercise 5

		Key words (possible answers)
paragraph 1	setting genre plot	Madrid in the future science-fiction comedy-drama students studying science experiment, something strange happens, special powers.
paragraph 2	characters favourite scene	Out a window, special powers, can fly
paragraph 3	why the writer likes it	unusual difficult funny exciting characters like real people

Exercises 6 & 7

Students' own answers.

Page 47

SPEAKING

Exercise 1

Students' own answers.

Exercise 2

Sara had a fun weekend.

🎧 Track 031

Sara: Hi, Iman! How are you?

Iman: Hi, Sara, I'm fine. How are you? Did you have a nice weekend? Did you go to the cinema to see that new film?

Sara: No, I didn't, but my weekend was still really good, thanks. I went shopping on Saturday and I got a really nice new top, then, well, do you remember Sam who was at school with us? Well, he's started his own restaurant, so I went there for dinner.

Iman: Of course I remember Sam! Do you often see him?

Sara: No, but I'm friends with some of his friends and he invited us all for food at his new place. We had a party till late. It was great! What about you? How was your weekend?

Iman: Well it wasn't great, to be honest. It was really quiet on Saturday. I stayed at home and finished some work. I didn't really want to work this weekend, but it was good to finish it! After that I cleaned the apartment and watched TV.

Sara: And what about Sunday? What did you get up to on Sunday?

Iman: Not much. I was really tired. I went for a run in the park. I tried to call you, but you were out! What did you do on Sunday?

Sara: This and that. It was quite busy. A group of us went for a bike ride. The weather was great and we had a picnic. Then we watched films at mine.

Iman: Your weekend sounds great. Mine was so boring! I'm coming home next month, little sister, so I hope you take me out at the weekend with you then!

Exercise 3

1 Did you have a nice weekend?
2 How was your weekend?
3 What did you get up to on Sunday?
4 What did you do at the weekend?

Exercise 4

S = really good, quite busy, this and that
I = not great, really quiet, not much

Exercise 5

1 c	3 a	5 b
2 d	4 f	6 e

Exercise 6

Students' own answers.

Page 48

EXAM FOCUS
READING PART 3

1 B	3 A	5 A
2 C	4 B	

Page 49

LISTENING PART 5

1 E	3 H	5 G
2 A	4 C	

🎧 **Track 032**

Narrator: For each question choose the correct answer.
You will hear Luis talking to his friend about a weekend trip to the city. What activity is each person going to do?

Woman: Hi, Luis. Are you ready for your weekend trip with your friends? What activity are you going to do on Saturday morning – visit a museum?

Luis: That's what I usually do, isn't it! Actually, I'm seeing a friend who I met on holiday.

Woman: Great! And Stella's going with you, isn't she?

Luis: Yes. She's going to do a bus tour, because it's her first time in the city. She said that's more important than concerts or shopping!

Woman: Is that what Marco's going to do – shopping?

Luis: That's his plan. He wants to go to the music shops in the area where the theatres are.

Woman: Who else is going?

Luis: Lili. She wanted to take a river trip, but it's too cold, so she's going to do a walking tour with a guide. She wants to see the museums, concert halls and other famous buildings from the outside.

Woman: And Richard?

Luis: He has a friend who's in a play, so he's going to see that.

Woman: What's Clara going to do?

Luis: There's a new art museum near the river that she's decided to go to.

Luis: Well I hope you're all going to eat together in the evenings!

Page 50

REAL WORLD

Exercise 1

Suggested answers

at the theatre, acting/performing, queueing for tickets

Exercise 2

1 What to see
2 Where to get tickets
3 Where to sit
4 Where to eat before the show
5 What to buy

Page 51

Exercise 3

1 T
2 F – It's more expensive to watch a show in the evening.
3 F – Sometimes you want to be further away to get a bigger picture of what's happening.
4 F – Restaurants around Times Square are usually expensive.
5 T

Exercise 4

1 a	3 b	5 a
2 b	4 b	

Exercise 5

Speaker	Show	Day	Evening or matinee	Seats
1	Wicked	Thursday	evening	balcony
2	School of Rock	Tuesday	evening	orchestra
3	Charlie and the Chocolate Factory	Saturday	matinee	mezzanine

🎧 **Track 033**

1

Tourist: I'd like to book four tickets for *Wicked* on Thursday.

Clerk: OK. Matinee or evening?

Tourist: Matinee if possible, please.

Clerk: Let's have a look. Hmm. No, the matinee's sold-out, I'm afraid. I have tickets for the evening.

Tourist: OK, the evening is fine.

Clerk: I have tickets in the balcony and the mezzanine.

Tourist: OK. Probably the balcony, I think. How much are the tickets?

Clerk: For the balcony, they're sixty-nine dollars.

Tourist: Yes, that's fine.

Clerk: OK. How would you like to pay?

Tourist: By card, please.

Clerk: OK. The machine's ready for you. If you could put your number in, please.

Tourist: Thanks.

Clerk: And here's your receipt and your tickets. Enjoy the show.

2

Tourist 2: Do you sell tickets for *School of Rock* here?

Clerk: Yes, we do. When are you looking to go?

Tourist 2: On Tuesday evening, if possible.

Clerk: And how many tickets do you need?

Tourist 2: Four, please.

Clerk: OK. I don't have four in a block. Is that a problem?

Tourist 2: What have you got?

Clerk: I have two twos in the orchestra, for $89 each. There's the plan, do you see?

Tourist 2: Yes, I think that would be OK. I've got a student card. Is there a discount for students?

Clerk: No, sorry. We don't offer any concessions.

Tourist 2: OK. No problem. I'll take the four tickets.

Clerk: Thank you. That'll be three hundred and fifty-six dollars in total.

3

Tourist 3: Can I book tickets for *Charlie and the Chocolate Factory* here?

Clerk: You certainly can. When would you like to go?

Tourist 3: Next Saturday, the matinee performance.

Clerk: Let's have a look. It's pretty full. OK, I have some in the mezzanine. Do you mind the back row?

Tourist 3: No, that's fine. I need two tickets.

Clerk: OK. I have two tickets in the back row at one hundred and twenty dollars each.

Tourist 3: That's great. Can I use these vouchers to pay for the tickets?

Clerk: Let me see the date on them. Yes, you can use these. They give you twenty per cent off, so your tickets will come to one hundred and ninety-two dollars in total.

Tourist 3: Thanks.

Exercise 6

1 I'd like
2 Do you sell
3 Is there
4 Can I
5 these vouchers

Exercise 7

1 c	3 d	5 b
2 a	4 e	

Exercises 8 & 9

1 c	3 a	5 f
2 e	4 b	6 d

Exercise 10

Students' own answers.

UNIT 4

Page 52

READING

Exercise 1

Students' own answers.

Exercise 2

1 A	3 B	5 E
2 D	4 C	6 F

Exercise 3

1 a	3 b	5 c
2 c	4 b	6 b

🎧 **Track 034**

Man: The fastest runners can run up to forty-four kilometres per hour.

Woman: Professional basketball players and dancers can jump nearly one point three metres.

Man: The fastest cyclists can cycle up to fifty-four kilometres in one hour.

Woman: Some divers can stay under water for over 20 minutes.

Man: Some skiers can ski up to two hundred and fifty kilometres per hour.

Woman: It's possible for a person to lift two thousand, eight hundred and forty kilos.

Exercise 4

Students' own answers.

Page 53

Exercise 5

1 T
2 F Only women dancers dance on their toes.
3 T
4 F They can. Small athletes run a lot.
5 T
6 F He couldn't play for three months.

Exercise 6

1 their feet
2 their knees, necks and shoulders

VOCABULARY

Exercise 1

1 neck
2 back
3 stomach
4 toe
5 brain
6 finger
7 heart
8 knee

Exercise 2

1 toes
2 back
3 neck
4 stomach
5 heart
6 fingers
7 brain
8 knee

Page 54

GRAMMAR

Exercise 1

1 can
2 could

Exercise 2

1 b	3 e	5 a
2 f	4 d	6 c

Exercise 3

1 couldn't
2 could
3 can't
4 could
5 can't
6 couldn't
7 can

Exercise 4

Can and *could* are unstressed:
- in the second question in each dialogue (*Can you? / Could you?*)
- in the positive statements in the last line of each dialogue (*I can walk on my hands, too / I could write quite well, too*)

🎧 **Track 035**

1

A: Can you stand on your head?
B: No, I can't. Can you?
A: Yes, I can and I can walk on my hands, too!

2

A: Could you read when you were six years old?
B: Yes, I could, a little. Could you?
A: Yes, I could and I could write quite well, too.

Exercise 5

Students' own answers.

Page 55

VOCABULARY

Exercise 1

1 C (Jack) has a headache
2 G (Alissa) has a broken arm
3 H (Mina) has backache.
4 D (Luca) hurt his knee
5 F (Harry) has a cold
6 A (Jenna) has a stomach ache and feels sick
7 B (Daniel) has a toothache.
8 E Sally hasn't got a health problem

🎧 **Track 036**

1

Woman: Are you OK, Jack? What's the matter?

Jack: I've got a headache. I think it's because of the sun. I was outside without a hat.

2

Man: Oh Alissa! How did you break your arm?

Alissa: I broke it when I was playing tennis with my friends.

Man: What happened?

Alissa: A friend called an ambulance and I went to hospital.

3

Woman: What's the matter, Mina?

Mina: I've got backache. I just need to sit down and have a rest.

4

Boy: Hi, Luca. How's your knee?

Luca: It's OK. I hurt it when I was playing football last weekend! Luckily, I didn't break it.

5
Woman: Have you got a cold, Harry?
Harry: Yes, I have.
Woman: Can I get you some medicine?
Harry: Oh no, it's OK. I went to the pharmacy and I got some already.
6
Man: Where's Jenna?
Woman: She's in bed. She ate some bad fish last night and now she's got a stomach ache and she feels sick.
Man: I'm sorry to hear that. I hope she gets better soon.
7
Woman: Have you got a headache, Daniel?
Daniel: No, I haven't. I've got toothache. It really hurts!
Woman: You should go to the dentist.
8
Man: How are you, Sally? Are you well?
Sally: I'm very well, thank you. I feel great!

Exercise 2
1 head
2 arm
3 backache
4 hurt
5 cold
6 stomach ache/feels
7 ache
8 fine

Exercise 3
1 e   **3** g   **5** a   **7** b
2 d   **4** f   **6** c

Exercise 4
1 matter
2 well
3 hurt
4 sorry
5 better
6 your

Exercise 5
1 1, 2, 3, 6
2 4, 5

Exercise 6
Students' own answers.

Page 56
GRAMMAR
Exercise 1
Students' own answers.

Exercise 2
1 5
2 25g
3 1.6
4 10

5 9
6 30

Exercise 3
1 should
2 shouldn't
3 Should
4 shouldn't

Exercise 4
1 should eat
2 Should … exercise, should
3 should drink
4 shouldn't drive, should walk

Exercise 5
Students' own answers.

SPEAKING
Exercise 1
Students' own answers.

🎧 **Track 037**
1
Woman: First of all, it's great that you are trying to start exercising, but perhaps you should start exercising more slowly! To begin with, what about walking for half an hour every day? Walking is great exercise. Also running isn't the only way to keep fit. Why don't you try some different types of exercise like dancing and swimming as well? It's important to do exercise that you enjoy.
2
Woman: Well, it's OK to eat fast food sometimes, but you shouldn't eat it all the time. It's bad for you because it has too much fat, salt and sugar in it. Why don't you try some other types of food? Healthy food tastes good too! And if you really want a burger, how about having a salad with it, or some fruit as a dessert?

Exercise 2
1 you should
2 how about
3 Why don't you
4 you shouldn't
5 Why don't you
6 how about

Exercise 3
Students' own answers.

Page 57
LISTENING PART 4: TRAINING
Exercise 1
🎧 **Track 038**
Narrator: One. Annie is talking to her friend at work. What's the matter with Annie?
Man: Are you OK, Annie? You look unwell.

Annie: I ate something yesterday that made me sick. I didn't sleep at all last night.
Man: Shall I help you with your work? I know you've got loads to do.
Annie: No, it's OK. I've finished everything for today. My stomach feels better today but I'm going home now – I just can't keep my eyes open.

Exercise 2
2 C   **3** C

🎧 **Track 039**
Narrator: Two, You will hear Victor phoning his friend Karen.
Why is Victor phoning?
Victor: Hi, Karen. It's Victor.
Karen: Hi, Victor. Do you still want to go for a walk after lunch?
Victor: I'd really like to, but I've got a problem with my leg. Whenever I try to walk, I'm in so much pain. I've made a doctor's appointment for 3 o'clock.
Karen: Oh dear. Then I'll fetch you from your house and drive you there.
Victor: Thanks.
Narrator: Three. You will hear Jake talking to his friend Naomi.
What's the matter with Jake?
Naomi: What's the matter, Jake? Have you got a headache?
Jake: Hi, Naomi. No, I was at the dentist yesterday. She took one of my teeth out.
Naomi: Ouch! Was it giving you a lot of pain?
Jake: It was, but not anymore. The thing is, I've hurt my neck. Probably my head was in the wrong position when I was lying in the dentist's chair.
Naomi: Poor you!

PUSH YOURSELF B1
Exercise 1
No, sports people often injure the parts of the body they use in their sports.

Exercise 2
1 ankles
2 lungs
3 shoulders
4 muscles
5 wrists
6 Bones
7 elbows
8 hips

Page 58
VOCABULARY
Exercise 1
Students' own answers.

Exercise 2
1 A on holiday in the mountains
   B in the garden

2 A last year

  B one afternoon

3 A A man skied in front of her and she bumped into him.

  B He was helping his nephew who was stuck in a tree and he got stuck too.

4 A her leg

  B his arm

Exercise 3

1 last year, one day, one sunny afternoon

2 then, after that, so, when

3 suddenly

Exercise 4

1 fell over

2 hit

3 got stuck

4 bumped into

Page 59

WRITING PART 7

Exercise 1

1 c   **3** a   **5** f

2 e   **4** d   **6** b

Exercise 2

Students' own answers.

SPEAKING

Exercise 1

When/where?	winter holidays, in the mountains
Who with?	cousin Gemma
What did they do?	They went ice-skating.
How did he feel?	worried, frightened
What happened?	A duck landed in front of him and he couldn't stop – he fell and hurt a finger.
What happened after that?	They didn't go skating again – his finger ached for the rest of the holiday.

🎧 Track 040

Alex: Last winter holidays, I went to visit my cousin Gemma in the mountains. It was very cold and the lake near her house was covered in thick ice so we decided to go ice-skating. I felt a bit worried because I'm not very good at ice-skating, but Gemma said it would be OK. When we got to the lake, I put on my ice-skates and went on to the ice for the first time. I was frightened, but I started skating slowly across the lake. Soon, I began to skate faster and it was actually quite fun! Then suddenly a duck flew down and landed on the ice in front of me. I tried to stop but I couldn't!

I lost control and I fell hard onto the ice! I didn't hit the duck, because it flew away, but I did hit my hand and I hurt one of my fingers. I didn't break anything, but my finger ached for the rest of the holiday and we didn't go skating again.

Exercises 2 & 3

Students' own answers.

Page 60

EXAM FOCUS
LISTENING PART 4

1 A   **3** C   **5** C

2 B   **4** B

🎧 Track 041

Narrator: For each question, choose the correct answer.

One. You will hear two friends talking about doing exercise. What does the man say about it?

Woman: I swam three kilometres yesterday!

Man: Wow, that's incredible! I can't swim that far. But don't you ever find swimming boring?

Woman: No, I love it. I like having time alone to think.

Man: I work harder when I do exercise with friends. That's why I like football or tennis.

Narrator: Two. You will hear a woman leaving a message for a doctor's receptionist. Why did the woman call?

Woman: Hello, this is Lily Williams. I called yesterday, and made an appointment to see the doctor next Monday. Now my boss says I have to work that day, so I was wondering if I could come on Tuesday instead. The time you gave me was 4 pm . Can I come at that time on Tuesday? Call me back, please.

Narrator: Three. You will hear a woman called Lara talking to a friend about going shopping. What does Lara want her friend to do?

Man: I'm looking forward to going to the new shopping centre, Lara. Is there plenty of parking there?

Woman: Yes, but my car's broken down. Can we go in yours? I'll pay you for the petrol.

Man: No problem and don't worry about the money! I'll pick you up at ten.

Woman: Thanks! I'm going to get a dress for Helena's wedding. I've seen the perfect one!

Narrator: Four. You will hear a man talking about his new job. How does the man feel about his new job?

Woman: How's the new job, Daniel?

Man: Pretty good. At first I wasn't sure, because the boss shouts, and he's always talking about how much money the

company is or isn't earning. But I guess that's his job – he's the boss! And there's no real end time. When we finish the day's work, we just go, so my days are shorter now, which is great.

Narrator: Five. You will hear two friends talking about an exhibition of photographs. Where will the exhibition be?

Woman: Lucy's chosen a great place for her photography exhibition!

Man: I know! A few of the photos will be behind the reception desk, so people will see them when they arrive, or as they're paying. There'll be others in the restaurant, too.

Woman: What about in the guest's rooms?

Man: No, but there'll be some on the walls between the lifts and the rooms.

Page 61

WRITING PART 7

Model answer

A man had toothache, so his wife phoned the dentist to make an appointment. He didn't want to see the dentist, so she pushed him into the room. She waited for him. When the man came out, he was smiling and didn't have toothache anymore. (45 words)

Page 62

REAL WORLD

Exercise 1

Suggested answer

to get help with health problems/if they are sick.

Exercise 2

1 C   **2** A   **3** B

Page 63

Exercise 3

1 c   **4** h   **7** e

2 f   **5** g   **8** b

3 a   **6** d

Exercise 4

1 from a supermarket, small shop or petrol station

2 from a supermarket, small shop or petrol station

3 from a pharmacy

4 find your nearest GP and phone to book an appointment

5 find out which doctor is on call and go to the medical centre

6 go to the A and E department of a hospital, or call 112 or 999 and ask for an ambulance

Exercise 5

1 b   **2** d   **3** a

1

Assistant: Hello. Can I help you?

Tourist: Yes. I have a prescription from the doctor.

Assistant: OK. Let me see … Yes, we can do this for you. Are you taking any other medicines?

Tourist: No, I'm not taking any medicines at the moment.

Assistant: Any other medical conditions?

Tourist: No.

Assistant: And have you taken this medicine before?

Tourist: Yes. In my own country.

Assistant: And you didn't have any side effects?

Tourist: No.

Assistant: That's good. Well, take a seat. It'll be about five minutes.

Tourist: Thank you.

Assistant: Here's your prescription. Take one tablet three times a day, with food. And you must finish the whole course.

Tourist: OK. Thank you.

2

Nurse: Maria Baldini, please. Could you come this way?

Nurse: OK. Just take a seat for me. Can I check your name first?

Maria: Yes, it's Maria Baldini.

Nurse: And what's your date of birth, Maria?

Maria: The tenth of December, 1999.

Nurse: So, can you tell me what's happened?

Maria: Yes. I was getting off a bus and I fell, and I've hurt my arm.

Nurse: And when was this?

Maria: About an hour ago.

Nurse: OK. Can I take a look?

Maria: Yes, of course.

Nurse: OK. Does this hurt here?

Maria: Ah, yes.

Nurse: Sorry. And what about this?

Maria: Yes, but that's not so bad.

Nurse: Can you move your fingers?

Maria: No, not really.

Nurse: OK, well I think we need to get it X-rayed. Any other medical problems?

Maria: No.

Nurse: Do you take any medicines regularly?

Maria: Yes, I take tablets for headaches.

Nurse: OK. Do you know the name?

Maria: I have it here.

Nurse: OK. Thanks. And where are you from, Maria?

Maria: I'm from Italy.

Nurse: Do you have your EHIC card with you?

Maria: Yes, it's in my bag. Here it is.

Nurse: Thanks. Are you in pain at the moment?

Maria: No, I'm OK, thanks.

Nurse: That's great. If you could wait back in the waiting area, you'll see a doctor within an hour, and they'll do an X-ray to see if anything's broken. Then they'll decide what to do next. There will be a charge for the emergency consultation, but you can probably claim that back when you get home.

Maria: OK. thanks.

3

Receptionist: Hi. How are you doing?

Tourist: OK, thanks, but I have a really bad sore throat and I need to get something for it.

Receptionist: OK. Do you think you need to see a doctor?

Tourist: No, I think it's OK. I just need some painkillers.

Receptionist: OK. Well, it's best to try the pharmacy on Argyle Street. It's only a five-minute walk from here, if you go out of the hotel and turn right, then first left, that's Argyle Street.

Tourist: OK. Thank you.

Exercise 6

1 prescription
2 medicines
3 tablets
4 sore
5 painkillers

Exercise 7

1 c   **3** a
2 d   **4** b

Exercises 8 & 9

the city: the capital of the Republic of Ireland, and also the biggest city; on the east coast of Ireland; has many old buildings and also modern buildings

pharmacies: have a green cross outside; you can buy medicines such as painkillers and also collect medicines when you have a prescription

medical centres: usually need to make an appointment to see a doctor, but at some medical centres you can go without an appointment. You will see a GP, a general doctor.

doctors on call: medical centres all open during the day; at night only one or two doctors are on call. Ask at your hotel to find out which doctors are on call.

hospital emergency departments: hospitals open 24 hours a day; you can go to the emergency department at any time, or dial 999 to call an ambulance if you are seriously ill or there is an emergency. Specialist doctors and nurses will look after you.

Exercises 10 & 11

Students' own answers.

UNIT 5

Page 64

VOCABULARY

Exercise 1

Students' own answers.

Exercise 2

1 B   **3** C   **5** E
2 A   **4** D

Exercise 3

Students' own answers.

Page 65

LISTENING

Exercise 1

1 Loli – the beach
2 Chloe and Lisa – the mountains
3 Jamie – the city

Loli: I love the beach but I'm a student and don't have much money at the moment, so I always try to find cheap destinations. If the weather is sunny and I can go swimming in the sea, I'm happy! My friends and I look for cheap flights and places to stay online. Some of them dream about staying in expensive hotels, but for me, staying with local people in their houses is the best kind of holiday accommodation.

Chloe: Well, for Lisa and me, a true holiday is when we are outside in nature. We like going to places where there aren't many tourists – or even any other people at all. We often go walking and camping in the mountains. We don't take much luggage – just a tent to sleep in and a backpack with food and water.

Lisa: Yes, that's right. Chloe loves camping like this and I do too, but I'm also happy when we can stay in a campsite where there are toilets and showers. I like meeting the local people and trying to talk to them. We enjoy going to places where we can't speak the language, but we do try to learn some important words before we go!

Jamie: An interesting city with lots of museums and restaurants is always a good destination for me! I work long hours in a bank and I like to pack a small suitcase on Friday night and fly to a city for the weekend. I always stay in the best hotels because I want to be really comfortable. When I visit a city for the first time, I take a proper city tour with a tour guide, so I can learn all about its history. In the evenings, I enjoy going to music concerts and I think that asking at the tourist information centre is a good way to find out about what's on. They can tell you about the best plays and concerts and book tickets for you.

Exercise 2

1 F She likes swimming.
2 T
3 F She's happy when they can stay in a campsite where there are toilets and showers.
4 F They often go to places where they can't speak the language, but they try to learn some important words before they go.
5 T
6 F He goes to the tourist information centre to find out about concerts.

Exercise 3

1 accommodation
2 miss, delay
3 luggage, tent, backpack
4 destination
5 suitcase
6 tour guide
7 tourist information centre

Exercise 4

1 d **3** f **5** c
2 e **4** a **6** b

Page 66

READING
Exercise 1

Students' own answers.

Exercise 2

1 He wanted something exciting to do. No.
2 He started to feel sick/was feeling bad.

Exercise 3

1 Camels are very friendly and they love their owners.
2 The camel didn't look friendly and made strange, loud noises.
3 She was saying hello to Jon.
4 so that people can get onto them
5 because riding a camel was like being in a boat
6 She was a nice animal.

GRAMMAR
Exercise 1

1 an action in progress at a time in the past
2 at the same time

Exercise 2

1 were … doing
2 wasn't raining, was snowing
3 were lying, watching
4 was packing, was doing
5 wasn't living, was studying
6 Was … looking for, wasn't

Page 67

Exercise 3

1 Where were you going yesterday afternoon?

2 The children weren't playing on the beach this morning.
3 Was she trying to take a photo?
4 Your friend wasn't staying at this hotel.
5 'Was he looking at her?' 'No, he wasn't.'
6 Which city were they visiting?

Exercise 4

A: Where were you last night? Were you at the party?
B: Yes, we <u>were</u>.
A: Was it good?
B: Yes, it was great! <u>Weren't</u> you invited?
A: Yes, we <u>were</u>. But we couldn't go because my mum was cooking us dinner.

Exercise 5

1 A unstressed, B stressed
2 A unstressed, B stressed
3 unstressed

🎧 Track 045
1
A: Was it hot that day?
B: No, it wasn't.
2
A: Was the exam really three hours long?
B: Yes, it was.
3
The actors in the play were really funny.

Exercise 6

Students' own answers.

LISTENING
Exercise 1

1 Mongolia and China
2 Students' own answers.

Exercise 2

Cold

🎧 Track 046
Man: Benedict Allen began to cross the Gobi Desert in Mongolia and China in August 1997. It was a journey of 1,600 kilometres and he was alone and on foot. He took three camels with him to carry his things and he decided not to use any modern technology to help him. He preferred to use a map.
He only had three months to make the journey because the Gobi Desert can be very cold and he needed to cross it before the beginning of winter. Many people thought that it was an impossible journey and one of Benedict Allen's camels did too. As they were doing the most difficult part of the journey, the camel decided that it didn't want to continue and it ran away. So Benedict Allen had to continue his journey with only two camels.
He never got lost but sometimes he didn't meet or speak to other people for weeks.

During his journey, one of Benedict Allen's biggest problems was the cold. Sometimes his food turned to ice before he finished eating it. On the 12th of October 1998, he reached the end of his journey and became one of the few people to cross the Gobi on foot.

Exercise 3

1 b **3** c **5** c
2 b **4** b **6** b

Exercise 4

Students' own answers.

Page 68

GRAMMAR
Exercise 1

1 in the middle of
2 after each other

Exercise 2

1 the dog ran out of the house
2 I realised I didn't have my passport

Exercise 3

1 were visiting, lost
2 stopped, got off
3 was having, reading
4 met, was walking

Exercise 4

1 were … going
2 were sailing, started
3 were driving, ran
4 was shining, came out

PUSH YOURSELF B1
Exercise 1

1 at the same time
2 after

Exercise 2

1 d **3** e **5** b
2 f **4** c **6** a

Page 69

VOCABULARY
Exercise 1

She works for a hotel company.
She doesn't enjoy cruises.

Exercise 2

1 e **3** d **5** a
2 b **4** f **6** c

Exercise 3

1 journey
2 trip
3 travel
4 cruise
5 flight
6 crossing

READING PART 4: TRAINING

Exercise 2

1 B   **3** A   **5** C
2 C   **4** B

Page 70

SPEAKING PART 2: TRAINING

Exercise 1

Students' own answers.

Exercise 2

Pablo – picture C
Julia – picture D
Arturo – picture A
Teresa – picture E
Picture B isn't mentioned.

🎧 **Track 047**

Pablo: My last holiday was in my country, in Mexico. I went to the beach with my family and some of our friends for a week and we had a great time. The weather was fantastic – really warm and sunny so there were lots of other people there. Sometimes the beach was very crowded but we didn't mind and we went swimming every day. I think that the best holidays are when you are with your friends.

Julia: Well I didn't have a good time on my last holiday. I went walking in the mountains with my boyfriend and it was really tiring. The weather was OK for the first two days and then it rained all the time. It was terrible! I hate being out in the rain.

Arturo: I came back from holiday last week. I went to New York with some friends. I didn't really enjoy it. For me, a holiday is a time to relax but New York is too noisy and crowded for that. My friends just wanted to go shopping and buy clothes but I'm not really interested in walking around shops so I was bored.

Teresa: In summer, I went camping for a week in the country. We were on a campsite by a lake. It was lovely – we lay on the grass under the trees all day or went swimming. The place was so quiet – it was really nice.

Exercise 3

Pablo and Teresa had a good time. Julia and Arturo didn't enjoy their holiday.

Exercise 4

1 I didn't have a good time
2 It was lovely.
3 For me, a holiday is a time to relax
4 The weather was fantastic.
5 I think that the best holidays are

Exercises 5 & 6

Students' own answers.

Exercise 7

The candidates:
ask each other questions.
give reasons using *because.*
use phrases like *I think,* and *In my opinion.*
They don't give longer answers.

🎧 **Track 048**

Examiner: Now, in this part of the test you are going to talk together. Here are some pictures that show different things to do on holiday. Do you like these different things to do on holiday? Say why or why not. I'll say that again. Do you like these different things to do on holiday? Say why or why not. All right? Now, talk together.

Elena: Let's talk about the first holiday, Ricardo – the people spending their holiday by the hotel swimming pool. Do you like doing this on holiday?

Ricardo: I like swimming – in the pool or in the sea – but I don't enjoy doing this every day on holiday. It's a bit boring for me.

Elena: I think swimming and sunbathing are very relaxing.

Ricardo: And what about the next picture? The people walking in the mountains.

Elena: Oh I think it's fantastic to enjoy nature on holiday. It could be tiring to climb a mountain.

Ricardo: Yes but you can see interesting things.

Elena: In my opinion, you can see more interesting things when you visit old cities on holiday, like in this picture. Do you agree?

Ricardo: Yes but I don't enjoy visiting cities when they're crowded. It's terrible.

Elena: That's true.

Ricardo: Do you enjoy visiting amusement parks on holiday?

Elena: Yes, why not?

Ricardo: I think amusement parks are noisy. I don't want to spend a whole day there.

Examiner: Do you think walking in the mountains is good for you, Ricardo?

Ricardo: Yes, the air is clean and you can stay fit.

Examiner: Do you think going to an amusement park is exciting, Elena?

Elena: Yes, because the rides are scary.

Examiner: So, Elena, which of these things to do on holiday do you like best?

Elena: I like going sightseeing.

Examiner: And you, Ricardo, which of these things to do on holiday do you like best?

Ricardo: Probably, walking in the mountains.

Examiner: Thank you. Now, do you prefer to go on holiday with your friends or your family, Ricardo?

Ricardo: With my friends, because it's more fun.

Examiner: What about you, Elena?

Elena: I like going on holiday with my family. My mum always goes shopping with me and buys me lots of things!

Examiner: What will you do on your next holiday, Elena?

Elena: I don't know. I'll probably visit my grandparents' house. I'll go swimming and windsurfing because they live by the beach.

Examiner: And you, Ricardo?

Ricardo: Sorry?

Examiner: What will you do on your next holiday?

Ricardo: I'll probably go sailing on a lake and ride my bike in the countryside.

Examiner: Thank you. That is the end of the test.

Page 71

WRITING

Exercise 1

1 on holiday in the mountains; camping
2 with her friends Thomas and Jo
3 No, she hates it.

🎧 **Track 049**

Lily: Hi, Carla, it's Lily here.

Carla: Lily! Where are you? You sound far away.

Lily: I am! We're in the mountains with my friends Thomas and Jo and I can't phone or text any of my friends most of the time – there's no signal. It's terrible. I have to sleep in a tent and it's really cold and uncomfortable.

Carla: Oh dear … So you don't enjoy camping then?

Lily: No, I hate it! I hate not having an indoor bathroom and I don't like walking or climbing up mountains like Thomas and Jo do. I prefer shopping and going to see interesting places when I'm on holiday.

Carla: What's the weather like, there? Can't you go swimming? Or at least do some sunbathing?

Lily: Well it's sunny but it's not warm enough for sunbathing. And the water in the lake is REALLY cold.

Exercise 2

It's now cold and raining. She isn't camping any more, she's staying in a hotel. She's enjoying her holiday.

Exercise 3

1 c   **3** d   **5** e
2 a   **4** b   **6** f

Exercise 4

1 In the evening
2 yesterday
3 right now
4 This morning
5 After that
6 Today

Exercises 5 & 6

Students' own answers.

Page 72

EXAM FOCUS
READING PART 4

1 C	3 C	5 B
2 A	4 A	6 B

Page 73

SPEAKING PART 2

Students' own answers.

Page 74

REAL WORLD

Exercise 1

A a hop on / hop off bus tour
B a walking tour
C a bike tour
D a Trabi safari

Page 75

Exercise 2

1 F You can get on and off when you want.
2 F You can buy tickets for more than one day.
3 T
4 T
5 F You can drive the car yourself.

Exercise 3

1 e	3 f	5 a
2 b	4 c	6 d

Exercise 4

1 d	2 c	3 a

🔊 Track 050

1

Receptionist: Hi. Can I help you?
Tourist: Yes, I'd like some information about the City Circle sightseeing tour.
Receptionist: OK. What would you like to know?
Tourist: How long does the tour take?
Receptionist: The whole tour takes about two hours from start to finish, but of course you can hop on and hop off as often as you like, and the ticket is valid all day, from ten till six.
Tourist: Great. And where does it go?
Receptionist: It takes in all the main sights – the Brandenburg Gate, Checkpoint Charlie, Potsdamer Platz, everywhere you want to see.

Tourist: That sounds good. How much are the tickets?
Receptionist: Tickets are 22 euros per person, but you can save 25% with the Welcome Card. Do you have one of those?
Tourist: Yes, I do.
Receptionist: OK. So with a Welcome Card it's 16 euros 50.
Tourist: Great. I'd like to buy two tickets for that, please.

2

Tourist: Hello. Do you sell Berlin Welcome Cards here?
Assistant: Yes, we do.
Tourist: Can you give me some information about the card? What do you get with it?
Assistant: There's free admission to the most popular tourist places, like the Berlin TV Tower, and also free admission to all museums, including the Berlin Wall Museum. You get one free tour, which can be bus, bike or on foot, and up to 30% discounts in some restaurants and theatres, plus a free information leaflet about travel in the city, and tourist map. There's also free public transport anywhere in the city. It's very popular, and most people find it really good value for money.
Tourist: OK. How much does it cost?
Assistant: Would you like 48 hours, 72 hours or 4 days?
Tourist: 48 hours.
Assistant: So, for 48 hours it's 19 Euros 90.
Tourist: OK. I'll buy one.

3

Tourist: Hello. Can we hire some bikes here?
Receptionist: Of course. Is it for a bike tour, or just for you?
Tourist: No. Not a bike tour. We just want to cycle round the city on our own.
Receptionist: That's fine. So, it's 10 euros per day per bike and you have to pay this before you take the bike. A helmet is included in the price if you want one. There's also a returnable deposit of 200 euros per bike, which must be paid straight away and we need some formal ID.
Tourist: OK. That's no problem.
Receptionist: And if you decide to extend the hire, it's one euro for each additional day.
Tourist: OK. that sounds good.
Receptionist: Great. So, do you want to hire one?
Tourist: Yes, please.

Exercise 5

1 some information
2 How long
3 How much
4 Do you sell
5 Can we hire

Exercise 6

1 c	3 a	5 b
2 e	4 f	6 d

Exercises 7 & 8

the Berlin Wall: built in 1961 to separate East Berlin from West Berlin; had guards to stop people crossing the city; came down in 1989; some sections still standing, tourists visit it.

the Brandenburg gate: built in 1700s, a major tourist attraction; important because it shows the city is now free and not divided.

Checkpoint Charlie: one of the official places where people could cross from East to West Berlin if they had the correct documents; now popular with tourists.

ghost stations: old East German train stations under Berlin that closed because of divided Berlin; people couldn't get off at them; now tourists can visit them.

Potsdamer Platz: public square that was divided by the Berlin Wall; now modern buildings and great place for shopping and eating.

Exercise 9

Students' own answers.

Page 76

PROGRESS CHECK 2

Exercise 1

1 B	3 C	5 E
2 F	4 A	6 D

Exercise 2

1 brain
2 fingers
3 neck
4 toes
5 knees
6 stomach
7 heart
8 back

Exercise 3

1 couldn't sleep
2 can speak
3 couldn't play
4 can't swim
5 could ride

Exercise 4

1
1 matter
2 ill
3 should
4 pharmacy

2
1 get up
2 much
3 streamed
4 shouldn't

3

1 How about
2 horror
3 comedy
4 Shall

4

1 trip
2 crowded
3 should
4 relaxing

5

1 ache
2 Why don't you
3 problem
4 rest

Page 77

Exercise 5

1 news
2 quiz shows
3 science fiction
4 crime drama
5 comedy
6 documentaries

Exercise 6

1 backpack
2 campsite
3 crossings
4 suitcase
5 journey
6 delay
7 cruise
8 tourist information centre

Exercise 7

1 Last night I **went** to a disco on the beach.
2 We **enjoyed** it when the country's team won.
3 Did you **go** anywhere for your summer vacation?
4 We **played** volleyball at the lake last summer.
5 The weather **was** warm and cloudy.
6 The T-shirt only **cost** me £5.

Exercise 8

1 called, didn't answer
2 was playing, hurt
3 went, was
4 didn't hear, was listening
5 were you doing, phoned
6 was, read

Exercise 9

1 was
2 found
3 Did
4 called / contacted
5 have
6 went
7 could

UNIT 6

Page 78

Exercise 1

A Someone is taking a photo with their phone.
B Someone is watching a cooking programme.
C Two men are cooking.
Students' own answers.

Exercise 2

taking photos of their food and posting them on social media

Exercise 3

1 F Many people don't want to cook and they say that they don't have time to cook.
2 T
3 T
4 F 70% take photos to share online.
5 F Some chefs don't want customers to take photos in their restaurants.

Exercise 4

Students' own answers.

Page 79

VOCABULARY

Exercise 1

1 Beef, chicken
2 Broccoli
3 Chillies, curry
4 yoghurt
5 cereal
6 mushroom
7 mango
8 omelette

Exercise 2

Students' own answers.

PUSH YOURSELF B1

Exercise 1

Speaker 1: fried potatoes (B)
Speaker 2: steak sandwich (C)
Speaker 3: sweet coconut rice (A)

🎧 **Track 051**

1

Woman: First I peel the skin off the potatoes and then I use a sharp knife to chop them into small rectangular pieces. After that I put some oil in a frying pan. When the oil is very hot, I put the potatoes in the pan and fry them until they are brown. I eat them with lots of salt. I love them!

2

Man: The best way to cook the meat is to grill it. I usually cook the steak for about 3–5 minutes on each side. You can cook it for longer if you want to but be careful not to burn it! When it's ready, I put the steak between two pieces of bread with some salad and then it's ready to eat. It's my favourite sandwich.

3

Woman: First, I steam the rice for 15 minutes above a saucepan of boiling water until it's soft. Then I put some coconut milk in another saucepan and add sugar or honey to make it sweet. I put the rice and the sweet coconut milk together and cook them gently for three minutes. I make sure that I stir the rice and coconut milk every few seconds. When the rice is ready, I eat it with fresh mango. Delicious!

Exercise 2

1 peel
2 chop
3 fry
4 grill
5 burn
6 steam
7 add
8 stir

Page 80

GRAMMAR

Exercise 1

1 One

Exercise 2

1 yoghurt U
2 bread U
3 apple C
4 mushroom C

Exercise 3

Students' own answers.

🎧 **Track 052**

Man: cakes
Woman: sandwiches
Man: bananas
Woman: pieces
Man: mangos
Woman: apples
Man: snacks
Woman: cups
Man: fridges

Exercise 4

/s/	/z/	/ɪz/
eat**s**	egg**s**	slic**es**
cakes	bananas	sandwiches
snacks	mangos	pieces
cups	apples	fridges

Exercise 5

1 countable
2 some
3 any
4 any

Exercise 6

1 any
2 Are, are
3 some
4 Is, isn't, are
5 some

Exercise 7

1 some
2 any
3 a
4 some
5 some
6 some
7 a
8 any

Exercise 8

Students' own answers.

Page 81

READING PART 1: TRAINING

Exercise 1

Students' own answers.

Exercise 2

C

Exercise 3

1 C   2 B   3 C

Page 82

GRAMMAR

Exercise 1

Students' own answers.

Exercise 2

1 a   3 a   5 a
2 b   4 b

🔊 Track 053

Vanessa: That smells delicious, Rob. What is it?

Rob: It's a vegetable chilli for tonight. For dinner with your friends.

Vanessa: What's in it?

Rob: All the vegetables I found in your fridge – onions, carrots, potatoes, mushrooms and tomatoes.

Vanessa: Is there a lot of chilli in it?

Rob: No, not much. I know you and your friends don't like hot and spicy food.

Vanessa: That's not true! I do! … I love spicy food. But some people don't. Can I taste it? Mmm, delicious … I don't like food that has a lot of salt in it, but this is just perfect! I'm going shopping now. Do you need anything?

Rob: I'm not sure. How much rice do we have in the cupboard?

Vanessa: Let's see. Not much. There's half a packet of rice.

Rob: OK, well can you get another two packets of rice, please? And do we have any lemons? I need a lot of lemons to make the dessert with.

Vanessa: Yes, we do, but not many. Just two.

Rob: Can you get me six lemons and a little cream. Oh, and also a few oranges, not many, just one or two.

Vanessa: OK, that's two packets of rice, six lemons, a little cream and a few oranges. OK, I'll get them. See you later!

Exercise 3

1 many, many
2 much, much
3 few
4 little
5 lot of

Exercise 4

1 a little
2 a few
3 much, much
4 How many
5 a few, a little
6 much

Exercise 5

1 many
2 any
3 some
4 much
5 much
6 many
7 an
8 an
9 some
10 a little
11 many
12 a lot of
13 a few
14 a few

Exercise 6

Students' own answers.

Page 83

LISTENING PART 3: TRAINING

Exercises 1 & 2

Students' own answers.

🔊 Track 054

Ben: Hi, Katie, how are you?

Katie: Hi, Ben. I'm fine. I went to dinner at Maria's house last night. You know, Maria, my Italian friend.

Ben: Yes, I remember Maria. I met her once at your mum's house. She's very nice! Is she a good cook?

Katie: I don't know. Maria's husband Dan did the cooking. It was delicious!

Exercise 3

2 B   3 A   4 B

🔊 Track 055

Ben: Hi, Katie, how are you?

Katie: Hi, Ben. I'm fine. I went to dinner at Maria's house last night. You know, Maria, my Italian friend.

Ben: Yes, I remember Maria. I met her once at your mum's house. She's very nice! Is she a good cook?

Katie: I don't know. Maria's husband Dan did the cooking. It was delicious!

Ben: What did you eat?

Katie: We had spicy chicken with fresh mango and rice. The rice had lots of salt in it – I couldn't eat it. But the mango was sweet and juicy and the chicken was delicious. I don't usually like spicy food but this was excellent.

Ben: What was for dessert?

Katie: Strawberries and a cake made with oranges. We didn't have coffee after the meal. We had a drink made with yoghurt instead. It was delicious after the sweet dessert.

Ben: Interesting! I made chocolate cake yesterday. Not from the book I got for my birthday – those recipes need too much chocolate – I found it online. The cake was delicious. I ate some while watching TV.

Katie: Mmmm.

Page 84

SPEAKING

Exercise 1

Students' own answers.

Exercise 2

1 Hi Izzy, Would you like to meet for lunch today? I'm free after 12.00. What about you?
2 Hi Henry, I'd love to. I have some things to do this morning, but I'm free at 12.30. Where shall we meet?
3 Shall we meet in front of the art museum? There are lots of restaurants near there.
4 OK. Great. I'll see you in front of the art museum at 12.30.

Exercise 3

1 cheese
2 the sushi restaurant

🔊 Track 056

Izzy: Hi, Henry. Sorry I'm late!

Henry: Hi, Izzy. That's OK. It's only just after half past twelve. We've got lots of time. Are you hungry?

Izzy: Yes, I am. I didn't have any breakfast!

Henry: Let's find somewhere to eat straight away then. Where shall we go?

Izzy: I don't mind. Do you like pizza? How about that pizza restaurant over there? My sister says it's very good.

Henry: I'm afraid I don't eat cheese. I don't like it.

Izzy: OK. How about going for an Indian meal? I know you like curry.

Henry: You're right. I love curry, but we ate it at Paul's house yesterday. Do you feel like eating fish? What about having some sushi? There's a sushi place over there.

Izzy: That's a great idea. Let's go to the sushi restaurant. Shall we sit outside?

Exercise 4

1 Izzy
2 Henry
3 Izzy
4 Henry
5 Izzy
6 Henry

Exercise 5

1 Let's
2 shall
3 mind
4 says
5 afraid
6 about
7 feel
8 What
9 idea
10 sit

Exercise 6

1 expressions 1, 2, 4, 6, 7, 8 and 10
2 expressions 3, 5 and 9

Exercises 7 & 8

Students' own answers.

Page 85

WRITING

Exercise 1

Students' own answers.

Exercise 2

curry

🔊 **Track 057**

Sunita: OK. So this is a really easy meal to make … and really lovely. First peel the garlic and ginger and chop them into small pieces. Then chop the onions and other vegetables. Fry the garlic, ginger and chopped onion lightly in some oil. When they are soft, add the curry powder. After that, add the other chopped vegetables and mix everything together. Cook for 15–20 minutes until the vegetables are soft. While the curry is cooking, wash the rice and put it into a saucepan. Add water and a pinch of salt. Cook for 20 minutes. Finally, serve the curry with the rice and enjoy!

Exercise 3

1 peel, chop
2 chop
3 Fry, add
4 add, mix
5 Cook
6 wash, put
7 Add
8 serve

Exercise 4

1 Peel
2 fry
3 serve
4 Mix
5 Chop

Exercise 5

Students' own answers.

Page 86

EXAM FOCUS
READING PART 1

1 A	3 C	5 A
2 B	4 B	6 C

Page 87

LISTENING PART 3

1 B	3 B	5 A
2 C	4 A	

🔊 **Track 058**

Narrator: For each question, choose the correct answer. You have 20 seconds to look at Part 3.
You will hear Lewis talking to his friend Laura about a cooking course.
Now listen to the conversation.

Lewis: Why didn't you come to our first cooking lesson yesterday, Laura?

Laura: Sorry, Lewis! I didn't forget, but my college teacher needed to speak to me after class, so I missed the bus. But I'll come next week!

Lewis: Well, it doesn't matter. You're such a good cook already.

Laura: You only think that because I always make the same things. I make so many omelettes, I should open an omelette restaurant! I need to learn to prepare new dishes. What did you make yesterday?

Lewis: The teacher said we could make soup or a dessert. I chose ice cream. Next week it's curry. I'll send you the list of things you'll need.

Laura: So what's the teacher like?

Lewis: She's okay. She explains things quite well, and shows people how to do things. But what I didn't like was that she shouted, and wasn't very nice about what someone cooked.

Laura: Oh dear! Can we go together next week?

Lewis: Sure. The class starts at 7 pm, but I like being early. I'll come to your college at 6.30, so we can arrive at 6.45. Okay?

Laura: Yes, thanks.

Page 88

REAL WORLD

Exercise 1

Students' own answers.

Exercise 2

1 T
2 T
3 F Water is always served with the coffee.
4 F Guests should feel welcome and shouldn't feel that they have to leave quickly.

Exercise 3

1 Café 100
2 Café Schokolade
3 Café 100
4 Café Vienna

Page 89

Exercise 4

1 a	3 b	5 a
2 a	4 a	6 a

Exercise 5

1 c	2 d	3 a

🔊 **Track 059**

1

Waiter: Hello. Are you ready to order?

Customer 1: Yes. I'd like a Viennese coffee, please.

Customer 2: And a black coffee for me, please.

Waiter: Anything to eat?

Customer 1: Yes. What's a *Kardinalschnitte*?

Waiter: It's a traditional Viennese cake. It has layers of vanilla sponge on the outside, then a layer of strawberry jam and a fresh cream filling.

Customer 2: Mmm. That sounds nice. Does it have nuts in it?

Waiter: No. There are no nuts, but it does have gluten. We do also have gluten-free options if you like.

Customer 2: That's OK. I'm allergic to nuts, but nothing else. So can we have one *Kardinalschnitte*, with two forks, please?

Waiter: Of course. Any whipped cream with that?

Customer: No, thank you.

Waiter: OK. That's fine.

2

Server: Who's next, please?

Customer: Hi, can I have a cheeseburger, please?

Server: Eat in or take away?

Customer: To eat in.
Server: Any fries with that?
Customer: Yes, please.
Server: And a drink?
Customer: A cola, please.
Server: Regular or large?
Customer: Regular, please.
Server: OK. One cheeseburger with fries, and a regular cola. Thank you.

3
Server: Hi. Can I help you?
Customer: Yes. Can I have a chicken sandwich, please?
Server: Sorry, we're out of chicken sandwiches at the moment. I've got a chicken wrap.
Customer: OK. Can I have a chicken wrap, please? And do you do decaf coffee?
Server: Yes, we do.
Customer: OK. I'd like a small decaf latte, please.
Server: No problem. Have you seen our combos? For 10 euros you can have any wrap or roll, plus a coffee and a cookie or muffin.
Customer: Oh. OK. What muffins do you have?
Server: Chocolate, lemon, or blueberry.
Customer: I'll have a chocolate muffin, please.
Server: Coming up! If you take a seat, someone will bring you your food.
Customer: Thank you.

Exercise 6
1 What's a
2 Does it have
3 allergic to
4 with two forks
5 Do you do
6 What muffins

Exercise 7
1 b   3 a   5 a
2 b   4 a   6 b

Exercises 8 & 9
the city: capital of Austria and the largest city; busy modern city, famous for old coffee shops
coffee shops and cafés: great place to relax and chat with friends, often have piano music; cakes, sandwiches, salads, sausages
types of desserts: *Apfelstrudel, Kardinalschnitte*
Wiener Schnitzel: flat steak of veal or pork, dipped in flour, eggs and breadcrumbs, fried in oil, served with chips and lemon

three famous cafés: Café Central, popular with writers and artists; Café Mozart, named after the musician and composer; Café Sacher, where *Sachertorte* was first made, a chocolate cake with smooth chocolate icing

Exercise 10
Students' own answers.

UNIT 7
Page 90
VOCABULARY
Exercise 1
Students' own answers.

Exercise 2
A photography
B doing nothing
C board games
D doing Massaoke
E baking
F doing exercise
G gigs
H going to the gym

Exercise 3
1 photography
2 gig
3 doing nothing
4 baking
5 board games
6 exercise
7 gym
8 does Massaoke

Exercise 4
Students' own answers.

Page 91
LISTENING
Exercise 1
1 photography
2 Massaoke

🔊 **Track 060**
1
Interviewer: Thanks for talking to me, Declan. Can I ask how old you are and where you are from?
Declan: I'm 22 and I come from Dublin in Ireland.
Interviewer: Thank you. And your hobby is photography, isn't it? So when did you start taking photos?
Declan: I started when I was at secondary school. I was doing a project and I needed some photos for it. I borrowed my dad's camera and I haven't stopped taking photos since then.
Interviewer: Does it take a long time to learn to take good photos?

Declan: Yes, and no. A person can always take good photos and it's a very personal thing. But photography is a big subject and you can spend your whole life learning about it. In fact, I've just been on a weekend course to learn some new techniques.
Interviewer: And do you use lots of special equipment? Is photography an expensive hobby?
Declan: Yes, I've got quite a lot of different cameras. But I bought them over a long time. You don't need an expensive camera to begin with. You can start with your phone and share photos with friends online.
Interviewer: And how good are you at photography now?
Declan: I don't know. Look at my photos and you decide! The important thing is that I love it.
Interviewer: So why do you like it? How does taking photos make you feel?
Declan: Taking photos makes me forget my problems. I look at the world through my camera and I see new things I have never noticed before.

2
Interviewer: I'm talking to Kimberley from Manchester, who is 19 years old, and Kimberley has done Massaoke for a year. Thank you for talking to us Kimberley. So how did you start singing and can you explain what massaoke is?
Kimberley: Well, I started singing because I've got two big sisters who sang a lot at home, and when my sisters started going to Massaoke clubs, I wanted to go along as well. Massaoke is a really fantastic night out. There's a brilliant live band, which plays the biggest pop or rock songs, and the crowd sings along. The words to the songs are on a big screen at the front, so everyone can join in. Have you ever been to a Massaoke club?
Interviewer: No, I haven't tried Massaoke, but it sounds great. So, how does singing Massaoke make you feel?
Kimberley: Singing along with hundreds of other people makes me feel really happy and full of energy! It's a great way to relax and have fun with my friends, so we try to do it every Saturday night if we can.
Interviewer: And where do you go to do it?
Kimberley: Well, it's becoming really popular. There are now two or three clubs in Manchester where you can do Massaoke, as a new club has just opened in the city centre.

Exercise 2

Interview 1
Name: Declan
Age: 22
Where from: Dublin, Ireland
Hobby: photography

Interview 2
Name: Kimberley
Age: 19
Where from? Manchester
Hobby: Massaoke

Exercise 3

1 D		**3** K		**5** D	
2 D		**4** D		**6** K	

Exercise 4

Students' own answers.

Exercise 5

1 When did you start taking photos?
2 Do you use lots of special equipment?
3 How good are you at photography?
4 Why do you like it?
5 How does singing Massaoke make you feel?
6 How often do you do it?

Exercise 6

Students' own answers.

Page 92

GRAMMAR

Exercise 1

2 have
3 ed

Exercise 2

1 take/taken
2 win/won
3 be/been
4 eat/eaten
5 sing/sung
6 speak/spoken
7 swim/swum
8 get/got

Exercise 3

2 Have … ever watched
3 have never been
4 has always enjoyed
5 Has … ever swum
6 have always lived

Exercise 4

/w/ sound before *you* (have you/w/ever)
/j/ sound before *I* and *they* (I/j/ever, they/j/ever)

🎧 **Track 061**

Man: Have you ever eaten sushi?
Woman: Yes, I have.
Man: Have they ever swum in a lake?
Woman: Yes, they have.
Man: Have I ever asked you to help me before?
Woman: No, you haven't.

Exercise 5

Students' own answers.

Exercise 6

1 a short time ago
2 after, before

Exercise 7

2 've/have just seen
3 have just painted
4 've/have just bought

Exercise 8

Students' own answers.

Page 93

READING PART 3: TRAINING

Exercise 1

Suggested answer
acting

Exercise 2

2 B   **3** C

VOCABULARY

Exercise 1

1 The audience are the people who watch a performance.
2 A performance is acting, playing music or dancing in front of people.
3 An actor's costume is the set of clothes he or she wears during the performance.
4 A rehearsal is when the actors practise the play.
5 The stage is the place where the actors perform.

Exercise 2

1 audience
2 stage
3 performance
4 rehearsal
5 costumes

Exercise 3

Students' own answers.

Page 94

LISTENING

Exercise 1

Students' own answers.

Exercise 2

1 They are children. They are from the city of Asunción in Paraguay.
2 They are made of recycled rubbish.

Exercise 3

1 rubbish
2 recycled

Exercise 4

Because he didn't have any money to buy them.

🎧 **Track 062**

Woman: In 2006, Favio Chavez began working in Asunción in Paraguay on a recycling project. He was also a musician and he started to give music lessons to some of the children in the local area in his free time. The problem was that he didn't have any money to buy instruments for the children to use. So he asked Cola, a local man who was very good at making things, if he could make some instruments out of old things. Cola made some drums and flutes and then violins and guitars. They sounded great and they cost nothing! It was also better for the children to have instruments like this and not expensive 'real' instruments that people would want to steal. Chavez formed an orchestra with his students and they started to give concerts in Asunción. They made beautiful music with their recycled instruments. They played classical music – Mozart, Beethoven and Bach – and they sounded fantastic. In 2012, a Paraguayan film director made a film about the orchestra and put it online and they started to become famous all over the world. They now get invited to play in different countries. One of the first countries they went to was Brazil. The young musicians were very excited to visit Rio de Janeiro, not just because it was a famous city in a different country but because they saw the ocean for the first time.

Exercise 5

1 b		**3** c	
2 b		**4** a	

Exercise 6

Students' own answers.

Page 95

VOCABULARY

Exercise 1

Students' own answers.

Exercise 2

1 Valeria and Diego perform music; Alex listens to music.
2 Valeria plays the guitar and the drums.

Exercise 3

1 a mix of pop and soul
2 They both write it.
3 female solo artist
4 the drums

Exercise 4

1 guitarist
2 solo artists
3 Songwriters
4 drummer
5 lead singer
6 musician

Exercise 5

1 lead singer
2 drummer
3 guitarist
4 songwriters
5 musicians
6 solo artists

Exercise 6

Students' own answers.

Page 96

WRITING

Exercise 1

Students' own answers.

Exercise 2

1 26–29 July, Charlsbury Park, Kent
2 an international music festival
3 four days
4 £185
5 yes, £70
6 £40 per tent
7 You can watch music and dance performances, buy things to eat and drink, do art and painting, learn music and dance styles.

Exercise 3

1 international, favourite
2 amazing, world famous
3 pleasant
4 excellent
5 fun
6 international
7 delicious

Exercises 4 & 5

Students' own answers.

Page 97

SPEAKING PART 1: TRAINING

Exercise 1

	Yannis	Carmen
Work or studies	student	works as a shop assistant
Age	17	19
Nationality	Greek	Spanish
City	Athens	Madrid

Track 063

Examiner: Good morning. What's your name?
Carmen: I'm Carmen.
Examiner: And what's your name?
Yannis: Yannis.
Examiner: Yannis, do you work or are you a student?
Yannis: Erm, erm … Student.
Examiner: How old are you?
Yannis: Seventeen.
Examiner: Where do you come from?
Yannis: Greece.
Examiner: Where do you live?
Yannis: What?
Examiner: Do you live in Athens?
Yannis: Yes, near the centre of Athens.
Examiner: Thank you. Carmen, do you work or are you a student?
Carmen: I'm working at the moment. I have a job as a shop assistant. But after the summer, I'm planning to go to university.
Examiner: How old are you?
Carmen: I'm nineteen years old.
Examiner: Where do you come from?
Carmen: I'm from Spain.
Examiner: Where do you live?
Carmen: I live in Madrid.
Examiner: Thank you.

Exercise 2

Carmen gives better answers because they are longer and have more information in them.

Exercise 3

1 Yannis: he plays sports in the evenings; he enjoys going to the cinema and sailing with his father at weekends.
2 Carmen: she likes watching and playing tennis; she'd like to try painting; she had a birthday party last weekend.

Track 064

Examiner: Now, let's talk about hobbies. Carmen, what's your favourite hobby?
Carmen: I love tennis. I like watching it, I like reading about tennis players, and best of all I love playing it.

Examiner: Yannis, how much time do you have for doing hobbies?
Yannis: Quite a lot of time. After school I play different sports, usually for one or two hours in the evening.
Examiner: Now, Carmen, please tell me something about a new hobby you would like to try.
Carmen: I'd like to try painting. I don't know if I could do it very well. But I'd like to paint some pictures, for example of my city. I could give them to my friends.
Examiner: Now, let's talk about weekends. Yannis, where do you enjoy going at weekends?
Yannis: I enjoy going to the cinema with my friends, and I enjoy going sailing with my father.
Examiner: Carmen, what was the best thing about last weekend?
Carmen: Oh, that's easy! It was my birthday, and I had a party on Saturday night.
Examiner: Now, Yannis, please tell me something about your plans for next weekend.
Yannis: I don't have any plans at the moment. I might have to do some homework, but I hope there's time to see my friends. I'll probably watch TV as well.

Exercise 4

1 favourite
2 much time
3 something about
4 enjoy going
5 was … best
6 Please tell me

Exercise 5

Students' own answers.

PUSH YOURSELF B1

Exercise 1

1 Lotti
2 Michael

Exercise 2

1 because
2 so that
3 so

Exercise 3

1 so that
2 because of
3 so
4 Because

EXAM FOCUS
READING PART 3

Exercise 1

1 one long text
2 five
3 three
4 choose
5 title of the text

Exercise 2

1 A	3 B	5 C
2 B	4 A	

Page 99

SPEAKING PART 1

Exercises 1 & 2

Students' own answers.

Page 100

REAL WORLD

Exercise 1

Students' own answers.

Exercise 2

A Street Art Tour
B Camden Market
C East End Food Tour

Exercise 3

1 F The tours change all the time.
2 F It started as an arts and crafts market.
3 T

Page 101

Exercise 4

1 a	3 b	5 b
2 a	4 a	6 b

Exercise 5

1 d	2 a	3 c

🎧 Track 065

1

Woman: Ooh, this is nice. I love cooking, and I love spicy things! Do you like it?
Man: Yes, it's really nice. It's very different. I didn't know that London had all these different kinds of food.
Woman: Oh, yes. London's a city with people from all over the world. I love it!
Man: Are you from London?
Woman: No, I'm from Cornwall, in the south west, but I've just moved up to London for my job. How about you?
Man: Oh, I'm a tourist. I'm here for two weeks.
Woman: Cool. Where are you from?
Man: I'm from Sevilla, in Spain. Spanish food is quite different.
Woman: Yeah. I love Spanish food, too.

Man: I really like this tour. You see a different side of the city when you think about its food.
Man: Yes, that's true.
Woman: Oh, it looks like we're on the move again!
Guide: Right, everyone, are you ready to go and …?
2
Man: I'm sorry I haven't got the colour you wanted. You could try again next week? Are you local?
Woman: No, I'm a tourist. I'm only here for one week.
Man: Oh, that's a shame. Is this your first time at the market?
Woman: Yes. I really like it. I collect vintage clothes and there are some really interesting clothes here. But it's very busy.
Man: Yeah. It's crazy some days! It's best to get here early. It's OK till lunch time, then it goes mad!
Woman: Yes, there are so many visitors. It's my first time in London, but I hope I'll be back next year.
Man: Well, if you are, nip down here again, and we'll see if we've got anything you like.
Woman: OK. Thank you.
Man: See you. Bye.
3
Man: Wow! That's amazing!
Woman: I know. I can't believe the city has so many artists!
Man: Where are you from?
Woman: I'm from the US.
Man: Really? Is street art a big thing where you come from?
Woman: In the big cities, yes. I'm from New York, and there's a lot of street art. But I've never seen a tour like this in my city. Are you from London?
Man: No. I'm from Manchester, and we don't have anything like this. I think it's great. I mean, you can always walk around and just look at the works yourself, but it's worth the few pounds to get the tour. You learn so much, and they know where the best pieces are. It'd be difficult to find them on your own.
Woman: That's true. And they take you to some really interesting places.
Man: Yeah. You get off the tourist track, that's for sure.

Exercise 6

1 Are you
2 I'm here
3 very busy
4 first time
5 never seen
6 true.
You can say 'That's true' to agree with someone.

Exercise 7

1 b	3 a	
2 a	4 b	

Exercises 8 & 9

1 a big wheel
2 30 minutes
3 a hop-on, hop-off ticket
4 Big Ben
5 to take photos on the famous crossing from a Beatles album
6 1,000 years; traditional British food and food from many different countries

Exercise 10

Students' own answers.

UNIT 8
Page 102

READING

Exercise 1

Students' own answers.

Exercise 2

1 villa E
2 houseboat C
3 cottage D
4 townhouse B
5 studio apartment/flat A

Exercise 3

Shanghai, China

🎧 Track 066

Ling: My name is Ling. I'm 43 years old and I live in Shanghai, a big city in China. I live with my sister in a small house in an old part of the city. It's in the centre of Shanghai, near the river. The house is 100 years old. My sister and I were born in it and we've lived there all our lives!
Huan: My name is Huan and I'm 25 years old. I live in an apartment in Shanghai in China. My apartment is very new. I moved into it four weeks ago! The building is modern and my apartment is on the 23rd floor so I have a great view across the whole of the city. It's not near the city centre but that's OK.

Exercise 4

1 c	3 c	5 a
2 b	4 b	6 a

Page 103

Exercise 5

Ling: Photo B
Huan: Photo A

Exercise 6

Students' own answers.

Exercise 7

1 because it's modern and has a balcony
2 the fantastic view
3 in the garage under the apartment building
4 three
5 on the roof
6 pay rent

VOCABULARY

Exercise 1

1 rent
2 roof
3 garage
4 view
5 building
6 balcony
7 furniture
8 ground floor
9 neighbours
10 basement

Exercise 2

1 How old is your home?
2 How many floors does it have?
3 What's your favourite room?
4 Do you have a garden or a balcony?

Page 104

LISTENING

Exercise 1

1 The house is in Beverly Hills, Los Angeles. An actress/singer lives there.
2 eight years
3 9.5 million dollars

Exercise 2

indoor swimming pool, gym, kitchen

🎧 **Track 067**

Reporter: Hello and welcome to Homes of the Rich and Famous. So, here I am standing in the hall of this amazing home. In front of me are the stairs. Let's go up … There are ten bedrooms in this house and five bathrooms, but the room I want to visit is the famous swimming-pool … Yes, here it is. A big, indoor swimming pool on the first floor. Wow! Next to the swimming pool is the gym. Let's go inside. Well, this gym has everything so it's the perfect house for fitness fans.

OK, Let's go downstairs now. I'd like to visit the kitchen … Yes, here it is, between the dining room and the hall. It's so big and everything is white … and gold. Just look at that big sink with gold taps. And is that really a fridge opposite the window? It's as big as a bus. I love it! There are loads of cupboards and the cooker and the oven are twice as big as normal ones! People who love cooking will be very happy here.

I think if we look out of the window, we can see the recording studio behind the house. Lots of famous musicians have recorded there. Let's see if we can look inside! There's a small cinema in the basement, under the recording studio, and there's also an amazing games rooms for adults and children.

Exercise 3

1 b	3 a	5 b
2 a	4 b	

VOCABULARY

Exercise 1

1 f	3 a	5 b
2 d	4 e	6 c

Exercise 2

a in front of
b between
c opposite
d under
e behind
f next to

Exercises 3 & 4

Students' own answers.

Page 105

Exercise 5

Students' own answers.

🎧 **Track 068**

Under the sink
Opposite the fridge
Behind the oven
Next to the tap
Between the cooker and the fridge
In front of the oven

GRAMMAR

Exercise 1

1 8 years ago / yes
2 last year / yes

Exercise 2

1 for
2 since

Exercise 3

1 for
2 since
3 for
4 since
5 since
6 for

Exercise 4

Students' own answers.

Page 106

SPEAKING

Exercise 1

1 Portugal
2 an apartment

🎧 **Track 069**

Woman: OK, Luzia, so where do you live?

Luzia: I live in Porto. It's a large city in the north-west of Portugal. It's on the Atlantic Ocean. It's a very old city and it's very beautiful.

Woman: And where do you live in the city? Who do you live with?

Luzia: I live in the centre, near the cathedral. I live in a big apartment with my parents, my sister, and my two brothers. It's on the third floor and it's old and big. There are eight rooms.

Woman: How long have you lived there?

Luzia: I've lived there all my life. I was born there.

Woman: Do you like your apartment? What's your favourite room?

Luzia: Yes, I like my apartment very much. The apartment building is old and the lift is broken, so we often have to climb lots of stairs, but it's still beautiful. My favourite room is the kitchen because it's where we eat and where the family spends time together.

Woman: Is there anything you don't like about your apartment?

Luzia: Yes, it's a bit noisy. I can often hear the noise from the street.

Woman: Do you have your own room?

Luzia: No, I don't. I share a room with my sister.

Woman: Can you describe your room?

Luzia: Yes, it's quite big. The walls are white. There isn't a carpet on the floor; there are wooden floorboards. The curtains are blue and in front of the window is a big desk where we do our homework. On the wall next to the door there are shelves with some books on them.

Exercise 2

1 And where do you live in the city?
2 Who do you live with?
3 How long have you lived there?
4 Do you like your apartment?
5 What's your favourite room?
6 Is there anything you don't like about your apartment?
7 Can you describe your room?

Exercise 3

noisy – quiet, old – modern, ugly – beautiful, big – small, cheap – expensive

Exercises 4 & 5

Students' own answers.

PUSH YOURSELF B1

Exercise 1

1 At the back of
2 In front of
3 In the middle of
4 On the left
5 on the wall

🔊 **Track 070**

Man: This is a photo of a living room. The walls are white and there's a grey rug on the floor. At the back of the room there are three big windows, but there aren't any curtains. In front of the window there's a round table with a white chair on each side of it. The part of the chair that we sit on – I don't know the name in English – is red. In the middle of the room there's a big glass table and on the table there are some pink flowers in … I don't know what it's called in English but it's a kind of pot for flowers. On the left there's a grey sofa and above the sofa, on the wall, there's a big picture. On the right of the table there are two black chairs and there's a dog standing in front of them.

Exercise 2

The part of the chair that we sit on – I don't know the name in English …
I don't know what it's called in English but it's a kind of …

Exercise 3

1 seat
2 vase
3 rug
4 lamp
5 bookshelf

Page 107

GRAMMAR

Exercise 1

Students' own answers.

Exercise 2

1 because he's got a new job
2 on the internet

🔊 **Track 071**

Anthony: Hi, Laura, it's Anthony. You know that job in Helsinki I told you about? Well, I got it! And I'm moving to Finland in ten days.
Laura: Wow! Congratulations about the job, but that doesn't give you much time to do everything! Have you found anywhere to live yet?
Anthony: Yes, I have actually. I've already found my new apartment.

Laura: That was quick! How did you do it?
Anthony: I found it online. I looked on the internet for apartments in Helsinki and I found it there.
Laura: So you've only seen photos of it online then? You haven't actually visited it yet?
Anthony: Yes, I have. I went to Helsinki last week to see it and I really like it. It's quite old but it's big – well big for me. It's got two bedrooms! It's near the centre and I've already paid the first month's rent and bought a new sofa. You must come and visit me. Helsinki is a great city.
Laura: I'd love to … But tell me about the job. Have you met your new boss yet?
Anthony: Yes, I've already met my boss. He offered me the job! I haven't visited the office yet. I haven't had time! Anyway, I must go now. There are some other people I need to phone. But come and visit me soon!

Exercise 3

1 found … yet
2 already found
3 visited … yet
4 already paid
5 yet
6 already met

Rule

1 already
2 yet

Exercise 4

1 Have you finished packing yet?
2 already said goodbye
3 have you texted your friends
4 haven't booked a taxi yet

Exercise 5

Students' own answers.

Page 108

GRAMMAR

Exercise 1

Students' own answers.

Exercise 2

Yes, she's met her neighbours and some girls from her exercise class.

Exercise 3

1 unfinished
2 for
3 finished
4 ago

Exercise 4

1 moved
2 's/has lived
3 haven't finished

4 bought
5 has been
6 put
7 found
8 has … been

Exercise 5

Students' own answers.

READING PART 5: TRAINING

1 on
2 is
3 the
4 go

Page 109

WRITING PART 6: TRAINING

Exercise 1

It's a party you have when you have just moved into/bought a new place to live.

Exercise 2

1 They go to the same language school.
2 She has just moved house.
3 7.30 pm on Saturday at 21, Lake Street
4 It's on the ground floor, is large, and has a beautiful modern kitchen and a garden. It's near the station on Lake Street.
5 other students from the language school and her brother Harry

Exercise 3

1 Hi + name
2 How are you?
3 I'm writing to …
4 Best wishes

Exercise 4

1 Dear + name; Hello + name
2 How are things?; I hope you're well.
3 I wanted to ask you; So, I wanted to know if …
4 See you soon!; All the best

Exercise 5

How are you getting to the party? Can we go together? Where shall/can we meet? What about the bus stop?

Exercises 6 & 7

Students' own answers.

Page 110

EXAM FOCUS
READING PART 5

1 it
2 of
3 Do / Would
4 to
5 your / the
6 the

Page 111

WRITING PART 6

Exercise 1

1 D	**3** E	**5** C
2 A	**4** B	

Exercise 2

Model answer

Dear Jamie, would you like to come and stay at my house next weekend? We can watch films and you can meet some of my friends. Bring some computer games too. Andres. (32 words)

Page 112

REAL WORLD

Exercise 1

Students' own answers.

Exercise 2

1 F They can come all year round.

2 T

3 F Adult classes are for all levels.

4 T

5 T

6 F There are different prices for the self-catering apartments.

Page 113

Exercise 3

1 a	**3** b	**5** b
2 a	**4** b	**6** a

Exercise 4

1 c	**2** d	**3** b

Track 072

1

Receptionist: Hello. International English College.

Rafael: Hello. My name's Rafael Lopez. I'm coming to your school in the summer with my family, and I'd like to book some accommodation.

Receptionist: OK. What was your name again?

Rafael: Rafael Lopez.

Receptionist: OK. Yes, I've got you here. Can you just give me the dates please?

Rafael: We're arriving on the twenty fifth of July, and we're leaving on the eighth of August.

Receptionist: Well, there are a couple of options available – you can go for a hotel or a self-catering apartment.

Rafael: We'd like an apartment, please.

Receptionist: That's fine. And how many of you are there?

Rafael: There are four people in my family.

Receptionist: That's great. So, I've got a lovely apartment here. It's quite new, so it's nice and fresh. Shall I send you the details? I've got your email address. And then if you want to go ahead, just send me an email and I can book it for you. Or we can have another look if this one's no good.

Rafael: Yes, thank you. That's perfect.

2

Teacher: Hi. Come in. You're a bit early, but that's OK. Are you Maria?

Maria: Yes.

Teacher: Well, welcome to Malta. When did you get here?

Maria: I arrived last night.

Teacher: And where are you from?

Maria: I'm from Slovakia.

Teacher: Lovely. I think you're with a host family, aren't you? Have you settled in OK?

Student: Yes, thank you. I've met my host family, they're really nice.

Teacher: Oh, that's good. Are you here with friends, or just on your own?

Student: I've come with two friends from Slovakia, but they're in different classes.

Teacher: OK. Well, you'll see this is a really friendly class and there are plenty of other students your age, so you'll soon feel at home. Have you dealt with all the formalities?

Student: Yes. I filled in all the forms and I've got my student card. And they told me to come to this class.

Teacher: That's perfect. Ah, here come the others. I'll introduce you, and then we can get started. Come in, everyone! This is Maria, …

3

Woman: Hello. You must be Jakob. Come on in. Here, let me take your bag.

Jakob: Thank you.

Woman: How was your flight?

Jakob: Yes, it was fine. The plane was on time.

Woman: Well, I'm Anna, and you'll be staying with us while you're here. You'll meet the rest of the family later when they get back. Shall I show you to your room first and we can get rid of these bags?

Jakob: OK. Thanks.

Woman: So, this is you in here. I'm sure you'll want to use the internet, so I've left the code for the Wi-Fi on the desk for you, so you can get that up and running.

Jakob: OK. Thanks.

Woman: So, just let me know if there's anything else you need. Now, with food, do you have any allergies?

Jakob: No. I don't have any allergies. I eat everything.

Woman: Well, that's nice and easy. And is there anything you don't like? Any particular preferences?

Jakob: I'm not very keen on spicy food. And I don't like fish very much. But I love pasta, and pizza.

Woman: OK. That's fine. I'm sure we can find things you'll like.

Exercise 5

1 like to book

2 There are

3 I've met

4 I've got

5 don't have

6 not very keen

Exercise 6

1 c	**3** d	**5** e
2 f	**4** a	**6** b

Exercises 7 & 8

towns and cities: largest city is Valletta, the capital, small streets and lovely buildings; Mdina is over 2,500 years old with narrow streets; St. Julian's is a more modern town, with lots of shops and restaurants and a great beach

history and culture: English is one of the official languages, many examples of British culture, such as telephone boxes and post boxes, double-decker buses

language schools: more than 40 language schools on the island

free-time activities: boat trips, sailing, scuba diving and horse-riding, relaxing on the beach

Exercises 9 & 10

Students' own answers.

Page 114

PROGRESS CHECK 3

Exercise 1

1 in

2 between

3 in front of

4 behind

5 under

6 next to

Exercise 2

1 solo artist

2 drummer

3 musicians

4 band

Exercise 3

1 broccoli

2 beef

3 chicken

4 omelette

5 mushroom

6 mango/melon

7 yoghurt

Exercise 4

1 some
2 a little
3 much
4 some
5 many
6 a few
7 a

Page 115

Exercise 5

1 going to the gym
2 baking, photography
3 going to gigs
4 playing board games
5 doing nothing, doing exercise

Exercise 6

1 **A:** Have you **ever** travelled somewhere by plane?
  B: Actually, I've **just** come back from New York. It was fantastic!
2 **A:** Have you finished that book **yet**?
  B: Of course! In fact, I've **already** started a new one.
3 **A:** What game is that you're playing? I have **never** seen it before.
  B: Oh, we've had this **for** years. My Dad bought it in China.

Exercise 7

1 I bought **some** jeans and **some** beautiful trainers.
2 It was good weather.
3 My favourite meal is pasta.
4 At the park no-one sells **any** food.
5 Don't forget to buy **some** juice.
6 We took **many** photos.

Exercise 8

1 bought
2 Has … had
3 left
4 haven't seen
5 haven't put
6 met

Exercise 9

1	A	4	C	7	A
2	B	5	A		
3	C	6	B		

UNIT 9

Page 116

READING

Exercise 1

Students' own answers.

Exercise 2

1	E	4	B
2	A	5	C
3	D		

Exercise 3

1 busy
2 confident
3 shy
4 friendly
5 generous
6 reliable

Exercises 4 & 5

	Friends	Where they met	When they met	Why they like their friend
1	Chris and John	at art school	20 years ago	He's friendly and generous with his time.
2	Emma and Sonia	at a birthday party	25 years ago	She's reliable and always there for her.
3	Enrique and Juan	at a tennis club	(about) 10 years ago	He's clever, funny makes him laugh, and he's never bored with him.
4	Helena and Jasmine	at a restaurant	last year	She's generous, gives people things and helps people.

🎧 Track 073

Chris: I met my best friend John when we were students at art school. That's 20 years ago now! We were both 18 and both very bad artists! I liked him immediately because he was so friendly but he's also generous with his time. He's always willing to help people.

Emma: My best friend's Sonia. I've known her all my life. That's 25 years now! We lived in the same street. We met at a friend's birthday party and we played together when we were small. She's like my sister. I love her because she's so reliable. I know she will always be there for me.

Enrique: Juan is probably my best friend. He's my tennis partner. We're professional tennis players, so it's an important relationship. I met him at the tennis club about 10 years ago. I get on so well with Juan because he's clever and funny. He makes me laugh and he's always telling me about something new he's read about. We spend a lot of time together but I'm never bored when I'm with him.

Helena: I met Jasmine last year in the restaurant where we both work after school. We haven't known each other very long but she's my best friend and I'm hers. I think she's the most generous person I've ever met. She's always giving people things and helping them.

Exercise 6

Students' own answers.

Page 117

Exercises 7 & 8

They met in Grace's restaurant in London when Matteo asked for a job 10 years ago. Grace is friendly and generous. She never gets angry with Matteo.
Matteo is always calm. He's a quiet person, but people never argue with him. They work in Grace's restaurant.

Exercise 9

1 her smile
2 ten years
3 Because she thought he was too young.
4 Because he's very calm. He's a quiet person but people listen to him and do what he says.

VOCABULARY

Exercise 1

1	b	3	e	5	d
2	f	4	a	6	c

Exercise 2

1 get on well
2 worried
3 bad mood
4 argue
5 stressed
6 angry

Exercise 3

Students' own answers.

GRAMMAR

Exercise 1

infinitive

Exercise 2

1 It was interesting to find out about life in a different country.
2 We were excited to hear that there's a trip to America next year.
3 They were sad to say goodbye to their friends.
4 She promised to help him in the evening.
5 I tried to learn how to ski but it was too difficult.

Exercise 3

1 easy to
2 learned to
3 want to
4 decided to
5 happy to
6 exciting to

Exercise 4

/tə/

🔊 **Track 074**

It's easy to get stressed.
I needed to get a job.
I didn't really want to give Matteo a job.
He's happy to pay for the drinks.

Exercises 5 & 6

Students' own answers.

Page 119

READING PART 2: TRAINING

Exercise 1

Students' own answers.

Exercise 2

2 C   4 C
3 A   5 A

Exercise 3

Students' own answers.

Page 120

GRAMMAR

Exercise 1

1 Paola
2 Tima
3 Monica
4 Fahad

🔊 **Track 075**

1
Paola: When I'm sad, I try to find something that will make me laugh. I love watching funny films, so I stream some of my favourite comedies – and before sitting down on the sofa to watch, I make some hot chocolate. This always cheers me up.

2
Tima: If I feel stressed, I try to find some friends to play a game of football with. I always enjoy running around, and thinking about the game helps me to forget my problems.

3
Monica: When I want to cheer myself up, I phone a friend. I soon stop thinking about sad things when we're talking and laughing. I have two or three good friends I can always call and I always feel better after talking to them.

4
Fahad: I clean my apartment when I'm feeling stressed. It always cheers me up! I hate being in a dirty, untidy place so washing up and making everything clean and tidy makes me happy.

Exercise 2

1 watching, sitting
2 running
3 thinking, talking
4 being

Exercise 3

Students' own answers.

Exercise 4

1 After
2 prepositions

Exercise 5

1 visiting
2 being
3 reading
4 going
5 playing
6 revising

Exercise 6

1 going, watching
2 to learn, taking
3 to help, to carry

Exercise 7

Students' own answers.

Page 121

LISTENING PART 4: TRAINING

Exercise 1

Conversation 1: angry
Conversation 2: worried
Conversation 3: excited
Conversation 4: sad

🔊 **Track 076**

Narrator: One. You will hear two friends talking. Why is Lisa angry with Alfie?
Alfie: What's the matter, Lisa?
Lisa: Don't you know, Alfie?
Alfie: I know I lost your tablet, but I got you a new one.
Lisa: It's not the tablet. You didn't come to my birthday party. I don't care about not getting a present, but how could you forget my party?! I'm so disappointed.
Narrator: Two. You will hear a mum and a dad talking about their daughter, Alison. Where's Alison now?
Dad: It's late. Why isn't Alison home?
Mum: She's with her friends. They went for a pizza. I expect she'll be back soon.
Dad: It's almost 10 o'clock. I rang her mobile just now and she didn't answer. I'm afraid something's happened.
Mum: Oh, they were planning to see a crime film called The Party after the pizza. She'll be at the cinema. That's why she didn't answer.
Narrator: Three. You will hear Jill and Lenny talking about Jill's holiday. What has Jill never done before?
Lenny: Are you ready for your holiday, Jill?
Jill: Yes, my suitcase is packed. I can't wait to get on the plane tomorrow.
Lenny: Is it your first holiday abroad?
Jill: No, I've been to Spain and France a couple of times, but I've never flown anywhere. My cousins are coming too, so there'll be 5 of us including my parents.
Lenny: Have fun.
Narrator: Four. You will hear Lara saying goodbye to her friend Tom. What's Tom going to do?
Lara: Bye, Tom, I'm so sorry you're leaving the company.
Tom: I'm not going far, Lara. I'm not leaving town! You know where I live. I'm staying in the same house. We'll still be friends. There'll be lots of chances to keep in touch.
Lara: But we won't see you so much, now you're moving to a different place of work. It won't be the same here.

Exercise 2

2 A   3 C   4 B

PUSH YOURSELF B1

Exercise 1

1 going to the park, getting wet and cold
2 coming to the beach, move
3 study computing, getting a good job
4 visiting Paris, go up the Eiffel Tower

Exercise 2

1 *to* + infinitive – can't be bothered to, plan to, hope to

-ing form – don't mind, can't stand, feel like, be keen on, excited about

Exercise 3

1 d	4 c	7 a
2 f	5 b	8 e
3 g	6 h	

Exercise 4

Students' own answers.

Page 122
SPEAKING
Exercise 1

Students' own answers.

Exercise 2

1 Sara
2 Tom
3 Mike

🎧 Track 077

1

Man: What's the matter, Sara?

Sara: My friend isn't speaking to me and I don't know why. It started a week ago. She doesn't say 'hello' to me when I arrive in the morning and she doesn't wait for me after classes, but she won't say why she's angry with me. She says I should know, but I don't! I'm really stressed about it.

2

Woman: You look tired, Mike. Are you OK?

Mike: Not really. I just can't sleep at the moment. I'm worried about my exams and my future and I can't get to sleep. Every night, I study until very late and I feel very tired, but when I go to bed I can't stop thinking. In the morning, I'm even more tired.

3

Man: You seem worried, Tom. Do you want to talk about it?

Tom: I'm having a bad time at work. My problem is that I don't get on with my boss – she's not a nice person. She never says 'good morning' or 'please' or 'thank you' and she often gets angry and talks to me in a rude way. When she does this, I feel really stressed! I like my job and the other people I work with but I can't stand her! Should I leave my job?

Exercise 3

1 She isn't speaking to her. She doesn't say 'hello' to her in the morning or wait for her after classes.
2 Because he's worried about his exams and his future and he can't sleep.
3 His boss. When she gets angry she speaks to him in a rude way.

Exercise 4

1 B   2 C   3 A

🎧 Track 078

A

Man: If this girl is really a friend, she should tell you why she's angry with you. Tell her that you're sorry that you upset her but there's nothing more you can do. Then stop worrying about it. A person like this is not a good friend. Try to spend time with other friends and forget about her.

B

Woman: You should stop studying so much and take some time to relax before you go to bed. It's not a good idea to work on a computer just before you sleep; try to do something different. Take a bath or read an interesting book. If you are worried about the future, why don't you talk to a friend about it? Talking about a problem makes most people feel better.

C

Man: You shouldn't leave your job if you enjoy it! Why don't you ask some other people if they feel the same? What about asking your boss very politely to change the way she speaks to you? If you're polite to her, it's more difficult for her to be rude to you.

Exercise 5

A

Tell her, stop worrying

B

You should, It's not a good idea to, try to, Why don't you

C

You shouldn't, Why don't you, What about

Exercises 6 & 7

Students' own answers.

Page 123
WRITING
Exercise 1

Students' own answers.

Exercise 2

He wants some advice because he has a problem.

Exercise 3

1 His English course is very difficult. The teachers talk very fast. He doesn't understand when people speak to him.
2 He doesn't want to spend time with students from his own country because they don't speak English.
He is shy and not confident about his English.

Exercise 4

Students' own answers.

Exercise 5

1 say thank you for an email: Thanks very much for your email; Thanks for getting in touch
2 say they are happy about receiving an email: It was great to hear from you; Good to hear from you
3 ask for advice (Felix): I'd like to ask you for some advice; What do you think I should do?
agree to give advice (Alice): Here's what I'd do
4 end an email: Hope to hear from you soon; Write soon and good luck!

Exercises 6 & 7

Students' own answers.

Page 124
EXAM FOCUS
READING PART 2
Exercise 1

1 T
2 F You answer seven questions.
3 T
4 F The questions come before the texts.
5 T

Exercise 2

1 B	4 C	7 C
2 A	5 B	
3 B	6 A	

Page 125
LISTENING PART 4
Exercise 1

1 5	3 1	5 3
2 2	4 1	

Exercise 2

1 B	3 A	5 B
2 C	4 C	

🎧 Track 079

Narrator: For each question, choose the correct answer.

One. You will hear two friends talking about a restaurant they've been to. What did they like about it?

Woman: What did you think of that restaurant? My steak wasn't really cooked enough.

Man: A bit raw, was it? Well you don't pay much there, so you can't expect the best food in town.

Woman: Yeah. The waiters did a good job, but they weren't very friendly. But you're right about the bill – it wasn't much at all.

Man: And that made the evening better!

Narrator: Two. You will hear a woman telling a friend about her new colleague. What's her new colleague like?

Man: What's your new colleague like?

Woman: Well, the important thing for me is that he does everything I ask – not like some of the others who do almost nothing! And he's happy to talk to anyone. His jokes are terrible though! I'm sure he'll be promoted soon!

Narrator: Three. You will hear a woman leaving a message for her husband. What does she want him to do?

Woman: Leo, on my way home from work I'm going to stop at the supermarket and do some shopping, so I'll be a little late. We can have roast chicken for dinner. Can you start getting it ready when you get in? You won't have to go to the shops – everything you need is in the fridge. Thanks!

Narrator: Four. You will hear two friends talking about an exhibition. How does the man know about it?

Man: There's an interesting art exhibition on at the moment.

Woman: Is that the one with paintings of flowers? There are posters all over town.

Man: Are there? I haven't noticed any posters. But yes, it is the flower paintings, at the museum near the station. My brother's a guide there, and he keeps talking about the artist. He knows her quite well.

Woman: Wow!

Narrator: Five. You will hear a man giving a message to passengers at a train station. Why is he giving them the message?

Man: This is a message for all passengers. Because of the bad weather, I'm afraid there were delays to some journeys at the weekend. If you experienced problems, please visit our website and click on 'refunds'. If your delay was more than 30 minutes, Central Trains will return the price that you paid for your ticket. Have a good journey!

Page 126

REAL WORLD

Exercise 1

Students' own answers.

Page 127

Exercise 2

1 F You should only accept invitations from people you know.

2 T

3 F It's often easier because people who are travelling are more interested in meeting new people.

4 F It takes time to meet people and become friends.

Exercise 3

1 make
2 enrol
3 have a lot
4 take up
5 get to
6 get on well

Exercise 4

1 b   2 d   3 a

🎧 Track 080

1

Receptionist: Hello, Melbourne Animal Rescue. How can I help you?

Student: Hello. My name's Maria and I've just moved to Melbourne. I love working with animals and I'd like to do some volunteering work. Is it possible to work here as a volunteer?

Receptionist: Yes, we do run a volunteer programme. I should warn you that our volunteers don't usually work with the animals. But we do use volunteers to help with collecting money. We have teams out on the streets most weekends, collecting money and giving out leaflets.

Student: That's great. Can I become a volunteer, please?

Receptionist: Yeah sure. You need to drop in here and fill out some forms, and you can meet the other members of our team. Then we can take it from there.

Student: OK. Thank you. Is it OK if I come to the centre this afternoon?

Receptionist: This afternoon would be great. We're open till six.

Student: OK. See you later. Bye.

Receptionist: Bye.

2

Receptionist: Hi. Can I help you?

Student: Yes. I'm interested in the photography course. Can you give me some information about it, please?

Receptionist: Sure. What would you like to know?

Student: Do I need an expensive camera to do the course?

Receptionist: No, not at all. As long as you have your own camera, that's fine, but it doesn't need to be a top of the range one and you can also use some of the cameras we have here at the college.

Student: That's great. And how many people will be on the course?

Receptionist: There are about ten people, so you'll get to know all the other students quite well.

Student: That's good. OK. I'd like to enrol on the course, please.

Receptionist: Sure. Have you done any courses here before?

Student: No. It's my first time.

Receptionist: OK. So, I'll just have to take some details from you, and I'll need to see your visa.

Student: Yes, I have my visa here.

Receptionist: OK, that's all in order. So, can you tell me your name and your date of birth?

3

Receptionist: Hi there. How can I help you?

Student: Hi. Is it possible to hire tennis courts here?

Receptionist: It certainly is.

Student: Oh, good. And do you have to be a member of the club, or can anyone use the courts?

Receptionist: Anyone can hire a court, but there are different rates for members and non-members. So, in the evenings, it's $24 per hour for non-members, and $12 an hour for members. If you think you'll play more than twice a week, you'd be better off joining, but if you're only going to play once a week, it's probably better just to pay each time you play.

Student: OK. I think I'll play maybe once a week.

Receptionist: OK, so it probably doesn't make sense for you to pay to become a member.

Student: So, how can I book a court?

Receptionist: You can call us, or you can do it online on the club website.

Student: OK. Thank you for your help.

Receptionist: You're welcome. Have a nice day!

Exercise 5

1 as a volunteer
2 OK if
3 interested in, give me
4 to enrol
5 have to be
6 book

Exercise 6

1 f   3 b   5 d
2 a   4 e   6 c

Exercises 7 & 8

the city: it's the capital of Victoria, on south-east coast of Australia, vibrant modern city, a good way
to see the city is on a sightseeing bus, or a boat on the river.

beaches and surfing: some amazing beaches near the city; Brighton Beach is famous for its beach huts used for changing; surfing is popular; there are lifeguards on most beaches to keep people safe.

sport: cricket is popular; Australia has one of the best cricket teams in the world, important games played at Melbourne Stadium.

Phillip Island: close to Melbourne, you can get there by boat; can see koalas and kangaroos, and in the evening you can watch the penguin parade, when penguins come out of the sea and walk along the beach to sleep in their burrows.

Exercise 9

Students' own answers.

UNIT 10
Page 128
VOCABULARY

Exercise 1

Students' own answers.

Exercise 2

1 C	3 B	5 D
2 A	4 F	6 E

Exercise 3

Students' own answers.

Page 129
LISTENING PART 1: TRAINING

Exercise 1

Students' own answers.

🔊 **Track 081**

Narrator: One. What time does the play begin tonight?
Anna: What time's the play tonight, Emma?
Emma: 7.00 I think, I'll look at the ticket. I'm wrong, it starts at 7.30, but we should get there early.
Anna: Shall we meet in front of the theatre at 7.15 – that gives us 15 minutes before the play begins.
Emma: I think we need more time, Anna. Shall we say 7 o'clock?
Anna: OK.

Exercise 2

2 A	3 C	4 C

🔊 **Track 082**

Narrator: Two. How far away is the best sports centre?
Man: Is there a sports centre near here?
Woman: Well there's a really good one in Yorkton. That's got everything. But that's 20km away.
Man: Isn't there one nearer?
Woman: Well, Barton, which is 15 km from here has one, but it's not very good. There is a small one in Linton, but that doesn't have a swimming pool. It's only 5 km away, so it depends what you want to do there I suppose.
Man: OK, thanks.

Narrator: Three. What are Carl and Jack going to see at the stadium?
Jack: Are you coming to rugby practice on Saturday, Carl?
Carl: No, I can't. I've got tickets for a big hockey match. The Rovers are playing! Do you want to come with me, Jack?
Jack: Thanks, I'd love to. Where's the match?
Carl: It's at the football stadium.
Narrator: Four. Where will the friends meet?
Man: So where shall we meet this evening? How about the bridge as usual?
Woman: Oh, my bus doesn't go that way anymore. What about meeting at the statue?
Man: It'll take me a long time to get there. The town square is better for me.
Man: No problem, I'll see you there at 7.

Page 130
READING

Exercise 1

Students' own answers.

Exercise 2

1 Manhattan
2 The High Line is a park. It is above the city. The Lowline is a project for a future park. It will be underground.

Exercise 3

1 a railway line
2 The line closed.
3 2.33 kilometres long
4 a great view of the city
5 a big, empty space under the city
6 They will use special technology to bring sunlight underground.

Exercise 4

1 railway line
2 benches
3 district
4 fresh air
5 path
6 middle
7 space
8 sunlight

Exercise 5

Students' own answers.

Page 131
GRAMMAR

Exercise 1

1 the future
2 sure
3 not sure
4 infinitive

Exercise 2

1 might
2 will
3 may
4 won't

Exercise 3

1 might/may come
2 won't grow
3 might/may turn
4 might/may not be

Exercise 4

1 It was a shoe factory.
2 It's a green space.
3 Students' own answers.

Exercise 5

Students' own answers.

Exercise 6

1 Mr Jones will offer the city €1 million euros for the land / to try to buy the land.
He might turn the land into a car park. He may build some apartments.
2 Mrs Greene says the city won't sell the land because it's a great space in the middle of the city. They might make it into a public park. They may build a new swimming pool.

🔊 **Track 083**

Mr Jones: I'll offer the city €1 million euros for the old factory and I might build a car park on the land. There's a lot of traffic in the city centre and not enough parking. I'll make a LOT of money from a car park without having to spend very much. I may also build some expensive apartments there to sell.
Mrs Greene: The city won't sell the land. We'll definitely keep it because it's a great space in the middle of the city. I think we might make it into a public park. We may also build a new swimming pool on it, if that's what the community wants.

Exercise 7

Students' own answers.

Page 132
VOCABULARY

Exercise 1

1 E	4 D	7 C
2 A	5 B	8 F
3 G	6 H	

Exercise 2

1 Come out of the library and turn right.
2 Go straight on down the main street.
3 Turn right at the traffic lights into Chester Road

4 Go over the bridge and go straight on
5 Take the first turning on the right into New Road.
6 You'll see it on your left.

Track 084
Woman: Come out of the library and turn right. Go straight on down the main street. Turn right at the traffic lights into Chester Road. Go over the bridge and go straight on. Take the first turning on the right into New Road. You'll see it on your left.

Exercise 3
the cinema

Exercise 4
1 supermarket
2 theatre

Track 085
1
Man: Excuse me. Do you know where the [beep] is?
Woman: Yes. Come out of the station and turn left. Then turn left into Main Street. Then take the first left and go straight over the roundabout. You'll see it on the right.
2
Man: Excuse me, where's the [beep]
Woman: Come out of the station and turn left. Then turn left into Main Street. Go straight on and turn left at the traffic lights into Chester road. It's on the right.

Exercise 5
1 c   3 b
2 d   4 a

Track 086
1 Excuse me. Do you know where the station is?
2 Can you tell me how to get to the library?
3 Excuse me. Could you give me directions to the town square?
4 Could you tell me where the museum is?

Exercise 6
1 a rising ↗, then falling ↘ intonation
2 a falling intonation ↘
3 a rising ↗, then falling ↘ intonation
4 a falling intonation ↘

Exercises 7 & 8
Students' own answers.

Page 133
SPEAKING PART 1: TRAINING
Exercise 1
Students' own answers.

Exercise 2
1 d   3 a   5 b
2 f   4 e   6 c

Exercise 3
Students' own answers.

Exercise 4
1 B   2 C   3 A

Track 087
Narrator: A
Student: One week ago I met two of my classmates at the bus station. We went to the cinema and afterwards we bought burgers and ate them in the park. It was good fun.
Narrator: B
Student: I don't want to stay in my home town because it's quite boring. I'd like to move to a big city because I could go shopping and go to restaurants and the theatre in the evenings.
Narrator: C
Student: There are houses and an apartment building but there aren't many cars. The houses have nice gardens and it's quiet. I've always lived there, and I like it very much.

Exercise 5
Students' own answers.

PUSH YOURSELF B1
Exercise 1
Students' own answers.

Exercise 2
1 public transport
2 polluted
3 traffic free
4 skyscraper
5 traffic jam
6 pedestrian
7 pavement
8 historic

Page 134
GRAMMAR
Exercise 1
A bank
B restaurant
C police station
D post office

Exercise 2
1 bank
2 restaurant
3 post office

Track 088
1
Woman: Hello, I'd like to change some money, please. Can I change €150 into American dollars?
Man: Yes. No problem. I'll check how much that will be in dollars. One euro is one point one seven American dollars. So €150 will give $174 American. Is that OK?
Woman: Yes, that's fine.
Man: Shall I put the money in an envelope for you?
Woman: Thank you.
2
Man: Have you finished?
Woman: Yes, thank you. It was delicious.
Man: OK, I'll take your plates. ... Would you like anything else? Shall I bring the dessert menu?
Woman: No, thank you. No dessert. But could I have a cup of coffee, please? Black, no sugar.
3
Man: I'd like to send this letter to France.
Woman: Certainly. That will be €1.75 for an ordinary letter or €2.50 if you send it express.
Man: How long will it take for an ordinary letter to arrive?
Woman: Two to three days.
Man: No that's too long ... I need it to get there as soon as possible.
Woman: Shall I send the letter express then?
Man: Yes, please.
Woman: OK. Can you sign here and I'll put the letter straight in the post bag.

Exercise 3
1 €150
2 no, coffee
3 France

Exercise 4
1 will
2 shall

Exercise 5
1 Shall
2 'll
3 Shall
4 'll

Exercise 6
1 shall we have
2 'll tell
3 Shall ... give?
4 'll phone

Exercise 7
Students' own answers.

Page 135

WRITING

Exercise 1
Students' own answers.

Exercise 2
1 to thank Julie for taking her to visit Paris
2 She visited the Louvre, went up the Eiffel Tower, went on a boat trip on the Seine
3 Her favourite moment was when they went up the Eiffel Tower because she has wanted to visit it for so long.
4 that she can come and visit her in Istanbul soon.
5 She is looking forward to showing Julie her favourite places.
6 Julie's friends, Marie and Lilou

Exercise 3
I had a great time!, I loved visiting …, it's the biggest … I've ever visited, I also really enjoyed …, my favourite moment was …, I'll never forget seeing …, It was great to meet them.

Exercise 4
1 great to meet
2 also really enjoyed
3 favourite moment
4 I've ever visited
5 never forget
6 had a great time
7 loved visiting

Exercises 5 & 6
Students' own answers.

Page 136

EXAM FOCUS
LISTENING PART 1

Exercise 1
1 F You hear five short recordings.
2 F You choose from 3 options.
3 T
4 T
5 F They're all dialogues.

Exercise 2
1 A   3 A   5 C
2 B   4 B

🎧 Track 089

Narrator: For each question, choose the correct answer.
Now we are ready to start. Look at question one. One. Where did Chris go yesterday?
Woman: Did you have a good day with your cousin, yesterday, Chris?
Man: Yes, thanks.
Woman: What did you do?

Man: Well, he really wanted to go to the theatre, but we couldn't get tickets. So we thought about the castle or the museum. We chose the castle because my cousin always goes to museums and he liked the idea of doing something different.
Narrator: Two. What is the woman looking for?
Man: Are you lost?
Woman: Yes! A man in the supermarket told me the station was around this corner, but I think he gave me the wrong information.
Man: Mm. Maybe you turned the wrong way when you came out. Just go back up this street, and turn right at the top. It's opposite the bank.
Woman: Turn right, opposite the bank. Thanks!
Narrator: Three. What is broken in the woman's house?
Man: Good afternoon, Mrs. Philips. I hope your cooker isn't broken again!
Woman: Hello. Come in. Don't worry, the cooker's worked well since you repaired it! It's something else I want you to look at – a door. It doesn't open very easily.
Man: No problem. Can you move that lamp before I start? I don't want to break it.
Woman: Yes, of course.
Narrator: Four. Why will the man stay at home this evening?
Woman: Why can't you come out this evening? Are you still ill with that cold?
Man: It's better now, thanks. I'm really upset I can't come.
Woman: Yes, it's such a shame.
Man: And I even finished work early, but then my sister called to say she can't come round to look after the children, so I have to stay at home. Helen will come without me.
Narrator: Five. How did the woman find out about the job?
Man: Your new job sounds great. Did you read about it in a magazine?
Woman: I don't think most companies do that type of advertising anymore. They just use the internet.
Man: So is that how you found your job?
Woman: Actually, my friend told me about it when I was out with her last week. That was before the company did any online advertising.

Page 137

SPEAKING PART 1

Exercise 1
1 live
2 two
3 tell
4 understand
5 three

Exercises 2, 3, 4 & 5
Students' own answers.

Page 138

REAL WORLD

Exercise 1
Students' own answers.

Exercise 2
Suggested answers
1 People fought wild animals or other fighters in front of crowds.
2 money
3 flying machines

Exercise 3
1 b   3 b
2 a   4 a

Exercise 4
1 T
2 T
3 F It's often hot.
4 F It's also open at night.
5 T

Page 139

Exercise 5
1 your tickets
2 early
3 queues
4 video guide
5 Take
6 Visit

Exercise 6
1 c   2 d   3 a

🎧 Track 090
1

Guide: So, now you can see how big the building really was and you can imagine what it was like for people to come here to watch the plays and fights. Are there any questions?
Tourist: Yes. How old is it?
Guide: It's nearly 2,000 years old.
Tourist: Wow! It's really big. How many seats were there?
Guide: We don't know for sure, but they reckon between 50,000 and 80,000. That's a lot of people!
Tourist: Yes. Wow!
Guide: Anything else?
Tourist: Yes. How long did it take to build?
Guide: It was actually quite fast. It took less than ten years to build, which is pretty amazing when you think that they had no machines and everything was done by hand.
Tourist 1: Yes. Oh, what's that hole in the ground?

Guide: That was one of the entrances they used to send gladiators and animals into the arena. There was a wooden door over the hole. The door opened, and animals or gladiators appeared. And in fact, that's where we're going now, so shall we move on?

2

Boy: This is lovely, isn't it?

Girl: Yes. It's so peaceful. I see you have a backpack. Are you travelling?

Boy: Yes. I'm travelling around Europe.

Girl: Me too! Have you been to any other cities in Italy?

Boy: Yes. I was in Florence last week. That was amazing!

Girl: Yes, everyone says it's beautiful. Maybe I'll go there next.

Boy: What other countries have you been to?

Girl: Lots! I was in Spain last week, and before that I was in France. But I love Italy!

Boy: Yes. Rome is an amazing city. But it's very hot. It's nice to be here, next to the water.

Girl: I agree. And the fountain's beautiful, isn't it?

Boy: Yes. Shall we throw some money in? They say that if you throw money in the Trevi Fountain, you'll come back to Rome one day.

Girl: Yes, good idea. Here we go.

3

Official: Next, please.

Tourist: Hello. Can I have two tickets, please? Is there a discount for students?

Official: Yes, there is. Do you have your student cards?

Tourist: Yes, here you are.

Official: OK. Thank you. That's 30 Euros, please.

Tourist: Thank you. Is it OK to take photos in the museum?

Official: Normal photos are fine, but there's no flash photography. And we also ask you not to spend too long taking photos, if you're holding other people up.

Tourist: OK. And what time does the museum close?

Official: It closes at 6.30 this evening. There'll be a bell 20 minutes before closing time, and we ask you to leave promptly.

Tourist: OK. And is there a gift shop?

Official: Yes. If you follow the audio guide tour through the museum, you'll end up in the gift shop. You can't miss it.

Tourist: Thank you.

Official: You're welcome. Enjoy your visit.

Exercise 7

1 Are you
2 Everyone says
3 Is there
4 Is it OK
5 What time

Exercise 8

| 1 a | 3 b | 5 b |
| 2 a | 4 a | |

Exercises 9 & 10

the Colloseum: theatre and gladiator fights during the Roman Empire

the Circus Maximus: horse and chariot races, up to 250,000 people watching, can't see much these days

the Trevi Fountain: 26m high, biggest fountain in Rome; statues of horses and people; built from same stone as the Colloseum

the Piazza Navona: large square, three fountains, live music and art

Exercise 11

Students' own answers.

UNIT 11
Page 140
READING
Exercise 1

| 1 B | 3 C |
| 2 A | 4 D |

Exercise 2

1 Carola
2 Rani
3 David

Exercise 3

1 Rani saves money by buying reduced items and items with a discount when she is shopping and never borrowing or lending money.
2 Carola likes upcycling things from fleamarkets.
3 He never keeps receipts.

Page 141
VOCABULARY
Exercise 1

1 salary
2 discount
3 receipt
4 sales
5 bill
6 reduced items

Exercise 2

1 costs
2 saving
3 waste
4 spent
5 lend
6 earn

Exercise 3

1 borrow
2 sales
3 discount
4 lend
5 cost
6 bill
7 paid
8 earn
9 salary
10 save

Exercise 4

Students' own answers.

Page 142
LISTENING
Exercise 1

Students' own answers.

Exercise 2

1 Marta – department store, garden centre
Josh – supermarket, music shop
2 Marta – summer clothes, birthday present for mum
Josh – food and drink for a party
3 Marta plans to go for dinner in a restaurant.
Josh plans to go to a party.

Exercise 3

1 to find something for her mum's birthday present. Her mum loves plants.
2 a surprise party

🔊 Track 091

Marta: I'm going shopping with my sister this Saturday. We're meeting in front of Darby's, the big department store, at 11.30 and we're going to go shopping for summer clothes. I saw a dress online that I liked and I'm going to try it on in the shop if they have it in my size. I hope so! I don't like the changing room there because it's always busy, but the shop assistants are really helpful. We're also going to look for a birthday present for my mum. She loves plants, so we're going to go to the garden centre to see if we can find something. In the evening, we're having dinner at a new restaurant called Milo's by the river. It opens at 7.00 pm and we've booked a table. I'm really looking forward to it!

Josh: Jez and I are going shopping for the food and drink for Alfie's surprise party on Saturday afternoon. The bus to town leaves at 2.00 pm and we're meeting outside the supermarket at 2.30. I'm going to pay for everything by card and I mustn't forget to ask for a receipt at the till. Alfie's friends want to share the cost of the food and drink, so we need to have something to show how much we spend. After the food shopping, we're going to the music shop. Alfie's parents have bought him some drums as a birthday present and they asked us to collect them. Alfie's dad gave me £50 in cash to pay for a taxi, but it's not going to cost that much, so I must remember to give him the change.
The party is starting at 7.00 so we're going to take everything straight to Alfie's house by taxi.

Exercise 4

1	b	3	a	5	b
2	b	4	a	6	a

VOCABULARY

Exercise 1

1 try it on, size
2 changing rooms, shop assistants
3 by card, till
4 in cash
5 change

Exercise 2

1 try on
2 size
3 changing room
4 shop assistant
5 by card
6 in cash
7 change
8 till

Exercise 3

Students' own answers.

Page 143

GRAMMAR

Exercise 1

the future

Rule

fixed plans

Exercise 2

1 are going
2 're visiting
3 're travelling
4 're staying
5 are … leaving
6 're flying
7 're coming
8 're not/aren't staying

9 's/is meeting
10 're going
11 're taking

Exercise 3

Suggested answers

1 On Tuesday, he's playing football at the leisure centre at 7.00 pm.
2 On Wednesday he's going to the dentist's at 9.00 am.
3 On Thursday, he's having a guitar lesson at 6.30 pm.
4 On Friday, he isn't working/going to work. He's going running in the park with Liz in the morning.
5 On Saturday afternoon, he's going shopping with Jez.

Exercise 4

Students' own answers.

Exercise 5

a schedule or timetable

Exercise 6

1 closes
2 is having
3 leaves
4 is visiting
5 're meeting, starts

Exercise 7

1 leaves
2 're/are going
3 ends
4 's/is meeting

Page 144

LISTENING PART 5: TRAINING

Exercises 1 & 2

Students' own answers.

🔊 Track 092

Paula: Maria, I'm going to buy some new clothes for my holiday. Has the supermarket got lots of summer clothes at the moment?

Maria: Not lots, Paula. I looked for a sun hat there last week. They didn't have any. You could get a swimsuit there – they've got a lot of them. I'm going to get one for myself.

Exercise 3

1	F	3	C
2	G	4	D

🔊 Track 093

Paula: Maria, I'm going to buy some new clothes for my holiday. Has the supermarket got lots of summer clothes at the moment?

Maria: Not lots, Paula. I looked for a sun hat there last week. They didn't have any. You could get a swimsuit there – they've got a lot of them. I'm going to get one for myself.

Paula: Great. … I could try the clothes shop near your college.

Maria: They've got some T-shirts you'd love – there's one that's perfect for you – but the dresses are expensive!

Paula: OK. What about the department store?

Maria: I think that's good for buying trainers, but not shirts and dresses. They have so many pairs to choose from.

Paula: Do you go shopping at the market?

Maria: I bought a sun hat there last year, but it didn't last long. The market's a good place for buying socks – you can get six pairs for a pound.

Paula: And I suppose I could get things online.

Maria: But you need to see swimsuits and shorts before buying them. I've just remembered. There are half-price sun hats on the Love-Clothes site.

Paula: Great.

GRAMMAR

Exercise 1

the future

Rule

our intentions

Exercise 2

1 is/'s going to go shopping
2 is she going to learn
3 are … going to get
4 'm/am not going to walk
5 Are … going to buy

Exercise 3

Students' own answers.

Exercise 4

/gəʊntə/ The 'g' at the end of going to is not pronounced and to is pronounced with the weak form /tə/.

🔊 Track 094

Man: What are you going to do this weekend? Do you have any plans?

Woman: Not really. I'm going to stay at home and watch TV this evening.

Man: Yes, so am I! And I'm going to go to bed early for once.

Exercise 5

Students' own answers.

Exercise 6

1 'm working
2 's going
3 starts
4 're going to watch
5 leaves
6 's taking

Page 145

READING PART 1: TRAINING

2 B   3 C   4 A

PUSH YOURSELF B1

Exercise 1

1 d   4 b   7 g
2 e   5 c   8 a
3 f   6 h

Exercise 2

Students' own answers.

Page 146

WRITING

Exercise 1

Students' own answers.

Exercise 2

1 the clothes department because of the on-trend clothes and the stylish changing rooms
2 They were friendly but there weren't many of them.
3 The reviewer had to wait a long time to pay and the prices were high.
4 good – the reviewer says 'I would recommend Bryson's'.

Exercise 3

Talking about good points
One of the best things about it is …
For me, the high point of Bryson's is …

Talking about bad points
The worst thing about Bryson's is …
Another negative point for me is …
Don't go there if …

Giving a final opinion
Overall …

Exercises 4, 5 & 6

Students' own answers.

Page 147

SPEAKING

Exercise 1

1 Do you enjoy shopping?
2 What sort of things do you like buying?
3 Where do you go shopping?
4 What's your favourite shop?
5 Have you bought anything recently?
6 Where and when did you buy them?

🎧 Track 095

1

Woman: So today I'm on the streets of London, interviewing people about their shopping habits. The first person I'm talking to is Ines. Hello, Ines! So, can you tell me – do you enjoy shopping?

Ines: No, I don't.

Woman: OK, but when you have to go shopping where do you go?

Ines: The supermarket near my house and online.

Woman: What's your favourite shop?

Ines: Well, I really don't have a favourite shop.

Woman: And other than food – have you bought anything recently? Something like new clothes or a new computer?

Ines: Yes, last month I bought a new bike.

Woman: OK! So tell me about it. Where did you buy it? What kind of bike is it?

Ines: I bought it in a sports shop. It's a road bike and it's very good. But I still don't like shopping.

2

Woman: And next up is Luca. So what about you, Luca? Do you enjoy shopping?

Luca: Yes, I do. I like shopping a lot. I especially like clothes shopping. That's why I love going to cities on holiday.

Woman: And what sort of things do you like buying? Where do you go shopping?

Luca: I really like wearing fashionable things, so when I have money, I like buying clothes and shoes a lot. There's a big shopping centre in my town and I go there. It's very crowded, but I really like it because it has a lot of shops!

Woman: And what's your favourite shop?

Luca: I don't know, there are so many. There's a clothes shop called *Place* that I like a lot. That's probably my favourite shop as the shop assistants are really helpful and I always see things I want to buy.

Woman: Have you bought anything recently?

Luca: Umm … Yes, I bought some boots – some really nice black boots – from a department store in London last weekend. Unfortunately, they weren't in the sale, so they were quite expensive, but they look great.

Exercise 2

	Ines	Luca
Enjoy shopping?	no	yes
Where shop?	supermarket, online	shopping centre
Favourite shop?	doesn't have a favourite shop	*Place* – a clothes shop
Bought recently?	a new road bike	black boots
When and where?	bought in a sports shop last month	bought in a department store in London at the weekend

Exercise 3

Suggested answers

Luca gives better answers than Ines because he gives more detail, including giving examples.

Exercise 4

1 That's why
2 so
3 because
4 as
5 so

🎧 Track 096

Woman: And next up, is Luca. So what about you, Luca? Do you enjoy shopping?

Luca: Yes, I do. I like shopping a lot. I especially like clothes shopping. That's why I love going to cities on holiday.

Woman: And what sort of things do you like buying? Where do you go shopping?

Luca: I really like wearing fashionable things, so when I have money, I like buying clothes and shoes a lot. There's a big shopping centre in my town and I go there. It's very crowded, but I really like it because it has a lot of shops!

Woman: And what's your favourite shop?

Luca: I don't know, there are so many. There's a clothes shop called *Place* that I like a lot. That's probably my favourite shop as the shop assistants are really helpful and I always see things I want to buy.

Woman: Have you bought anything recently?

Luca: Umm … Yes, I bought some boots – some really nice black boots – from a department store in London last weekend. Unfortunately, they weren't in the sale, so they were quite expensive, but they look great.

Exercise 5

A

Exercises 6 & 7

Students' own answers.

Page 148

EXAM FOCUS
READING PART 1

Exercise 1

Shorter texts – label on a product, sign on a wall, shop notice

Longer texts – email, text message, post-it note, web message, notice on a work/school/club noticeboard

Exercise 2

1 C	3 C	5 B
2 A	4 A	6 B

Page 149

LISTENING PART 5

Exercise 1

1 a conversation between two people
2 five
3 You hear these in the order you read them.
4 eight
5 will not

Exercise 2

1 A	3 G	5 D
2 H	4 B	

🎧 **Track 097**

Narrator: For each question, choose the correct answer.
You will hear Alicia talking to a friend about her party. What job will Alicia do each day?
Man: Hi, Alicia. Are you ready for your party?
Alicia: Nearly. I've decided to do one job each day, starting on Monday, when I'm going to get some new plates and glasses. I haven't got enough.
Man: Right. And what about Tuesday? Don't you have an appointment at the hairdresser's?
Alicia: I decided I don't need to do that. I'm going shopping for a new dress that day instead.
Man: And on Wednesday?
Alicia: I don't know yet.
Man: Have you remembered to ask everyone to the party? The people who live near you, for example?
Alicia: I forgot about them! I'll do that on Wednesday. And on Thursday I'm planning to clean the house.
Man: It'll get dirty again before the party!

Alicia: You're right. I'll download the music that day, instead.
Man: Good idea. What are you going to do on Friday?
Alicia: Get the snacks. I'm not going to cook anything. It's too much work.
Man: And on Saturday?
Alicia: In the morning I'll clean the house. So I'll have lots of time to put my dress on and do my make up before the party.
Man: Great! See you there!

Page 150

REAL WORLD

Exercise 1

1 A	3 D
2 C	4 B

Exercise 2

They use cards or smartphones.

Page 151

Exercise 3

1 F Most shops only accept kronor.
2 T
3 F You can pay by credit card for most things.
4 T
5 F There are cash machines all over the city.
6 F You need to use your pin.

Exercise 4

1 b	4 d	7 a
2 h	5 f	8 c
3 e	6 g	

Exercise 5

1 d	2 a	3 c

🎧 **Track 098**

1
Tourist: Can I have two tickets please?
Official: Certainly. Full price?
Tourist: Is there a student discount?
Official: Yes, there is. The full price is 130 kronor, but it's 110 kronor with the student discount. Do you have your student ID card?
Tourist: Yes, here it is.
Official: That's fine. So two tickets will be 220 kronor, please.
Tourist: Here you are.
Official: Oh, I'm sorry. We don't take cash. Only cards and smartphone payments.
Tourist: Oh, OK. I've got my card. Can I use contactless?
Official: Yes, of course. There you go.
Official: Yes, that's gone through. So, here are your tickets. Enjoy your visit.
Tourist: Thank you.

2
Tourist: Excuse me. Is there a cash machine near here?
Man: A Bankomat? Yes, let me think. There's one near the Royal Palace. I'm just trying to think of the best way for you to get there. It's quicker to use the back streets, but you might get lost. So, I think maybe it's best to go straight along this road until you see the Nobel Museum on your right. Then take a right turn, any one will do, and you'll see the Royal Palace. There's a Bankomat just on the right there, opposite the palace. You can't miss it.
Tourist: OK. Thanks. How far is it?
Man: Oh, it's only a five-minute walk. Not too far.
Tourist: OK. Thank you.

3
Tourist: Hello. Can I have these things, please?
Shopkeeper: Of course. That's 175 kronor, please.
Tourist: Do you take cards?
Shopkeeper: Oh, no. I'm sorry. We don't take credit cards. We're only a small shop and it's expensive for us to process the payments.
Tourist: Oh. This isn't a credit card. It's a debit card.
Shopkeeper: Oh, OK. Problem solved. Is it contactless?
Tourist: No. I need to use my pin number.
Shopkeeper: OK, no problem. That's ready for you now. No. The other way round. Thank you. Now, if you can just put in your pin number.That's fine. If you could take your card? And here's your receipt. Thank you. Have a nice day.
Tourist: Thank you. Bye.

Exercise 6

1 discount
2 use
3 cash machine
4 far
5 take
6 pin number

Exercise 7

1 b	3 a	5 a
2 a	4 b	

Exercises 8 & 9

old town: called Gamla Stan; it's on an island, you have too cross a bridge to get there; Royal Palace, home of the Swedish Royal Family; Nobel Museum has information about the Nobel Prize.

currency: the krona, most common banknotes are 20, 50, 100, 200, 500; there are 1, 2, 5 and 10 kronor coins; bankomats all over the city, always the same colour.

paying for things: use your credit or debit card to take out money; some small shops don't accept credit cards; some shops still have chip and pin machines, but many now accept contactless and smartphones; new ways of paying for things are becoming popular, e.g. using your eyes to recognise you and using fingerprints.

Exercises 10 & 11
Students' own answers.

Page 152
PROGRESS CHECK 4
Exercise 1
1	D	**3**	B	**5**	A
2	F	**4**	C	**6**	E

Exercise 2
1 earn
2 lend
3 cost
4 save
5 pay
6 waste

Exercise 3
1	h	**4**	a	**7**	d
2	e	**5**	b	**8**	c
3	f	**6**	g		

Exercise 4
1 happy to
2 learned to
3 prefer to
4 ask

Page 153
Exercise 5
1 size, changing room
2 by card, change
3 receipt, till

Exercise 6
1 corner
2 roundabout
3 main square
4 district

Exercise 7
1 … because I don't like **cooking**.
2 I want **to invite** you …
3 You need **to buy** some food …
4 … it stopped **raining** …
5 … have **to study** hard …
6 I'd like **to know** which …

Exercise 8
1 I'm going
2 leaves
3 I have
4 will be

5 I'm going to buy
6 Are you going
7 might
8 may

Exercise 9
1 Are
2 'll / will / might
3 can / shall
4 Do
5 am / 'm
6 be / get

UNIT 12
Page 154
VOCABULARY
Exercise 1
Students' own answers.

Exercise 2
1 maths
2 modern languages
3 history
4 biology
5 geography
6 chemistry
7 physics
8 drama

Exercise 3
1 write (an) essay
2 do (some) research
3 do equations
4 do (an) experiment
5 take part (in a) performance
6 find out

Exercise 4
Students' own answers.

Page 155
READING
Exercise 1
Fung – wants to go to university. We don't know what job she wants to do.
Angeles – wants to be an engineer.
Massimo – wants to be an accountant.
Massimo already has a job.

Exercise 2
1 so she could study in the city
2 the *gaokao*. She hopes that she will get a place at university.
3 because it's one of the best universities for studying her subject
4 a physics exam
5 to become an accountant
6 when he has a qualification and can change jobs

Exercise 3
1	f	**3**	b	**5**	d
2	e	**4**	c	**6**	a

Exercise 4
1 revise for, take, pass, study for, fail

Exercise 5
1 revised for
2 fail
3 pass
4 studying for
5 taken

Exercise 6
Students' own answers.

Page 156
GRAMMAR
Exercise 1
1 facts that are generally true
2 present

Exercise 2
2 doesn't understand, asks
3 feel, is
4 take, fail

Exercise 3
1 in the future
2 present, future

Exercise 4
2 will be, don't pass
3 get, won't give
4 'll fail, doesn't work

Exercise 5
1 What will happen if I don't pass the exam?
2 If students arrive late for the class, the teacher never lets them in.
3 If he studies late tonight, he'll be tired in the morning.
4 What will you give me if I help you with your essay tomorrow?

PUSH YOURSELF B1
Exercise 1
1 not sure
2 sure
3 unless

Exercise 2
1 unless
2 If
3 unless
4 when
5 unless
6 If

READING PART 4: TRAINING

Exercises 1 & 2

Students' own answers.

Exercise 3

2 B   **4** A
3 C   **5** B

GRAMMAR

Exercise 1

1 No, No, Yes

Rule

1 don't know, not important
2 to be
3 by

Exercise 2

1 c   **3** a   **5** b
2 e   **4** d

Exercise 3

1 was asked
2 isn't taught
3 was taken
4 are collected
5 was given

LISTENING

Exercise 1

Students' own answers.

Exercise 2

1 farmer
2 receptionist
3 dentist
4 engineer
5 businesswoman
6 journalist

🎧 Track 099

1

Farmer: Everyone knows that farmers don't earn much money, but that's not the most important thing to me. I really enjoy my work. I love being outside all day in the fresh air. The problem is that I never have any holidays or days off – it's too difficult to find someone to look after the animals.

2

Receptionist: I enjoy my work because I like talking to people and helping them. The receptionist knows everything that's happening in the hotel. It's a very interesting job! The only problem is that there are only two receptionists, so we don't get many breaks during the day. One of us has to be at the front desk all the time.

3

Dentist: In my country it takes eight years to study to be a dentist. I have a couple of degrees and diplomas! I earn a good salary, but I don't really enjoy my work. Nobody likes coming to the dentist and I often work with people who think I am going to hurt them.

4

Engineer: The good thing about my job as an engineer is that it is always interesting. I love working on big international projects with people from all over the world. The only difficult thing is that I often need to give instructions to people in English, so I really need to improve it.

5

Businesswoman: I have my own company with a staff of 500 people. I work long hours and my diary is full every week. I'm in the office by 7.00 in the morning every day and I often don't get home before 9 pm. But I love my job. It's very exciting to have your own business.

6

Journalist: I love doing research and finding exciting new stories. I always try to give true information – as a journalist that's my job. The only thing I don't like about my job is my boss. I hate people telling me what to do! Luckily, we don't see each very much.

Exercise 3

1 a   **3** a   **5** b
2 a   **4** a   **6** b

VOCABULARY

Exercise 1

1 e   **3** d   **5** c
2 b   **4** a   **6** f

Exercise 2

1 time off
2 breaks
3 diplomas
4 staff
5 long hours
6 boss

Exercise 3

Students' own answers.

LISTENING PART 3: TRAINING

2 C   **3** C   **4** A

🎧 Track 100

Mick: Hi, Annie. I hear you left your computer programming job.

Annie: Yes, Mick. I had to spend so much time away from home. Staying in hotels every week was lonely and boring. So I decided to change my life completely. I've started my own business and I'm working at home.

Mick: How exciting! So what's your new business?

Annie: I was never very interested in computer programming and I wanted to do something completely different. I'm making and selling cakes.

Mick: Wow! That's amazing. I mean, I knew you didn't enjoy computer programming, but I didn't know that you liked baking! It's great you can work at home.

Annie: Exactly.

Mick: How do you sell the cakes? Where do your customers come from?

Annie: I have several customers who order cakes through my website and I sell a few in the baker's shop in town, but nearly all of my cakes are sold at the market.

Mick: And do you like having your own business?

Annie: Well, I earned a lot more in my old job and was always going on holiday, but I don't really care about money. The hardest thing now is I have to decide everything by myself. When I had a job, I could talk to the people I worked with.

WRITING

Exercise 1

Students' own answers.

Exercise 2

A 1
B 2

Exercise 3

	Job 1	Job 2
Place of work	with a circus which will travel in Europe	at the Sea World Aquarium
Tasks	perform as a trapeze artist in a new show	clean the shark tank
Salary	€25–€35,000 per year	€40–€45,000 per year
Hours	6–8 performances a week	35 hours a week
Qualifications	no formal qualifications	degree in marine biology
Things to send	photos and videos of performances	CV and letter

Exercise 4

a 2   d 3   g 8
b 5   e 6   h 7
c 4   f 1

Exercise 5

1 I am writing to apply for the job of English teacher as advertised on your website.
2 I am attaching my CV and a copy of my teaching diploma.
3 I am a patient, friendly teacher.
4 As you will see from my CV, I have worked for several schools in Granada.
5 I look forward to hearing from you.

Exercise 6

Students' own answers.

Page 161

SPEAKING

Exercise 1

Students' own answers.

Exercise 2

1 21
2 Circus Arts
3 a year and a half

🎧 **Track 101**

Billy: Hello, Talia. I'm Billy Cain. Please take a seat.
Talia: Thank you.
Billy: So, you're 21 years old, is that right?
Talia: Yes, I am.
Billy: We liked your videos of your performances. Can you tell us about your qualifications and experience? It says on your CV that you have a Diploma in Circus Arts.
Talia: Yes, I studied for two years at the National Centre for Circus Arts in London and at the end of the course I got a diploma.
Billy: OK, that's interesting but for us, experience of performing is more important, so how many years' experience of trapeze work do you have?

Talia: I started when I was 16, but I didn't perform all the time. I have a year's experience at the Melodia Variety Theatre and six months with Smith's Circus – so in total I have a year and a half's experience.
Billy: Can you tell us something about your other skills? Can you drive?
Talia: Yes I can. I've got my driving licence.
Billy: Good. And we'll be travelling through a lot of different European countries. Which other languages do you speak?
Talia: Well my mother is Russian, so I speak Russian, English and a little Italian.

Exercise 3

1 e   3 a   5 c
2 d   4 b

Exercise 4

1 What salary are you offering?
2 Are the costumes provided?
3 Will I get my own hotel room?
4 Am I going to perform with other people?
5 Who will be my boss?
6 How many hours will we practise?
7 How much time off will I get per week?

Exercise 5

1 b   4 a   7 e
2 g   5 c
3 f   6 d

Exercise 6

1 c
2 a

🎧 **Track 102**

Man: What time do we start in the mornings?
Woman: Where is the photocopier?
Man: Can I park here?
Woman: Is this my chair?

Exercises 7, 8 & 9

Students' own answers.

Page 162

EXAM FOCUS
READING PART 4

Exercise 1

1 e
2 d
3 c
4 a
5 b

Exercise 2

1 C
2 B
3 A
4 A
5 C
6 B

Page 163

LISTENING PART 3

Exercise 1

1 two
2 five
3 no
4 three
5 yes

Exercise 2

1 A
2 B
3 C
4 A
5 B

🎧 **Track 103**

Narrator: For each question, choose the correct answer.
You will hear Lena and Max talking about a course which Max has done. Now listen to the conversation.
Lena: Max, that course on working in a team – is it good?
Max: It's not bad. When my boss sent me I was worried – I thought he was angry with me for being bad at working in a team!
Lena: What's the teacher like?
Max: Some people thought she needed to help them more – she often seemed to explain things to only a few students. But she included lots of good examples. And it was interesting. We did lots of different things.
Lena: Was there anything that you didn't like?
Max: Getting to that college in the morning is hard – there's so much traffic. One day, most students didn't arrive until the coffee break! They should start later. Why, are you going to do the course?

Lena: Well, my job's different now from when I first got it. Before, I worked alone – now I'm part of a group. It's like having a completely new job – but without any extra money!

Max: So are you going to do it soon?

Lena: Well, next week's course is full. And so was next month's. But then someone decided not to go next month, so I can do it then. Better than waiting until next year!

Max: Enjoy it!

Page 164

REAL WORLD

Exercise 1
Students' own answers.

Exercise 2
1 C	3 A
2 D	4 B

Exercise 3
1 T
2 F You can study any subject.
3 F You can go skiing in the winter.
4 F It's quite small.

Page 165

Exercise 4
1 d	3 e	5 f
2 c	4 a	6 b

Exercise 5
1 d	2 a	3 c

🔊 **Track 104**

1

Receptionist: Hello. Can I help you?

Student: Yes. I'm a new student. Can you give me some information about the welcome event, please?

Receptionist: Of course. What would you like to know?

Student: What time does it start?

Receptionist: It starts at 7 o'clock this evening. You might want to get there nice and early. It can get quite crowded.

Student: OK, thanks. And which room is it in?

Receptionist: It's in the main hall. That's just by the main entrance to the building. You can't miss it. There are signs up all over the place.

Student: Thank you. Do I need to take anything with me?

Receptionist: Just your student card. I think that's it.

Student: Is there food at the event?

Receptionist: There are a few snacks, but not a full meal. And drinks, of course.

Student: OK. Thank you. Bye.

Receptionist: Bye. Enjoy the event.

2

Woman: Oh, hi, Xavier. How are things?

Man: Hi. I'm OK, thanks. There's a lot to do when you first arrive in a new place.

Woman: That's true. And it's quite hard to find your way around, too.

Man: Yes. And you don't want to ask for help all the time!

Woman: Yeah. Are you going to the welcome event later today?

Man: Yes, I want to go. How about you?

Woman: Yeah, I'm definitely going. It should be good, and hopefully we'll meet lots of people, too.

Man: Shall we go together?

Woman: That's a good idea. Where shall we meet?

Man: Let's meet in the student café near the main entrance at 6.30. We can have a coffee, then go to the event.

Woman: That sounds great. See you later.

Man: See you.

3

Man: Hi. Are you a new student?

Woman: Yes. My name's Maria.

Man: Nice to meet you. I'm Bartek.

Woman: Where are you from?

Man: I'm from Poland. And you?

Woman: From Italy.

Man: Oh, nice. I went to Rome last year. I really liked it. When did you arrive?

Woman: Last week, on Wednesday.

Man: Oh. I just arrived yesterday. What are you studying?

Woman: International Business. It's a one-year course, and I hope I can get some work experience in the holidays. What about you?

Man: I'm studying Biology.

Woman: Oh, that's interesting. Shall we go and find some food? I think there's some over there.

Man: Good idea. I think there are some
…

Exercise 6
1 Can you give me
2 What time
3 Which room
4 Do I need to
5 Is there
6 about you

Exercise 7
1 a	3 a
2 b	4 b

Exercises 8 & 9

the city: Switzerland, close to the Alps, high mountains all around it, old and modern and lots of young people study there. One of the most famous sights in the city is the Water Jet, the water goes up to 140 metres into the air.

organisations in the city: a lot of well-known organisations have their main buildings in Geneva, such as the United Nations and the Red Cross. Also a lot of big companies have offices there, so a great place to study and get work experience.

the university: one of the best universities in the world, attracts students from all over the world, nearly 40% of the students from other countries; has a lot of modern scientific equipment, great place to study science; halls of residence all over the city, and most students choose to live in these, but some choose to live in apartments.

life in the city: quite expensive, but clean and safe; good public transport, lots of cafés and restaurants, and in the winter you can try skiing

Exercises 10 & 11
Students' own answers.

UNIT 13
Page 166

READING

Exercise 1
Students' own answers.

Exercise 2
A Aidan
B Jasmine

Exercise 3
1 She hasn't got any.
2 how to draw and paint
3 She's getting married.
4 six
5 younger
6 move to/get his own flat

Exercise 4
1 only child
2 single
3 engaged, fiancé
4 stepfather
5 stepsister
6 relatives
7 important person in my life

Exercise 5
Students' own answers.

Page 167

VOCABULARY

Exercise 1

Students' own answers.

Exercise 2

A Harry

B Leo

🔊 **Track 105**

Jane: Oh, let me see that photo … are those little girls your stepsisters?

Aidan: Yes, that's Minnie on the right and Lulu on the left. Aren't they sweet?

Jane: Yes, they are! I wish I had little sisters like that. But what about your brothers? They aren't in the photo? What do they look like?

Aidan: Well Harry is the oldest and he's very tall already. He's taller than me – and thinner. He goes running and to the gym a lot so he's quite thin and very fit. He's got straight brown hair and brown eyes and he wears glasses. He looks a lot like me – you can see that we are brothers. However, he's much cleverer than I am – he's really brilliant! He's studying maths at university and he's really good at it – he gets great marks in all his exams. Leo's the youngest. He's got very fair curly hair and blue eyes. He's not very tall, but he's quite good-looking – much better-looking than and me and Harry! And he's funnier. He's always making people laugh. All the girls like him. But Leo and I don't get on very well. He's not my favourite brother.

Jane: Really, why's that. What's he like?

Aidan: He's just very annoying! To start with he's a bit lazy. He doesn't help around the house and I often do his jobs for him. And he's also not very kind to Harry. Leo's younger than Harry but he's much more confident and sociable. He has lots of friends and goes out a lot, but Harry is quiet and shy. Leo makes jokes about Harry and laughs at him in front of his friends.

Jane: No, that isn't very kind – poor Harry! Does he get upset?

Aidan: No, I don't think he notices. He's thinking about other things, but I notice – and I don't like it.

Exercise 3

1 sweet

2 brilliant

3 annoying, lazy

4 kind

5 confident, sociable

6 quiet

Exercise 4

1 brilliant

2 sweet

3 Sociable

4 quiet

Exercise 5

Students' own answers.

Exercise 6

1	A	3	A
2	B	4	B

Exercise 7

1	B	3	A	5	A
2	B	4	B		

Exercise 8

Students' own answers.

Page 168

GRAMMAR

Exercise 1

1 -er

2 more

3 than

4 better

Exercise 2

1 older

2 taller

3 more successful

4 stronger

5 faster

6 quicker

Exercise 3

Students' own answers.

PUSH YOURSELF B1

Exercise 1

a the same

b different

Exercise 2

1 not as shy as

2 as good as

3 not as expensive as

4 not as dangerous as

5 as boring as

6 as long as

Page 169

LISTENING PART 2: TRAINING

Exercise 1

Students' own answers.

Exercise 2

1 D casual

2 C sporty

3 B smart

4 E fashionable

5 A cool

Exercise 3

1 1st October

2 teenagers

3 7.30

4 Derrick

🔊 **Track 106**

Woman: A fantastic new shop is opening in town. It's called Lily's Fashion Boutique and it's going to open in the town centre. You'll need to know the address; it's 149 High Street. There will be an opening party on September 30th and the store will open on the first of October. As you know, there are already many shops here selling ladies' and men's clothes but Lily's Fashion Boutique will be the only store where you can buy things for teenagers to wear. The store will open at 9.30 in the morning and shut at 7.30 in the evening. This is later than most shops in town, which close at 7 o'clock. If you're looking for work in the new shop, contact the manager. His name's Mr Derrick. I'll spell that for you – D-E-double-R-I-C-K. He'll be happy to give more information.

READING PART 5: TRAINING

1 went/was

2 than

3 to

4 lot

5 more

Page 170

READING

Exercise 1

Students' own answers.

Exercise 2

1	B	2	C	3	A

Exercise 3

1 Rihanna

2 Eddie Redmayne

3 Lupita Nyong'o

4 Rihanna

5 Eddie Redmayne

Exercise 4

1 jewellery

2 brands

3 suits, ties

4 fashions

5 trainers

6 handbag

7 sunglasses

8 sandals

Exercise 5

Students' own answers.

GRAMMAR

Exercise 1

1 -est
2 most
3 the
4 best

Exercise 2

1 the most boring
2 the cheapest
3 the ugliest
4 the most famous
5 the best, the most expensive
6 the hottest

Exercise 3

1 more important
2 the most interesting
3 more difficult
4 more expensive
5 happier

Exercise 4

/ɪst/

🔊 Track 107

hottest, biggest, thinnest, prettiest, funniest, ugliest

Exercises 5, 6 & 7

Students' own answers.

WRITING

Exercise 1

Students' own answers.

Exercise 2

1 People can buy the trainers now, online and in sports shops.
2 He likes the colours; they are light and comfortable to wear; they are so cool they will make all your other clothes look good.
3 They are expensive, not good value for money, not strong or practical; his feet got wet when he went out in the rain.
4 You shouldn't buy them if you want trainers to wear every day. You should buy them if you want trainers that look great.

Exercise 3

1 I fell in love with… They are the best-looking trainers I've seen for a long time … for me, the best thing about them is…
2 On the less positve side…
3 So do I recommend… It depends on what you want… (aren't) a good buy…

Exercise 4

'sell out' means that the shops/websites will sell all the trainers and none will be left to buy.

Exercise 5

Paragraph 1
d introduction where/when you can buy the product
Paragraph 2
c the good things about the product
Paragraph 3
a the bad things about the product
Paragraph 4
b conclusion: overall opinion of the product / recommendation

Exercise 6

1 Paragraph 2
2 Paragraph 4
3 Paragraph 3
4 Paragraph 2
5 Paragraph 4
6 Paragraph 3

Exercises 7 & 8

Students' own answers.

SPEAKING

Exercises 1 & 2

Students' own answers.

Exercise 3

1 A
2 A & B
3 A & B
4 B
5 B
6 B

Exercise 4

1 B   **2** A

🔊 Track 108
1
Man: Well, I think the people in the middle of the photo are friends. I'm sure they're having a really good time because they look very happy. They are wearing casual clothes like jeans and shirts and the tall man with the dark hair is wearing sunglasses too. One of the young women has got long red hair and she's got something on her face – it might be face paint. Perhaps they are at a music festival or gig. The women are holding some fruity drinks, but the men haven't got any. It's a sunny day, but I don't think it's very hot because I can see some people with jackets in the background. There are trees with lots of green, so I think it's probably summer. It could be in Britain.

2
Woman: So, I can see a little café in a street. It's really quiet there because there are only two people walking along the street. I think it's probably in a town or city because there are lots of parked cars, but maybe it's early in the morning. In the middle of the photo I can see two people sitting at a small round table. There are some coffee or tea cups, so maybe they're having breakfast. The people are young, maybe 25 to 30 years old and I think they are going to work because they are wearing smart clothes. They look quite serious – maybe they're thinking about work. The woman has got red hair and is wearing a dark jacket and skirt and the man has got short dark hair and is wearing jeans and a jacket. The woman is holding something, but I can't see what it is. I think one of them goes to work by bike because I can see a bike and a bike helmet behind them.

Exercise 5

1 I think
2 I'm sure
3 it might be
4 Perhaps
5 I don't think
6 probably
7 could be
8 maybe

Exercise 6

Students' own answers.

EXAM FOCUS
READING PART 5

Exercise 1

1 F It tests your grammar.
2 F There are no options.
3 F There may be two shorter texts.
4 T
5 T

Exercise 2

1 than
2 of
3 Did
4 Was
5 there
6 Would

Page 175

LISTENING PART 2

Exercise 1
1 c   3 e   5 a
2 d   4 b

Exercise 2
1 9.15 / quarter past nine
2 Tuesday
3 Wralstone
4 smartphone
5 dress

🎧 Track 109

Narrator: For each question, write the correct answer in the gap. Write one word or a number or a date or a time.
You will hear a woman talking at the start of a course on fashion.
Woman: Welcome to this short summer course on fashion. When I've finished speaking, your teacher will take you to the North room for your classes. Thank you for being here at quarter to eight. The early start was because there's so much information to give you. Classes begin at nine fifteen today, and every other day. There's been a change to the timetable: on the one we sent you, it says Wednesday for the lesson on drawing, but it's actually going to be on Tuesday. Then on Thursday a famous fashion photographer is coming to talk to you. His name is Peter Wralstone – you spell that W-R-A-L-S-T-O-N-E.
We'll give you most of the things you need for the course – a pen, notepad, etc., but please make sure you have your smartphone to take photos – you'll use that every day. On the last day, you'll make something. I'm sure you've all made a skirt at least once already, so it'll be a dress. That's a little more difficult!

Page 176

REAL WORLD

Exercise 1
Students' own answers.

Exercise 2
prices are lower

Exercise 3
1 B   2 A   3 C

Exercise 4
1 F There are lots of malls.
2 F Mornings are a good time because it's quieter.
3 T
4 F The prices aren't fixed so they can change.
5 T
6 T

Page 177

Exercise 5
1 a   3 a   5 b
2 a   4 b   6 a

Exercise 6
1 d   2 c   3 b

🎧 Track 110

1
Assistant: Hello. Can I help you?
Customer: Yes. I really like this dress, but it's too small. Do you have a bigger size? I'm not sure what size this one is.
Assistant: Let me see. This is a size 36. With designer clothes like this, the sizes are all international, so we use the same sizes here as in most countries in Europe. We usually have all sizes in stock, so let me see if we've got a size 38. Do you want the same colour?
Customer: Yes, I like this colour. But do you have it in other colours? Maybe I could see those, too?
Assistant: No problem. Ah, yes. Here we are. This is a 38. We've got it in red or green. Would you like to try it on?
Customer: Yes, please. Can I try them both?
Assistant: Of course. There you go. The changing rooms are just over there, on your left.
Customer: Thank you.
2
Assistant: Hello. Can I help you?
Customer: Yes, please. Are these shoes in the sale?
Assistant: I'm afraid not. They're full price.
Customer: Oh. So, how much are they?
Assistant: They're 450 Dirham.
Customer: Oh, OK. Is there a discount for students?
Assistant: No, I'm sorry, we don't offer any discounts. But there are plenty of other shoes in the sales. If you come this way, I can show you our special offers. Here you are. These are all the sale items. There are some very good price reductions at the moment. Everything on this shelf is half price, so it's worth taking a look.
Customer: OK, thanks for your help.
3
Customer 3: So, what do you think? How do they look?
Customer 4: They're lovely jeans and they look great on you. That colour really suits you. Do you like them?
Customer 3: I'm not sure about them. They're a bit loose. What do you think?
Customer 4: Hmm. I can see what you mean. What about these jeans?

Customer 3: I'll go and try them on. Back in a minute!
Customer 3: Right. How do they look?
Customer 4: Wow! They look amazing! Do you like them?
Customer 3: Yes, I really like these ones. They fit me perfectly and they're really comfortable to wear, too.
Customer 4: Yes. And the colour's nicer than the other one. How much are they?
Customer 3: That's the other good thing about them. They're on special offer for the shopping festival, so they've got 30% off.
Customer 4: A bargain!
Customer 3: Yeah. I think I'll get them!

Exercise 7
1 bigger
2 colours
3 sale
4 How much
5 discount
6 look
7 suits
8 fit

Exercise 8
1 b   3 b
2 a   4 a

Exercise 9
the city: in the United Arab Emirates; a big, modern city important for business; lots of interesting modern buildings and some of the tallest buildings in the world; on the coast, popular with tourists, lots of beaches, some on islands built especially for tourism; gets very hot in summer, sometimes 50 degrees.
shopping malls: more than 70 shopping malls; Dubai Mall is the biggest shopping mall in the world; designer clothes are often cheaper than in other countries; malls also have other interesting things, like an aquarium and an indoor ski slope!
the souks: the place to go if you want cheaper clothes, colourful scarves, carpets, gold jewellery, tasty spices for cooking with, and foods grown in the country, like dates.
the shopping festival: started in 1995, now takes place for one month every year; entertainment in the streets, people come all over the world to find cheap designer clothes; Dubai Global Village has stalls selling clothes and other things from over 40 different countries; there are fireworks at night.

Exercise 10
Students' own answers.

UNIT 14
VOCABULARY
Exercise 1
Students' own answers.

Exercise 2
Photos:
A basketball
B rugby
C cricket
D athletics
E tennis
F football
Quiz:
1 tennis
2 football
3 athletics
4 rugby
5 cricket
6 basketball

Exercise 3
Most popular to least popular: football, basketball, cricket, tennis, athletics, rugby

Track 111
Man: Football is the most popular sport in the world. People play and watch football in every country and on every continent in the world. The second most popular sport is basketball. The game comes from the USA and is very popular in North and South America, but there are also lots of basketball fans in China and Europe. Cricket is the world's third most popular sport. This might be a surprise for some people because cricket is not well known in many countries. But you will find a lot of cricket fans in countries like India, Pakistan, the UK, Australia and New Zealand. Tennis is the world's fourth most popular sport. Both men and women play and enjoy tennis all over the world on indoor or outdoor courts. One of the most popular sports in the summer Olympic Games is athletics and it's the fifth most popular sport in the world. In sixth place is rugby. People mostly play rugby in Europe and English-speaking countries like Australia and New Zealand, but it's also very popular in Argentina.

Exercise 4
Students' own answers.

Exercise 5
1 kick
2 throw, team
3 winning, scored
4 racket
5 races
6 net
7 bat, match

READING
Exercises 1 & 2
Students' own answers.

Exercise 3
1 T
2 F It was called football because you played it on foot and not riding on a horse.
3 F You couldn't play football in the street or in public places.
4 F Women used the same pitches as men before 1921 and then again after 1971.
5 F It's becoming more popular.

Exercise 4
1 teams
2 pitch
3 goal
4 score
5 loses
6 match
7 rules
8 referee
9 red card
10 send
11 off

GRAMMAR
Exercise 1
1 can
2 mustn't
3 have to
4 don't need to

Exercise 2
1 c **3** e **5** d
2 f **4** b **6** a

Exercise 3
1 have to/need to, can't
2 don't have to/don't need to, can
3 Can, can't
4 must/have to/need to
5 don't have to/don't need to
6 must/need to/have to
7 must/need to/have to, must/needs to/has to
8 Do … have to/need to

Exercise 4
Students' own answers.

LISTENING
Exercise 1
Students' own answers.

Exercise 2
1 long-distance races
2 the mountains above the Rift Valley

Exercise 3
Because they run all the time as they are poor and don't have transport.
For example, they have to run to school every day because their families don't have cars and there aren't any buses.
Because they live in the mountains, they often have to run up and down hills. This makes their legs strong and is good for their breathing.

Track 112
Interviewer: I'm here in the Rift Valley in Kenya, at a school which specialises in training local children to become long-distance runners. With me is Florence Kipoge, a teacher at the school. Florence, I've just watched some of the students from the school running and they all look like future champions to me. What do you think are the reasons there are so many amazing runners here?
Florence: Well, the children you saw today don't come from rich families. This means that all their lives they have to walk – and run – everywhere. For example, they have to run to school every day because their families don't have cars and there aren't any buses. When I was a teenager, I lived five kilometres from school and I ran there and back every day.
Interviewer: So people here need to be good at running because there's very little transport?
Florence: Yes. Also, because we live in the mountains, we often have to run up and down hills. This makes our legs strong and is good for our breathing.
Interviewer: Lots of the children run barefoot, without shoes, don't they? Do you think that helps?
Florence: Yes, it's very good for your whole body to run and walk without shoes. It makes your feet strong and you have to use your legs and body in a different way. It gives you a good running style.
Interviewer: But doesn't it hurt your feet?
Florence: You mustn't run long distances on hard, flat roads without shoes – that would hurt your feet. But the roads here are not like city roads. When students from our school start winning competitions and get some money, they often buy running shoes, but sometimes they don't like wearing them!
Interviewer: All the students I see seem very serious and they train very hard. Is this another reason why they do so well?
Florence: Absolutely. This part of Kenya is beautiful but there aren't many jobs. For the young people here, becoming a professional runner or getting a sports scholarship is a dream. It can change their lives and the lives of their families. So they work very, very hard.

Exercise 4

1 b	**4** a	**7** b
2 a	**5** b	
3 b	**6** a	

Exercise 5

Students' own answers.

VOCABULARY

Exercise 1

1 do

2 play

3 go

Exercise 2

Do	Play	Go
aerobics	handball	horse riding
gymnastics	baseball	cycling
judo	volleyball	fishing
yoga		snowboarding
		surfing
		rock climbing
		skiing
		sailing
		windsurfing

Exercise 3

Students' own answers.

Page 182

WRITING PART 7: TRAINING

Exercise 1

1 B

2 C

3 A

Exercise 2

Students' own answers.

Exercise 3

Tenses used: past continuous and past simple

Exercise 4

1 It's longer because some words have been added. It's more interesting because of the adjectives used.

2 adjectives – they give you more information to help you imagine and 'see' what is happening in the story.

Page 183

Exercise 5

Suggested answers

1 One day I was sitting in a busy/quiet café when I noticed that there was a big/colourful bag on the round table next to me.

2 A beautiful woman was walking through the quiet/big park when suddenly she saw a shiny/strange/big/ colourful object on the small path in front of her.

3 One afternoon, as I crossing the busy road to my house, a/an expensive/ new/big car stopped in the street next to me and a/an angry/strange man put his big head out of the window to speak to me.

Exercise 6

Model answer

Charlotte was playing basketball with her friends. When she threw the ball, the wind carried it away. It landed on a roof. 'Why did you do that, Charlotte?' shouted her friend. Charlotte was upset because everyone was angry. She climbed up and got the ball. Everyone was happy because they could play again. (53 words)

GRAMMAR

Exercise 1

1 was born

2 began

3 was … studying

4 won

5 has taken part

6 has won

7 stopped

8 works

9 is working

Exercise 2

Past simple is used in gaps 1, 2, 4 and 7 as they are referring to finished actions or events in the past.

Past continuous is used in gap 3 as it describes a background event.

Present perfect is used in gaps 5 and 6 as they are referring to experiences in Trischa's life.

Present simple is used in gap 8 as it refers to a present routine.

Present continuous is used in gap 9 because it refers to a temporary action.

Exercise 3

All the words have the same vowel sound.

🎧 Track 113

Woman: bought, thought, taught, saw

PUSH YOURSELF B1

Exercise 1

1 when something happened

2 how something happened

3 how the speaker or writer feels about something

Exercise 2

Adverbs of time: Afterwards

Adverbs of manner: slowly, carefully, quickly

Sentence adverbs: Surprisingly, Luckily

Exercise 3

1 afterwards

2 fortunately

3 suddenly

4 before

5 Unfortunately

Page 184

LISTENING

Exercise 1

A Arno

B Loli

C Sandra

Exercise 2

1 Sandra

2 Arno

3 Loli

🎧 Track 114

1

Sandra: I went to my first rugby match when I was living in Cardiff. I was about 18 years old and I wasn't interested in sport at all. I only went because my friends were going, but I loved it! It was cold and raining, but the game was very exciting. The other great thing was the way the fans in the stadium never stopped singing. It was fantastic! Now I'm a serious fan and I have a season ticket to watch the Cardiff Blues, the team I support. I go to all the Blues' home matches and I sometimes follow them to the away matches too.

2

Arno: I started going to race tracks with my father when I was six. He was a big fan all his life so I became one too. Some people can't understand why I like it. They ask things like: 'Why do you want to watch cars go round and round on a race track? Doesn't it get boring?' The answer is 'No, never!' It's easier to follow what is happening in a race if you watch it on TV but, for me, that isn't as exciting. I prefer to be there. I love the atmosphere, the smell of the petrol and the noise.

3

Loli: I got interested in basketball out of love! I started going to matches at college when I was about 20 because my college boyfriend was a basketball player. For a long time, I was bored. Basketball rules are very complicated, so I didn't know what was happening. But then, slowly, I started to understand the game. Now I like it and find it interesting because it's complicated and because it's a team game. I love watching how the team play together on the court – this is very important in basketball and it changes all the time.

Exercise 3

	Sandra	Arno	Loli
Age when he/she started watching the sport	18	6	20
Why he/she started watching the sport	because her friends were going	because his father was a fan – he started going to races as a child	because her boyfriend was a basketball player
Where the sport is played/practised	stadium	race track	(basketball) court
What the person likes about the sport / feels when watching a match	It's exciting – she likes the singing during matches.	He loves the atmosphere, the smell of the petrol and the noise.	It's a complicated, interesting game. She loves watching the team play together.

Exercise 4

1 c   3 d
2 a   4 b

Exercise 5

1 season ticket
2 home matches
3 away matches
4 live

Exercise 6

Students' own answers.

Page 185

SPEAKING PART 2: TRAINING

Exercise 1

Students' own answers.

Exercise 2

	Mei	Luca
basketball	✗ played a little at school She's not very good very fast game	✓ game popular in his country *Olimipia Milano* is a good team played in basketball team in college
running	✓ likes running alone it's good to keep fit was in running competitions	✗ doesn't like running a long way
swimming	✓ lives near the beach – goes often	✓ swims a lot in summer when goes to visit grandfather
tennis	✗ learned at school difficult to hit the ball makes her arms hurt	✓ goes to a tennis club likes watching tennis – exciting

Track 115

Examiner: Now, in this part of the test you are going to talk together. Here are some pictures that show different sports. Do you like these different sports? Say why or why not. I'll say that again. Do you like these different sports? Say why or why not? All right? Now, talk together.

Luca: This is basketball, isn't it? This game is very popular in my country. I like it. I come from Milan and Olimpia Milano is a good team. Do you play basketball?

Mei: I played a little at school, but I don't like it very much. I'm not very good … It's a very fast game. What about you? Do you play basketball?

Luca: Yes, I play basketball sometimes with my friends, when we have time. And I played in the basketball team in my college, but not this year.

Mei: And this one is running. I like running alone. It's good for exercise and to keep fit. In the past I was in running competitions – races. What about you? Do you like running?

Luca: No, not very much. I don't like running a long way. I like this sport – swimming. In the summer, I go to stay with my grandfather. His house is near a lake and I swim a lot.

Mei: I live near the beach so I go swimming very often. It's great.

Luca: And this sport is tennis. I enjoy playing tennis. In the summer I go to a tennis club – and I like watching it too. Do you play tennis?

Mei: I learned tennis at school, but I think it's difficult. I'm often too slow to hit the ball and it makes my arms hurt.

Exercise 3

Students' own answers.

Exercise 4

Do you think playing basketball is difficult?
Do you think swimming is fun?
Which of these sports do you like best?

Track 116

Examiner: Do you think playing basketball is difficult, Luca?

Luca: I suppose it's not easy to score goals. You have to be very tall to be a good basketball player.

Examiner: Do you think swimming is fun, Mei?

Mei: In my opinion, swimming is fun but I don't like swimming in cold water. Also, it's a cheap sport to do.

Examiner: So, Luca, which of these sports do you like best?

Luca: Definitely tennis. I think it's fun to play and exciting to watch.

Examiner: And you, Mei, which of these sports do you like best?

Mei: From these sports, I like running best. But actually, my favourite sport is football.

Examiner: Thank you.

Exercise 5

Students' own answers.

Exercise 6

Luca would like to try snowboarding.
Mei prefers watching sports.

🔊 **Track 117**

Examiner: Now, which new sport would you like to learn, Mei?

Mei: I'm interested in learning how to water-ski.

Examiner: Why?

Mei: Because it looks awesome. Some people say it's a dangerous sport, but I think it's amazing.

Examiner: And what about you, Luca?

Luca: I'd like to try snowboarding. My cousins are very good snowboarders and I'd like to go snowboarding with them. I think you need a lot of lessons to stay safe, and they're quite expensive.

Examiner: Which do you prefer, watching sports or playing sports, Luca?

Luca: I don't know really. It's different for different sports. But probably playing sports, because it's fun and it's good for you.

Examiner: And you, Mei?

Mei: Definitely watching sports. My favourite thing is to go to a football match to watch my team.

Examiner: Thank you. That is the end of the test.

Exercise 7

1 it looks awesome; I think it's amazing
2 I'd like to go
3 it's good for you
4 My favourite thing is

Exercise 8

Students' own answers.

Page 186

EXAM FOCUS
WRITING PART 7

Exercise 1

1 pictures
2 tell
3 decide
4 write
5 words

Exercise 2

Model answer

The women were playing football in the park. One player kicked the ball into the lake. The players were sad because they couldn't play anymore, but the people in the boat picked up the ball and returned it to the players. The players were happy.
(45 words)

Page 187

SPEAKING PART 2

Exercise 1

1 b   3 d   5 c
2 e   4 a

Exercises 2, 3, 4 & 5

Students' own answers.

Page 188

REAL WORLD

Exercises 1 & 2

Students' own answers.

Exercise 3

1 a   3 d   5 e
2 f   4 b   6 c

Page 189

Exercise 4

KizziGrand

Exercise 5

1 KizziGrand
2 ClareM
3 TomR44
4 KizziGrand
5 TomR44
6 ClareM

Exercise 6

1 b   2 c   3 d

🔊 **Track 118**

1

Customer: Hello. I'd like to buy two tickets for the match next Saturday.

Official: OK. Let's see what we've got. Yes, I've got tickets available at most prices. Which part of the stadium did you have in mind?

Customer: Well, where are the cheapest seats?

Official: They're at both ends, behind the goals. There are a few seats in the North Stand for 40 Euros each. They're right at the top.

Customer: Will I get a good view of the game?

Official: Well, it's hard to say. It depends how the game goes. If the action's all at your end, you'll be fine. If the action's all at the other end of the pitch, you won't see so well. There are some tickets in the side stands for 55 euros. You should get a better view from there.

Customer: Oh, OK. I'll take those ones.

Official: OK. No problem.

Customer: And what time do the gates open?

Official: They open 45 minutes before the game starts. And next Saturday, the game starts at 7.30, so it will be 6.45.

Customer: OK. Thanks.

2

Guide: So, this is where the players come out onto the pitch. Can you imagine coming out and seeing the stadium full of people, all cheering for you?

Male: Wow! The stadium's amazing, isn't it?

Female: Yeah. It's so big!

Male: I can't imagine playing in front of a big crowd like this!

Female: No! I'd be really scared! But I don't play football. I only watch it.

Male: Which team do you support?

Female: Well, I'm from Paris, so I support Paris St Germain. They're doing quite well this season. What about you?

Male: I support Arsenal. I go and watch them play quite a lot, with my uncle.

Female: Cool.

Guide: Right, if you'd like to come this way, we'll go and see the changing rooms.

3

Girl: That was a great game – so exciting!

Boy: Yeah. I'm so glad Real Madrid won.

Girl: Me too. They played well. And their first goal was amazing.

Boy: Yeah, a brilliant shot. The goalkeeper had no chance!

Girl: They were lucky to get a penalty in the second half.

Boy: Yeah, I don't think it was really a penalty. I think the referee got that wrong.

Girl: Yes, but that's football.

Exercise 7

1 support
2 What
3 great
4 too
5 chance
6 referee

Exercise 8

1 a   3 b   5 b
2 b   4 a

Exercises 9 & 10

Madrid: the capital city of Spain, also the country's biggest city, home to the Spanish royal family; important government buildings; Plaza Mayor, or Main Square, 400 years old, buildings on the square are expensive flats.

football teams in the city: two big teams – Real Madrid and Atlético Madrid, both teams have thousands of fans and are good at winning; Real Madrid has won 64 trophies in Spain and 24 trophies in European and world competitions; one of the most successful clubs in the world; Atlético Madrid has won the Spanish League and Europa Cup recently, used to play at the Vicente Calderón Stadium but now Wanda Metropolitano; Real Madrid plays at the Bernabéu Stadium.

stadium tours: can go on a tour of stadiums in Madrid; the Bernabéu Stadium first opened in 1947 and can hold 81,000 fans; can sometimes see the players practising on the pitch before a game.
buying tickets for matches: cheapest tickets are about 40 euros, most expensive are over 400 euros; best to book your tickets in advance.

Exercise 11

Students' own answers.

Page 190
PROGRESS CHECK 5

Exercise 1

1	D	3	C
2	A	4	B

Exercise 2

1 sociable
2 funny
3 quiet
4 kind
5 lazy
6 clever

Exercise 3

1 relatives
2 small family
3 only child
4 married
5 important person in my life
6 fiancé

Exercise 4

1 have to
2 need to
3 don't have to
4 can
5 must
6 mustn't

Exercise 5

1 going, train, competition
2 played, catch, bat
3 play, red card, matches
4 team, do, races
5 went, do, rules

Page 191
Exercise 6

1 bigger
2 more interesting
3 best
4 friendliest
5 worse
6 busier

Exercise 7

1 ~~better~~ best
2 ~~more fast~~ faster
3 ~~sport more popular~~ most popular sport
4 one of my ~~most~~ favourite games
5 ~~more~~ safer

Exercise 8

1	f	3	a	5	c
2	d	4	b	6	e

Exercise 9

1	B	3	C	5	A
2	A	4	C	6	B

Exercise 10

1 doing – maths
2 taking – drama
3 do – chemistry
4 revising – history
5 doing – journalist
6 qualifications – farmer

Exercise 11

1 The dentist pulled my tooth out. / The dentist pulled out my tooth.
2 A really famous engineer built that bridge.
3 Our geography teacher asked us to find out about rivers.
4 My modern languages teacher gave me really good marks.

GRAMMAR REFERENCE
Page 196
STARTER UNIT
BE

Exercise 1

1 You're
2 isn't
3 I'm not
4 aren't, We're
5 She's

Exercise 2

1 is/'s
2 am/'m
3 are
4 Is, isn't, is/'s
5 Are, am

HAVE GOT

Exercise 3

1 hasn't
2 have
3 have
4 Have, haven't
5 have

Exercise 4

1 've got
2 haven't got
3 has got
4 Have … got, haven't
5 haven't got

CAN/CAN'T/LIKE/DON'T LIKE

Exercise 5

1 She can't paint very well.
2 We don't like dogs.

3 Correct
4 Correct
5 I like watching films on TV.
6 Correct

WH- QUESTION WORDS

Exercise 6

1 Where
2 Who
3 How
4 When
5 Whose

Exercise 7

1 What
2 Where
3 How
4 Whose
5 When

THE APOSTROPHE 'S

Exercise 8

1 This is my best friend's car.
2 Steve Brown's in my class.
3 The children's books are on the teacher's desk.
4 The new pilots' uniforms are dark blue.
5 It's very noisy here.
6 Peter's so friendly, he's always helping me.

3RD PERSON S IN THE PRESENT SIMPLE

Exercise 9

1 like
2 eats
3 loves
4 come
5 walks

Page 198
UNIT 1
PRESENT SIMPLE

Exercise 1

1 plays
2 get up
3 likes
4 live
5 goes

Exercise 2

1 Paul doesn't play the piano every evening.
2 I don't get up at 6 o'clock every day.
3 My brother doesn't like football.
4 My friends don't live near me.
5 Hannah doesn't go to school by bus.

Exercise 3

1 My brother **works** in Moscow.
2 Tom **doesn't** play the piano.
3 I **play** football every weekend.

4 Does she **start** work at 9 o'clock every morning?

5 My parents **don't** watch TV in the afternoon.

ADVERBS OF FREQUENCY

Exercise 4

1 I never go to work in the evening.

2 I sometimes help my brother with his homework.

3 My sister and I walk to college every day.

4 I am sometimes late for work.

5 I always work hard at college.

Exercise 5

Students' own answers.

Exercise 6

1 He doesn't like to go camping.

2 They don't like getting up early.

3 He loves to drink iced coffee.

4 We don't want to go shopping this morning.

5 She wants to wear her new top to the party.

Page 200

UNIT 2
PRESENT CONTINUOUS

Exercise 1

1 are not/aren't watching, are/'re listening

2 am/'m writing

3 Are you doing?, 'm not, am/'m playing

4 is/'s running

5 isn't washing

Exercise 2

1 reading

2 putting

3 cooking

4 sitting

5 dancing

PRESENT SIMPLE OR PRESENT CONTINUOUS?

Exercise 3

1 go

2 's doing

3 love

4 's starting

5 play

6 have

Exercise 4

1 ~~we are usually getting~~ we usually get

2 ~~I listen~~ I'm listening

3 ~~my family is hating~~ my family hates

4 ~~Mateo is having~~ Mateo has

5 ~~Jon has~~ Jon is having

6 ~~Are you understanding~~ Do you understand

Page 202

UNIT 3
PAST SIMPLE

Exercise 1

1 were, broke, walked

2 did … have, ate, drank

3 did … get, got, gave

4 Did … go, did, went

5 Did … watch, didn't, took, was

6 came, weren't, was

Exercise 2

1 left

2 won, felt

3 made

4 met, bought

5 began

Page 204

UNIT 4
CAN/CAN'T, COULD/COULDN'T + INFINITIVE WITHOUT TO

Exercise 1

1 can't

2 can, can

3 can't

4 couldn't, could

5 Can, can't

Exercise 2

2 Could you swim when you were three?
Yes, I could. / No, I couldn't.

3 Can you speak more than two languages?
Yes, I can. / No, I can't.

4 Can you skateboard?
Yes, I can. / No, I can't.

5 Can both of your parents drive?
Yes, they can. / No, they can't.

SHOULD/SHOULDN'T

Exercise 3

You should: go to bed early, ask parents or friends to help you.

You shouldn't: work late the day before, spend too much time alone, worry

Exercise 4

1 should drink

2 should wear

3 shouldn't eat

4 shouldn't ride

5 should get

6 shouldn't arrive

Page 206

UNIT 5
PAST CONTINUOUS

Exercise 1

1 were listening/listened, were having

2 was sleeping, phoned

3 was doing

4 woke up, was raining

5 were you doing

Exercise 2

1 were driving

2 were travelling

3 were reading

4 were listening

5 saw

6 was standing

7 was telling

8 passed

9 was coming

10 was

PAST CONTINUOUS AND PAST SIMPLE

Exercise 3

1 was watching

2 often phoned

3 realised

4 was shining, were singing

5 won

Exercise 4

1 was tidying, found

2 was leaving, realised

3 was watching, cooked/was cooking

4 heard, stopped, were doing, walked

5 crashed, was updating

Page 208

UNIT 6
COUNTABLE AND UNCOUNTABLE NOUNS

Exercise 1

Countable nouns: baby, box, child, knife, man, person, school, strawberry, student, teacher

Uncountable nouns: bread, coffee, juice, milk, money, rice, tea, water

Exercise 2

babies, boxes, children, knives, men, people, schools, strawberries, students, teachers

Exercise 3

1 an

2 any

3 Some

4 some

5 any

6 a

Exercise 4

1 How much

2 How many

3 A lot of

4 a few

5 a lot of

6 no

7 a little

8 a few

IMPERATIVES

Exercise 5
1 Don't use
2 Don't shout, Talk
3 Don't run, Walk
4 Don't come, Use

Exercise 6
2 Wash them.
3 Don't forget to buy her a present.
4 Turn it off.
5 Go to bed.

Page 210

UNIT 7
PRESENT PERFECT

Exercise 1
1 has met
2 have/'ve never been
3 Have … travelled
4 has/'s won
5 has never swum

Exercise 2
1 didn't see
2 Have you ever been
3 haven't
4 have been
5 have been

PRESENT PERFECT WITH *JUST*

Exercise 3
1 I'm really hot. I've just run home from college.
2 We've just finished eating.
3 I've just texted my brother.
4 He's just told me he passed his exam.
5 They've just arrived back from India.

Page 212

UNIT 8
PRESENT PERFECT WITH *FOR* AND *SINCE*

Exercise 1

for	since
24 hours	6 o'clock
400 years	last November
ten minutes	my birthday
three weeks	October 12th
12 months	the end of May
	yesterday

Exercise 2
1 two weeks
2 25 years
3 last weekend
4 January
5 23 years
6 the age of nine

PRESENT PERFECT WITH *YET* AND *ALREADY*

Exercise 3
1 Have you tidied your bedroom yet?
2 They've already finished their college project.
3 I don't want to watch that programme. I've already seen it twice.
4 Tania doesn't want to go to bed yet. She isn't tired.

Exercise 4
1 I haven't worn my new shoes yet.
2 We've already finished eating.
3 I've already texted all my friends. / I've texted my friends already.
4 Have you finished reading that book yet?
5 I've already phoned my older sister.

Page 214

UNIT 9
–ING OR *TO* INFINITIVE AFTER VERBS, ADJECTIVES AND PREPOSITIONS

Exercise 1
1 to tell
2 to help
3 playing
4 watching
5 playing
6 helping

Exercise 2
1 My friends and always enjoy **meeting** in town on Saturdays.
2 I hope **to visit** Brazil one day.
3 I'm sorry **to hear** you're ill.
4 All my friends enjoy **watching** football.
5 Do you mind **waiting** a little longer?

Exercise 3
1 to visit
2 playing
3 having
4 to finish
5 to spend
6 to pass
7 being
8 going

Page 216

UNIT 10
THE FUTURE WITH *WILL*

Exercise 1
1 won't have
2 will go
3 Will … be, won't
4 won't pass, will be
5 will meet

Exercise 2
1 We'll probably go to Spain for our holiday next year.
2 I think it will be colder tomorrow.
3 Perhaps we'll have a new teacher next term.
4 Are you sure you'll be OK?
5 He probably won't come to our party.

Exercise 3
1 Shall
2 I'll
3 Will
4 won't
5 will
6 I'll

Exercise 4
1 b	3 e	5 f
2 c	4 a	6 d

MAY/MIGHT

Exercise 5
Tom and Julie are going. The others are not sure.

Exercise 6
1 e	3 a	5 c
2 f	4 b	6 d

Page 218

UNIT 11
BE GOING TO

Exercise 1
1 're going to miss
2 're going to ride
3 'm going to do
4 aren't going to need
5 are going to visit

Exercise 2
2 **A:** What are you going to do this evening?
   B: I'm going to play a video game.
3 **A:** Is it going to rain tomorrow?
   B: No, Look at the red sky. It's going to be sunny all day.
4 **A:** What are you going to do when you leave college?
   B: I'm going to look for a good job.
5 **A:** Is your team going to win the match?
   B: No, the other team is much better. We're going to lose.

PRESENT CONTINUOUS FOR THE FUTURE

Exercise 3
1 going to eat
2 catching
3 seeing
4 going to do, going to phone
5 having

PRESENT SIMPLE TO TALK ABOUT THE FUTURE

Exercise 4

1 leaves
2 's having
3 is coming
4 starts
5 finish

Page 220

UNIT 12
ZERO AND FIRST CONDITIONAL

Exercise 1

1	d	3	b	5	c
2	a	4	e	6	f

Exercise 2

1 see, 'll/will tell
2 'll/will hurt, fall
3 don't catch, 'll/will have
4 'll/will be, don't leave
5 is, 'll/will wake

Exercise 3

1 If I get a new job, I'll earn more money.
2 I'll buy a car if I have enough money.
3 If I buy a car, I'll use it to go to work.
4 I'll get fit if I ride my bike to work.
5 I won't get fit if I go to work by bus.

CONJUNCTIONS: *WHEN, IF, UNLESS* + PRESENT , FUTURE

Exercise 4

1 Unless
2 unless
3 If
4 if
5 unless
6 When/If
7 If
8 when

THE PASSIVE

Exercise 5

1 is grown
2 are sold
3 are shown
4 is made
5 is closed

Exercise 6

1 was built
2 were told
3 was closed
4 was given
5 were taken
6 was sent

Page 222

UNIT 13
COMPARATIVES AND SUPERLATIVES

Exercise 1

1 bigger
2 more interesting
3 heavier
4 warmer
5 worse
6 larger

Exercise 2

1 I am the **best** footballer at my college.
2 Anna is **happier** than she was this morning.
3 I want to be **fitter** so I do lots of exercise.
4 What is the **most expensive** thing you have?
5 Ben's apartment is **larger** than mine.
6 Tom is **taller than** his father.

TO BE LIKE AND *TO LOOK LIKE*

Exercise 3

1 What does he look like?
2 What are your new neighbours like?
3 What is their new baby like?
4 What does she look like?

AS… AS, NOT AS… AS

Exercise 4

1 He is **as tall as** his father now.
2 The climate in England is **as pleasant as** the climate in Ireland.
3 You must play **as hard as** you can, if you want to win the match.
4 This ice cream's not **as tasty as** the one we bought yesterday.
5 I'm making **as many mistakes as** I did yesterday.

Page 224

UNIT 14
MUST/MUSTN'T

Exercise 1

1 mustn't be
2 must wear
3 mustn't run
4 mustn't talk
5 mustn't use
6 must finish

Exercise 2

1 You must visit / go to
2 You mustn't use
3 You must try
4 You mustn't lose
5 You must see / visit

HAVE TO

Exercise 3

1 have to help
2 do you have to do

3 have to tidy
4 Does she have to tidy
5 she does
6 has to wash
7 don't have to do

Exercise 4

1 have to
2 don't have to
3 don't have to
4 have to
5 have to

NEED TO/DON'T NEED TO

Exercise 5

1 You don't need to finish the project by Friday.
2 I need to phone home to check that everything is OK.
3 I really need to work harder or I won't get very good marks.
4 She needs to buy some food for dinner tonight.

CAN/CAN'T

Exercise 6

1 Anyone can become rich and famous.
2 Learning a foreign language can be very hard.
3 A room in a small hotel can't cost more than fifty pounds.
4 When you have small children, you can't leave objects around the house.

PHRASAL VERB BANK

Page 227

GETTING ABOUT

Exercise 1

get back = return
take off = leave the ground (a plane)
come round = visit someone's house
come in = enter a place
pick (someone) up = collect someone from somewhere

Exercise 2

1 takes off
2 get back
3 picked me up
4 come in
5 came round

Exercise 3

Students' own answers.

IN THE MORNING

Exercise 1

take something off = stop wearing
wake up = stop sleeping
get up = get out of bed
go out = leave
put something on = start wearing

Exercise 2
1 wake up
2 get up
3 take off
4 put (my school uniform) on
5 go out

Exercise 3
Students' own answers.

PEOPLE AND COMMUNICATION
Exercise 1
grow up = become an adult
call someone back = return a phone call
find out = get information about
look after = take care of
get on with someone = be friendly with someone

Exercise 2
1 look after
2 get on
3 find out
4 call (you) back
5 grew up

Exercise 3
Students' own answers.

OTHER PHRASAL VERBS
Exercise 1
lie down = usually something you do before you go to sleep
turn off = stop a machine or light from working
fill in = write information on a form
give back = give something to the person who gave it to you
try on = put on clothes to see if they fit

Exercise 2
1 lie down
2 turn off
3 try (shoes) on
4 fill in
5 give back

Exercise 3
Students' own answers.

WRITING BANK
Page 229

HOW TO MAKE YOUR WRITING BETTER: ADJECTIVES
Exercise 1
2b We had lunch in a small, friendly restaurant.
3b A kind woman showed me the way home.
4b I knew I had made a big mistake.

Exercise 2
1 true
2 false
3 true

Exercise 3
1 heavy
2 important
3 modern/lovely
4 lovely
5 expensive

Exercise 4
1 exciting, funny
2 beautiful, lovely
3 brilliant, great
4 friendly, kind
5 sunny, pleasant
6 great, excellent

Exercise 5
1 wonderful
2 terrible
3 amazing
4 horrible
5 awful
6 fantastic

very good	very bad
wonderful	terrible
amazing	horrible
fantastic	awful

HOW TO MAKE YOUR WRITING BETTER: ADVERBS AND INTERESTING VERBS
Exercise 1
2b The children were playing happily in the garden.
3b I read the invitation carefully.
4b She opened the letter slowly.
5b I couldn't see well because it was cloudy.

Exercise 2
1 true
2 true
3 false
4 true

Exercise 3
1 loudly
2 hungrily
3 clearly
4 fast
5 carefully
6 easily
7 well
8 beautifully

Exercise 4
2 I quickly read the letter.
3 She closed the door quietly.
4 He carefully carried the hot drinks into the sitting room.
5 We walked slowly through the park.
6 Mark didn't sleep well last night.

Exercise 5
1 hurried
2 shouting
3 relaxing
4 jumped
5 threw
6 cried

Exercise 6
1 ran
2 shouted
3 relaxed
4 jumped
5 threw

USE VERB FORMS CORRECTLY TO TALK ABOUT THE PAST, PRESENT AND FUTURE
Exercise 1
Hi Jo,
I go swimming next Saturday. My cousin are here at the moment, and he love films. Are you want to come too? There's a new cinema on Wood Road. We can to get the bus. I meet you at the bus stop.
Sam

Exercise 2
Hi Jo,
I'm going swimming next Saturday. My cousin is here at the moment, and he loves films. Do you want to come too? There's a new cinema on Wood Road. We can get the bus. I can/will meet you at the bus stop.
Sam

Exercise 3
1 'm going
2 is
3 loves
4 Do you want
5 've never been
6 went
7 get
8 can meet

Exercise 4
1 'm going
2 went
3 've never been
4 can get, can meet

Exercise 5
1 'm going
2 bought
3 starts
4 to come
5 have met
6 go

Exercise 6

Model answer

Hi Max,

I'm going to a water park next Saturday. Would you like to come? My friend Paul is coming too. He went there last month and loved it. We can get there by train. I think it will be amazing!

Stan

USE LINKING WORDS AND RELATIVE PRONOUNS TO MAKE SENTENCES LONGER

Exercise 1

10 sentences

Exercise 2

Dan woke up <u>and</u> got out of bed. He didn't look at his clock. He opened the fridge, <u>but</u> it was almost empty. He was hungry, <u>so</u> he decided to go out for some food. He went to a café, <u>but</u> it was closed <u>because</u> it was only 6.30 in the morning!

Exercise 3

1 but
2 and
3 so
4 because
5 but
6 so

Exercise 4

1 which
2 who
3 who
4 that

Exercise 5

1 who
2 which

Exercise 6

1 who
2 which
3 which
4 who

Page 233

WRITING PART 6: A SHORT MESSAGE

Exercise 1

Write about three things. Write 25 words or more.

Exercise 2

1 don't
2 could
3 Shall
4 Let's
5 Why

Exercise 3

1 c   3 d   5 b
2 a   4 e

Exercise 4

2 I'm afraid I can't come to your party.
3 I'm sorry, but I'll be a bit late.
4 Guess what! I won the competition!

Exercise 5

Hi Joe,

My cousin <u>Beth is</u> (Beth's) coming to visit on Saturday, and I <u>am</u> (I'm) really excited. <u>She is</u> (She's) very good at computer games <u>I have</u> (I've) got a new game and <u>we are</u> (we're) going to play some games together. Do you want to come too? <u>I will</u> (I'll) call you later.

Sam

Exercise 6

You should say that you can't go to the concert, give a reason why you can't go and suggest another day when you can go.

Exercise 8

Model answer

Hi Laura,

I'm sorry, but I can't go to the concert on Saturday. I have to stay at home because my grandparents are coming to visit. Why don't we meet on Sunday and go to the cinema?

See you soon,

Ana

Page 234

WRITING PART 7: A STORY

Exercise 1

35 words or more

Exercise 2

1 was feeling
2 was raining
3 arrived
4 was carrying
5 ate
6 played

Exercise 3

1 First
2 Next
3 Finally
4 Suddenly
5 Then
6 Finally

Exercise 4

1 tall
2 empty
3 pleased
4 quick
5 high
6 ready

Exercise 5

Students' own answers.

Exercise 6

Model answer

Alice wanted to watch TV, but her TV was broken. She told her sister. They looked on their computer and quickly found a big, new TV online. It wasn't expensive, so Alice's sister bought it. The next day, the new TV arrived, and Alice felt really happy.

Exercise 7

Students' own answers.

SPEAKING BANK

Page 237

GIVING PERSONAL INFORMATION

Exercise 1

	Pablo	Lucia
Age	17	18
From	Madrid	Milan

Exercise 2

1 b   2 c   3 d   4 a

🎧 Track 119

Pablo: Hello. My name's Pablo and I'm 17 years old. I'm Spanish and I come from Madrid.

Lucia: Hi. My name's Lucia. I'm 18 years old, and I'm Italian. I live in Milan.

TALKING ABOUT HABITS, LIKES AND DISLIKES

Exercise 1

doing homework, meeting friends, playing tennis, watching TV

Exercise 2

1 always get up
2 am never
3 usually do
4 often watch
5 on Saturdays
6 sometimes meet

🎧 Track 120

Girl: I always get up early on school days, and I'm never late for school. I usually do my homework when I get home from school. I don't often watch TV. I usually play tennis on Saturdays, and I sometimes meet my friends at the weekend too.

Exercise 3

basketball

Exercise 4

1 like
2 don't
3 listening
4 prefer
5 favourite

Track 121

Boy: I like maths and science, but I don't like art. I enjoy listening to music, but I don't like singing because I'm not a very good singer. I love sport! I like tennis, but I prefer football to tennis. Basketball is my favourite sport because it's very exciting.

GIVING OPINIONS AND REASONS

Exercise 1

cycling

Exercise 2

1 Do
2 do
3 about
4 don't
5 think
6 going
7 What
8 prefer
9 fun
10 love

Track 122

Girl: Do you like swimming?
Boy: Yes, I do. It's fun. What about you?
Girl: No, I don't like swimming. I think it's boring. But I love going to the cinema. It's really interesting. What do you think?
Boy: No, I think going to the cinema is expensive. I prefer to watch films at home. My favourite activity is cycling. Do you think cycling is fun?
Girl: Yes, I do. I love cycling!

Exercise 3

1 b   2 a   3 a

Track 123

Narrator: One
Boy: I often travel to other countries with my family. I like travelling because you visit interesting places and you learn about different countries.
Narrator: Two
Girl: My brother loves skateboarding, but I don't like it because I think it's dangerous. You can fall down and hurt yourself.
Narrator: Three
Boy: This is my new computer game. I play it a lot. I'm not very good at it, but I love it because it's exciting. Oh, no!

Exercise 4

Students' own answers.

Track 124

Narrator: One
Girl: I like reading because it's relaxing and you can learn about a lot of different things.

Narrator: Two
Boy: I love football because it's an exciting game, and you feel really good when you win.
Narrator: Three
Boy: I don't like shopping because there aren't any good shops here.

AGREEING AND DISAGREEING

Exercise 1

1

Exercise 2

1 not sure about
2 That's true
3 agree with you
4 Yes, but

Track 125

Girl: Do you play any musical instruments?
Boy: Yes, I'm learning to play the guitar. What about you?
Girl: I'm learning the piano. I think it's very difficult to learn an instrument.
Boy: I'm not sure about that. The guitar isn't very difficult, but it's important to practise every day.
Girl: That's true. I agree with you that it's important to practise so that you can get better. I think that lessons are very expensive, too.
Boy: Yes, but you can watch lessons online and teach yourself. That isn't expensive.

DEALING WITH PROBLEMS

Exercise 1

1 Could you repeat
2 Can you repeat
3 say that again

Exercise 2

1 Could you repeat ~~again~~ that <u>again</u>, please?
2 Can you repeat ~~me~~ the question, please?
3 Could you say <u>that</u> again, please?

Track 126

Narrator: One
Teacher: Don't forget the trip to the museum tomorrow. We're meeting at 9.45.
Girl: Could you repeat that, please?
Teacher: Yes. It's 9.45 tomorrow morning.
Girl: Thank you.
Narrator: Two
Teacher: Do you think swimming in the sea is dangerous?
Boy: Can you repeat the question, please?
Teacher: Of course. Do you think swimming in the sea is dangerous?
Boy: Yes, I think that sometimes it can be dangerous, especially in bad weather.

Narrator: Three
Girl: I'm glad you can come to my party. It's at my house. I live at 29, West Street.
Boy: Could you say that again, please? I need to write it down.
Girl: Sure. It's 29, West Street. It isn't far from here.

Exercise 3

1 c   2 a   3 b

Exercise 4

1 not, word
2 what, called
3 know, is

Track 127

Man: I'm not sure what the word is, but you often play this on the beach, with your friends. You have a ball, and you hit the ball with your hand.
Woman: I'm not sure what this is called, but it's something you wear around your neck in winter, when it's very cold.
Man: I don't know what the word is, but it's something you eat. It's sweet, and very cold, and you often eat it in the summer.

Page 240

SPEAKING PART 1

Exercise 1

Yes, she does.

Exercise 3

1 or
2 because
3 because

Track 128

Examiner: Now, let's talk about weekends. What do you do at weekends?
Ana: I often go shopping, or I sometimes go to the cinema.
Examiner: And who do you like spending your weekends with?
Ana: I like spending my weekends with friends, because we laugh and have fun together.
Examiner: Now, let's talk about shopping. Where do you like going shopping?
Ana: I like going shopping in London because there are lots of good shops.
Examiner: And what do you like buying?
Ana: I like buying clothes and shoes because I'm interested in fashion.

Exercise 4

1 love
2 buy
3 bought
4 liked
5 'm going to take

Track 129

Examiner: Now, please tell me something about presents that you buy for other people.

Ana: Well, I love buying presents for people. I usually buy presents for people when it's their birthday. For example, last month I bought a T-shirt for my brother and he really liked it. It's my friend's birthday next week, and I'm going to take her to the cinema as a present.

Exercise 5

1 b	**3** b	**5** b
2 a	**4** a	**6** b

Exercise 6

1 have – present
2 'm going to meet – future
3 watch – present
4 cooked – past
5 'm going to play – future
6 bought – past

Exercise 7

1 c	**3** e	**5** a
2 d	**4** b	

Track 130

Examiner: Tell me something about what you like doing at home.

Ana: I like watching films, and I enjoy playing video games. I've just got a new game, so I'm quite excited about that.

Examiner: Tell me something about what you like to eat with friends.

Ana: I sometimes go to restaurants with my friends, and I prefer Italian food. We went to a pizza restaurant last weekend, and it was very nice.

Examiner: Tell me something about the clothes you like to buy.

Ana: I love buying new clothes, and my favourite thing to buy is jeans, because I like wearing them. I bought some really nice jeans last week, so I was happy.

Examiner: Tell me something about the places you like to visit.

Ana: I don't like going to big cities because there's too much traffic. I like visiting places that are near the sea. I love swimming when the weather's hot.

Examiner: Tell me something about the sports you like to do.

Ana: I like playing football. I play for a team, and we have a game every Saturday. My team doesn't often win, but it's still fun.

Exercise 8

Students' own answers.

Page 241

SPEAKING PART 2

Exercise 1

Yes, they do.

Track 131

Girl: So, do you like playing video games?

Boy: Yes, I do. I've got a lot of video games, and I often play with my friends. I think they're exciting. What do you think?

Girl: I'm not sure about that. I sometimes play video games, but I think they're a bit boring.

Boy: What about taking photos? Do you like taking photos?

Girl: I often take photos when I'm with my friends, but I don't have a camera. I take photos on my phone. What about you?

Boy: I like taking photos, too. I have got a camera, and I love taking photos of animals and the countryside.

Girl: What about cycling? I love cycling because it's fun, and it's healthy. I always go cycling at weekends. What do you think about it?

Boy: I agree with you that it's fun and it's also good exercise. What about music? Do you play any instruments?

Girl: No, I don't. But I enjoy listening to music. What about you? Do you play an instrument?

Boy: I'm learning to play the drums. I'd like to be in a band one day.

Girl: And what about reading books? Do you like reading?

Boy: Yes, I like reading books, for example adventure books. But I prefer films to books.

Girl: Yes, I agree with you. I think films are more exciting than books.

Exercise 2

Yes, she does.

Track 132

Examiner: So, which of these hobbies do you like best?

Girl: I like cycling the best because I enjoy being active and I like spending time outside, and I think that cycling keeps you fit and healthy.

Exercise 3

1 think
2 sure
3 like
4 about
5 do
6 agree

Track 133

Boy: I think video games are exciting. What do you think?

Girl: I'm not sure about that.

Boy: What about taking photos? Do you like taking photos?

Girl: I often take photos when I'm with my friends.

Girl: I take photos on my phone. What about you?

Boy: I like taking photos, too. I've got a camera.

Girl: I always go cycling at weekends. What do you think about it?

Boy: I agree with you that it's fun.

Exercise 4

1 d	**3** e	**5** c
2 a	**4** b	

Exercise 5

Students' own answers.

Track 134

Boy: Well, I love music festivals because I'm a music fan. I think they're great. What about you?

Girl: I agree with you. I like going to music festivals with my friends. And do you like going to the beach?

Boy: Yes, I do. I like swimming in the sea and playing with a ball on the beach. What about you?

Girl: Yes, I agree. Going to the beach is fun when the weather's hot. And what about walking in the mountains? I don't like that because it's really difficult. What do you think?

Boy: I'm not sure. I like it because you can see the beautiful countryside. I like camping, too because it's fun and you're outside. Do you agree?

Girl: No, I don't agree. I hate camping because I prefer to sleep in a comfortable bed! But I like picnics. I often go for picnics with my friends in the summer. Do you like picnics?

Boy: Yes, I do. When it's sunny, it's lovely to eat outside in a nice place, for example near a river.

Exercise 6

Students' own answers.

Track 135

Examiner: Which of these activities do you like the best?

Boy: I like going to music festivals because you can listen to some exciting bands and also spend time with your friends and have fun.

Examiner: Do you prefer to go on holiday to the beach or the countryside?

Boy: I prefer to go to the beach because in the countryside it's sometimes a bit boring, because there aren't many people and there are no restaurants or cafés. At the beach there are lots of people, so it's more exciting.

Examiner: Do you prefer swimming in the sea or in a swimming pool?

Boy: I prefer swimming in the sea. It's more interesting because you can see different things around you, but in the swimming pool you just have to go up and down all the time, so I think it's a bit boring.

ACKNOWLEDGEMENTS

The authors and publishers would like to thank the following contributors:

Grammar on the move: Lucy Passmore
Grammar reference: Bryan Goodman-Stephens

The authors and publishers are grateful to the following for reviewing the material during the writing process:
Italy: Cressida Hicks, Rachael Smith; Portugal: Liliana Moreira; Spain: Vicky Gibney, Chris Johnson

The authors and publishers acknowledge the following sources of copyright material and are grateful for the permissions granted. While every effort has been made, it has not always been possible to identify the sources of all the material used, or to trace all copyright holders. If any omissions are brought to our notice, we will be happy to include the appropriate acknowledgements on reprinting and in the next update to the digital edition, as applicable.

Photography
Key: ST = Unit Starter, U = Unit, CA = Communication activities, GR = Grammar Reference, PVB = Phrasal verb builder, WRB = Writing Bank, SPB = Speaking Bank.

The following images are sourced from Getty Images.

ST: Ben Pipe Photography/Cultura; Hero Images; Sam Edwards/OJO Images; Eric Audras/ONOKY; mediaphotos/E+; Jose Luis Pelaez Inc/Blend Images; Klaus Vedfelt/DigitalVision; Tom Werner/DigitalVision; Klaus Tiedge; Mike Lawrie/Getty Images Entertainment; NurPhoto; Jean Baptiste Lacroix/WireImage; **U1:** Maskot; Westend61; Peathegee Inc./Blend Images; bymuratdeniz/E+; dardespot/E+; Sergey Ryumin/Moment; LWA/Sharie Kennedy/Blend Images; Blend Images-Hill Street Studios/Brand X Pictures; GiorgioMagini/iStock/Getty Images Plus; RoBeDeRo/E+; Keith Wood/The Image Bank; ERproductions Ltd/Blend Images; Chris Ryan/Caiaimage; Er Creatives Services Ltd/Photodisc; Vladimir Godnik; Digital Vision/Photodisc; Yellow Dog Productions/The Image Bank; aurmios000720/Aurora Photos; Echo/Juice Images; Hero Images; Hill Street Studios/Blend Images; Juanmonino/E+; ©fitopardo.com/Moment; fitopardo.com/Moment Open; Thomas Barwick/Stone; **U2:** Tetra Images; Kangheewan/Moment Open; Philippe Sainte-Laudy Photography/Moment; mikroman6/Moment; Sergey Ryumin/Moment; DEA/G.SIOEN/De Agostini; Stefan Christmann/Corbis NX; Shaji Manshad/Moment Open; Mariia Kamenska/EyeEm; David Crespo/Moment; Daniel Delgado/Moment; Jeremy Walker/The Image Bank; John Coletti/The Image Bank; VukasS/E+; Klaus Tiedge; Nico Tondini/Photographer's Choice RF; nullplus/iStock/Getty Images Plus; LightFieldStudios/iStock/Getty Images Plus; Justin Lewis/Taxi; Henn Photography/Cultura; Caiaimage/Trevor Adeline; Kieran Stone/Moment; annhfhung/Moment; James O'Neil/Stone; 1001slide/iStock/Getty Images Plus; Kim Rogerson/Moment; PeopleImages/E+; Blend Images-JGI/Jamie Grill; BFG Images; RYO/a.collectionRF; Don Hammond; imagenavi; Fertnig/E+; Echo/Juice Images; SolStock/E+; Klaus Vedfelt/DigitalVision; Compassionate Eye Foundation/DigitalVision; Thomas Northcut/DigitalVision; **U3:** Pekic/E+; Peter Dazeley/The Image Bank; Colin Anderson/Blend Images; stilletto82/DigitalVision Vectors; Resolution Productions; Tom Merton/Caiaimage; Nattapong Wongloungud/EyeEm; Tim Robberts/The Image Bank; ISAAC LAWRENCE/AFP; Westend61; Sofie Delauw/Cultura; DougSchneiderPhoto/iStock/Getty Images Plus; Walter McBride/WireImage; Rob Kim/Getty Images Entertainment; tomch/iStock/Getty Images Plus; Zsolt Hlinka/Moment; **U4:** Matthew Leete/DigitalVision; GibsonPictures/E+; MoMo Productions/Stone; Laurence Monneret/The Image Ban; Peter Muller/Cultura; alvarez/E+; skynesher/E+; Oliver Burston/Ikon Images; Stockbyte; Westend61; PhotoAlto/Eric Audras; Ebby May/The Image Bank; Michael Heim/EyeEm; amanaimagesRF; elenaleonova/E+; interstid/iStock/Getty Images Plus; Pollyana FMS/Moment; Ian Lishman/Juice Images; Sally Anscombe/Moment; svetikd/E+; Maskot; Adie Bush/Image Source; Nick David/DigitalVision; powerofforever/iStock/Getty Images Plus; kulicki/iStock/Getty Images Plus; David Soanes Photography/Moment; Samarskaya/DigitalVision

Vectors; **U5:** franckreporter/iStock/Getty Images Plus; Matthias Tunger/Photodisc; traumlichtfabrik/Moment; Jose A. Bernat Bacete/Moment; Yaorusheng/Moment; Miss Pearl/Moment; Alex B. Huckle/FilmMagic; Image Source; Keystone-France/Gamma-Rapho; Geber86/E+; DEA/V.GIANNELLA/De Agostini; Sean Gallup Getty Images News; fhm/Moment; Schöning/ullstein bild Dtl; martin-dm/E+; Maskot; kosmos111/iStock/Getty Images Plus; Neustockimages/E+; Tom Merton/OJO Images; Todd Pearson/Photodisc; Westend61; Nutexzles/Moment; kbeis/DigitalVision Vectors; **U6:** Image Source; Sigrid Gombert/MITO images; Westend61; FotografiaBasica/E+; Jupiterimages/Taxi; ATU Images/Photographer's Choice; David Murray/Dorling Kindersley; The Real Tokyo Life/Moment; Keiko Iwabuchi/Moment; Steven Puetzer/Photolibrary; Paolo De Santis/EyeEm; markos86/E+; Pekic/E+; Andrea Chu/DigitalVision; andresr/E+; Alina555/E+; Lumina Images/Blend Images; Mathias Kniepeiss/Getty Images News; Digital Vision/Photodisc; Basilios1/iStock/Getty Images Plus; Maica/E+; Maskot; Sandeep Kapoor/EyeEm; Halfpoint Images/Moment; **U7:** mikroman6/Moment; FatCamera/E+; BraunS/E+; zeljkosantrac/E+; EmirMemedovski/E+; Yuri_Arcurs/DigitalVision; Mike Harrington/DigitalVision; Westend61; De Agostini Picture Library; CRIS BOURONCLE/AFP; Peathegee Inc; Philippa Langley/Cultura; Dave J Hogan/Getty Images Entertainment; Steve Prezant/Image Source; Hero Images; Matt Anderson Photography/Moment; Loop Images/Universal Images Group; jax10289/iStock Editorial/Getty Images Plus; Eye Ubiquitous/Universal Images Group; Caiaimage/Tom Merton; **U8:** Amer Ghazzal/Moment; mbtaichi/iStock/Getty Images Plus; thyme/E+; a40757/iStock/Getty Images Plus; Martin Barraud/OJO Images; shen wei/Moment Open; Westend61; simonlong/Moment; rappensuncle/E+; Martin Deja/Moment; Jumping Rocks/Universal Images Group; Katherine Frey/The Washington Post; Miemo Penttinen-miemo.net/Moment; Halfpoint/iStock/Getty Images Plus; patrickheagney/E+; Fancy/Veer/Corbis; WLADIMIR BULGAR/SCIENCE PHOTO LIBRARY; Dieter Weck/500px Prime; Tara Moore/DigitalVision; diane39/iStock/Getty Images Plus; Westend61; Jed Share/Kaoru Share; **U9:** Westend61; Martin Novak/Moment; praetorianphoto/E+; Ariel Skelley/DigitalVision; Francesco Piacentini/EyeEm; Gary John Norman; Echo/Juice Images; Hill Street Studios LLC/DigitalVision; BananaStock/Getty Images Plus; Ezra Bailey/DigitalVision; Dougal Waters/Photodisc; DGLimages/iStock/Getty Images Plus; PeopleImages/E+; PeopleImages/iStock/Getty Images Plus; Steve Debenport/E+; Boy_Anupong/Moment; maydays/Moment; WILLIAM WEST/AFP; Dean Fikar/Moment; Igor Ustynskyy/Moment; **U10:** Jeff Greenberg/Universal Images Group; Sasha Mordovets/Getty Images News; Tom Shaw/Getty Images Sport; E_Rojas/iStock Editorial/Getty Images Plus; Elizabeth Beard/Moment; kasto80/iStock/Getty Images Plus; Sascha Kilmer/Moment; Dmitry Lopatin/EyeEm; PeopleImages/E+; Jutta Klee/Canopy; xavierarnau/E+; DuKai photographer/Moment; zoranm/E+; DavidCallan/iStock/Getty Images Plus; Hero Images; Prapass Pulsub/Moment; GARDEL Bertrand/hemis.fr; Miles Ertman/All Canada Photos; joe daniel price/Moment; Pablo Cersosimo/robertharding; **U11:** Hero Images; JGI/Jamie Grill; GCShutter/E+; Eric Audras/ONOKY; Tetra Images; Nikada/E+; Cristian Bortes/EyeEm Premium; martin-dm/E+; vgajic/E+; piola666/E+; Portra/E+; SolStock/E+; Isabel Meinhold/EyeEm; Doug Armand/Photolibrary; poba/E+; Juanmonino/E+; Marco Bottigelli/Moment; brittak/iStock/Getty Images Plus; Johner Images; Anna Bizon; olaser/iStock/Getty Images Plus; Vijay Patel/DigitalVision Vectors; **U12:** Monty Rakusen/Cultura; Sebastián Crespo Photography/Moment; SolStock/E+; Hill Street Studios/Blend Images; bo1982/iStock/Getty Images Plus; Sergio Mendoza Hochmann/Moment; Sam Edwards/Caiaimage; Ariel Skelley/DigitalVision; davidf/E+; Jose Luis Pelaez Inc/DigitalVision; Amanda Edwards/WireImage; SusanHSmith/E+; Seth Joel/The Image Bank; BJI/Blue Jean Images/Collection Mix: Subjects; kali9/E+; Blend Images-Peathegee Inc; track5/E+; Bastiaan Slabbers/NurPhoto; Boston Globe; Artyom Geodakyan/TASS; Janina Laszlo/STOCK4B; GlobalVision Communication/GlobalVision 360/Moment; MichalLudwiczak/iStock Editorial/Getty Images Plus; Elenarts/iStock/Getty Images Plus; John Wildgoose/Caiaimage; **U13:** Caiaimage/Robert Daly; Hero Images; martinedoucet/E+; Christie Goodwin/Redferns; Csondy/E+; Fred Duval/FilmMagic; Nicholas Hunt/Getty Images Entertainment; MPI02/Bauer-Griffin/GC Images; Megan Maloy/Image

Video still photography

Video

one80: Signature; **U13:** AhmetovRuslan/Creatas Video+/Getty Images Plus; creuxnoir/Creatas Video; Henglein And Steets/Image Bank Film; Aerial Filmworks; Spotmatik/Photolibrary Video; Martin Puddy/Image Bank Film; Pierre Ogeron/one80; Geoff Tompkinson/Iconica Video; ImageDB/Creatas Video+/Getty Images Plus; pictafolio/Creatas Video; viafilms/Creatas Video+/Getty Images Plus; Robert Harding Video/ Photolibrary Video; FluxFactory/Creatas Video; nk87/Creatas Video+/ Getty Images Plus; DeReGe/Creatas Video+/Getty Images Plus; **U14:** AhmetovRuslan/Creatas Video+/Getty Images Plus; piola666/Creatas Video; GoranQ/Creatas Video; vichie81/Creatas Video; Mattia Bicchi Photography/Moment Video RR; Denis Doyle/Getty Images Sport; Clippn/Getty Images Editorial Footage; ITN; Anadolu Agency/Footage.

Illustrations

Chris Chalik; Denis Cristo; Niall Harding (In the style of Steven Johnson); Derren Toussaint (In the style of Steven Johnson).

Audio

Produced by Creative Listening and recorded at Tileyard Studios, London.

Speaking bank produced by Dan Strauss and recorded at Triangle, Cambridge.

Grammar on the move audio produced by Dan Strauss and recorded at Triangle, Cambridge.

Real World documentary audio produced by Dan Strauss and recorded at Half-ton Studios, Cambridge.

The following audios are sourced from Getty Images.

U1: Lenny Marcus/Soundexpress; **U2:** Mike Bridge/Soundexpress; **U3:** EasyTunes/Soundexpress; **U4:** Emerson Swinford/Soundexpress; **U5:** Claudio Giovann Colombo/SoundExpress; **U6:** Streicher Trio/ SoundExpress; **U7:** Vytenis Misevicius/SoundExpress; **U8:** Dmitriy Shironosov/SoundExpress; **U9:** Sergii Pavkin/SoundExpress; **U10:** juqboxmusic/SoundExpress; **U11:** CagdasTakmaz/SoundExpress; **U12:** Claudio Giovann Colombo/SoundExpress; **U13:** Francesco Biondi/ SoundExpress; **U14:** RFM/SoundExpress.

Page make up

EMC Design Ltd